SELECT WORKS OF EDMUND BURKE

VOLUME 1

Select Works of Edmund Burke

A NEW IMPRINT OF THE PAYNE EDITION

VOLUME 1

Thoughts on the Cause of the Present Discontents

The Two Speeches on America

VOLUME 2

Reflections on the Revolution in France

VOLUME 3

Letters on a Regicide Peace

Miscellaneous Writings

[Payne I]

EDMUND BURKE

SELECT WORKS OF EDMUND BURKE

A NEW IMPRINT OF THE PAYNE EDITION

Foreword and Biographical Note by Francis Canavan

VOLUME 1

THOUGHTS ON THE PRESENT DISCONTENTS

THE TWO SPEECHES ON AMERICA

LIBERTY FUND

INDIANAPOLIS

This book is published by Liberty Fund, Inc., a foundation established to encourage study of the ideal of a society of free and responsible individuals.

[cuneiform logo]

The cuneiform inscription that serves as our logo and as the design motif for our endpapers is the earliest-known written appearance of the word "freedom" (*amagi*), or "liberty." It is taken from a clay document written about 2300 B.C. in the Sumerian city-state of Lagash.

Frontispiece is a mezzotint by J. Jones of George Romney's portrait of Edmund Burke. By courtesy of the National Portrait Gallery, London.

99 00 01 02 03 C 5 4 3 2 1
99 00 01 02 03 P 5 4 3 2 1

Library of Congress Cataloging-in-Publication Data

Burke, Edmund, 1729–1797.
[Selections. 1999]
Select works of Edmund Burke : a new imprint of the Payne edition / foreword and biographical note by Francis Canavan.
p. cm.
Vols. 1–3 originally published: Oxford : Clarendon Press, 1874–1878.
Includes bibliographical references.
Contents: v. 1. Thoughts on the cause of the present discontents. The two speeches on America—v. 2. Reflections on the revolution in France—v. 3. Letters on a regicide peace—[4] Miscellaneous writings.
ISBN 0-86597-162-5 (v. 1 : hc : alk. paper).—ISBN 0-86597-163-3 (v. 1 : pb : alk. paper)
1. Great Britain—Politics and government—18th century. 2. Great Britain—Colonies—America. 3. France—History—Revolution, 1789–1799. 4. Great Britain—Relations—France. I. Canavan, Francis, 1917- . II. Payne, Edward John, 1844–1904. III. Title.
JC176.B826 1999
320.9'033—dc21   97-34325

ISBN 0-86597-253-2 (set : hc : alk. paper)
ISBN 0-86597-254-0 (set : pb : alk. paper)

LIBERTY FUND, INC.
8335 Allison Pointe Trail, Suite 300
Indianapolis, IN 46250-1687

Contents

Editor's Foreword

The first three volumes of this set of *Select Works* of Edmund Burke, fully edited by Edward John Payne (1844–1904), were originally published by the Clarendon Press, Oxford, from 1874 to 1878. Liberty Fund now publishes them again, with a fourth volume of additional writings by Burke. The original set has been praised by Clara I. Gandy and Peter J. Stanlis as "an outstanding critical anthology of Burke's essential works on the American and French revolutions"; and they went on to say: "The scholarship and criticism is perhaps the best on Burke during the last quarter of the nineteenth century."[1]

E. J. Payne was born in England to parents "in humble circumstances," as the *Dictionary of National Biography* phrases it. No doubt for that reason, the *Dictionary* goes on to say that he "owed his education largely to his own exertions."[2] Nonetheless he was able at age twenty-three to matriculate at Magdalen Hall, Oxford, from which he transferred to Charsley's Hall. He graduated B.A. in 1871, with a first class in classics. The following year he was elected to a fellowship in University College, Oxford. He was married in 1899 and therefore had to resign his fellowship, but was re-elected to a research fellowship in 1900. To the end of his days he took an active part in the management of College affairs.

He was called to the bar at Lincoln's Inn in 1874, but devoted himself mainly to research and writing, especially

---

1. *Edmund Burke: A Bibliography of Secondary Studies to 1982* (New York and London: Garland Publishing, 1983), no. 916.

2. Second Supplement (1912), 3:85.

on English colonial history and exploration, on which subjects he published rather widely. He also wrote on music, and
was an accomplished violinist. His introductions and notes to
these *Select Works* show him also to have been well versed in
English, French, Italian, and classical literature as well as in
history.

The first of these volumes contains Burke's great speeches
on the crisis between Great Britain and her American colonies, *On American Taxation* (1774) and *On Conciliation with the
Colonies* (1775). They are preceded by his pamphlet *Thoughts
on the Cause of the Present Discontents* (1770), which sets forth
the political creed of the Whig faction led by the Marquis of
Rockingham, for whom Burke acted as spokesman. The uni-
fying theme of all three documents is Burke's fear of arbitrary
power divorced from political prudence. In the *Present Discontents* it was the power of the Crown and in the American
speeches it was the sovereignty of the Mother Country that
he argued were being exercised in an arbitrary and foolish
manner.

The second volume is devoted wholly to Burke's best-
known work, *Reflections on the Revolution in France* (1790); the
third, to his *Letters on a Regicide Peace* (between Great Britain
and revolutionary France), which were written in 1796 and
1797. In these volumes he again expresses a detestation of
arbitrary power, in this case of the sovereign people, which
in practice was really the power of an oligarchy posing as a
democracy.

The fourth volume contains writings that express Burke's
views on representation in Parliament, on economics, on the
political oppression of the peoples of India and Ireland, and
on the enslavement of African blacks.

One of the attractive features of Burke's political thought
is his keen awareness of the way in which reason operates
in political judgments. He so heavily emphasized the roles
of tradition, even to the point of calling it prejudice, and of

sentiment and emotion in politics that it is easy to overlook his insistence that it was reason, not will, that should govern in the affairs of men. Mere will was arbitrary; reason recognized and took into account the complexity of reality. But it was practical, prudential reason, not abstract ideology, that should determine political decisions.

Thus, in his American speeches, while he did not deny Great Britain's right to tax the colonies, he severely questioned the wisdom of trying to do so without the consent of the colonists. His objection to the French Revolution, and to the British radicalism that agreed with it, was not to democracy in the abstract (though he thought it unsuited to any large country), but to the doctrine of the "rights of men," which the new French government had stated early in the Revolution in these terms: "The Representatives of the people of France, formed into a National Assembly, considering that ignorance, neglect, or contempt of human rights, are the sole causes of public misfortunes and corruptions of government, have resolved to set forth in a solemn declaration those natural imprescriptible, and unalienable rights."

Noble as that sentiment may be, it presumes that the purpose of politics and of the state can be reduced to a question of rights. The end of all political associations is the preservation of rights, and denying or ignoring them is the sole cause of public misfortunes. It follows that if a nation were to get its conception of rights straight, it would have solved all the problems of society. Burke was a strong and sincere defender of people's rights in other contexts, but he was repelled by the ideological simple-mindedness of the French *Declaration of the Rights of Man and Citizen* (1789).

Despite what Burke often seems to mean in his denunciations of "theory" and "metaphysics," he did not reject principles or an overarching natural moral order. On the contrary, he often appealed to them, particularly in his arguments against political oppression in India and Ireland. His objection was to the ideological mind that reasoned in politics as if it were engaged in an exercise in geometry, proceeding from an initial principle to practical conclusions that followed with necessary logic, without regard to "the wisdom of our ancestors," present circumstances, and the nature of the people as conditioned by their history. "For you know," Burke wrote to Sir Hercules Langrishe in 1792, "that the decisions of prudence (contrary to the system of the insane reasoners) differ from those of judicature; and that almost all of the former are determined on the more or the less, the earlier or the later, and on a balance of advantage and inconvenience, of good and evil." [3] But the decisions of prudence were nonetheless rational judgments that should not be considered irrational because they were not modelled on mathematics.

Burke believed in a common human nature created by God as the supreme norm of politics. But he knew that human nature realizes itself in history through conventional forms, customs, and traditions, which constitute what he called the second nature of a particular people. Convention can and often enough does distort our nature, but it is not of itself opposed to it. Burke would have agreed with the remark of the late Sir Ernest Barker: "Once oppose Nature to Convention, and the whole inherited tradition of the ages goes by the board." [4] Convention, made as it should be to satisfy the needs of nature, is not nature's enemy, but its necessary clothing. The statesman must therefore frame his policies with a practical wisdom that understands his people, their history, their traditions, their inherited rights and liberties, and their present circumstances. To do otherwise is to court disaster.

Burke thought that in the French Revolution it was the National Assembly that was courting disaster; in the Ameri-

3. *Letter to Sir Hercules Langrishe,* in *Miscellaneous Writings,* the companion volume to *Select Works of Edmund Burke* (Indianapolis: Liberty Fund, 1999), p. 202.

4. *Greek Political Theory: Plato and His Predecessors* (New York: Barnes and Noble, 4th ed., 1951), p. 75.

can Revolution it was the British government. He never favored America's independence from Britain, because he always strove to be an enlightened imperialist for whom the British Empire could and should be a blessing to all its member countries. But when American independence came, he was able to accept it gracefully, and he even praised the new Constitution of the United States. Or so, at least, he is reported as saying in the House of Commons on May 6, 1791: "The people of America had, he believed, formed a constitution as well adapted to their circumstances as they could." It was, to be sure, a republican constitution, but, given the circumstances of the Americans, it had to be one: "They had not the materials of monarchy or aristocracy among them. They did not, however, set up the absurdity that the nation should govern the nation; that prince prettyman should govern prince prettyman: but formed their government, as nearly as they could, according to the model of the British constitution."[5]

In regard to France, however, he was uncompromising. There he saw the Revolution as an attack not only on monarchy and aristocracy, but on the religion, morals, and civilization of Christendom, inspired by a rationalistic ideology — "rationalistic" because it was founded not on reason, but on intoxication with abstract theory.

Nor did Burke divorce reason from emotion. On the contrary, he held that our reason can recognize our nature through our natural feelings and inclinations. To cite but one example, he is reported to have said in the Commons on May 14, 1781, that the obligation of kings to respect the property even of conquered enemies "is a principle inspired by the Divine Author of all good; it is felt in the heart; it is recognized by reason; it is established by consent."[6] Burke

5. *The Parliamentary History of England* (London: Hansard, 1806–1820), 29:365–66.

6. Ibid., 22:230.

was well aware, of course, that man is subject to disordered passions as well as to natural feelings. But for that reason he said that "the wise Legislators of all countries [have] aimed at improving instincts into morals, and at grafting the virtues on the stock of the natural affections."[7] Reason cultivates rather than tries to exterminate natural affections, because it is through them that it recognizes our natural good.

Man of his times though he was and defender of a now-defunct aristocratic order of society, Burke still speaks to us today. Harold Laski was a Marxist who did not mourn the demise of the aristocratic order; nonetheless he said that Burke "wrote what constitutes the supreme analysis of the statesman's art" and was "the first of English political thinkers." Laski therefore concluded that "Burke has endured as the permanent manual of political wisdom without which statesmen are as sailors on an uncharted sea."[8] This set of Burke's *Select Works* offers a valuable introduction to that wisdom.

FRANCIS CANAVAN
Fordham University

7. *First Letter on a Regicide Peace,* in *Select Works of Edmund Burke,* vol. 3 (Indianapolis: Liberty Fund, 1999), p. 127.

8. *Political Thought in England from Locke to Bentham* (London: Thornton Butterworth, 1920), pp. 15, 26, 172.

Biographical Note

Since E. J. Payne does not furnish the details of Edmund Burke's biography, it will be useful to the modern reader to include a brief sketch of Burke's life here. (See also the chronological table in volume 2 of this edition.)

He was born in Dublin on January 12, 1729, of a Roman Catholic mother and a father who, according to the most likely account, had conformed to the Established Anglican Church of Ireland (whose head, as in England, was the King of Great Britain and Ireland) in order to be able to practice law, a profession forbidden to Catholics under the Penal Laws. Of the children of that marriage who lived to maturity, the boys, Garrett, Richard, and Edmund, were raised as Protestants; the one girl, Juliana, as a Catholic.

Since Edmund was a somewhat sickly child, he was sent to live from 1735 to 1740 with his mother's Catholic relatives, the Nagles, in the country air of County Cork. He maintained cordial relations with them throughout his life. If Burke had a personal religious problem as a result of this mixed religious family background, he solved it by maintaining that all Christians shared a common faith which subsisted in different forms in the several nations of the commonwealth of Christendom. The points on which they differed were the less important ones which could be left for the theological schools to argue about. When the French Revolution came, Burke found it easy to insist that all Christian kingdoms and churches must forget their quarrels and unite against what he called "an armed doctrine" hostile to all religion and civilization. (On a visit to France many years earlier, in 1773, he had been shocked by the rationalism and even atheism that he encountered in Paris.)

BIOGRAPHICAL NOTE

From 1741 to 1744, he attended a school in County Kildare that was conducted by a Quaker, Abraham Shackleton. Again, Burke maintained friendly relations with the Shackleton family for many years. In 1744, he entered Trinity College, Dublin, the intellectual stronghold of Irish Protestantism; he graduated with an A.B. degree in 1748 and received an M.A. degree in 1751.

By that time, he had gone to London to study law in the Inns of Court. But although in later life he displayed a considerable knowledge and understanding of law, he found the method of study distasteful and, much to his father's annoyance, abandoned the law for a literary career.

He began this with two books that attracted much attention: *A Vindication of Natural Society,* a satire on the Deism of the Enlightenment, in 1756; and a treatise on aesthetics, *A Philosophical Enquiry into the Origin of Our Ideas of the Sublime and Beautiful,* in 1757. In the latter year, he married Jane Nugent, the daughter of a Catholic doctor; Jane herself may or may not have been brought up as a Catholic and, if she was, may or may not have continued to practice that religion after her marriage to Burke. In any case, the two children of the marriage, Christopher and Richard (who alone survived to maturity), were brought up in their father's religion.

In 1758, Edmund became the editor of a yearly review of events and literature, the *Annual Register,* which continues publication to the present day. He also became private secretary to William Gerard Hamilton and went with him to Dublin in 1761 when Hamilton became Chief Secretary (a powerful post) to the Lord Lieutenant of Ireland. It was there that Burke began, but never finished, his *Tracts Relative to the Laws against Popery in Ireland.* He returned to London with Hamilton in 1764 and, after a bitter break with him, became private secretary to the Marquis of Rockingham in 1765. The Marquis, one of the wealthiest men in both England and Ireland, was the leader of a Whig faction that resisted the efforts of the new young king, George III, to reassert the personal power of the monarch.

In 1765, a reluctant King George appointed Rockingham First Lord of the Treasury (Prime Minister). In the same year, Burke was elected to the House of Commons from the nomination borough of Wendover through the influence of Lord Verney, with whom the Burke family had become friendly. Burke immediately made a reputation in the Commons as an orator. The Rockingham administration fell from power in 1766, after it repealed the Stamp Act that had so outraged the American colonies. Burke remained one of Rockingham's followers, however, and so spent most of the rest of his parliamentary life in opposition. In 1768, Burke bought an estate in Buckinghamshire, which made him a country gentleman but kept him in debt to the end of his days.

In the Commons, he quickly became the intellectual spokesman for the Rockingham Whigs. In that capacity, he wrote the party's creed, *Thoughts on the Cause of the Present Discontents*. During the American crisis, he argued for the Rockingham Whigs' position and against the British government's policies in his great speeches on American taxation and on conciliation with the colonies, and in other documents, such as his *Letter to the Sheriffs of Bristol*.

Burke lost his seat in Parliament when Lord Verney, strapped for money, had to sell it (a practice fully acceptable in that time). But, now well known, Burke was elected to the Commons from the city of Bristol, where he delivered his famous speech on the role of a parliamentary representative (see *Miscellaneous Writings*, published with this set). Burke's disagreements with his constituents on a number of issues (his *Two Letters to Gentlemen in Bristol* describe one of them) led him to withdraw from the Bristol election in 1780. The Marquis kept him in Parliament, however, by having him elected from the Yorkshire borough of Malton, a seat that Burke held until his retirement in 1794.

A second Rockingham ministry came into office in 1782 to make peace with the rebellious Americans. Burke, who was never invited to sit in a Cabinet, became Paymaster of the Forces. The post was supposed to be lucrative to its holder, but Burke chose to reform it. He also carried on the Rockingham policy of combatting royal influence in Parliament with a bill designed to reduce the king's power of patronage. Unfortunately, the Marquis died in the same year, and Burke was again out of a job.

He became Paymaster again in 1783, however, when a coalition government led by Charles James Fox, who succeeded the Marquis as leader of the Rockingham Whigs, and the Tory Lord North, who had been King George's prime minister during the American war, had a brief period in power. During this time, Burke delivered his *Speech on Fox's East India Bill* (see *Miscellaneous Writings*).

Burke was again out of office when the coalition fell in 1783 and was replaced by a Tory ministry under the younger William Pitt. The following year, Pitt's Tories won a smashing victory in a general election and remained in power for the rest of Burke's life.

Two of the great causes that engaged Burke began in the 1780s: the impeachment of Warren Hastings, the Governor-General of Bengal, which began in 1788 and ended with Hastings's acquittal in 1795; and the French Revolution, which began in 1789. Burke's principal and most famous writing on the latter subject is his *Reflections on the Revolution in France*. The most important of his other writings on that great cataclysm, *A Letter to Charles-Jean-François Depont, A Letter to a Member of the National Assembly, An Appeal from the New to the Old Whigs, Thoughts on French Affairs,* and *Letter to William Elliot,* have been published by Liberty Fund in *Further Reflections on the Revolution in France,* edited by Daniel E. Ritchie. Burke's last and increasingly severe attacks on the Revolution are the *Letters on a Regicide Peace.*

BIOGRAPHICAL NOTE

Burke was also active in Irish affairs during this period, mostly through private correspondence, and he had a significant influence in the continued relaxation of the Penal Laws against Catholics in Ireland. His *Letter to Sir Hercules Langrishe* is one piece of his writing on Irish affairs that was published in his lifetime.

Burke became a man without a party after his break in 1791 with Charles James Fox over the attitude to be taken toward the French Revolution. Burke's last years were sad and bitter ones. Rejected by his own party, he was not received by the governing Tories except as an occasionally useful ally. The Prime Minister, William Pitt, dismissed *Reflections on the Revolution in France* as "rhapsodies in which there is much to admire, and nothing to agree with." Burke retired from Parliament in 1794, having completed the prosecution of Warren Hastings, and was utterly disgusted, though not surprised, when the House of Lords acquitted Hastings in the following year. In 1794, Burke also suffered the loss through death of both his brother Richard and his son Richard, Jr. His son was the apple of his father's eye and had been, Burke said, his main reason for continuing to live after the end of his parliamentary career.

But Burke did keep on living and writing. Abandoned politically at home, he became through his writings, as a friend of his said, "a sort of *power*" in Europe as well as in England. The aristocratic order he so strenuously defended eventually died, and he can be praised or blamed only for having delayed its passing. But Burke lives on in his writings. Today it would be too much to say, as Payne did in 1874, that "the writings of Burke are the daily bread of statesmen, speakers, and political writers."[1] Yet they are still reprinted, read, and quoted, because each new generation finds something of lasting value in them.

1. P. 7 below.

EDITOR'S NOTE

In this volume, the pagination of E. J. Payne's edition is indicated by bracketed page numbers embedded in the text. Cross references have been changed to reflect the pagination of the current edition. Burke's and Payne's spellings, capitalizations, and use of italics have been retained, strange as they may seem to modern eyes. The use of double punctuation (e.g., ,—) has been eliminated except in quoted material.

All references to Burke's *Correspondence* are to the 1844 edition.

SELECT WORKS OF EDMUND BURKE

VOLUME 1

THOUGHTS ON THE
PRESENT DISCONTENTS

THE TWO SPEECHES
ON AMERICA

INTRODUCTION

BY E. J. PAYNE

A̲ N ACCOMPLISHED CRITIC[1] has observed, with much truth, that the only specimen of Burke is "all that he wrote," because every product of his pen contains additional proofs of his power. Those who wish to understand the nature and importance of his multifarious labours should make the acquaintance of his writings in the mass, and master them singly in detail. It has long been understood that he who gives his nights and days to this task will acquire a knowledge of the principles of general politics, of the limitations which modify those principles in our own national policy, of the questions with which that policy deals, and of the secret of applying the English tongue to their illustration, which cannot be acquired in any other way. In the prosecution of this task the student will learn the practical importance of the maxim laid down in the Preface to a previous volume of this series, that all study, to be useful, must be pursued in a spirit of deference. He will find it necessary to exert an unusual degree of patience, and to acquire the habit of continually suspending his own judgment. He will find himself in contact with much that seems dry and uninviting. It may therefore be well to caution him at the outset, that Burke, like all writers of the first class, will not repay a prejudiced or a superficial perusal. He gains upon us, not altogether by the inherent interest of what he presents to us, but very much by the skill and force with which he presents it, and

1. Hazlitt.

3

these qualities do not immediately strike the mental eye in all their fulness. The reader must meet his author half-way; he must contribute something more than a bare receptivity. It has been well said of Paradise Lost, that while few general readers are attracted by [vi] the subject, and fewer read it through, or often enough to discern the art with which it is written, every one who has once mastered it recurs to it with never-failing delight. There could not be a finer definition of a classical author, and it exactly describes Burke.

The details of Burke's biography, and the general lessons of the period in which he played his part, must be sought from other sources. As a party politician he seems to stand too near to our own times to permit of our regarding him fairly and comprehensively. Why this should be so, in a case separated by a whole century from the present generation, it is difficult to see; but sufficient evidence of the fact may be gathered from the writings of party men down to our own day. Political parties will always divide civilised nations, and no Englishman can altogether dismiss the party relations of any celebrated politician. Liberals will always be disposed to forget the originality, the consistency, and the humanity of Burke's views in the fact that he refused, at an important crisis, to sacrifice them in the mass to the opinion of a leader of far less wisdom and experience, though of more influence, than himself, and thereby broke up his party; while Conservatives will always see in him a determined Whig, a zealous advocate of religious liberty, and an audacious reformer. The coalition of 1782, in which he took an active part, is not one of the most creditable incidents in our political annals,[1] and he

---

1. The coalition should be judged, not by the better standard of political morality which dates its prevalence from the younger Pitt, but by that of the early part of the century, to which it properly belongs. The fruits of a long and honourable opposition were far more prodigally cast away, by the selfishness of a few, on the occasion of the fall of Walpole, and that by the hands of such men as Pulteney and Carteret.

Introduction

shared fully in the bitter and ungenerous hostility with which his party treated its Whig rivals.[1] His party services do not form the most memorable parts of his career. The "Observations on a late state of the Nation," and the "Present Discontents," for instance, only served to widen the breach between the Rockinghams and the other sections of the Whigs, without gaining them [vii] any additional strength in the court or in the popular party. His best efforts, if we except his advocacy of the cause of American liberty, are outside the policy of his party. Whiggism had small sympathy with religious freedom for Ireland, with humane and rational government in India, with the abolition of Slavery, or with the denunciation of its own caricature in the first French Republic. We must therefore regard Burke in a light different from that of party statesmanship.

The first question that is suggested on finding the political writings of an eminent party leader ranked among literary classics, is—What marks distinguish these writings from the common mass of political ephemera? Why should their author be remembered in respect of them, whilst more than one of those who equalled or exceeded him in contemporary reputation survives indeed as a great name, but in regard of permanent influence has passed away "as the remembrance of a guest that tarrieth but for a day"? By the virtue of what elements was a value communicated to them, extending, in the eyes of contemporaries, far beyond that of the arguments they enforced, the expedients they favoured, and the present effect they produced; and in the eyes of posterity, equally far beyond their worth as part of the annals of party, and as ma-

---

1. See the remark on Lord Chatham, post, p. 63. Burke, in a letter to a private friend, calls Lord Shelburne, who was Chatham's lieutenant and the link between the elder and the younger Pitt, "weak, wicked, stupid, false, and hypocritical," in one breath, and exults in having at length "demolished" and "destroyed" him. Time has placed things in another light. Chatham and Shelburne founded the modern school of independent statesmen.

terials for general history? It is an insufficient answer to such questions to say that Burke was a politician and something more, in the sense in which we should say the same, for instance, of Sheridan. The personal triumphs of Sheridan may indeed be said to exceed, in the mass, those of any genius on record, not excepting Pericles himself. To speak all the day, with overpowering effect, in Westminster Hall—to go in succession to the theatres, and see in each a masterpiece of his own, played by the first of actors—at night, to repeat in Parliament the feat of the morning—in all these, constantly to have the eyes of a nation upon him, and the plaudits of a nation in his ears—this seems like the realisation of as wild a dream as ever flattered the ignorance of young ambition. The triumphs of Burke were of another kind. From the first he astonished: but he never attained the art of carrying a Parliamentary audience with him. He was too severe to persuade, and too bold to convince, a body to most of whom his philosophy was a stumblingblock and his statesmanship foolishness. In his latter years he commanded so little attention that the wits of the House [viii] called him the "dinner-bell." Nothing is more melancholy than to read of the fate of the last Parliamentary speech which he gave to the world through the press, that on the Nabob of Arcot's Debts (1785). Brougham considered this by far the finest of his orations, and it certainly contains his finest exordium. But no one listened to it, or seemed to understand it. Erskine slept through the five hours which it occupied in delivery, though he afterwards thumbed the printed copy to rags. Yet this was the speech in which the orator's feelings were most thoroughly roused—in which there is more wealth of imagery, more invective, and more sarcasm than in any other. Never, says Dr. Goodrich, was there a greater union of brilliancy and force, or a more complete triumph over the difficulties of a subject. Near its close, Pitt asked Lord Grenville whether it would be necessary to reply. The answer was, "No! not the slightest impres-

INTRODUCTION

sion has been made. The speech may with perfect safety be passed over in silence."

But while the speeches of Sheridan are read once, and then laid on the shelf, the writings of Burke are the daily bread of statesmen, speakers, and political writers. We cannot take up a review or newspaper without finding some trace, however faint, of their effect. Similarly, as Coleridge says, the very sign-boards of our inns afford evidence that there was once a Titian in the world. We cannot peruse the speeches of any successful modern orator, without observing how much they owe to the method, the phraseology, the images, and even the quotations of Burke. To him may be applied with truth the epitaph of Ennius.[1] The speeches of Canning are especially recommended as an example of what a clever man, without much originality, may make of himself with the aid of Burke. The difficulty is not, indeed, to see where Burke's influence is to be found, but to preserve our own vision unaffected by it. His genius is of so peculiarly brilliant a nature, that it seems to affect the mind's eye the more, the more the mind's eye becomes accustomed to it. It seems to dazzle the strong intellect more effectually than the feeble. It has been well said that Burke sways the mass of intelligent and cultivated readers with almost as little resistance as a demagogue experiences from a mob. In the endeavour [ix] to penetrate the cause of this we shall not be much assisted by any criticism specially directed to the subject, though many capable men have penned such criticisms at greater or less length. Hazlitt, who has left two contradictory estimates of Burke, is the most conspicuous exception: and he, in another work, has admitted the futility of the attempt. The student will beware of falling into this error. He will aim at a minute knowledge of the relics of Burke's genius, a comprehension of their method, and a perception of their relation to each

---

1. *Volito vivu' per ora virom.*

other. In this way will an idea gradually be created, not to be got at second-hand, and a species of faith in his author will be generated, which will end in the disappearance of seeming discrepancies. He will supplement this by the interesting task of tracing the influence of Burke's views upon those of more modern writers, an influence quite unparalleled, except in the history of theology. Burke's reputation is full of variety. He devoted much of his toil to demolishing the modern school of philosophy, but the philosophers, both in Germany and in France, have forced him into their systems. He was born to a position outside the religious controversies of the day,[1] and he confirmed himself in it by deliberation; but his extreme tolerance has exposed him to the claims of both parties. The Catholics tell us that he was really a Catholic, or would have been so if he had lived in our own time. He has often been quoted, like Scripture, for and against the same doctrine. Even the democrats admire him and approve him exceedingly, although they have somewhat against him. They did the same in his lifetime. "These priests (of the Rights of Man) begin by crowning me with their flowers and their fillets, and bedewing me with their odours, as a preface to the knocking me on the head with their consecrated axes." Some charm forces from them an unbelieving homage, before they stamp him to pieces, and scatter his fragments to the winds.

This multifarious praise is balanced by a general outcry against him for deserting his early convictions. Burke's consistency has always been a trite point of controversy, and many acute minds have been deceived by appearances. The charge against him will be found forcibly stated in Moore's Life of Sheridan:

1. Burke's father was a Protestant and his mother a Catholic. The girls of the family were brought up in the faith of the mother, the boys in that of the father. Mrs. Burke was born in a family similarly circumstanced.

INTRODUCTION

[x] He has left behind him two separate and distinct armouries of opinion, from which both Whig and Tory may furnish themselves with weapons, the most splendid, if not the most highly tempered, that ever Genius and Eloquence have condescended to bequeath to Party. . . . Burke was mighty in either camp: and it would have taken two great men to effect what he, by this division of himself, achieved. His mind, indeed, lies parted asunder in his works, like some vast continent severed by a convulsion of nature—each portion peopled by its own giant race of opinions, differing altogether in features and language, and committed in eternal hostility with each other.

This view has descended from Whig politicians of Burke's time to the philosophical writers of our own day. This inconsistency was accounted for easily enough—in the last decade of his life he was alleged to be mad. The French Revolution at any rate, if it did not turn his brain, was said to have turned the current of his opinions, and made him a Conservative, as the horrors of Münster made More and Erasmus persecutors. Even Mr. Cobden echoed this cry.[1] He admitted, however, a certain method in this madness. "Burke's strictures on the Revolution," he says, "began with criticism, grew into menace, and ended in a cry for war." The story of his madness is stated in its most absurd form by Mr. Buckle. Burke lent support to this silly notion, by speaking of the decay of his powers in his last years, while he was preaching his crusade against the Republic with a force that seemed superhuman, and with a spirit that bordered on fanaticism. But it was reserved for Mr. Buckle to clothe this with the "dignity of history," and to make lamentation over the "ruins of that mighty intellect." It is sufficient in this place to say that the whole story is utterly without foundation. Burke's intellect was never more firmly settled, never exerted more widely its magical influence, and never expressed itself in sager utterances, than in these last years. Let the student examine the "Letters on a Regicide

1. "1793 and 1853," Works, vol. i.

Peace," and he will find Burke's folly wiser than the wisdom, and his madness saner than the reason, of his critics.[1]

The term inconsistency may be used in different ways to imply charges of very various kinds. In the shifting circumstances [xi] of political life, the statesman is often forced into "inconsistent" positions. He often acts, in consequence, in ways which seem, and may really be, inconsistent. He reaches the climax of inconsistency by deliberately changing his opinions, and with them his course of policy. Such a change, accompanied by a frank avowal of the fact, and an exposition of his reasons, was that of a great modern statesman on the question of the Irish Church. But the inconsistency which lies in acting differently under different circumstances, with the same radical views, does not come under any of these heads. The physician may, one day, order the patient's chamber window to be kept open, and the next, order it to be kept shut. But on the first day the wind was in the south-west, on the second day in the north-east. Of this nature was the inconsistency of Burke. He maintained to the last the perfect consistency of his political opinions. He valued himself upon it. "I believe," he writes in the third person, "if he could venture to value himself upon anything, it is on the virtue of consistency that he would value himself the most. Strip him of this, and you leave him naked indeed."[2] In order to gain a first idea of the opinions to which Burke adhered so tenaciously, the student is advised to set out with the idea that Burke was always what would now be called a *Conservative.* Party distinctions are of so perishable a nature that unless we can fix on something belonging to our own times, and "coming home to our business and bosoms," we are in dan-

---

1. Hazlitt says with great truth, that those who looked upon him as a man of disordered intellect, did so "because he reasoned in a style to which they had not been used, and which confounded their dim perceptions."

2. From the *Appeal from the New to the Old Whigs,* written to vindicate himself from this charge.

INTRODUCTION

ger of becoming the victims of words. We will not limit this term to the attitude or principles of the political party which is at this day in possession of it. By conservatism is meant that preference for and indulgence to what is already established, that faith in what has been tried, and that distrust of what exists only in speculation, which never wholly forsakes every sound politician, of whatever party. Passing from sentiment to logic, we might describe it, in the words of a German philosopher, as a system which holds the thinking away of what exists, and the thinking back in its place of what does not, to be the root of fallacies. Passing to practice, we use it to express briefly that policy in a commonwealth which, in the words of Hallam, "favours possession." The word is attempted, for the nonce, to be changed from a counter into [xii] a coin. It indicates that memorable group of principles which are enforced in the *Reflections on the French Revolution*.[1] In that work is contained, though not the first use of the idea, the first application in all its bearings of the doctrine of "conservation." The principles of that work were eagerly adopted by the politicians of the restoration, and it was to these, and to their principles respectively, that the words *conservateur* and *conservatif* came to be first generally applied, about the years 1820–1830. Mr. Croker, in the *Quarterly Review*, is said to have first given the term an English application, and Canning, who drew so largely from the later statesmanship of Burke, seems to have fixed it in English parlance. Since it has become a party name, it has of course incurred the liability common to all party names of losing not only its original meaning, but all vestige of any meaning whatsoever. The vicissitudes of such names are curious. The term "Whig," for instance, near the time of its first appearance, was interpreted by a lexicographer,[2] *homo fanaticus, factiosus*. "Whig-

1. Contained in vol. ii. of these Select Works.

2. Littleton.

gism" he translated by *enthusiasmus, perduellio.* In the middle of the last century, however, "Whig" was a most honourable title, claimed by politicians of all parties. Supporters of the court, of the great families, and of the rights of the people, all boasted of it, much as contending sectaries might claim the honoured title of Christian. It was understood to imply exalted sentiments of constitutional liberty. When anything occurred in Parliament to offend these sentiments, men used to say, "it made all the Whig blood boil in their veins." Whiggism seems now to be in its dotage, and to mean a spurious kind of Conservatism, which nobody is very eager to profess. The history of the term "Tory" is yet more curious. When it was introduced into our classical literature, the loyalty of a Tory was compared with the courtesy of a fasting bear.[1]

Now the Whiggism of the last century was in nearly every respect more conservative than are the principles of any party which exists at present. Nearly all reforming measures proceeded from the Tories, and jealousy for the constitution was [xiii] the cardinal virtue of the Whigs. "As respects the practical questions then pending," writes Macaulay, in his Essay on the Earl of Chatham, "the Tory was a reformer, and indeed an intemperate and indiscreet reformer, while the Whig was conservative even to bigotry." The Whig was sneered at for maintaining a standing army to be the bulwark of liberty, septennial parliaments a protection against corruption, the electoral dominions an important accession to the wealth and strength of the country, and the public debt a blessing to the nation. The army, the national debt, and the septennial parliament were indeed important protections to the settlement of the crown made on the Revolution, and they gradually grew so firmly into the framework of the state

---

1. Oldham, Second Satire on the Jesuits:
Think Tories loyal, or Scotch Covenanters;
Robbed tigers gentle; courteous, fasting bears.

that these sneers in time lost their place among the common-
places of Toryism. As the Tories became reconciled to the
Hanoverian succession, they took up a more practicable line.
The influence enjoyed by Whig ministers was enormous. The
first and second Georges were mere puppets in their hands.
Within the limits of their court, these sovereigns were encouraged to do as they pleased, but they were never suffered
to take part in the actual conduct of the state. Bolingbroke,
in his celebrated "Patriot King," had cleverly shown how this
state of things might be reversed, and during the last twenty
years of the reign of George II, the blow was being prepared
which paralysed the Whig party for a whole generation, and
from which they only recovered when they had identified
themselves seriously and thoroughly with the interest of the
mass of the nation. Frederick, Prince of Wales, had resolved
to destroy the Whigs, and his plans were inherited by his
son George III, with the commencement of whose reign
Burke's political career begins. If the old phalanx of Whigs
had held together, they might have despised their assailants.
But when Burke entered political life, the great Whig party,
which included most of the great territorial families, had
split into sections. What may be called the *legitimate* section
of the party, that which had for several years been under
the leadership of a member of the house of Pelham, had degenerated into a remnant, or as it was called in coarse old
political English, a Rump. There was a section of "Bedfords,"
headed by the Duke of Bedford, and another of "Grenvilles,"
under Earl Temple. A fourth section, that which could have
lent overwhelming weight to either of the others, and had
from [xiv] 1757 to 1763 constituted the strength of the legitimate section, but which, standing by itself, was the weakest,
was composed of the followers of the popular war minister, Lord Chatham. Such divisions were naturally the one
thing needful to give effect to a policy of aggression on the
part of the court. It was the first, which we have called the

legitimate section of the party, then headed by the Marquis of Rockingham, into which Burke happened to be thrown. The sympathies of readers of the present day will probably be divided, as the sympathies of the mass of the people at the time were probably divided, between this party and that which lay under the influence of Chatham. Chatham, with the legitimate Whigs at his back, had been a brilliant, a popular, and a successful minister. But Chatham was no Whig at heart. His powerful influence was of a personal nature, and he despised Whiggism. The best men, by this system, were excluded from the highest offices. The chief arts which recommended to these were private deceit and public corruption. The whipper-in of an old premier, being an influential peer or near relative of an influential peer, had a right to expect the premiership in his turn. His business was to study the temper of the House of Commons, and to lead it by the nose; to cajole or intimidate the monarch, and to drain the Treasury to enrich his friends, supporters and parasites. It was not likely that under such a system statesmanship could rise to a very high level. Chatham became gradually weary of the supremacy of men whose title to power lay outside their personal capabilities. His own following was small; but he refused to coalesce with either of the parties, and, with childish vanity, never rested until he had constructed an administration in which he himself took the place of a Whig potentate by becoming a mere *fainéant* minister, whose name was necessary to enable government to proceed. It was a signal failure, and was probably the most miserable administration that England has ever seen. The consequences were disastrous. Chatham's influence with his own cabinet speedily waned, and all that he had accomplished was to pave the way for a ministry in which the King's will was supreme. The Whigs went over to it in bodies, America was lost, and England was brought to the verge of Revolution.

The principal historical thread which runs through the

present volume is that of this contest between the King and the Whigs. [xv] The King fought his battle manfully, held each position, as it yielded to him, tenaciously, and gained his victory—though ingloriously. It would have been otherwise had America been compelled to submission. But America and Reform were the sacrifices made to secure his success. A dispassionate critic might possibly sympathise with him in this struggle for what many would regard as his natural rights. "There is something," says Thackeray, "grand about his courage. . . . He bribed; he bullied; he darkly dissembled on occasion; he exercised a slippery perseverance, which one almost admires, as one thinks his character over. His courage was never to be beat. It trampled North under foot; it beat the stiff neck of the younger Pitt; even his illness never conquered that indomitable spirit." It is impossible not to feel a certain satisfaction on seeing "the engineer hoist with his own petard," and the poisoned chalice returned in its just circulation to the lips of those who mingled it. Corruption, in fact, was the only weapon with which to combat corruption. The King's plan was to take the packed cards out of the hands of the Whigs, and play off their tricks upon themselves. The chief point for the student to observe is, that all his measures were innovations, attacks on existing interests, and reforms more or less impolitic and mischievous. The setting up of Lord Bute was intended as a reform. The whole system of the *double cabinet,* exposed in the "Present Discontents," was intended to effect what Bute had failed in. The sham Chatham cabinet, however, was at bottom the boldest innovation, and if Townshend had carried out, as he probably would had he lived, the idea of parcelling out America into Royal Governments, the foundation would have been laid of a reform which, supposing a little less public spirit than actually existed among the upper classes, might have ended in reducing England to the model of contemporary continental governments. The taxation of America was the thin end of the wedge, and it was a happy thing for England and the world that it was so heroically resisted. The experiment of a ministry headed by a favourite was a conspicuous failure: but the succeeding administrations were an apprenticeship in kingcraft, and with Lord North as an instrument, the King appears, if not a finished master, at least as something better than a bungler. Like most monarchs by hereditary title, he was totally unfitted to direct the policy [xvi] of his country. He was wanting in that knowledge of the mass of social and political facts which forms the first requisite of the statesman, and in the philosopher's familiarity with the general laws of human nature and of history. He was, however, a fair specimen of the active and popular monarch. Modelling himself, not on those who preceded him, but on the noblemen by whom he was surrounded, he devoted such talents as he had to the duties which he conceived to claim them, and he was rewarded by a full measure of popularity. The impression he left on the hearts of the nation, an index not without its value, comes nearer than any other we could mention to that left by the great Queen Elizabeth. Much of the policy of his reign was false, but historians have laid too much of the blame upon the King's own shoulders. He was certainly not more ignorant or prejudiced than the bulk of his subjects. Where he erred, he erred with the nation. The reaction against the Whigs, which ended in their practical extinction, was a national reaction. The American War was favoured by pampered national pride, and its great failure was a national lesson.

The "Present Discontents" is chiefly interesting on account of the admirable method which it exhibits, the skilful alternation of the arguments, and the force and purity of the style. The topics of Whiggism in 1770 do not in themselves greatly stir the reader of history. Some of them were stale, others worn to rags. Years before the terrible spectre of a Double Cabinet arose to confound the Whigs and alarm the susceptibilities of a free nation, statesmen were pretty well agreed as to the meaning of Parliamentary independence. The whole nation, writes Pulteney to Swift, is so abandoned and corrupt, that the Crown can never fail of a majority in both Houses of Parliament. "I am convinced," he says, "that our constitution is already gone; and we are idly struggling to maintain what in truth has been long lost." The conclusion which he drew was to desist from an useless struggle against corruption. The precarious nature of the Whig domination, for which Burke contends as earnestly as for some elementary principle of morals, had long been known. Their fall, under changed circumstances, was imminent. Bolingbroke had found a plan for bringing it about, which he embodied in his famous tract "The Idea of a Patriot King"—a work important equally as a historical document, and as a model of style. [xvii] Chesterfield said that until he read that tract he did not know what the English language was capable of. The seed of the "Patriot King" was intended for the mind of Frederick, Prince of Wales, the King's father, but it sprang up and bore its fruits in the son. It contains nothing specially of a Tory nature in its arguments, and is in fact a piece of the purest Whiggism.[1] But it was an attack on existing interests in the guise of Reform; suggested an ideal Whiggism, purified from corruption and faction; and teemed with the common Whig claptrap of liberty and patriotism. The "Present Discontents," which is intended as its refutation, has been considered the "text-book" of Whiggism, and Burke intended it to be the creed of his party. But the student must bear the "Patriot King" in mind, and be cautious of accepting the former as expounding the ultimate form which Whiggism was capable of assuming. Modern liberalism has a creed which differs

1. A friendly critic has called this (which is borrowed from Hallam) a "hard saying." What can be more of the essence of Whiggism than the fundamental doctrine of the pamphlet that the title of Kings merely *descends*, and is not in any way strengthened by its descent?

widely from either. Bolingbroke had no hopes except from a
liberal monarch. Burke rested his system upon an oligarchy
of liberal noblemen and landowners. We can now, thanks to
the diffusion of wealth and education, appeal securely to a
liberal people.

How shall we reconcile all this with the reputation which
Burke justly enjoys of being himself a great reformer, and
the father of the present generation of reformers? The fact
is, that liberalism has always rested upon the positions which
it has won, and that the same man may often be fairly regarded in two aspects. Burke's liberalism may seem moderate
in quantity, but it had the merit of consistency. An early employment of his pen was to ridicule, by imitation, the Irish
democrat Lucas. Another was to expose in a similar way the
all-unsettling speculations of Bolingbroke. Indeed, the "Vindication of Natural Society" contains neither more nor less
than the germs of the "Reflections on the French Revolution." Very early in his career he declared in the House of
Commons that being warned by the ill effect of a contrary
procedure in great examples, he had taken his ideas of liberty very low; in order that they should stick to him, and
that he might stick to them, to the end of his life. Johnson
bore a remarkable testimony [xviii] to the nature of these
early principles. He hated the party in which his friend had
found himself by accident, and confirmed himself by consideration; and he charged Burke with selling himself, and
acting contrarily to his convictions. "*We* know what his genuine principles were!" said this honest Tory, who had been one
of Burke's intimates long before he became the instrument
of great men—"We are sure that he acts from interest!"[1] But
there were finer threads in reasoning than entered into the
web of Dr. Johnson's political philosophy. It is certain that
Burke never thought he was deserting any principle of his
own, in joining the Rockinghams. He had an old and most re-

---

1. Boswell, Life of Johnson, p. 509, ed. Croker.

spectable connexion to support, and a new and disreputable one to oppose; and his party were at the time devoted to opposing certain most impolitic innovations. Burke's conservatism was brought out to the full in fighting their battles.

Hazlitt has observed a remarkable anticipation of the political method of Burke in a speech of the Earl of Egmont,[1] a nobleman of remarkable originality and capacity who had been the head of opposition to Dodington in the court of Leicester House. Without exalting him to the place of Burke's master, we may agree with Hazlitt that the following passage contains the germ of Burke's general reasoning on politics:

Sir, it is not common sense, but downright madness, to follow general principles in this wild manner, without limitation or reserve; and give me leave to say one thing, which I hope will be long remembered and well thought upon by those who hear me, that those gentlemen who plume themselves upon their open and extensive understanding, are in fact the men of the narrowest principles in the kingdom. For what is a narrow mind? it is a mind that sees any proposition in one single contracted point of view, unable to complicate any subject with the circumstances and considerations that are, or may, or ought to be, combined with it. And pray, what is that understanding that looks upon naturalization only in this general view, that naturalization is an increase of the people, and an increase of the people is the riches of the nation? Never admitting the least reflection, what the people are you let in upon us; how in the present bad regulation [xix] of our police, they are to be employed or maintained; how their principles, opinions, or practice may influence the religion or politicks of the State, or what operation their admission may have upon the peace and tranquillity of the country; is not such a genius equally contemptible and narrow with that of the poorest mortal upon earth, who grovels for his whole life within the verge of the opposite extreme?

"In this speech," says Hazlitt, "we find the first denunciation of the intrusion of abstract theorems and metaphysical

1. Speech on the Jews' Naturalization Bill, 1750. Eloquence of the British Senate, i. 521. Lord Egmont published in 1742 a capital pamphlet called "Faction Detected." On his character and abilities see Walpole's Memoirs of George III, vol. i.

generalities into the science of politics." It is certain, however, that something very like it is to be found in the "Politics" of Aristotle. It is not difficult to trace this anti-theoretical and conservative method in the works before us, written whilst Burke was labouring on the Whig side. In the following volume, containing the "Reflections on the French Revolution," it will be found to be the burden of every page.

We have already remarked that the system denounced in the "Present Discontents," and the aggressions on America, were intended as Reforms. Never did the spirit of conservatism appear more plainly than in the two famous Speeches contained in the present volume, which he composed, delivered, and wrote out for the press on two important occasions in the debates before the war actually broke out. But it is plain enough in the "Present Discontents." Many historical allusions are introduced, all bearing on unsalutary innovation, and "alterations to the prejudice of our constitution."[1] It is not easy to say what may have been Burke's real opinion on the constitution as exhibited at the time when this pamphlet was written. Bentham's memorable "Fragment on Government" was as yet unwritten, though probably not unmeditated. The view of Montesquieu, Blackstone, and De Lolme was not yet treated, as it came to be treated in the succeeding generation, as a plausible romance. But the false picture of a supposed Saxon constitution was constantly held up to view by reformers, in contrast with that which subsisted. This picture Burke treated with the slight regard it deserved.[2] Yet we find in the pamphlet no indication of a jealous attachment on his part to the forms of the "control" which "the higher people and the lower" are jointly to exercise.[3] On the contrary, the House of Peers is treated as a form of popular rep-

1. p. 76.

2. Ibid.

3. p. 99.

resentation:[1] "the people [xx] by their representatives and grandees." The "great peers" are included in a mass with the "leading landed gentlemen, the opulent merchants, and the substantial yeomanry," as the natural strength of the kingdom, which is to be roused into exertion against the court faction.[2] The climax of this popular theory is reached at p. 118, where he maintains King and Lords to be representatives of and trustees for the people, as well as the Commons, and the whole scheme of government to "originate with the People." This seems like the Whig doctrine of the Revolution with deductions. But these are themselves historical. It is well known that every title in the House of Lords was anciently, if not elective, intended to represent local interests. The Lords represented themselves, and those who stood in the relation of homage to them. The Knights of the Shires and Burgesses represented themselves, and those freemen who, being in homage with no man, would otherwise have had no voice in the national deliberations. When Edward III demanded an aid in the fourteenth year of his reign, an answer was made by "the Prelates, Earls, and Barons, *for themselves and for all their tenants,* and the Knights of the Shires, *for themselves and for the Commons of the land.*" Similarly, Burke's theory of the constitution is in its real elements simply *the King and the People.* The People deliberating and making laws, and the King controlling by his negative; the King deliberating and making choice of ministers, and the People having the control of *their* negative by refusing to support them. In all this there is a remarkable likeness to Harrington's views on the proper place of a nobility and gentry in a popular government, and of the resolution of politics into "dividing and choosing," like the two girls with the apple. There is also a remarkable tendency to transcend all narrow views as to "fixed forms in a mixed

1. p. 101.

2. p. 105.

government." There is no sign whatever of a disposition to regard King, Lords, and Commons as making up a precious and complete mosaic, preserved by a magical balance, which it would be perilous to disturb, much less to regard any fixed forms as the normal and final state of man.

It is here that Burke's conservatism enters into the question. Here, he says in effect, I lay before you the established rights of the nation; and here, too, is the system by which these rights have always been carried into effect. That system has been [xxi] deranged by an interested and wicked faction, and we claim to have it restored; because it is not only the best possible, but the only possible system by which these rights can be secured. If it were answered that representation, as it then existed, was a miserable farce, and that the peers really governed the country by their control of elections, Burke's answer was that the system, if not theoretically perfect, was good in working, and had acquired its title by prescription. Possession, he said in one of his writings, passed with him for title. This was in a particular case; but where interests were large, and meddling with them would be hazardous, it became his general maxim. "The old building stands well enough, though part Gothic, part Grecian, and part Chinese, until an attempt is made to square it into uniformity. Then indeed it may come down upon our heads, all together, in much uniformity of ruin; and great will be the fall thereof" (1769). "No man examines into the defects of his title to his paternal estate, or to his established government" (1777). The Whig oligarchy, according to this convenient theory, had an established title to govern the kingdom. And rotten and incongruous as was the parliamentary system through which alone their influence could be maintained, none was to disturb it. Hence a conspicuous difference between the theory and the practice contemplated in Burke's pamphlet. A Ministry accountable to Parliament, and a Parliament accountable to the People, are plausible demands, and they are demands which a happier generation has realised. But the consequences of a considerable majority for a single Whig minister, as in the palmy days of Walpole, were a ministry accountable to no one, and a parliament forced on the people whether they liked it or no. A true family likeness subsisted between Whiggism and the domination of the King's friends, and hence the deadly struggle which ensued between them. Radical reform, as between the two, was as far off as ever, and the Whig opposed it with the most bitterness. The King's man had something to hope, under any circumstances, for his master's influence was permanent and indefinite. A slight concussion might destroy that of his rival, and hence the strongholds of Whiggism were guarded with great jealousy and vigilance. The Whig, in short, was a true Conservative.

The cry for radical reform is usually supported by some plausible [xxii] general maxim. Conservatism is averse from the employment of abstract principles in political reasoning, and in general to what metaphysicians call the philosophical method. "Das Christenthum ist keine Philosophie," wrote a metaphysical theologian, at the end of his wearisome efforts to square religion with abstract principles. "Die Politik ist keine Philosophie," is the summary of Burke. It is a matter of observation and of practice, and its laws are those of individual human nature enlarged. Abstract principles, like most things, have their use and their abuse: and the confusion of these has been a main difficulty to the thinking world. To the use of them we owe all our systems, and the effect of our systems, of religion, of law, and of education. All great changes for the better have been produced by engrafting upon the growing understanding of mankind, not bare statements of facts, but generalisations based on facts past and present, and proceeding transitively to other facts present and future. But while these principles in their use have been to civilisation as the dew and the rain, in their abuse they have been a mildew and a pestilence. What they have nourished they have the power to corrupt and to destroy. As an instance of an abstract principle often misapplied, let us take that which asserts the cheapest government to be the best. Burke, though he knew something of Economical Reform, was not of opinion that the statesman's business consisted mainly in reducing the expenses of government to a minimum. The way in which this question stood in his mind connected with others is lucidly explained by Hazlitt, in the following extract, which will furnish a clue to an important section of Burke's political theory:

He did not agree with some writers, that that mode of government is necessarily the best which is the cheapest. He saw in the construction of society other principles at work, and other capabilities of fulfilling the desires and perfecting the nature of man, besides those of securing the equal enjoyment of the means of animal life, and doing this at as little expense as possible. He thought that the wants and happiness of man were not to be provided for as we provide for those of a herd of cattle, merely by attending to their physical necessities. He thought more nobly of his fellows. He knew that man had his affections, and passions, and powers of imagination, as well as hunger and thirst, and the sense of heat and cold. He took his idea of political society from the pattern of private life, wishing, as he himself [xxiii] expresses it, to incorporate the domestic charities with the orders of the state, and to blend them together. He strove to establish an analogy between the compact that binds together the community at large, and that which binds together the several families which compose it. He knew that the rules that form the basis of private morality are not founded in reason; that is, in the abstract properties of those things which are the subjects of them, but in the nature of man, and his capacity of being affected by certain things from habit, from imagination, and sentiment, as well as from reason. Thus, the reason why a man ought to be attached to his wife and family is not, surely, that they are better than others (for in this case every one else ought to be of the same opinion), but because he must be chiefly interested in those things which are nearest to him, and with which he is best acquainted, since his understanding cannot reach equally to everything;[1] because he must be most

---

1. Hazlitt borrows his argument from Bishop Taylor's Discourse on Friendship.

attached to those objects which he has known the longest, and which by their situation have actually affected him the most, not those which are in themselves the most affecting, whether they have ever made any impression on him or no: that is, because he is by his nature the creature of habit and feeling, and because it is reasonable that he should act in conformity to his nature. He was therefore right in saying, that it is no objection to an institution, that it is founded on *prejudice,* but the contrary, if that principle is natural and right: that is, if it arises from those circumstances which are properly subjects of feeling and association, not from any defect or perversion of the understanding in those things which fall properly under its jurisdiction. On this profound maxim he took his stand. Thus he contended that the prejudice in favour of nobility was natural and proper, and fit to be encouraged by the positive institutions of society, not on account of the real or personal merit of the individual, but because such an institution has a tendency to enlarge and raise the mind, to keep alive the memory of past greatness, to connect the different ages of the world together, to carry back the imagination over a long tract of time, and feed it with the contemplation of remote events: because it is natural to think highly of that which inspires us with high thoughts, which has been connected for many generations with splendour, with power, and with permanence. He also conceived that by transferring the respect from the person to the thing, and thus rendering it steady and permanent, the mind would be habitually formed to habits of deference, attachment, and fealty, to whatever else demanded its respect: that it would be led to fix its views on what was elevated and lofty, and be weaned from the low and narrow jealousy which never willingly or heartily admits of [xxiv] any superiority in others, and is glad of any opportunity to bring down all excellence to a level with its own miserable standard. Nobility did not therefore exist to the prejudice of the other orders of the state, but by and for them. The inequality of the different orders of society did not destroy the unity and harmony of the whole. The health and well-being of the moral world was to be promoted by the same means as the beauty of the natural world; by contrast, by change, by light and shade, by variety of parts, by order and proportion. To think of reducing all mankind to the same insipid level, seemed to him the same absurdity as to destroy the inequalities of surface in a country for the benefit of agriculture and commerce. In short, he believed that the interests of men in society should be consulted, and their several stations and employments assigned with a view of their nature not as physical, but as moral beings, so as to nourish their hopes, to lift their imagination, to enliven their fancy, to rouse their activity, to strengthen their virtue, and to furnish the greatest number of objects of pursuit and means of employment, to beings constituted as man is, consistently with the order and stability of the whole.

The same reasoning might be extended further. I do not say that his arguments are conclusive: but they are profound and *true* as far as they go. There may be disadvantages and abuses necessarily interwoven with his scheme, or opposite advantages of infinitely more value, to be derived from another state of things and state of society. This, however, does not invalidate either the truth or importance of Burke's reasoning; since the advantages he points out as connected with the mixed form of government are really and necessarily inherent in it; since they are compatible in the same degree with no other; since the principle itself on which he rests his argument (whatever we may think of the application), is of the utmost weight and moment; and since on whatever side the truth lies, it is impossible to make a fair decision without having the opposite side of the question fully stated to us. This Burke has done in a masterly manner. He presents to you one view or face of society. Let him who thinks he can, give the reverse side with equal force, beauty, and clearness. It is said, I know, that truth is *one;* but to this I cannot subscribe, for it appears to me truth is *many.* There are as many truths as there are things, and causes of action, and contradictory principles, at work in society. In making up the account of good and evil, indeed, the final result must be one way or the other; but the particulars on which that result depends are infinite and various.[1]

[xxv] The discovery of these things, these causes of action, these contradictory principles, is the first business of the statesman. No man can speculate properly on what things ought to be, who has not previously devoted his whole energies to the discovery of what they are. No man is entitled to criticise the abuse, who has not fully mastered the idea of the use of an institution. Here, indeed, we have arrived at the main point in Burke. Just as, in his Treatise on the Sublime

1. Eloquence of the British Senate, vol. ii. The student is also recommended to the Section on the "Use and Abuse of General Principles in Politics," in Dugald Stewart's Philosophy of the Human Mind, Part i. ch. iv.

and Beautiful, he did not aim at shewing the defects of these venerable ideas, or that people often judged by a false standard, but that the traditional ideas of the mass of mankind are sure, in the long run, to be correct, and to be confirmed by being explained and elucidated, so in dealing with social and political ideas, he always took his stand upon those in general currency, and sought to explain and confirm them. The best instructor is not he who describes the excellences of some wonderful thing which we cannot get, but he who explains and shows us how to use or to improve something which we have got. It is easy to imagine other states of society, but it is difficult to learn the true bearings of our own. The sense of political objects does not come by nature. A partial view, in politics, distorts the judgment, and destroys the mental balance; in no science is it so true that a little learning is a dangerous thing. Burke will always stand forth as a man whose political knowledge was complete. He was therefore, though a reformer, incapable of rash and inconsiderate action. The man who has arrived at a view of the whole plan of civil society, and taken in the mutual relations and dependencies of distant parts, is not in danger of being consumed by an irrational zeal for or against any established element in that society. "Sanguine and inconsiderate projects of reformation," says Dugald Stewart, "are frequently the offspring of clear, and argumentative, and systematical understandings; but rarely of comprehensive minds. For checking them, nothing is so effectual as a general survey of the complicated structure of society." It is only to him who has attained this point, that everything fills its proper space, and no more, in the mind's eye. It is only then that a man gains what Burke calls that "elevation of reason, which brings things to the true point of comparison." To the Englishman who wishes to gain this elevation, Burke will prove of valuable assistance. Burke will help him at once to comprehend the [xxvi] plan of his national polity, and the materials with which it deals. A German philosopher thought that the vast combination of interests which constituted the British Empire demanded a whole lifetime to be adequately understood.[1] He recommended the learner to study the writings of Burke, in which this combination would be found concentrated and reflected, as in a mirror. The reader may be sure that he is following the track of a vigorous, acute, comprehensive intelligence; unsparing of fatigue, intent on and always arriving at some valuable result. It is this quality of solid bullion value which makes it impossible to *distil* Burke. Of the intellectual labour which prepared the way for this unlimited mastery over fact—which annihilates all obstacles between the group of facts and the intellect—it is not the place here to speak. It was commenced early, and carried on without intermission to the end. Once, in the vigour of his manhood, his constitution sank under his labours. It was with a just indignation that he said in defence of his pension, "I did not come into Parliament to con my lesson. I had earned my pension before I set my foot in St. Stephen's Chapel." These labours have made the works of Burke not only what Erskine termed them, "an immense magazine of moral and political wisdom," but an immense magazine of moral and political fact. They will be to future ages what the works of Cicero are to us—we can reconstruct from them alone, with certainty and ease, the social and political scene in which their author lived.

Burke knew very well that nothing could stand long which did not stand on its merits. He led the way in Reform while raising his voice against innovation. The spirit of Conservatism and the spirit of Reform are really the necessary complements of each other. No statesman ever pretends to separate them. "A state without the means of some change," Burke wrote, "is without the means of its conservation." He was fond of tracing the operation of "the two principles of correction and conservation" at different periods in English history. The

1. A. H. Müller, Verm. Schr. Th. i.

way in which these two principles are blended in Burke's system, has been pointed out in a pamphlet by Professor Opzoomer.[1] The student, however, [xxvii] will probably prefer to seek Burke's doctrines of Reform, like those of Conservatism, in his own writings. Nowhere else, except in the Politics of Aristotle, shall we find these two principles so well harmonised. With Aristotle, he thinks the spirit of Conservatism the first requisite of the statesman, and its general diffusion the first condition of a well-ordered state. With Aristotle, he allows the fullest share of importance to the reform[2] of existing institutions. In the older politician, indeed, we find a greater tendency, owing to the excessively analytical bent of the Greek mind, to regard the two principles as opposites; and the same distinction may be observed in the treatment of contrary elements in his moral philosophy. Burke traced the concurrent effect of these two principles everywhere; and he delighted to regard them in their concrete elements, as well as in the abstract form. He writes, for instance, of Parliaments:

Nothing is more beautiful in the theory of Parliaments, than that principle of renovation and union of permanence and change, that are happily mixed in their constitution: that in all our changes we are never wholly old or wholly new: that there are enough of the old to preserve unbroken the traditionary chain of the maxims and policy of our ancestors, and the law and custom of parliament; and enough of the new to invigorate us, and bring us to our true character, by being taken from the mass of the people: and the whole, though mostly composed of the old members, have, notwithstanding, a new character, and may have the advantage of change without the imputation of inconstancy.[3]

It was chiefly in connexion with Irish and Indian questions, and on the economy of the Royal revenue, that his

1. It can be read in the German translation, "Conservatismus und Reform, eine Abhandlung über E. Burke's Politik," Utrecht, 1852.

2. Variously termed διόρθωσις, ἐπανόρθωσις, or βοηθεία.

3. Notes for Speech on the Amendment on the Address, Nov. 30, 1774.

exertions in the cause of Reform were made.[1] Burke had also his views of Parliamentary Reform;[2] but his observations on the temper and tendencies of the age inclined him to postpone indefinitely all practical dealing with the question. The knowledge we possess of the times, and the history of the great battle in the succeeding generation, when the position of the Reformers was much strengthened, induces us to think that he was right. It may also be observed that there is in Burke a *bona fide* [xxviii] dealing with the question, which is wholly wanting in some later opponents of Parliamentary Reform, and notably in Canning.

In the beginning of the Speech on the East India Bill four canons of reform are laid down. They are indeed immediately applicable to a particular case, but they are substantially those which he applies generally. There must be abuses, he says, in all governments. But there are great abuses and small abuses. Small abuses ought indeed to be reformed, if possible, but if impossible, difficult, or dangerous to be reformed, they may be left alone. Great abuses stand on a different footing; and these are the conditions on which we are justified in violating standing rights (for this is the real point in all Reform) with a view to their correction: "1st. The object affected by the abuse should be great and important: 2nd. The abuse affecting this great object ought to be a great abuse: 3rd. It ought to be habitual, and not accidental: 4th. It ought to be utterly incurable in the body as it now stands constituted." "All this," Burke proceeds, "ought to be made as visible to me as the light of the sun, before I should strike off an atom of their charter." Conservative as he was, this alone would clearly entitle him to be considered the forerunner of the modern Reformers. In one of his latest works he proudly declared that it had been the business of his strength to re-

1. See the chapters in Mr. Morley's "Edmund Burke, a Historical Study."

2. See note to p. 116, l. 34, inf.

form abuses in government; and he classed his last efforts against the French Republic under the same head. His book on the Revolution, he said, spared no existing abuse. "Its very purpose is to make war with abuses; not indeed to make war with the dead, but with those which live, and flourish, and reign."[1]

Very widely removed from this harmonious contrast of Conservatism and Reform, stands a darker and less reconcileable antithesis. In the Introduction to the succeeding volume it will be our business to follow the footsteps of Burke around the "Serbonian bog" of certain speculations, which were supposed to be at the bottom of the vast convulsion of France which commenced in 1789 and continues unfinished to this day. With that convulsion those speculations had little enough to do. Revolutions are never produced by opinions, but by political facts, such as actual badness of government, or oppression of one class by another. The wildest political opinions usually thrive best under [xxix] the strongest governments. Burke in his earlier years had traced the germs of Rousseau's ideas in the writings of Bolingbroke, and exposed their tendency in his "Vindication of Natural Society." Such ideas are not fraught with great danger, for they take fast hold only of crooked or ill-educated minds, and they rarely take so original a form as to rise to the level of an intellectual curiosity. Minds, however, once imbued with them do not soon relinquish them. It is the slow pressure of facts which imperceptibly modifies them. Fact is the best teacher in political science, and every man who has actually touched the political facts which surround him will recognise the soundness of the following emphatic words, addressed to the general public by one of the most memorable Reformers of our times. "The necessity," says Lord Brougham, "of some considerable degree of restraint to the well-being of society—the impos-

1. Appeal from the New to the Old Whigs.

sibility of the supreme power being left in the hands of the whole people—the fatal effects of disregarding the right of property, the great corner-stone of all civil society—the interest which all classes, down to the humblest, have in the protection afforded by law to the accumulation of capital—the evils of resistance to established government, except in extreme, and therefore very rare cases—the particular interest which the whole people, low as well as high, must ever have in general obedience to the supreme power in the state—the almost uniform necessity of making all changes, even the most salutary, in any established institution, gradually and temperately—all these are the very first lessons which every political teacher must inculcate if he be fit for his office, and commonly honest." Unequal distribution of power seems to be necessary for all government, and unequal distribution of property essential to its very existence. "Too much and too little," says Burke, "are treason against property." When a man pretends to invent a form of society in which there shall be no superior power, no property, and no religion to give effect to moral obligations, we know him at once to be a presumptuous sophist. As Siéyès said of Rousseau, "Croyant remonter aux *principes,* il s'arrête aux *commencements.*"

Burke was no democrat; but he thought that under certain circumstances a pure democracy might be a necessary and desirable form of government. This was consonant to the old [xxx] Whiggism; but it was going further than Cicero, who denies to democracy the very name of Republic. Burke's objections to it under ordinary circumstances are most clearly stated in the Appeal from the New to the Old Whigs; the chief one being that the very frame of a democracy excludes all restraints upon the depraved ambition which its spirit fosters. He was no friend to aristocracy properly so called; which in these pages he stigmatises as "an austere and insolent domination."[1] Monarchy Burke preferred upon principle, and he

1. Page 89, l. 26.

naturally preferred the limited monarchy of England, which
general opinion then held up to the envy of Europe. Montesquieu had recently given an impetus to the study of politics
by a work in which the English constitution received a full
measure of praise, and which Burke had studied with much
care. There are many works which, after being exceedingly
useful to mankind in their day, appear after a certain time
to lose their importance, and such has been in a remarkable
degree the fate of the "Esprit des Lois." But it has been justly
remarked,[1] that it is chiefly to that work itself that we owe
its present comparative uselessness. It was foolish to force
a work of so miscellaneous a nature into any semblance of
system. But this mass of ill-authenticated facts, of opinions
derived from ignorant antiquity, of the theories of a modern
recluse—this imperfect cyclopaedia of a science which can
never be perfectly understood, is also rich with sound reflection, and brilliant with true philosophical genius. It is best
known to the present generation by the caricature of Macaulay, contained in an essay written when he was fresh from
college, and which his maturer judgment must have almost
wholly disapproved. Sir James Mackintosh thought highly of
it, while Burke made use of its materials, and was decidedly
influenced by its spirit.

There is much in the mode of thinking of Montesquieu
that reminds us of Burke. There is a similar power of approxi-
mating to truth by a rapid and exact glance at the object,
and a similar determination always to keep his theory, as
Mackintosh expresses it, "in the immediate neighbourhood
of practice." With Burke, Montesquieu thought that wisdom
was often shown in leaving an evil uncorrected;[2] that the evil
of change might be greater than [xxxi] the evil of sufferance;
that conjunctures must be awaited, and can rarely or never

1. Edinburgh Review, vol. xlviii. p. 519.

2. "Il ne faut pas tout corriger." So Erasmus: "Scio quidvis esse ferendum
potius quam ut publicus orbis status turbetur in pejus."

be forced on; that political genius consisted in a great measure in knowing where uniformity was necessary, and where inequalities might be tolerated; that there was a difference between legislation and government, between parsimony and economy, between taxation and revenue. He did not think much of the inherent wisdom of the masses. He thought the people always had either too much or too little action. "Quelquefois avec cent mille bras il renverse tout; quelquefois avec cent mille pieds il ne va que comme les insectes."[1] He had equally small faith in appeals to the *reason* of mankind in the mass. He more than eulogised the English constitution; and said with equal wit and truth of Harrington, what might be said of all who plan new forms of government without understanding the excellences of the old, that he had built Chalcedon when he had the shore of Byzantium before his eyes. He has been accused, like Burke, of degenerating into a solemn and mysterious enunciation of truisms. But there are some truths which are considered unimportant, because they are undisputed; so true that they may be safely neglected, or even tossed into the limbo of the most exploded errors. When they are brought to light, they are called truisms. Such truisms neither Montesquieu nor Burke disdained.

The political essays of Hume exhibit an order of mind equally rare with that of Burke. Both had derived their stimulus in different ways from the restless intellect of Bolingbroke. But Hume's metaphysical studies, which had produced his marvellous power of contracting the mental eye to the subtleties of abstraction, had weakened the power of dilating it so as to take in the wide and complicated relations of fact. Hume, in dealing with contemporary topics, was an acute observer, but a bad reasoner: his mind played idly, and, as it were, in patches, on the surface of things which the less exquisite intellect of Burke penetrated in their depths and illuminated

1. Liv. ii. c. 2.

in their entirety. Burke stands apart from the metaphysical politics of Sidney and Locke, from whom the Whig writers of the early part of the century, and notably Hoadly and Tindal, had derived their tone, though he is occasionally indebted to them for an idea. He was familiar with Swift; but no trace is to be found in Swift's writings of the large way of thinking which [xxxii] pervades Burke's. The former is almost as remarkable for his reluctance to commit himself to broad and general views, as the latter for his eagerness to fortify his particular case by appealing to them. Swift indeed usually reasoned by a chain of minute particulars, and made his arguments turn in some form on personalities, which Burke, as far as was possible, avoided. Swift laboured, says Jeffrey, "not to point out the wrongs of Ireland, in the depression of her Catholic population, her want of education, or the discouragement of her industry; but to raise an outcry against an amendment of the copper or the gold coin, or against a parliamentary proposition for remitting the tithe of agistment." Burke, like Demosthenes, preferred to treat a variety of topics in such a way as to bear with irresistible force on a single argument. Gordon, the English Machiavelli, supplied him with some hints; and from Bolingbroke he learned a philosophical mode of treatment, and an easy and powerful style. The "Vindication of Natural Society" is a singular proof that genius is, if not the child, at least the foster-child of imitation. But though Burke was never ashamed of borrowing a good idea, the sum of his obligations to the strictly political writers of this or any other country is small. He had the run of a wider field. The literature of England is remarkable for the extent in which it is pervaded by political ideas. Poets, divines, dramatists, and historians, alike illustrate the leading tendency of the English mind. In the two former of these classes Burke had an especial interest. Hooker and South, Milton and Dryden, were often to him a real fount of inspiration. His philosophical mind readily discerned any analogy which was convertible to his own purpose, and this faculty in him was rarely misused. Burke knew general English literature well; and he turned all his knowledge to such account that next to facts and reasonings upon facts, it became his chief resource. Burke moreover, like Cicero, had received the training, not of a politician, but of a man of letters. When Cicero first appeared in the character of a statesman, politicians used contemptuously to call him "the Greek," and "the Scholar." Every one of Burke's productions exhibits a mind thoroughly tinctured with scholarship, in the widest sense of the word, and perfected in it by continuous practice. His scholarship is of the Roman rather than the Greek model. Cicero, Livy, and Tacitus were familiarised to [xxxiii] him by sympathy with their subject-matter. He was equally acquainted with the poets, and was often indebted to them for an illustration.

The general resemblance which may certainly be traced between the style (though not the method) of Burke and that of Cicero, is due rather to similarity of circumstances than to intentional imitation. There is an amusing passage in Boswell's Life of Johnson,[1] which contains the opinion of the great critic on this point in 1773. Being asked what was the particular excellence of Burke's eloquence, Johnson says, "Copiousness and fertility of allusion; a power of diversifying his matter by placing it in new relations. Burke has great information, and great command of language; though in my opinion it has not in every respect the highest elegance." *Boswell:* "Do you think, Sir, that Burke has read Cicero much?" *Johnson:* "I don't believe it, Sir. Burke has great knowledge, great fluency of words, and great promptness of ideas; so that he can speak with great illustration on any subject that comes before him. He is neither like Cicero, nor like Demosthenes, nor like any one else, but speaks as well as he can." What Johnson indicated by this deficiency in the highest ele-

1. Ed. Croker, p. 336.

INTRODUCTION

gance was the *familiarity* of Burke's style. In his own writings
he rarely lost a certain formal and academical air, which does
not disappear altogether in his conversations. Even in the
delightful writings of Goldsmith there is a constant savour of
the press. Burke's political writings, on the other hand, have
always the air of a spoken *appeal* from man to man. He is
always forcible and earnest, but, in spite of the compass of
his thought and the prodigality of his illustrations, the ab-
sence of self-consciousness is as remarkable as in the writings
of Hooker and Taylor. As is usual in the case of men of good
feeling, strong conviction, and high principles, there is no
sense of labour or display in anything that he writes, and in
this respect he even contrasts advantageously with such comparatively unambitious writers as Bolingbroke, Shaftesbury,
and Swift.

Changes have been traced in the progress of Burke's style,
but they are not worth considering. A remarkable identity
connects his earliest and his latest works, but the greater dif-
fuseness of the latter is attributable, of course, to the habit of
public speaking. [xxxiv] Burke's eloquence introduced a new
model into Parliament. The conventional style of speaking in
the middle of the last century may be best described in the
words of Lord Hervey, who thus characterises the speaking of
Lord Lyttelton, whose speech on the Jew Bill was considered
a model of oratory: "He had a great flow of words, that were
uttered in a lulling monotony, and the little meaning they had
to boast of was generally borrowed from commonplace maxims of moralists, philosophers, patriots, and poets, crudely
imbibed, half digested, ill put together, and confusedly re-
funded." Walpole describes this nobleman as "talking hero-
ics through his nose, with the gesticulations of a puppet."
Nothing can be more removed from this mixture of commonplace and falsetto, than the candour and profundity which
mark the manner of Burke. He expressed his ideas with all
the grandeur in which they were conceived; but the expres-

sion was always natural, and occasionally agreeably relieved by familiarity. It approaches to that manner of "good conversation" which he himself attributes, as a high excellence, to Cicero. Burke reprehended any attempt to separate the English which is written from the English which is spoken.[1] Plautus and Terence, and the "beautiful fragments of Publius Syrus," he considered to be models of good speaking and writing. He often casts to the winds all literary formality, and writes just as he may have spoken in public or private, freely and unrestrainedly. In this way Burke gave a lasting stimulus to English prose literature, as Wordsworth soon afterwards gave a stimulus to poetry, by the introduction of a fresher and more natural diction. His writings have ever since been the model of all who wish to say anything forcibly, naturally, freely, and in a comparatively small space. The common-sense politician recognises him as his master, and modern satire is indebted to him for originating the "Saturday Review" style.[2] He fell naturally into that manner which was best adapted to take and to keep hold of the [xxxv] practical English mind, and he brought that manner at once to its perfection.

The chief art of the speaker and writer consists in giving every part of his work its due degree of force, and its proper shade of colour.[3] This is remarkably exemplified in the products of the pen of Burke. "His words," says Hazlitt, "are the

1. See his letter to Murphy, upon his Translation of Tacitus.

2. See, for instance, the Letter to W. Elliott, Esq., 1795. "There may be sometimes too much even of a good thing. A toast is good, and a bumper is not bad; but the best toast may be so often repeated as to disgust the palate; and ceaseless rounds of bumpers may nauseate and overload the stomach. The ears of the most steady-voting politicians may at last be stunned with 'Three times three.'"

3. "Is erit eloquens," says Cicero, "qui poterit parva summisse, modica temperate, magna graviter dicere. . . . Qui ad id, quodcunque decebit, poterit accommodare orationem. Quod quum statuerit, tum, ut quidque erit dicendum, ita dicet, nec satura jejune nec grandia minute nec item contra, sed erit rebus ipsis par et aequalis oratio" (Orat. c. 29, 36).

most like *things:* his style is the most strictly suited to the subject. He unites every extreme and every variety of composition: the lowest and the meanest words and descriptions with the highest." This is strictly true. Shakspere is no less conspicuously equal to himself whether drawing his greatest or his least characters, than Burke, on the occasion of the impeachment of Hastings, now preparing the highest flights of his rhetoric, and now employed upon the humble task of the legal draftsman.[1] His addresses to the King and to the American Colonists should be noticed as specimens of the most difficult of all eloquence, that which produces its effect by extreme gravity and simplicity, avoiding all rhetorical ornament. There is a passage in the former which Lord Grenville thought the finest that Burke ever wrote—perhaps the finest in the English language—beginning, "What, gracious Sovereign, is the empire of America to us, or the empire of the world, if we lose our own liberties?" which was evidently suggested by the passage in St. Matthew,[2] "What shall a man give in exchange for his soul?" In the sections of his works in which this grave simplicity is most prominent, Burke frequently employed the impressive phrases of the Holy Scriptures, affording a signal illustration of the truth, that he neglects the most valuable repository of rhetoric in the English language who has [xxxvi] not well studied the English Bible.[3] Refined tastes prefer the simpler parts of Burke's works to

1. There is a product of his pen which is raised by the nature of the subject from that description, but which is altogether a lawyer's work, full of patient research and mature judgment, the Report of the Committee to examine the Lords' Journals in relation to proceedings on the same occasion. Charles Butler, the eminent conveyancer, considered this an ample refutation of the notion that he was not equal to the subtleties of abstract jurisprudence. "It is one of the most valuable productions of his pen. It abounds in learning and profound observation, and embraces the whole of the subject" (Reminiscences, vol. i. p. 139).

2. xvi. 26.

3. See South's Sermon, "The Scribe Instructed."

the more ornate. Sir Samuel Romilly considered the best of his speeches, and indeed the best piece of oratory in the language, to be that "at Bristol previous to the Election," which he contrasted with that on American Taxation, much to the disadvantage of the latter. The comparison is unjust. The latter, though premeditated in some of its parts, was delivered in haste, in the heat of a debate; the former was a skilful and elaborate address, carefully prepared, embracing a wide field of subjects, and intended as a lasting vindication of his policy. The Speech on Conciliation, however, which has generally been the most admired, both by contemporaries and posterity, is almost faultless. "It unites," says Sir James Mackintosh, "the careful correctness of his first manner to the splendour of his second." It may be added, that it is a masterpiece of method; of what Goldsmith called Burke's way of "winding into his subject, like a serpent."

Of the characteristics of Burke's higher flights of rhetoric, it is difficult to say anything of value. Hazlitt confesses himself in despair at the task of analysing the style. "Its severe extravagance; its literal boldness; its matter-of-fact hyperboles; its running away with a subject, and from it, at the same time—but there is no making it out, for there is no example of the same thing anywhere else. We have no common measure to refer to; and his qualities contradict even themselves." There is indeed something about the best rhetoric which baffles the analysis of the critic, as life evades the scalpel of the anatomist. And in Burke's profuse employment of imagery to extend and amplify the thought—never merely echoing or repeating it—it is true that incongruity sometimes made its appearance. Sometimes, again, the brilliancy is overwrought, and instead of enforcing and illustrating the leading idea, draws off the attention to its picturesque accompaniment. But Burke's mind was by nature generative and progressive. "Some collateral adjunct of the main proposition," says De Quincey, "some temperament or restraint,

INTRODUCTION

some oblique glance at its remote affinities, will invariably be found to attend the progress of his sentences, like the spray from a waterfall, or the scintillations from the iron under the blacksmith's hammer." It is less wonderful that a few errors of taste or [xxxvii] method should find their way into such a train of ideas, than that these errors should be so few and so insignificant. It is hazardous to approach this fiery element too nearly. "Rhetoric," says Selden, "is very good, or stark naught: there's no medium in Rhetoric." These higher beauties will be imitated at the student's peril. In the manner of them, as in that of Pindar, there is no harbour for mediocrity: you must either succeed or fail. And the continual study of the finest passages is not to be recommended. "If dwelt on exclusively as models of style," says Dr. Goodrich, "they are sure to vitiate the taste. It is like taking all our nutriment from highly seasoned food and stimulating drinks."[1]

The favourite epithet of Shakspere is "sweet"; that of Milton, "bright"; that of Taylor, "eternal." That of Burke takes several forms, the chief being "great," "noble," "manly," and "liberal." Such epithets afford an index to the tendency of the works in which they abound. Taylor bears the thought of his reader in an irresistible current from the things of time to the things of eternity. Shakspere, above all things, refines the taste: Milton quickens and exalts the imagination. The peculiar effect of Burke is to enlarge, strengthen, liberalise, and ennoble the understanding. In following the train of his arguments, even in their minor particulars, he must be a wise man indeed who does not constantly perceive lights that never fell on him before. He must be an extraordinary man, and have laboured in an unusual degree in the study of the interests of Britain, who does not find his power of methodically compre-

---

1. Bishop Hurd well says: "The more generally the best models are understood, the greater danger of running into that worst of literary faults—affectation."

hending those interests assisted and expanded by the perusal of every one of Burke's political works, from the "Present State of the Nation" of 1769, to the posthumous Third Letter on the Regicide Peace. In the latter work Burke has been compared to an Atlas; not labouring, but sporting with the burden of a world on his shoulders. This Letter has been held to exceed in intellectual magnitude all other single efforts of the human brain. Compared to that astounding work, said a man fresh from perusing it, the most famous effusions of ancient and modern eloquence sink into child's play.[1]

[xxxviii] In his manner of working Burke was unlike Sydney Smith, who composed slowly, and seldom corrected what he wrote. Charles Butler tells us that he never sent a manuscript to the press which he had not so often altered that every page was almost a blot, and never received from the press a first proof which he did not almost equally alter.[2] Often the printers never attempted to correct his proofs, finding it less trouble to take the whole matter to pieces and begin afresh. Most writers have constantly beside them as a model some favourite classical author. Voltaire's model for prose was the "Petit Carême" of Massillon: for poetry, Racine. Burke, according to Butler, always had a "ragged Delphin Virgil" not far from his elbow. Milton, Pope, and Dryden were quite as familiar to him. He is said to have known Young's Night Thoughts by heart; but, if this is true, it is somewhat strange that not a single quotation from that author is to be found in all his writings. In his illustrations, no less than in the body of his work, he is remarkable for an exquisite instinct of *selection;* which is the polar opposite of what is often called, by a false application of a mathematical term, *exhaus-*

1. Green, Diary of a Lover of Literature.

2. "I ask pardon for my blots (i.e. erasures and corrections). It is not proper, I am sensible, to send you a paper in that fashion; but I am utterly incapable of writing without them." Correspondence, vol. iii. p. 196.

tiveness—formerly much practised by the Germans, and consisting, to use the phrase of Goldsmith, in a certain manner
of "writing the subject to the dregs"; saying all that can be
said on a given subject, without considering how far it is to
the purpose; and valuing facts because they are true, rather
than because they are significant. Burke also excels in the
selection of words and epithets, in which he was assisted by
his knowledge of the writers of Queen Anne's period; but he
did not aim at the perfection attained in the most carefully
elaborated works of Bolingbroke. Bolingbroke, like Pope in
verse, loved to assemble specimens of the finer lights and
shades of words. "He can bribe, but he cannot seduce; he can
buy, but he cannot gain; he can lie, but he cannot deceive."
Burke, though not incurious of such effects, never stops in
his course to seek for them. It was rather his practice to bring
out the hidden force of common words and phrases, in such
a way as to give dignity even to vulgarisms. This habit was
early acquired. A passage in one of his earliest works (The
"Sublime and Beautiful"), beginning, "In the morning of our
days, when [xxxix] the senses are unworn and tender," &c., is
as worthy of note in this respect, as any of the most brilliant
passages of his latest writings. Indeed the remarkable unity
of Burke's writings is produced, as much as by anything, by
the ever fresh, natural, energetic air of his diction. He never
appears to go out of his way for beauties, and yet his work is
full of them. The study of law-books and state papers never
blunted his keen sense of literary beauty and propriety, nor
was the necessity of grappling with a definite mass of dry facts
enough to defeat its habitual operation. Everything that he
wrote charms in the reading. To understand the full meaning
of these remarks the reader must be familiar with the manner,
at once dry and verbose, of the speeches of the younger Pitt.

It is a well-known canon of rhetoric, that, in the selection
of words with a view to energy, we must always prefer those
terms which are the least abstract and general. Campbell and

Whately have pointed out as a remarkable instance of this rule, the well-known passage, "Consider the lilies, how they grow," &c.[1] To illustrate the effect produced by its systematic employment, we will take a passage from the present volume, and compare it with a passage to the same purpose, in the ordinary style, from an early work of Lord Brougham:

In large bodies, the circulation of power must be less vigorous at the extremities. Nature has said it. The Turk cannot govern Aegypt and Arabia, and Curdistan, as he governs Thrace; nor has he the same dominion in Crimea and Algiers, which he has at Brusa and Smyrna. Despotism itself is obliged to truck and huckster. The Sultan gets such obedience as he can. He governs with a loose rein, that he may govern at all; and the whole of the force and vigour of his authority in his centre is derived from a prudent relaxation in all his borders (pp. 242–43).	In all the despotisms of the East, it has been observed, that the further any part of the empire is removed from the capital, the more do its inhabitants enjoy some sort of rights and privileges; the more inefficacious is the power of the monarch; and the more feeble and easily decayed is the organisation of the government, &c. (Brougham's Inquiry into the Colonial Policy of the European Powers).

[xl] This particularising style is of the essence of poetry; and in prose it is impossible not to be struck with the energy which it produces. Brougham's passage is excellent in its way; but it pales before the flashing lights of Burke's sentences. The best instances of this energy of style are to be found in the classical writers of the seventeenth century. When South says, "An Aristotle was but the rubbish of an Adam, and Athens but the rudiments of Paradise," he communicates more effectually his notion of the difference between the intellect of fallen and of unfallen humanity than in all the philosophy of his sermon put together.

1. St. Luke xii. 27, 28.

INTRODUCTION

Almost every device of the accomplished prose-writer may be learned from Burke. One of the first things to be learned is to avoid the opposite errors of extreme conciseness and of extreme prolixity. The practised rhetorician does this by an instinct which is bound by no rule. It is, however, a safe maxim to employ *Repetition;* not in our vulgar sense, but as answering to what the Rhetoricians called *Interpretatio;* in the words of Archbishop Whately, "to repeat the same sentiment and argument in many different forms of expression; each in itself brief, but all, together, affording such an expansion of the sense to be conveyed, and so detaining the mind upon it, as the case may require." "Cicero among the ancients," he proceeds, "and Burke among the modern writers, afford the most abundant practical exemplifications of this rule." Almost every page of the "Present Discontents" will afford one or more of such exemplifications. The following passage from the First Letter on a Regicide Peace is one of the most remarkable examples of the employment of this effect:

Even when men are willing, as sometimes they are, to barter their blood for lucre, to hazard their safety for the gratification of their avarice, the passion which animates them to that sort of conflict, like all short-sighted passions, must see its objects distinct and near at hand. The passions of the lower order are hungry and impatient. Speculative plunder; contingent spoil; future, long-adjourned, uncertain booty; pillage which must enrich a late posterity, and which possibly may not reach to posterity at all; these, for any length of time, will never support a mercenary war. The people are in the right. The calculation of profit in all such wars is false. On balancing the account of such wars, ten thousand hogsheads of sugar are purchased at ten [xli] thousand times their price. The blood of man should never be shed but to redeem the blood of man. It is well shed for our family, for our friends, for our God, for our country, for our kind. The rest is vanity; the rest is crime.

Burke commonly practises the method of *Interpretatio* by first expanding the sense, and then contracting it into its most compendious and striking form. This device is indispensable when the author is dealing with a subject which is presumed to be unfamiliar to his readers. "The hearers," says Dr. Whately, "will be struck by the forcibleness of the sentence which they will have been prepared to comprehend; they will *understand* the longer expression, and *remember* the shorter.[1] Nor does any writer, not even Macaulay, excel him in producing effect by that less methodical interspersion of short, pointed, and forcible sentences throughout the performance, which is so necessary to the energetic and suggestive style.

The concluding periods of the paragraph last quoted form a remarkable example of what Fuller has called work "sewn together with strong stitches." When once heard, it is almost impossible that they should ever drop out of the memory. The following passage, which occurs later in the same work, will further illustrate this way of working, combined with more periodic structure:

> And is then example nothing? It is everything. Example is the school of mankind, and they will learn at no other. This war is a war against that example. It is not a war for Louis the Eighteenth, or even for the property, virtue, fidelity of France. It is a war for George the Third, for Francis the Second, and for all the dignity, property, honour and virtue of England, of Germany, and of all nations.

Here, as usual with Burke, the *sententia* ("Example is the school," &c.) is introduced early in the passage, forming as

---

1. The student must beware of abusing this useful figure, as in the following passage: "No individual can be happy unless the circumstances of those around him be so adjusted as to conspire with his interest. For, in human society, no happiness or misery stands unconnected and independent. Our fortunes are interwoven by threads innumerable. We touch one another on all sides. One man's misfortune or success, his wisdom or his folly, often by its consequences reaches through multitudes." Blair, Sermon VIII. Here the same proposition is repeated five times, without any material addition or illustration, the impression left being that of great poverty of thought. See note to p. 116, l. 34, infra.

it were [xlii] a light to lighten the reader's path to the end. Passages such as these should be committed to the memory as standard examples of the Syntax of modern Rhetoric. This Syntax differs materially from the system employed by the earlier and equally great English rhetoricians, Milton and Taylor. The method of the latter has been called *cumulative;* that of Bolingbroke and Burke, *constructive* or *artificial.* The difference lies partly in the mode of connecting the members of the sentence, and partly in a studied variety in the grouping of the ideas. The transition from the one style to the other answers to the transition in poetry from a style of unsymmetrical redundance to one in which (to quote the editor of Pope in this Series) the chief end was *form* or *art.* Not that specimens of the earlier style are wanting in Burke, but they are rare. The manner of the following passage will be instantly recognised by the reader of Taylor:

> But when the fear, and the evil feared, come on together, and press at once upon us, deliberation itself is ruinous, which saves upon all other occasions; because when perils are instant, it delays decision; the man is in a flutter, and in an hurry, and his judgment is gone, as the judgment of the deposed King of France and his ministers was gone, if the latter did not premeditately betray him.[1]

We have here a passage which consists of what the Greeks called κόμματα, or short separate members, connected in a primitive way, by conjunctions. The modern or French method is to unite the members of the passage by a connexion of ideas; as Dr. Whately expresses it, "to interweave or rather *felt* them together," by making the thought pass over from one member to the other; by concealing the sutures, and making the parts fit into and complement each other. This method leaves better opportunities for marking boldly the transitions in the argument, and, if appropriate, making

---

1. Speech on the Petition of the Unitarians, 1792.

corresponding changes in the style. In the literary art, as in all others, unprepared transition from one main member of the composition to another is an unfailing mark of barbarism.[1] The Speech on Conciliation, which is the most remarkable of the works in this volume as a specimen of method, is full of illustrations of this canon. Of the boldness with which Burke sometimes broke [xliii] through his method for the sake of the method we have a striking instance at page 235, where he inserts in the first part, which consists of a description of the condition of America, and of American character, a series of objections to the employment of force against the Colonists, properly belonging to the second part of the speech.[2]

Burke employed with great effect the device, so fashionable in literary works of the age which immediately preceded him, of diversifying his writings by the introduction of what were called "characters." Under this general denomination were included compendious sketches not only of what was most remarkable in remarkable persons, but also of places, nationalities, opinions, curious or obsolete manners—of anything, in short, of a particular nature, not being altogether foreign to the general purpose, which could be turned to account so as to relieve or to illustrate the performance. The characters of Mr. Grenville, of Charles Townshend, of the Chatham Ministry, and of the American Colonists, in this volume, are specimens. They should be compared with those of Walpole, Montesquieu, Fox, Savile, Howard, and others, in other parts of his writings, and with similar compositions of Clarendon and Bolingbroke. The student should also refer to the characters in the spurious "History of the Last Four Years of Queen Anne," printed among the works of Swift. Burke had read this work, and had remarked the peculiarities of the style, though he never thought of pronouncing it a

1. This remark belongs, of course, only to prose.

2. See Argument, p. 221.

forgery. Burke excels in putting his characters in the peculiar light which suits his work, without seeming directly to intend it. They are drawn in a few easy, broad, and masterly strokes, fulfilling in a striking degree the canon that works of true art must always appear to have been done easily. They remind one of the description of a famous portrait by Velasquez, of which a painter said that every part seemed to have been "touched in with a wish"; and that the spectator could not help feeling that he could take up the brush and do the same thing himself.[1]

Burke possessed the secret of being methodical without the appearance of method. The "Present Discontents," which was originally cast in the form of a letter, and the "Reflections on the French Revolution," which retains that form, appear at first sight [xliv] devoid of arrangement, though really as methodical as the epic of Tasso or the Hamlet of Shakspere. The unity of feeling which reinforces this unity of composition was derived from the tone of the author's mind. It is evident that he wrote them, especially the latter, under the influence of some mental excitement. He appears even to have cultivated this excitement, on the ground that it stimulates the faculties, and in his own words, "suffers not a particle of the man to be lost." Even vehement passion he considered to be so far from indicating an infirm judgment, that it was often not merely the accompaniment and auxiliary, but the actuating principle, of a powerful understanding.

In touching slightly on the points of contact between Burke and his contemporaries, it will be necessary to do what has hitherto been avoided—to consider separately his separate characters of orator and author. No man of modern times has united these characters with equal success. He was the only man of his day who had pursued the only and infallible path to becoming a real orator, that of *writ-*

---

1. Hazlitt, Conversations of Northcote.

ing much, and assiduously cultivating literary excellence.[1] Bolingbroke, by universal consent the greatest orator of his time, had done the same thing: so had Chatham, in his early years, although scarcely anything of his labours saw the light. But most of Burke's contemporaries had attained their proficiency in public speaking by the common and less troublesome plan of trying to do it as often as opportunity offered, and hardening themselves against failure. In this way fluency and [xlv] self-possession are always to be gained, eloquence never. The former go to make up the practical debater: and a few pointed remarks and striking images will be enough, with a clever man, to conceal want of art in combining his ideas, and incompetency to present them in their most effective form. The oratory of the younger Pitt, which is a good example of the speaking of a business-like, practical statesman, has much of this character. It is marked by a certain mechanical fluency, well adapted for bearing the speaker up while he is meditating what he shall say next, but accompanied by a baneful tautology and confusion of method. It is wanting in organic elasticity.

---

1. It may be useful to subjoin the opinions of two authorities well qualified to pronounce upon this point. In the first extract, Crassus is criticising the system of "debating societies."

"In quo fallit eos, quod audierunt, dicendo homines, ut dicant, efficere solere. Vere enim etiam illud dicitur, PERVERSE DICERE HOMINES PERVERSE DICENDO FACILLIME CONSEQUI. Quamobrem in istis ipsis exercitationibus, etsi utile est, etiam subito saepe dicere, tamen illud utilius, sumpto spatio ad cogitandum, paratius atque accuratius dicere. Caput autem est, quod (ut vere dicam) minime facimus; (est enim magni laboris, quem plerique fugimus:) quam plurimum scribere, STILUS OPTIMUS ET PRAESTANTISSIMUS DICENDI EFFECTOR AC MAGISTER." Cic. De Orat. Lib. i. cap. 33.

"I should lay it down as a rule, admitting of no exception, that a man will speak well in proportion as he has written much; and that with equal talents he will be the finest extempore speaker, when no time for preparing is allowed, who has prepared himself the most sedulously when he had an opportunity of delivering a premeditated speech. All the exceptions which I have ever heard cited to this principle are apparent ones only." Brougham, Address to the Glasgow Students, 1825.

INTRODUCTION

Excellent as is the first part of the Speech on American taxation, the student must look elsewhere than in Burke for the best specimens of the art of Parliamentary debate. The fine perception of the fitnesses of time and circumstances, and the habit of waiting assiduously upon the temper of individuals, and upon the nameless caprices of a collective body, were incompatible with the preoccupation of the state-philosopher. As a debater Burke was the inferior of Pitt, and in an increased degree, of Fox. The speeches of Fox, in spite of the indifferent state in which they have come down to us, are the classical models for debating, the most important being those on the Westminster Scrutiny and the Russian Armament. The first part of the latter, to repeat the advice of Brougham to the father of Macaulay on the subject of his son's education, the student should "pore over till he has it by heart." Among the few other models recommended by Brougham were Burke's Thoughts on the Present Discontents, and Speech on Conciliation with America. With his usual enthusiasm for the ancient orators Brougham goes on to say that he must by no means conclude his studies with the moderns. "If he would be a great orator, he must go at once to the fountain-head, and be familiar with every one of the great orations of Demosthenes."

How is it that so few speeches of modern times, out of so many which survive, grandly constructed, and finely adapted to their purpose, obtain a permanent place in literature? For this doubtless there must be something which shall touch the permanent nature of mankind at large, not only the temporary disposition of particular assemblies. Burke dealt largely in questions of great permanent interest, but this was hardly sufficient in itself [xlvi] to account for the extent in which his writings and speeches have been cherished. The first requisite for preservation is a certain amount of literary skill employed either in their original construction or in their preparation for the press. The same may be said of forensic oratory. Most of the speeches of Windham and Canning, of Erskine and

Curran, have for succeeding generations an interest which hardly rises above that of the subjects with which they are concerned. Those of Grattan and Brougham possess something of the same interest which attaches to those of Burke.

The writings of Burke have often been classed, in point of style, with those of Johnson and Gibbon. The resemblance is only partial. Johnson conceived it to be his mission to reform his native tongue, and in his own words, to clear it from colloquial barbarisms, licentious idioms, and irregular combinations. "Something, perhaps," he wrote at the end of the *Rambler,* "I have added to the elegance of its construction, and something to the harmony of its cadence." This elegance is generally considered to be mechanical, and this harmony monotonous. It is the sound and painstaking commonsense—the candid and profound judgment, which give body and worth to the "alternate coruscations" of verbiage in which Johnson delighted. If we imagine Bolingbroke—whom nature intended for a demagogue, and endowed with a natural flow of exquisite and expressive language, coupled with a natural flimsiness and quackery of reasoning—possessed, instead, of this Johnsonian sense and judgment, we have something approaching to the manner of Burke. To write in the closet with the ardour inspired by the surroundings of the senate; to be copious, even to a fault; to flow in a torrent, regardless of measure and symmetry, unstudious of phrase and parenthesis; to shift the argument into different lights, as careless of the "harmony" or "unity" of the picture, and as successful in the effect of it, as Rubens; there is nothing of Johnson, nor of Gibbon in this. Gibbon set before himself a higher literary ideal than ever governed the pen of Burke. Whatever may be faults of the style of Gibbon, it possesses one excellence of a high order—that its graces are not destroyed by translation. The censure of unnaturalness and affectation is, in general, unjustly applied to it. There is a constant elevation of expression: if monotonous, it is always dignified. But the tastes, studies, and objects of Burke were wholly diverse from those of Gibbon: [xlvii] and there are too few points at which their works can be said to touch to enable us, as to their style, to draw a just comparison.

Of authors who were Burke's contemporaries, the most characteristic of the manner of his age, but as manifested in an upper and non-literary class, is Walpole. The best literary artist is Goldsmith. The few first-class men of the time stand towards the popular authors of the day in a fixed relation which will be best understood by comparing Goldsmith as a writer of fiction with Richardson and Sterne. The literary vice of the age was a sickly and demoralising species of sentimentality. In oratory, it may be traced in some passages of Sheridan's Indian speeches. Hardly one of the sentimental poets of the century is free from the taint. What it was in its culmination the reader may see in the once popular poems of Charlotte Smith. Bowles and Coleridge illustrate it at the time when it was about to disappear before the examples of Cowper, Rogers, and Wordsworth. A hundred forgotten novels exemplify it in prose. Rousseau, Goethe, and many others, show in what way it spread to the literature of neighbouring countries. Fielding and Smollett afford evidence of it, even whilst protesting against it by their example. A large section of the literature of the age is turned by it into a mass of unqualified rubbish, as worthless as the copper-plate page illustrations that adorned the volumes which contained it. Yet without reference to these it would be impossible to estimate the greatness of Reynolds and his school. Similarly, to estimate the importance of the manly tone of thought which Burke and Johnson exhibit, the student should glance at some of the best known among the didactic works of the age, such as Hervey's Meditations, once one of the most popular books in the world. "The distemper of the age," said Burke on one occasion, "is a poverty of spirit and of genius": and he went on to say that it was characterised by "the politics and morals of girls at a boarding-school, rather than of men and statesmen."[1]

Johnson and Goldsmith, who were original thinkers by nature, and men of letters by profession, derived no literary stimulus from communication with Burke, and there is, in fact, a balance on the other side of the account. It was otherwise with Reynolds. Attracted by the profound appreciation of the fine arts expressed in the Treatise on the Sublime and Beautiful, the [xlviii] great painter had sought Burke's acquaintance at an early period in his career. The powers of Burke as a critic and philosopher of art are clearly proved by that work, and by his letters to the painter Barry. But their best testimony is the fact that the Discourses of Reynolds are guided by a method, and expressed in a manner, which none who are familiar with Burke's writings can hesitate for a moment in pronouncing to be his. Until the appearance of Malone's edition of the works of Reynolds, it had been generally believed that Burke was the sole author of these Discourses. Many years afterwards, Northcote, who had good means of knowing, avowed his belief in what Malone had denied, that Burke had supplied much that was necessary to complete their literary form. To the reader of the present day, judging from these works themselves, it seems more probable that Burke composed them with facts supplied by Reynolds, than that the work of Reynolds was brought into shape and finished off by Burke. But the direct evidence is wholly in favour of the latter view. The "Discourses" are, however, pervaded by the mode of thought, as well as full of the expressions and illustrations, with which the reader of Burke is familiar. They bear evidence of a double influence. The philosophical critic guided the views of the artist, and his friendly pen corrected and embellished the writings in which they were expressed. Whatever may have been the exact share of

1. Speech on a Bill for shortening the Duration of Parliaments.

Burke in them, they are models, in their kind, of style and expression, and part of the standard literature of England; and Sydney Smith, without any reference to Burke, has described them by the terms which Goldsmith so justly applied to his friend, as "full of all wisdom."

Burke, in the history of English letters, represents the transition from the formal style of the early part of the last century to the far less constrained one which has prevailed in the present. He restores to literature, in some measure, the wealth and freedom which it had enjoyed in the days of the great dramatists and philosophical divines. In the spirit of his writings, however, he is distinctly the son, and not the changeling, of his age. His philosophy recalls the didactic school of Young, Johnson, and Armstrong; he sometimes partakes the satirical vein of Churchill and Smollett; more rarely we trace in him a tone akin to that of the "patriot poets," of Thomson, Akenside, and Glover. The influence of the great literary school of France, and of the [xlix] English copyists of their style and phrase, is often noticeable. He has, however, none of that habitual stiffness on which Johnson sometimes congratulated his contemporaries,[1] which had been diffused by the effect of French examples. If the aims of writing could be reached by simple reasoning and description, closely and concisely expressed, much of the poetry and the prose of the last century would be unsurpassable. The more sensitive elements in human nature, however, will not consent to be thus desolated, and the formal writer is thwarted at every step by the recoil of his own mechanism. In the literary art, as in all others, nature must be patiently studied. Burke, who never aimed at merely literary fame, and never once, in his mature years, cherished the thought of living to future ages in his

---

1. "There is now an elegance of style universally diffused." Again, on the Divines: "All the latter preachers have a good style. Indeed, nobody now talks of style; every body composes pretty well." Boswell, April 7, 1778.

works, was well acquainted with the economics of his art. He devoted himself solely to the immediate object before him, with no sidelong glance at the printing press or the library shelf. He reasoned little, or not at all, when he conceived reason to be out of place, or insufficient for his purpose. He never rejected a phrase or a thought because it did not reach the standard required by literary dignity. With all this, his writing always reaches a high standard of practical excellence, and is always careful and workmanlike. It is, moreover, well attuned to the ear. The cadence of Burke's sentences always reminds us that prose writing is only to be perfected by a thorough study of the poetry of the language. Few prose writers were so well acquainted with the general body of English verse, and few have habitually written so fully, so delicately, and so harmoniously.

This slight general sketch could not be better concluded than with the beautiful inscription composed by Dr. Parr for a national monument to Burke. Such a monument was demanded by public opinion, and the project was favoured by most of Burke's friends and admirers; but the House was never moved on the subject, partly from a scruple lest the wishes expressed in Burke's will should be violated, and partly on account of the disturbed state of popular opinion. The inscription is considered the best that Parr ever wrote: and as that eminent scholar was most eminent in inscriptions, it may be regarded as a masterpiece.

[1]   EDMUNDO . BURKE

VIRO

MULTIS . ET . EXQUISITIS . LITTERIS . IMBUTO

ET . SUMMA . INGENII . PRAEDITO . GLORIA

SODALI

SUIS . AMABILI

ET . IN . OMNI . GENERE . FACETIARUM . ORNATISSIMO

INTRODUCTION

CIVI

QUI . REMPUBLICAM . PROPRIAM . BRITANNORUM

IDCIRCO . ESSE . OPTIMAM . STATUEBAT

QUOD . REGALIS . SENATORII . POPULARISQUE . JURIS

CONSENSU . FUNDATA . ESSET

ET . COMMUNIONE . UTILITATIS . STABILITA

CRITICO

QUI . E . RECONDITA . VI . VERBORUM . QUOTIDIANORUM[1]

QUOD . AUT . VERUM . EST

AUT . AD . ID . QUAM . PROXIME . ACCEDIT

ACUTE . ARGUTEQUE . ELICUIT

INTIMOS . QUOSDAM . ANIMI . SENSUS . PATEFECIT

ET . ADUMBRATAS . IN . EODEM . A . NATURA

RERUM . IMAGINES

MULTO . EXPRESSIORES . DEFINIENDO . ET . EXPLICANDO . REDDIDIT

PHILOSOPHO

QUI . MULTIPLICES . ET . ABSTRUSAS . REI . POLITICAE . RATIONES

CUM . DISCIPLINA . MORALI . CONJUNCTAS

UBERRIME . ET . GRAVISSIME . ILLUSTRAVIT

ORATORI

QUI . COPIOSE . ERUDITE . SPLENDIDE . DICENDO . EFFECIT

UT . OMNES . ARTES . SE . PRAEBERENT

COMITES . ELOQUENTIAE . AC . MINISTRAS

QUI . VIXIT . ANN . LXVII . MENS . V . DIES . XXVII

DECESSIT . VIII . ID . QUINTIL . ANNO . SACRO . M . DCC . LXXXXVII

ET . BEACONSFIELDIAE . IN . AGRO . BUCKINGENSI

SEPULTUS . EST

REX . SENATUSQUE . BRITANNICUS

H . M . P . P . IMPEN . PONENDUM . JUSSERUNT.

1. "Sublime" and "Beautiful."

INTRODUCTION

[li] Burke is so copious and so clear a writer that the text of his works is, in general, amply sufficient to make him intelligible to an intelligent reader. It is believed that all additional illustration which is necessary is included in the Notes at the end of the volume; but those who require still further information may refer to the works mentioned in the footnote.[1] It only remains to give some particulars of the history of the works in the present volume.

The "Present Discontents" is a political pamphlet of the old school. The style is mainly pedestrian, relieved by some touches of humour, and by a few passages of a descriptive character. It contains much solid reasoning, but no rhetoric, except that of facts, or alleged facts. Great attention has been paid to style and finish, though no superfluities have been admitted, and there is a certain affectation of plainness, intended to sustain the author's assumed character of a private citizen. The facts are admirably marshalled, and it is

1. HISTORY. The Histories of Bisset, Belsham, Adolphus, Massey, Phillimore, Bancroft, and Stanhope; Wraxall's Historical and Posthumous Memoirs; Walpole's Memoirs; Jesse's Memoirs of George III; Rockingham Memoirs; Bedford Correspondence; Grenville Papers; The Annual Register; Almon's Biographical Anecdotes; Letters of Junius; Chesterfield's Letters; Macaulay's Essays; May's Constitutional History.

BIOGRAPHY. Boswell's Life of Johnson; Butler's Reminiscences; The Lives of Burke by M'Cormick, Bisset, Prior, and the recent work of Mr. Macknight, which, however, does not supplant the work of Sir James Prior as the standard biography; the brief Life of Burke by Mr. Sergeant Burke; Mr. Morley's Edmund Burke, a Historical Study; the admirable Lecture on the Life of Burke to the Dublin Young Men's Christian Association, 1862, by Sir Joseph Napier; Professor Robertson's Lectures on Burke.

GENERALLY. Professor Goodrich's Select British Eloquence; Hazlitt's Political Essays and Eloquence of the British Senate; Rogers's Biographical and Critical Introduction to Holdsworth and Ball's Edition of Burke's Works, 1834; Allibone's Critical Dictionary, art. Burke; De Quincey on Style and Conversation; Mackintosh's Memoirs and Works; Winkelmann's (German) edition of the two Speeches in this volume; Müller's Lectures, and Miscellaneous Writings (German).

clear that long meditation in the writer's mind has given the principal arguments a well-rounded form. Burke had already written and printed an historical *jeu-d'esprit,* shadowing forth the principal matters in the pamphlet under the figment of an insurrection against the Crown of Spain, in the form of a remonstrance from the supposed insurgents. The pamphlet itself seems to have been commenced shortly after the unusually early prorogation of parliament in May 1769, [lii] when the turbulence of the freeholders of Middlesex was extending to the country at large. The nation was indignant that a ministry labouring under an unprecedented weight of odium should continue to stand their ground. Most of the counties were holding meetings for petitions of remonstrance to the King on the subject of the Middlesex election. The administration adopted the singular course of endeavouring to repress the symptoms, instead of to cure the disease. They moved heaven and earth, in the words of Burke, to prevent the progress of the spirit of petitioning. Rigby got it under in Essex: then proceeded to Norfolk, and was busy, when the first mention of this pamphlet occurs in Burke's letters, opposing it in Northamptonshire. The ministry were looking with anxious eyes to Yorkshire, where the influence of Lord Rockingham was sufficient to authorise or to prevent a county petition; and the Whig leader seems to have hesitated on a matter so little in accordance with Whig traditions. Burke, however, urged him to this measure; and the Petition, which bears the marks of Burke's pen, was signed by more than 10,000 freeholders.[1] Lord Temple, in Buckinghamshire,

---

1. Addresses were sent in the early part of the year from the counties of Essex, Kent, Surrey and Salop, the towns of Bristol, Liverpool, Leicester, Coventry, &c., and from almost every part of Scotland. The county of Middlesex led the way in petitions on May 24: and was followed by the livery of London, the electors of Westminster, and the freeholders of Surrey, Cornwall, Devon, Somerset, Wilts, Gloucester, Worcester, Hereford, Northumberland, and the most important cities and boroughs.

was less scrupulous; and Burke assisted to present the remonstrance of the freeholders of that county at St. James' on the 29th of November.

Burke had much difficulty in continuing his pamphlet from time to time, in adapting it to the frequent changes in the unsettled state of affairs.[1] At first it seems to have been drawn out in the form of a letter, addressed to a retired member of the Rockingham party (John White, formerly M.P. for Retford). In October he sent a large portion of the manuscript to Lord Rockingham, with a request that it might be circulated among the party. He writes:

> The whole is in a manner new cast, something to the prejudice of the order, which, if I can, I will rectify, though [liii] I fear this will be difficult. The former scheme would no ways answer, and I wish I had entirely thrown it aside, as it has embarrassed me a good deal. The whole attack on Pitt's conduct must be omitted, or we shall draw the cry of the world upon us, as if we meant directly to quarrel with all mankind.

Burke wished the responsibility of the pamphlet to be divided fairly with all the other supporters of Lord Rockingham:

> In order that it should be truly the common cause, make it at your meeting what you please. Let me know what ought to be left out, what softened, and what strengthened. On reading it to Will and Dick,[2] they thought some things a little too ludicrous. I thought much otherwise, for I could rather wish that more had occurred to me (as more would, had my spirits been high) for I know how ill a long detail of politics, not animated by a direct controversy, wants every kind of help to make it tolerable.

Burke, in his desire to remove the responsibility as far as possible from himself, even suggested to the party "whether

---

1. "More difficult . . . . than to produce something altogether new." Letter to Rockingham, July 30.

2. Burke's brother Richard, and distant kinsman William Burke.

a thing of this nature should appear at all"; on the ground that it attacked the dearest objects of the court, did nothing to conciliate the Grenville party, and at the same time avowed doctrines which were the reverse of popular. He continued his work at the pamphlet in November. He then writes:

I find I must either speak very broad, or weaken the matter, and render it vulgar and ineffectual. I find some difficulties as I proceed; for what appear to me self-evident propositions, the conduct and pre-tences of people oblige one formally to prove; and this seems to me, and to others, a dull and needless labour. However, a good deal of it will soon be ready, and you may dispose of it as you please. It will, I am afraid, be long.[1]

A week after this he writes:

I cannot now send the rest of my pamphlet. It is not in order, nor quite finished even in the scheme; but I wish that, if you approve what is done, you may send it back, for it ought not now to have a mo-ment's delay.

The conclusion was written, and the whole submitted to Lord Rockingham in December, about the time of the appearance of Junius' celebrated Letter to the King. On the 23rd of that [liv] month Rockingham sent the manuscript to Dowdeswell. Rockingham writes: "I wish it was possible that this work could soon make its appearance. I am only fearful that my own delay may have made it difficult." The Duke of Portland warmly approved of the work, but justly remarked that the king was not "so absolute a thing of straw" as he was represented in it. He objects also to the "softening or sliding over" the conduct of the Earl of Bute. The Duke writes:[2]

I myself can speak of Lord Bute's public avowal of the principles on which the present Court system is formed, at least eighteen years agone (a time that you will think his professions must have been re-

1. Burke to Rockingham, Nov. 6, 1769.

2. Rock. Mem. ii. 145.

markable to have struck so young a boy as I then was); and though he may possibly not have had sense enough to form all the plan himself, he has had villany enough to adopt it, and introduce it in a manner that perhaps nobody had the means of doing so effectually as himself.

In reply to the question of the policy of the publication, the Duke of Portland says:

What hurt the publication can do, I can't foresee. "It will make you enemies." So it will; but those only, that for your own sake you would be ashamed to call friends, except one,[1] who never will like you till he sees he can't go on without you; and when that is the case, if he has as much honesty as sense, he will feel and own a pleasure that he never as yet can have experienced. As to serious, thinking people, men of weight and property either in a landed or commercial way, what injury can it do you in their opinions? Don't they see and feel every day the mischiefs of the present system? You join with them in their complaint; you shew exactly where the sore arises, and point out the remedy; nay, pledge yourself (at least I hope the pamphlet may be understood in that light) to apply it. And as to the young men of property and independent people in both Houses, it is holding out a banner for them to come to, where, surely, interest cannot be said to point out the way, and where nothing but public good is to be sought for on the plainest, honestest, and most disinterested terms.

Internal evidence shows that the work was accommodated to circumstances which occurred early in 1770, and it does not appear to have been published until the month of April. Two quarto and two octavo editions were sold in that year, besides an [lv] Irish reprint. A fifth edition was published in 1775, and a sixth in 1784.

The pamphlet contains indications of that relaxation of the formal literary manner which we have noted above. A literary friend in Ireland remarked that the business of the House of Commons had had its effect on Burke's style, and that the phraseology was "not so elegant as usual." He erred,

1. The King.

however, in ascribing this to the author's admitting insertions from other hands, to which he did not take the trouble to give his own colouring; for every line of the work is unmistakeably from the pen of Burke.

The pamphlet had little or no effect on the position of the Court party. They were even pleased with the liberal hostility it displayed.[1] Compared with the scorpionlike flagellations of Junius, the stripes of Burke seemed like the chastisement of one who loved them. It was otherwise with the popular party. The "Answer" of Mrs. Macaulay, which was published in May 1770,[2] embodies their opinions of it. This otherwise worthless production is valuable as a testimony to Burke's political consistency. In it he is considered to be as determined and formidable an enemy to democracy as in the "Rights of Man," twenty years afterwards.

Lord Chatham, the professed champion of an ideal anti-factious Whiggism, declared in a letter to Lord Rockingham, that the pamphlet had "done much hurt to the cause." On the back of this letter the following memorandum, dated July 13, 1792, was written by Burke:

Looking over poor Lord Rockingham's papers, I find this letter from a man wholly unlike him. It concerns my pamphlet ("The Cause of the Discontents"). I remember to have seen this knavish letter at the time. The pamphlet is itself, by anticipation, an answer to that great artificer of fraud.[3] *He* would not like it. It is pleasant to hear *him* talk of *the great extensive public,* who never conversed but with a parcel of low toad-eaters. Alas! alas! how different the *real* from the ostensible public man! [lvi] Must all this theatrical stuffing and raised heels be necessary for the character of a great man?

EDMUND BURKE.

1. Burke's Correspondence, i. 229.

2. "No heroine in Billingsgate can go beyond the patriotic scolding of our republican virago. You see I have been afraid to answer her." Burke to Shackleton, Aug. 15, 1770.

3. Milton (Par. Lost, iv. 121) names Satan "Artificer of Fraud."

Oh! but this does not derogate from his great, splendid side. God forbid!

E. B.

The Speech on American Taxation was delivered in the debate on the Repeal of the Tea-duty, the sole remnant of the taxes imposed by Townshend in 1767, purposely left to assert the *right* of taxation, when the rest were repealed in 1770, and in itself nothing, in the words of Lord Rockingham, but "an uncommercial, unproductive, pepper-corn rent." The attempted enforcement of this duty produced that resistance which terminated in American independence.

The first official notice of this resistance was contained in an ominous message from the throne, March 7, 1774, produced by the advices of the outrages committed on board the teaships at Boston. A mob, disguised as Mohawk Indians, had boarded the ships, broken open the tea-chests, and poured their contents into the sea. In this message, and the address which was voted upon it, the objects aimed to be secured by the Boston Port Bill were only too clearly shadowed forth. This fatal measure, which removed the custom-house officers of Boston, and prohibited the "landing and discharging, lading and shipping of goods, wares and merchandizes at the said town of Boston or within the harbour thereof," passed the House on the 25th, was immediately carried up to the Lords, and received the royal assent on the 31st of March. The more statesmanlike politicians, however, entertained the gravest apprehensions of the results of this measure: and, with the concurrence of some who had voted for it on general grounds, the motion in the debate upon which this speech was made, which had been so often proposed in former sessions, was again brought forward. It was negatived: and the numbers in its favour were much smaller than upon former occasions. The policy of coercion was further followed up by the monstrous attempt to subvert the constitution of the province of which the offending port was the capital, which appeared in due time under the form of a "Bill for the better regulating government in the Province of Massachusett's Bay." The purpose of this bill was, in the words of Burke in [lvii] the Annual Register, "to alter the constitution of that province as it stood in the charter of King William; to take the whole executive power out of the hands of the democratic port, and to vest the nomination of counsellors, judges, and magistrates of all kinds, including sheriffs, in the Crown, and in some cases in the King's governor, and all to be removable at the pleasure of the Crown."

Burke consented to the publication of this speech at the earnest solicitation of his friends. It is difficult to realise the great effect which it seems to have produced. Colonel Barré declared, in his excitement, that if it could be written out, he would nail it on every church door in the kingdom. Sir George Savile called it the greatest triumph of eloquence within his memory. Governor Johnstone said on the floor of the House that it was fortunate for the noble lords (North and Germaine) that spectators had been excluded during that debate, for if any had been present, they would have excited the people to tear the noble lords in pieces on their way home.

It seems to have been from a generous wish to give the ministry an opportunity of doing their best to restore tranquillity, and from an indisposition to appear in the light of a demagogue, while equally unwilling to soften down the terms in which he had spoken, that Burke deferred the publication of the Speech until the beginning of the ensuing year. It was several times reprinted, and, like most of Burke's publications, provoked an "Answer," which is not worthy of attention.

As to the Speech on Conciliation with America, and its relation to the former, the student is commended to the following note by Dr. Goodrich:

It would hardly seem possible that in speaking so soon again on the same subject, he could avoid making this speech to some extent an echo of his former one. But never were two productions more entirely different. His stand-point in the first was *England*. His topics were the inconsistency and folly of the ministry in their "miserable circle of occasional arguments and temporary expedients" for raising a revenue in America. His object was to recall the House to the original principles of the English colonial system—that of *regulating* the trade of the colonies and making it subservient to the interests of the mother country, while in other respects she left them "every characteristic mark of a free people in all their internal concerns." [lviii] His stand-point in the second speech was *America*. His topics were her growing population, agriculture, commerce, and fisheries; the causes of her fierce spirit of liberty; the impossibility of repressing it by force, and the consequent necessity of some concession on the part of England. His object was (waiving all abstract questions about the right of taxation) to show that Parliament ought "to admit the people of the colonies into an interest in the Constitution" by giving them (like Ireland, Wales, Chester, Durham) a share in the representation; and to do this by leaving internal taxation to the Colonial Assemblies, since no one could think of an actual representation of America in Parliament at the distance of three thousand miles. The two speeches were equally diverse in their spirit. The first was in the strain of incessant attack, full of the keenest sarcasm, and shaped from beginning to end for the purpose of putting down the ministry. The second, like the plan it proposed, was conciliatory; temperate and respectful towards Lord North; designed to inform those who were ignorant of the real strength and feeling of America; instinct with the finest philosophy of man and of social institutions; and intended, if possible, to lead the House *through* Lord North's scheme, into a final adjustment of the dispute, on the true principles of English liberty. It is the most finished of Mr. Burke's speeches; and though it contains no passage of such vividness and force as the description of Hyder Ali in his Speech on the Nabob of Arcot's debts, it will be read probably more than any of his other speeches, for the richness of its style and the lasting character of the instruction it conveys. Twenty years after Mr. Fox said, in applying its principles to the subject of parliamentary reform, "Let gentlemen read this speech by day, and meditate on it by night; let them peruse it again and again, study it, imprint it on their minds, impress it on their hearts: they will then learn that *representation* is the sovereign remedy for every evil."

Nowhere else, according to Dr. Goodrich, who is well qualified to speak, notwithstanding all that has been written since, is there to be found so admirable a view of the causes which produced the American Revolution as in these two speeches. "They both deserve to be studied with the utmost diligence by every American scholar."[1]

The history of the events which happened between the dates of the two speeches, the action of the Congress which had now assembled, the renewed penal measures of the government, and [lix] the respective merits of the various conciliatory measures which were advocated by Chatham, North, Burke, and Hartley, though desirable to be known, are not material to the understanding of this speech. If any testimony were wanted to the principles of colonial statesmanship which it embodies, it is to be found in the use made of them by Sir Robert Peel in his Speech on the Jamaica Government Bill, May 3, 1839.[2]

It is believed that the sources from which help and information have been derived, in the compilation of this edition, are sufficiently indicated by the references. In addition, the Editor has to express his grateful acknowledgment of the assistance and encouragement he has received from many friends, and particularly from Dr. Watson and Mr. Boyes, both of St. John's College, Oxford.

London,
March 1874.

---

1. Select British Eloquence, by Chauncey A. Goodrich, D.D., Professor in Yale College.

2. See also Peel's Speeches on the East Retford Franchise, May 5, 1829, and on New Zealand, June 17, 1845.

Thoughts on the Cause

of the Present Discontents

[1770. Sixth Edition, Dodsley, 1784.]

[Argument

Hoc vero occultum, intestinum ac domesticum malum, non modo non existit, verum etiam opprimit, antequam prospicere atque explorare potueris. —CICERO.

Thoughts on the Present Discontents

It is an undertaking of some degree of delicacy to examine into the cause of public disorders. If a man happens not to succeed in such an enquiry, he will be thought weak and visionary; if he touches the true grievance, there is a [2] danger that he may come near to persons of weight and consequence, who will rather be exasperated at the discovery of their errors, than thankful for the occasion of correcting them. If he should be obliged to blame the favourites of the people, he will be considered as the tool of power; if he censures those in power, he will be looked on as an instrument of faction. But in all exertions of duty something is to be hazarded. In cases of tumult and disorder, our law has invested every man, in some sort, with the authority of a magistrate. When the affairs of the nation are distracted, private people are, by the spirit of that law, justified in stepping a little out of their ordinary sphere. They enjoy a privilege, of somewhat more dignity and effect, than that of idle lamentation over the calamities of their country. They may look into them narrowly; they may reason upon them liberally; and if they should be so fortunate as to discover the true source of the mischief, and to suggest any probable method of removing it, though they may displease the rulers for the day, they are certainly of service to the cause of Government. Government is deeply interested in everything which, even through the medium of some temporary uneasiness, may tend finally to compose the minds of the subject, and to conciliate their affections. I have nothing to do here with the abstract value of the voice of the people. But as long as reputation, the most precious possession of every individual, and as long as opinion, the great support of the State, depend entirely upon that voice, it can never be considered as a thing of little consequence either to individuals or to Government. Nations are not primarily ruled by laws; less by violence. Whatever original energy may be supposed either in force or regulation; the operation of both is, in truth, merely instrumental. Nations are governed by the same methods, and on the same principles, by which an individual without authority is often able to govern [3] those who are his equals or his superiours; by a knowledge of their temper, and by a judicious management of it; I mean, when public affairs are steadily and quietly conducted: not when Government is nothing but a continued scuffle between the magistrate and the multitude; in which sometimes the one and sometimes the other is uppermost; in which they alternately yield and prevail, in a series of contemptible victories, and scandalous submissions. The temper of the people amongst whom he presides ought therefore to be the first study of a Statesman. And the knowledge of this temper it is by no means impossible for him to attain, if he has not an interest in being ignorant of what it is his duty to learn.

To complain of the age we live in, to murmur at the present possessors of power, to lament the past, to conceive extravagant hopes of the future, are the common dispositions of the greatest part of mankind; indeed the necessary effects of the ignorance and levity of the vulgar. Such complaints and humours have existed in all times; yet as all times have *not* been alike, true political sagacity manifests itself, in distinguishing that complaint which only characterizes the general infirmity of human nature, from those which are symptoms of the particular distemperature of our own air and season.

NOBODY, I BELIEVE, will consider it merely as the language of spleen or disappointment, if I say, that there is something particularly alarming in the present conjuncture. There is hardly a man, in or out of power, who holds any other language. That Government is at once dreaded and contemned; that the laws are despoiled of all their respected and salutary terrors; that their inaction is a subject of ridicule, and their exertion of abhorrence; that rank, and office, and title, and all the solemn plausibilities of the world, have lost their reverence and effect; that our foreign politicks [4] are as much deranged as our domestic oeconomy; that our dependencies are slackened in their affection, and loosened from their obedience; that we know neither how to yield nor how to enforce; that hardly anything above or below, abroad or at home, is sound and entire; but that disconnexion and confusion, in offices, in parties, in families, in Parliament, in the nation, prevail beyond the disorders of any former time: these are facts universally admitted and lamented.

This state of things is the more extraordinary, because the great parties which formerly divided and agitated the kingdom are known to be in a manner entirely dissolved. No great external calamity has visited the nation; no pestilence or famine. We do not labour at present under any scheme of taxation new or oppressive in the quantity or in the mode. Nor are we engaged in unsuccessful war; in which, our misfortunes might easily pervert our judgement; and our minds, sore from the loss of national glory, might feel every blow of Fortune as a crime in Government.

IT IS IMPOSSIBLE that the cause of this strange distemper should not sometimes become a subject of discourse. It is a compliment due, and which I willingly pay, to those who administer our affairs, to take notice in the first place of their speculation. Our Ministers are of opinion, that the increase of our trade and manufactures, that our growth by colonization and by conquest, have concurred to accumulate immense wealth in the hands of some individuals; and this again being dispersed amongst the people, has rendered them universally proud, ferocious, and ungovernable; that the insolence of some from their enormous wealth, and the boldness of others from a guilty poverty, have rendered them capable of the most atrocious attempts; so that they have trampled upon all subordination, and violently borne down the unarmed laws of a free Government; barriers too feeble

[5] against the fury of a populace so fierce and licentious as ours. They contend, that no adequate provocation has been given for so spreading a discontent; our affairs having been conducted throughout with remarkable temper and consummate wisdom. The wicked industry of some libellers, joined to the intrigues of a few disappointed politicians, have, in their opinion, been able to produce this unnatural ferment in the nation.

Nothing indeed can be more unnatural than the present convulsions of this country, if the above account be a true one. I confess I shall assent to it with great reluctance, and only on the compulsion of the clearest and firmest proofs; because their account resolves itself into this short, but discouraging proposition, "That we have a very good Ministry, but that we are a very bad people"; that we set ourselves to bite the hand that feeds us; that with a malignant insanity we oppose the measures, and ungratefully vilify the persons, of those whose sole object is our own peace and prosperity. If a few puny libellers, acting under a knot of factious politicians, without virtue, parts, or character, (such they are constantly represented by these gentlemen,) are sufficient to excite this disturbance, very perverse must be the disposition of that people, amongst whom such a disturbance can be excited by such means. It is besides no small aggravation of the public misfortune, that the disease, on this hypothesis, appears to be without remedy. If the wealth of the nation be the cause of its turbulence, I imagine it is not proposed to introduce poverty, as a constable to keep the peace. If our dominions abroad are the roots which feed all this rank luxuriance of sedition, it is not intended to cut them off in order to famish the fruit. If our liberty has enfeebled the executive power, there is no design, I hope, to call in the aid of despotism, to fill up the deficiencies of law. Whatever may be intended, these things are not yet professed. We [6] seem therefore to be driven to absolute despair; for we have no other materials to work upon, but those out of which God has been pleased to form the inhabitants of this island. If these be radically and essentially vitious, all that can be said is that those men are very unhappy, to whose fortune or duty it falls to administer the affairs of this untoward people. I hear it indeed sometimes asserted, that a steady perseverance in the present measures, and a rigorous punishment of those who oppose them, will in course of time infallibly put an end to these disorders. But this, in my opinion, is said without much observation of our present disposition, and without any knowledge at all of the general nature of mankind. If the matter of which this nation is composed be so very fermentable as these gentlemen describe it, leaven never will be wanting to work it up, as long as discontent, revenge, and ambition have existence in the world. Particular punishments are the cure for accidental distempers in the State; they inflame rather than allay those heats which arise from the settled mismanagement of the Government, or from a natural ill disposition in the people. It is of the utmost moment not to make mistakes in the use of strong measures; and firmness is then only a virtue when it accompanies the most perfect wisdom. In truth, inconstancy is a sort of natural corrective of folly and ignorance.

I am not one of those who think that the people are never in the wrong. They have been so, frequently and outrageously, both in other countries and in this. But I do say, that in all disputes between them and their rulers, the presumption is at least upon a par in favour of the people. Experience may perhaps justify me in going further. When popular discontents have been very prevalent; it may well be affirmed and supported, that there has been generally something found amiss in the constitution, or in the conduct of Government. The people have no interest in disorder. [7] When they do wrong, it is their error, and not their crime. But with the governing part of the State, it is far otherwise. They certainly may act ill by design, as well as by mistake. "*Les révolutions qui arrivent dans les grands états ne sont point un effect du hazard, ni du caprice des peuples. Rien ne révolte* les grands *d'un royaume comme* un Gouvernement foible et dérangé. *Pour la* populace, *ce n'est jamais par envie d'attaquer qu'elle se soulève, mais par impatience de souffrir."* These are the words of a great man; of a Minister of state; and a zealous assertor of Monarchy. They are applied to the *system of Favouritism* which was adopted by Henry the Third of France, and to the dreadful consequences it produced. What he says of revolutions, is equally true of all great disturbances. If this presumption in favour of the subjects against the trustees of power be not the more probable, I am sure it is the more comfortable speculation; because it is more easy to change an administration than to reform a people.

UPON A SUPPOSITION, therefore, that, in the opening of the cause, the presumptions stand equally balanced between the parties, there seems sufficient ground to entitle any person to a fair hearing, who attempts some other scheme beside that easy one which is fashionable in some fashionable companies, to account for the present discontents. It is not to be argued that we endure no grievance, because our grievances are not of the same sort with those under which we laboured formerly; not precisely those which we bore from the Tudors, or vindicated on the Stuarts. A great change has taken place in the affairs of this country. For in the silent lapse of events as material alterations have been insensibly brought about in the policy and character of governments and nations, as those which have been marked by the tumult of public revolutions.

[8] It is very rare indeed for men to be wrong in their feelings concerning public misconduct; as rare to be right in their speculation upon the cause of it. I have constantly observed, that the generality of people are fifty years, at least, behindhand in their politicks. There are but very few, who are capable of comparing and digesting what passes before

their eyes at different times and occasions, so as to form the whole into a distinct system. But in books everything is settled for them, without the exertion of any considerable diligence or sagacity. For which reason men are wise with but little reflexion, and good with little self-denial, in the business of all times except their own. We are very uncorrupt and tolerably enlightened judges of the transactions of past ages; where no passions deceive, and where the whole train of circumstances, from the trifling cause to the tragical event, is set in an orderly series before us. Few are the partizans of departed tyranny; and to be a Whig on the business of an hundred years ago, is very consistent with every advantage of present servility. This retrospective wisdom, and historical patriotism, are things of wonderful convenience; and serve admirably to reconcile the old quarrel between speculation and practice. Many a stern republican, after gorging himself with a full feast of admiration of the Grecian commonwealths and of our true Saxon constitution, and discharging all the splendid bile of his virtuous indignation on King John and King James, sits down perfectly satisfied to the coarsest work and homeliest job of the day he lives in. I believe there was no professed admirer of Henry the Eighth among the instruments of the last King James; nor in the court of Henry the Eighth was there, I dare say, to be found a single advocate for the favourites of Richard the Second.

No complaisance to our Court, or to our age, can make me believe nature to be so changed, but that public liberty will be among us, as among our ancestors, obnoxious to some [9] person or other; and that opportunities will be furnished for attempting, at least, some alteration to the prejudice of our constitution. These attempts will naturally vary in their mode, according to times and circumstances. For ambition, though it has ever the same general views, has not at all times the same means, nor the same particular objects. A great deal of the furniture of ancient tyranny is worn to rags; the rest is entirely out of fashion. Besides, there are few Statesmen so very clumsy and awkward in their business, as to fall into the identical snare which has proved fatal to their predecessors. When an arbitrary imposition is attempted upon the subject, undoubtedly it will not bear on its forehead the name of *Ship-money*. There is no danger that an extension of the *Forest laws* should be the chosen mode of oppression in this age. And when we hear any instance of ministerial rapacity, to the prejudice of the rights of private life, it will certainly not be the exaction of two hundred pullets, from a woman of fashion, for leave to lye with her own husband.

Every age has its own manners, and its politicks dependent upon them; and the same attempts will not be made against a constitution fully formed and matured, that were used to destroy it in the cradle, or to resist its growth during its infancy.

Against the being of Parliament, I am satisfied, no designs have ever been entertained since the Revolution. Every one must perceive, that it is strongly the interest of the Court, to have some second cause interposed between the Ministers and the people. The gentlemen of the House of Commons have an interest equally strong, in sustaining the part of that intermediate cause. However they may hire out the *usufruct* of their voices, they never will part with the *fee and inheritance*. Accordingly those who have been of the most known devotion to the will and pleasure of a Court, have, at the same time, been most forward in asserting an [10] high authority in the House of Commons. When they knew who were to use that authority, and how it was to be employed, they thought it never could be carried too far. It must be always the wish of an unconstitutional Statesman, that an House of Commons who are entirely dependent upon him, should have every right of the people entirely dependent upon their pleasure.

It was soon discovered, that the forms of a free, and the ends of an arbitrary Government, were things not altogether incompatible.

The power of the Crown, almost dead and rotten as Prerogative, has grown up anew, with much more strength, and far less odium, under the name of Influence. An influence, which operated without noise and without violence; an influence, which converted the very antagonist, into the instrument, of power; which contained in itself a perpetual principle of growth and renovation; and which the distresses and the prosperity of the country equally tended to augment, was an admirable substitute for a Prerogative, that, being only the offspring of antiquated prejudices, had moulded in its original stamina irresistible principles of decay and dissolution. The ignorance of the people is a bottom but for a temporary system; the interest of active men in the State is a foundation perpetual and infallible. However, some circumstances, arising, it must be confessed, in a great degree from accident, prevented the effects of this influence for a long time from breaking out in a manner capable of exciting any serious apprehensions. Although Government was strong and flourished exceedingly, the *Court* had drawn far less advantage than one would imagine from this great source of power.

AT THE REVOLUTION, the Crown, deprived, for the ends of the Revolution itself, of many prerogatives, was found too weak to struggle against all the difficulties which pressed so [11] new and unsettled a Government. The Court was obliged therefore to delegate a part of its powers to men of such interest as could support, and of such fidelity as would adhere to, its establishment. Such men were able to draw in a greater number to a concurrence in the common defence. This connexion, necessary at first, continued long after convenient; and properly conducted might indeed, in all situations, be an useful instrument of Government. At the same time, through the intervention of men of popular weight and character, the people possessed a security for their just proportion of importance in the State. But as the title to the Crown grew stronger by long possession, and by the constant increase of its influence, these helps have of late seemed to certain persons no better than incumbrances. The powerful managers for Government were not sufficiently submissive to the pleasure of the possessors of immediate and personal favour, sometimes from a confidence in their own strength natural and acquired; sometimes from a fear of offending their friends, and weakening that lead in the country, which gave them a consideration independent of the Court. Men acted as if the Court could receive, as well as confer, an obligation. The influence of Government, thus divided in appearance between the Court and the leaders of parties, became in many cases an accession rather to the popular than to the royal scale; and some part of that influence, which would otherwise have been possessed as in a sort of mortmain and unalienable domain, returned again to the great ocean from whence it arose, and circulated among the people. This method therefore of governing by men of great natural interest or great acquired consideration, was viewed in a very invidious light by the true lovers of absolute monarchy. It is the nature of despotism to abhor power held by any means but its own momentary pleasure; and to annihilate all intermediate situations between boundless [12] strength on its own part, and total debility on the part of the people.

To get rid of all this intermediate and independent importance, and *to secure to the Court the unlimited and uncontrouled use of its own vast influence, under the sole direction of its own private favour,* has for some years past been the great object of policy. If this were compassed, the influence of the Crown must of course produce all the effects which the most sanguine partizans of the Court could possibly desire. Government might then be carried on without any concurrence on the part of the people; without any attention to the dignity of the greater, or to the affections of the lower sorts. A new project was therefore devised by a certain set of intriguing men, totally different from the system of Administration which had prevailed since the accession of the House of Brunswick. This project, I have heard, was first conceived by some persons in the court of Frederick Prince of Wales.

The earliest attempt in the execution of this design was to set up for Minister, a person, in rank indeed respectable, and very ample in fortune; but who, to the moment of this vast and sudden elevation, was little known or considered in the kingdom. To him the whole nation was to yield an immediate and implicit submission. But whether it was from want of firmness to bear up against the first opposition; or that things were not yet fully ripened, or that this method was not found the most eligible; that idea was soon abandoned. The instrumental part of the project was a little altered, to accommodate it to the time, and to bring things more gradually and more surely to the one great end proposed.

The first part of the reformed plan was to draw *a line which should separate the Court from the Ministry.* Hitherto these names had been looked upon as synonymous; but for [13] the future, Court and Administration were to be considered as things totally distinct. By this operation, two systems of Administration were to be formed; one which should be in the real secret and confidence; the other merely ostensible, to perform the official and executory duties of Government. The latter were alone to be responsible; whilst the real advisers, who enjoyed all the power, were effectually removed from all the danger.

Secondly, *A party under these leaders was to be formed in favour of the Court against the Ministry:* this party was to have a large share in the emoluments of Government, and to hold it totally separate from, and independent of, ostensible Administration.

THOUGHTS ON THE PRESENT DISCONTENTS

The third point, and that on which the success of the whole scheme ultimately depended, was *to bring Parliament to an acquiescence in this project*. Parliament was therefore to be taught by degrees a total indifference to the persons, rank, influence, abilities, connexions, and character of the Ministers of the Crown. By means of a discipline, on which I shall say more hereafter, that body was to be habituated to the most opposite interests, and the most discordant politicks. All connexions and dependencies among subjects were to be entirely dissolved. As hitherto business had gone through the hands of leaders of Whigs or Tories, men of talents to conciliate the people, and to engage their confidence, now the method was to be altered; and the lead was to be given to men of no sort of consideration or credit in the country. This want of natural importance was to be their very title to delegated power. Members of Parliament were to be hardened into an insensibility to pride as well as to duty. Those high and haughty sentiments, which are the great support of independence, were to be let down gradually. Point of honour and precedence were no more to be regarded in Parliamentary decorum, than in a Turkish [14] army. It was to be avowed, as a constitutional maxim, that the King might appoint one of his footmen, or one of your footmen, for Minister; and that he ought to be, and that he would be, as well followed as the first name for rank or wisdom in the nation. Thus Parliament was to look on, as if perfectly unconcerned, while a cabal of the closet and back-stairs was substituted in the place of a national Administration.

With such a degree of acquiescence, any measure of any Court might well be deemed thoroughly secure. The capital objects, and by much the most flattering characteristicks of arbitrary power, would be obtained. Everything would be drawn from its holdings in the country to the personal favour and inclination of the Prince. This favour would be the sole introduction to power, and the only tenure by which it was to be held: so that no person looking towards another, and all looking towards the Court, it was impossible but that the motive which solely influenced every man's hopes must come in time to govern every man's conduct; till at last the servility became universal, in spite of the dead letter of any laws or institutions whatsoever.

HOW IT SHOULD HAPPEN that any man could be tempted to venture upon such a project of Government, may at first view appear surprizing. But the fact is, that opportunities very inviting to such an attempt have offered; and the scheme itself was not destitute of some arguments, not wholly unplausible, to recommend it. These opportunities and these arguments, the use that has been made of both, the plan for carrying this new scheme of government into execution, and the effects which it has produced, are in my opinion worthy of our serious consideration.

His Majesty came to the throne of these kingdoms with more advantages than any of his predecessors since the Revolution. Fourth in descent, and third in succession of [15] his Royal family, even the zealots of hereditary right, in him, saw something to flatter their favourite prejudices; and to justify a transfer of their attachments, without a change in their principles. The person and cause of the Pretender were become contemptible; his title disowned throughout Europe, his party disbanded in England. His Majesty came indeed to the inheritance of a mighty war; but, victorious in every part of the globe, peace was always in his power, not to negociate, but to dictate. No foreign habitudes or attachments withdrew him from the cultivation of his power at home. His revenue for the civil establishment, fixed (as it was then thought) at a large, but definite sum, was ample, without being invidious. His influence, by additions from conquest, by an augmentation of debt, by an increase of military and naval establishment, much strengthened and extended. And coming to the throne in the prime and full vigour of youth, as from affection there was a strong dislike, so from dread there seemed to be a general averseness, from giving anything like offence to a Monarch, against whose resentment opposition could not look for a refuge in any sort of reversionary hope.

These singular advantages inspired his Majesty only with a more ardent desire to preserve unimpaired the spirit of that national freedom, to which he owed a situation so full of glory. But to others it suggested sentiments of a very different nature. They thought they now beheld an opportunity (by a certain sort of Statesmen never long undiscovered or unemployed) of drawing to themselves, by the aggrandisement of a Court Faction, a degree of power which they could never hope to derive from natural influence or from honourable service; and which it was impossible they could hold with the least security, whilst the system of Administration rested upon its former bottom. In order to facilitate the execution of their design, it was necessary to [16] make many alterations in political arrangement, and a signal change in the opinions, habits, and connexions of the greatest part of those who at that time acted in publick.

In the first place, they proceeded gradually, but not slowly, to destroy everything of strength which did not derive its principal nourishment from the immediate pleasure of the Court. The greatest weight of popular opinion and party connexion were then with the Duke of Newcastle and Mr. Pitt. Neither of these held their importance by the *new tenure* of the Court; they were not therefore thought to be so proper as others for the services which were required by that tenure. It happened very favourably for the new system, that under a forced coalition there rankled an incurable alienation and disgust between the parties which composed the Administration. Mr. Pitt was first attacked. Not satisfied with removing him from power, they endeavoured by various artifices to ruin his character. The other party seemed rather pleased to get rid of so oppressive a support; not perceiving that their own fall was prepared by his, and involved in it. Many other reasons prevented them from daring to look their true situation in the face. To the great Whig families it was extremely disagreeable, and seemed almost unnatural, to oppose the Administration of a Prince of the House of Brunswick. Day after day they hesitated, and doubted, and lingered, expecting that other counsels would take place; and were slow to be persuaded, that all which had been done by the Cabal, was the effect not of humour, but of system. It was more strongly and evidently the interest of the new Court Faction, to get rid of the great Whig connexions, than to destroy Mr. Pitt. The power of that gentleman was vast indeed and merited; but it was in a great degree personal, and therefore transient. Theirs was rooted in the country. For, with a good deal less of popularity, they possessed a far more natural [17] and fixed influence. Long possession of Government; vast property; obligations of favours given and received; connexion of office; ties of blood, of alliance, of friendship (things at that time supposed of some force); the name of Whig, dear to the majority of the people; the zeal early begun and steadily continued to the Royal Family: all these together formed a body of power in the nation, which was criminal and devoted. The great ruling principle of the Cabal, and that which animated and harmonized all their proceedings, how various soever they may have been, was to signify to the world, that the Court would proceed upon its own proper forces only; and that the pretence of bringing any other into its service was an affront to it, and not a support. Therefore when the chiefs were removed, in order to go to the root, the whole party was put under a proscription, so general and severe as to take their hard-earned bread from the lowest officers, in a manner which had never been known before, even in general revolutions. But it was thought necessary effectually to destroy all dependencies but one; and to show an example of the firmness and rigour with which the new system was to be supported.

Thus for the time were pulled down, in the persons of the Whig leaders and of Mr. Pitt, (in spite of the services of the one at the accession of the Royal Family, and the recent services of the other in the war,) the *two only securities for the importance of the people; power arising from popularity; and power arising from connexion.* Here and there indeed a few individuals were left standing, who gave security for their total estrangement from the odious principles of party connexion and personal attachment; and it must be confessed that most of them have religiously kept their faith. Such a change could not however be made without a mighty shock to Government.

[18] To reconcile the minds of the people to all these movements, principles correspondent to them had been preached up with great zeal. Every one must remember that the Cabal set out with the most astonishing prudery, both moral and political. Those, who in a few months after soused over head and ears into the deepest and dirtiest pits of corruption, cried out violently against the indirect practices in the electing and managing of Parliaments, which had formerly prevailed. This marvellous abhorrence which the Court had suddenly taken to all influence, was not only circulated in conversation through the kingdom, but pompously announced to the publick, with many other extraordinary things, in a pamphlet which had all the appearance of a manifesto preparatory to some considerable enterprize. Throughout, it was a satire, though in terms managed and decent enough, on the politicks of the former Reign. It was indeed written with no small art and address.

In this piece appeared the first dawning of the new system; there first appeared the idea (then only in speculation) of *separating the Court from the Administration;* of carrying everything from national connexion to personal regards; and of forming a regular party for that purpose, under the name of *King's men*.

To recommend this system to the people, a perspective view of the Court, gorgeously painted, and finely illuminated from within, was exhibited to the gaping multitude. Party was to be totally done away, with all its evil works. Corruption was to be cast down from Court, as *Atè* was from heaven. Power was thenceforward to be the chosen residence of public spirit; and no one was to be supposed under any sinister influence, except those who had the misfortune to be in disgrace at Court, which was to stand in lieu of all vices and all corruptions. A scheme of perfection to be realized in a Monarchy, far beyond the visionary [19] Republick of Plato. The whole scenery was exactly disposed to captivate those good souls, whose credulous morality is so invaluable a treasure to crafty politicians. Indeed there was wherewithall to charm every body, except those few who are not much pleased with professions of supernatural virtue, who know of what stuff such professions are made, for what purposes they are designed, and in what they are sure constantly to end. Many innocent gentlemen, who had been talking prose all their lives without knowing anything of the matter, began at last to open their eyes upon their own merits, and to attribute their not having been Lords of the Treasury and Lords of Trade many years before, merely to the prevalence of party, and to the Ministerial power, which had frustrated the good intentions of the Court in favour of their abilities. Now was the time to unlock the sealed fountain of Royal bounty, which had been infamously monopolized and huckstered, and to let it flow at large upon the whole people. The time was come, to restore Royalty to its original splendour. *Mettre le Roy hors de page*, became a sort of watchword. And it was constantly in the mouths of all the runners of the Court, that nothing could preserve the balance of the constitution from being overturned by the rabble, or by a faction of the nobility, but to free the sovereign effectually from that Ministerial tyranny under which the Royal dignity had been oppressed in the person of his Majesty's grandfather.

These were some of the many artifices used to reconcile the people to the great change which was made in the persons who composed the Ministry, and the still greater which was made and avowed in its constitution. As to individuals, other methods were employed with them; in order so thoroughly to disunite every party, and even every family, that *no concert, order, or effect, might appear in any future opposition.* And in this manner an Administration without [20] connexion with the people, or with one another, was first put in possession of Government. What good consequences followed from it, we have all seen; whether with regard to virtue, public or private; to the ease and happiness of the Sovereign; or to the real strength of Government. But as so much stress was then laid on the necessity of this new project, it will not be amiss to take a view of the effects of this Royal servitude and vile durance, which was so deplored in the reign of the late Monarch, and was so carefully to be avoided in the reign of his Successor. The effects were these.

In times full of doubt and danger to his person and family, George the Second maintained the dignity of his Crown connected with the liberty of his people, not only unimpaired, but improved, for the space of thirty-three years. He overcame a dangerous rebellion, abetted by foreign force, and raging in the heart of his kingdoms; and thereby destroyed the seeds of all future rebellion that could arise upon the same principle. He carried the glory, the power, the commerce of England, to an height unknown even to this renowned nation in the times of its greatest prosperity: and he left his succession resting on the true and only true foundation of all national and all regal greatness; affection at home, reputation abroad, trust in allies, terror in rival nations. The most ardent lover of his country cannot wish for Great Britain an happier fate than to continue as she was then left. A people emulous as we are in affection to our present Sovereign, know not how to form a prayer to Heaven for a greater blessing upon his virtues, or an higher state of felicity and glory, than that he should live, and should reign, and, when Providence ordains it, should die, exactly like his illustrious Predecessor.

A great Prince may be obliged (though such a thing cannot happen very often) to sacrifice his private inclination [21] to his public interest. A wise Prince will not think that such a restraint implies a condition of servility; and truly, if such was the condition of the last reign, and the effects were also such as we have described, we ought, no less for the sake of the Sovereign whom we love, than for our own, to hear arguments convincing indeed, before we depart from the maxims of that reign, or fly in the face of this great body of strong and recent experience.

One of the principal topicks which was then, and has been since, much employed by that political school, is an effectual terror of the growth of an aristocratic power, prejudicial to the rights of the Crown, and the balance of the constitution. Any new powers exercised in the House of Lords, or in the House of Commons, or by the Crown, ought certainly to excite the vigilant and anxious jealousy of a free people. Even a new and unprecedented course of action in the whole Legislature, without great and evident reason, may be a subject of just uneasiness. I will not affirm, that there may not have lately appeared in the House of Lords a disposition to some attempts derogatory to the legal rights of the subject. If any such have really appeared, they have arisen, not from a power properly aristocratic, but from the same influence which is charged with having excited attempts of a similar nature in the House of Commons; which House, if it should have been betrayed into an unfortunate quarrel with its constituents, and involved in a charge of the very same nature, could have neither power nor inclination to repell such attempts in others. Those attempts in the House of Lords can no more be called aristocratic proceedings, than the proceedings with regard to the county of Middlesex in the House of Commons can with any sense be called democratical.

It is true, that the Peers have a great influence in the kingdom, and in every part of the public concerns. While [22] they are men of property, it is impossible to prevent it, except by such means as must prevent all property from its natural operation: an event not easily to be compassed, while property is power; nor by any means to be wished, while the least notion exists of the method by which the spirit of liberty acts, and of the means by which it is preserved. If any particular Peers, by their uniform, upright, constitutional conduct, by their public and their private virtues, have acquired an influence in the country; the people on whose favour that influence depends, and from whom it arose, will never be duped into an opinion, that such greatness in a Peer is the despotism of an aristocracy, when they know and feel it to be the effect and pledge of their own importance.

I am no friend to aristocracy, in the sense at least in which that word is usually understood. If it were not a bad habit to moot cases on the supposed ruin of the constitution, I should be free to declare, that if it must perish, I would rather by far see it resolved into any other form, than lost in that austere and insolent domination. But, whatever my dislikes may be, my fears are not upon that quarter. The question, on the influence of a Court, and of a Peerage, is not, which of the two dangers is the most eligible, but which is the most imminent. He is but a poor observer, who has not seen, that the generality of Peers, far from supporting themselves in a state of independent greatness, are but too apt to fall into an oblivion of their proper dignity, and to run headlong into an abject servitude. Would to God it were true, that the fault of our Peers were too much spirit! It is worthy of some observation, that these gentlemen, so jealous of aristocracy, make no complaints of the power of those peers (neither few nor inconsiderable) who are always in the train of a Court, and whose whole weight must be considered as a portion of the settled [23] influence of the Crown. This is all safe and right; but if some Peers (I am very sorry they are not as many as they ought to be) set themselves, in the great concern of Peers and Commons, against a back-stairs influence and clandestine government, then the alarm begins; then the constitution is in danger of being forced into an aristocracy.

I rest a little the longer on this Court topick, because it was much insisted upon at the time of the great change, and has been since frequently revived by many of the agents of that party: for, whilst they are terrifying the great and opulent with the horrors of mob-government, they are by other managers attempting (though hitherto with little success) to alarm the people with a phantom of tyranny in the Nobles. All this is done upon their favourite principle of disunion, of sowing jealousies amongst the different orders of the State, and of disjointing the natural strength of the kingdom; that it may be rendered incapable of resisting the sinister designs of wicked men, who have engrossed the Royal power.

THUS MUCH OF THE TOPICKS chosen by the Courtiers to recommend their system; it will be necessary to open a little more at large the nature of that party which was formed for its support. Without this, the whole would have been no better than a visionary amusement, like the scheme of Harrington's political club, and not a business in which the nation had a real concern. As a powerful party, and a party constructed on a new principle, it is a very inviting object of curiosity.

It must be remembered, that since the Revolution, until the period we are speaking of, the influence of the Crown had been always employed in supporting the Ministers of

State, and in carrying on the public business according to their opinions. But the party now in question is formed [24] upon a very different idea. It is to intercept the favour, protection, and confidence of the Crown in the passage to its Ministers; it is to come between them and their importance in Parliament; it is to separate them from all their natural and acquired dependencies; it is intended as the controul, not the support, of Administration. The machinery of this system is perplexed in its movements, and false in its principle. It is formed on a supposition that the King is something external to his government; and that he may be honoured and aggrandized, even by its debility and disgrace. The plan proceeds expressly on the idea of enfeebling the regular executory power. It proceeds on the idea of weakening the State in order to strengthen the Court. The scheme depending entirely on distrust, on disconnexion, on mutability by principle, on systematic weakness in every particular member; it is impossible that the total result should be substantial strength of any kind.

As a foundation of their scheme, the Cabal have established a sort of *Rota* in the Court. All sorts of parties, by this means, have been brought into Administration, from whence few have had the good fortune to escape without disgrace; none at all without considerable losses. In the beginning of each arrangement no professions of confidence and support are wanting, to induce the leading men to engage. But while the Ministers of the day appear in all the pomp and pride of power, while they have all their canvas spread out to the wind, and every sail filled with the fair and prosperous gale of Royal favour, in a short time they find, they know not how, a current, which sets directly against them; which prevents all progress; and even drives them backwards. They grow ashamed and mortified in a situation, which, by its vicinity to power, only serves to remind them the more strongly of their insignificance. They are obliged either to execute the orders of their inferiors, or to [25] see themselves opposed by the natural instruments of their office. With the loss of their dignity, they lose their temper. In their turn they grow troublesome to that Cabal, which, whether it supports or opposes, equally disgraces and equally betrays them. It is soon found necessary to get rid of the heads of Administration; but it is of the heads only. As there always are many rotten members belonging to the best connexions, it is not hard to persuade several to continue in office without their leaders. By this means the party goes out much thinner than it came in; and is only reduced in strength by its temporary possession of power. Besides, if by accident, or in course of changes, that power should be recovered, the Junto have thrown up a retrenchment of these carcases, which may serve to cover themselves in a day of danger. They conclude, not unwisely, that such rotten members will become the first objects of disgust and resentment to their antient connexions.

They contrive to form in the outward Administration two parties at the least; which, whilst they are tearing one another to pieces, are both competitors for the favour and protection of the Cabal; and, by their emulation, contribute to throw everything more and more into the hands of the interior managers.

A Minister of State will sometimes keep himself totally estranged from all his collegues; will differ from them in their counsels, will privately traverse, and publicly oppose, their measures. He will, however, continue in his employment. Instead of suffering any mark of displeasure, he will be distinguished by an unbounded profusion of Court rewards and caresses; because he does what is expected, and all that is expected, from men in office. He helps to keep some form of Administration in being, and keeps it at the same time as weak and divided as possible.

However, we must take care not to be mistaken, or to [26] imagine that such persons have any weight in their opposition. When, by them, Administration is convinced of its insignificancy, they are soon to be convinced of their own. They never are suffered to succeed in their opposition. They and the world are to be satisfied, that neither office, nor authority, nor property, nor ability, eloquence, counsel, skill, or union, are of the least importance; but that the mere influence of the Court, naked of all support, and destitute of all management, is abundantly sufficient for all its own purposes.

When any adverse connexion is to be destroyed, the Cabal seldom appear in the work themselves. They find out some person of whom the party entertains an high opinion. Such a person they endeavour to delude with various pretences. They teach him first to distrust, and then to quarrel with his friends; among whom, by the same arts, they excite a similar diffidence of him; so that in this mutual fear and distrust, he may suffer himself to be employed as the instrument in the change which is brought about. Afterwards they are sure to destroy him in his turn; by setting up in his place some person in whom he had himself reposed the greatest confidence, and who serves to carry off a considerable part of his adherents.

When such a person has broke in this manner with his connexions, he is soon compelled to commit some flagrant act of iniquitous personal hostility against some of them (such as an attempt to strip a particular friend of his family estate), by which the Cabal hope to render the parties utterly irreconcileable. In truth, they have so contrived matters, that people have a greater hatred to the subordinate instruments than to the principal movers.

As in destroying their enemies they make use of instruments not immediately belonging to their corps, so in advancing their own friends they pursue exactly the same [27] method. To promote any of them to considerable rank or emolument, they commonly take care that the recommendation shall pass through the hands of the ostensible Ministry: such a recommendation might however appear to the world, as some proof of the credit of Ministers, and some means of increasing their strength. To prevent this, the persons so advanced are directed in all companies, industriously to declare, that they are under no obligations whatsoever to Administration; that they have received their office from another quarter; that they are totally free and independent.

When the Faction has any job of lucre to obtain, or of vengeance to perpetrate, their way is, to select, for the execution, those very persons to whose habits, friendships, principles, and declarations, such proceedings are publicly known to be the most adverse; at once to render the instruments the more odious, and therefore the more dependent, and to prevent the people from ever reposing a confidence in any appearance of private friendship, or public principle.

If the Administration seem now and then, from remissness, or from fear of making themselves disagreeable, to suffer any popular excesses to go unpunished, the Cabal immediately sets up some creature of theirs to raise a clamour against the Ministers, as having shamefully betrayed the dignity of Government. Then they compel the Ministry to become active in conferring rewards and honours on the persons who have been the instruments of their disgrace; and, after having first vilified them with the higher orders for suffering the laws to sleep over the licentiousness of the populace, they drive them (in order to make amends for their former inactivity) to some act of atrocious violence, which renders them completely abhorred by the people. They who remember the riots which attended the Middlesex Election; the opening of the present Parliament; and the [28] transactions relative to Saint George's Fields, will not be at a loss for an application of these remarks.

That this body may be enabled to compass all the ends of its institution, its members are scarcely ever to aim at the high and responsible offices of the State. They are distributed with art and judgement through all the secondary, but efficient, departments of office, and through the households of all the branches of the Royal Family: so as on one hand to occupy all the avenues to the Throne; and on the other to forward or frustrate the execution of any measure, according to their own interests. For with the credit and support which they are known to have, though for the greater part in places which are only a genteel excuse for salary, they possess all the influence of the highest posts; and they dictate publicly in almost every thing, even with a parade of superiority. Whenever they dissent (as it often happens) from their nominal leaders, the trained part of the Senate, instinctively in the secret, is sure to follow them; provided the leaders, sensible of their situation, do not of themselves recede in time from their most declared opinions. This latter is generally the case. It will not be conceivable to any one who has not seen it, what pleasure is taken by the Cabal in rendering these heads of office thoroughly contemptible and ridiculous. And when they are become so, they have then the best chance for being well supported.

The members of the Court Faction are fully indemnified for not holding places on the slippery heights of the kingdom, not only by the lead in all affairs, but also by the perfect security in which they enjoy less conspicuous, but very advantageous, situations. Their places are, in express legal tenure, or in effect, all of them for life. Whilst the first and most respectable persons in the kingdom are tossed about like tennis balls, the sport of a blind and insolent caprice, no Minister dares even to cast an oblique glance at [29] the lowest of their body. If an attempt be made upon one of this corps, immediately he flies to sanctuary, and pretends to the most inviolable of all promises. No conveniency of public arrangement is available to remove any one of them from the specific situation he holds; and the slightest attempt upon one of them, by the most powerful Minister, is a certain preliminary to his own destruction.

Conscious of their independence, they bear themselves

with a lofty air to the exterior Ministers. Like Janissaries, they derive a kind of freedom from the very condition of their servitude. They may act just as they please; provided they are true to the great ruling principle of their institution. It is, therefore, not at all wonderful, that people should be so desirous of adding themselves to that body, in which they may possess and reconcile satisfactions the most alluring, and seemingly the most contradictory; enjoying at once all the spirited pleasure of independence, and all the gross lucre and fat emoluments of servitude.

Here is a sketch, though a slight one, of the constitution, laws, and policy, of this new Court corporation. The name by which they chuse to distinguish themselves, is that of *King's men,* or the *King's friends,* by an invidious exclusion of the rest of his Majesty's most loyal and affectionate subjects. The whole system, comprehending the exterior and interior Administrations, is commonly called, in the technical language of the Court, *Double Cabinet;* in French or English, as you chuse to pronounce it.

Whether all this be a vision of a distracted brain, or the invention of a malicious heart, or a real Faction in the country, must be judged by the appearances which things have worn for eight years past. Thus far I am certain, that there is not a single public man, in or out of office, who has not, at some time or other, borne testimony to the truth of what I have now related. In particular, no persons have [30] been more strong in their assertions, and louder and more indecent in their complaints, than those who compose all the exterior part of the present Administration; in whose time that Faction has arrived at such an height of power, and of boldness in the use of it, as may, in the end, perhaps bring about its total destruction.

It is true, that about four years ago, during the administration of the Marquis of Rockingham, an attempt was made to carry on Government without their concurrence. However, this was only a transient cloud; they were hid but for a moment; and their constellation blazed out with greater brightness, and a far more vigorous influence, some time after it was blown over. An attempt was at that time made (but without any idea of proscription) to break their corps, to discountenance their doctrines, to revive connexions of a different kind, to restore the principles and policy of the Whigs, to reanimate the cause of Liberty by Ministerial countenance; and then for the first time were men seen attached in office to every principle they had maintained in opposition. No one will doubt, that such men were abhorred and violently opposed by the Court Faction, and that such a system could have but a short duration.

It may appear somewhat affected, that in so much discourse upon this extraordinary Party, I should say so little of the Earl of Bute, who is the supposed head of it. But this was neither owing to affectation nor inadvertence. I have carefully avoided the introduction of personal reflexions of any kind. Much the greater part of the topicks which have been used to blacken this Nobleman, are either unjust or frivolous. At best, they have a tendency to give the resentment of this bitter calamity a wrong direction, and to turn a public grievance into a mean personal, or a dangerous national, quarrel. Where there is a regular scheme of operations carried on, it is the system, and not any individual [31] person who acts in it, that is truly dangerous. This system has not risen solely from the ambition of Lord Bute, but from the circumstances which favoured it, and from an indifference to the constitution which had been for some time growing among our gentry. We should have been tried with it, if the Earl of Bute had never existed; and it will want neither a contriving head nor active members, when the Earl of Bute exists no longer. It is not, therefore, to rail at Lord Bute, but firmly to embody against this Court Party and its practices, which can afford us any prospect of relief in our present condition.

Another motive induces me to put the personal consideration of Lord Bute wholly out of the question. He communicates very little in a direct manner with the greater part of our men of business. This has never been his custom. It is enough for him that he surrounds them with his creatures. Several imagine, therefore, that they have a very good excuse for doing all the work of this Faction, when they have no personal connexion with Lord Bute. But whoever becomes a party to an Administration, composed of insulated individuals, without faith plighted, tie, or common principle; an Administration constitutionally impotent, because supported by no party in the nation; he who contributes to destroy the connexions of men and their trust in one another, or in any sort to throw the dependence of public counsels upon private will and favour, possibly may have nothing to do with the Earl of Bute. It matters little whether he be the friend or the enemy of that particular person. But let him be who or what he will, he abets a Faction that is driving hard to the ruin of his country. He is sapping the foundation of its liberty, disturbing the sources of its domestic tranquillity, weakening its government over its dependencies, degrading it from all its importance in the system of Europe.

[32] It is this unnatural infusion of a *system of Favouritism* into a Government which in a great part of its constitution is popular, that has raised the present ferment in the nation. The people, without entering deeply into its principles, could plainly perceive its effects, in much violence, in a great spirit of innovation, and a general disorder in all the functions of Government. I keep my eye solely on this system; if I speak of those measures which have arisen from it, it will be so far only as they illustrate the general scheme. This is the fountain of all those bitter waters of which, through an hundred different conduits, we have drunk until we are ready to burst. The discretionary power of the Crown in the formation of Ministry, abused by bad or weak men, has given rise to a sys-

tem, which, without directly violating the letter of any law, operates against the spirit of the whole constitution.

A PLAN OF FAVOURITISM for our executory Government is essentially at variance with the plan of our Legislature. One great end undoubtedly of a mixed Government like ours, composed of Monarchy, and of controuls, on the part of the higher people and the lower, is that the Prince shall not be able to violate the laws. This is useful indeed and fundamental. But this, even at first view, is no more than a negative advantage; an armour merely defensive. It is therefore next in order, and equal in importance, *that the discretionary powers which are necessarily vested in the Monarch, whether for the execution of the laws, or for the nomination to magistracy and office, or for conducting the affairs of peace and war, or for ordering the revenue, should all be exercised upon public principles and national grounds, and not on the likings or prejudices, the intrigues or policies, of a Court.* This, I said, is equal in importance to the securing a Government according to law. The laws reach [33] but a very little way. Constitute Government how you please, infinitely the greater part of it must depend upon the exercise of the powers which are left at large to the prudence and uprightness of Ministers of State. Even all the use and potency of the laws depends upon them. Without them, your Commonwealth is no better than a scheme upon paper; and not a living, active, effective constitution. It is possible, that through negligence, or ignorance, or design artfully conducted, Ministers may suffer one part of Government to languish, another to be perverted from its purposes, and every valuable interest of the country to fall into ruin and decay, without possibility of fixing any single act on which a criminal prosecution can be justly grounded. The due arrangement of men in the active part of the State, far from being foreign to the purposes of a wise Government, ought to be among its very first and dearest objects. When, therefore, the abettors of the new system tell us, that between them and their opposers there is nothing but a struggle for power, and that therefore we are no-ways concerned in it; we must tell those who have the impudence to insult us in this manner, that, of all things, we ought to be the most concerned, who and what sort of men they are, that hold the trust of everything that is dear to us. Nothing can render this a point of indifference to the nation, but what must either render us totally desperate, or soothe us into the security of ideots. We must soften into a credulity below the milkiness of infancy, to think all men virtuous. We must be tainted with a malignity truly diabolical, to believe all the world to be equally wicked and corrupt. Men are in public life as in private, some good, some evil. The elevation of the one, and the depression of the other, are the first objects of all true policy. But that form of Government, which, neither in its direct institutions, nor in their immediate tendency, has contrived to throw its affairs into [34] the most trust-worthy hands, but has left its whole executory system to be disposed of agreeably to the uncontrouled pleasure of any one man, however excellent or virtuous, is a plan of polity defective not only in that member, but consequentially erroneous in every part of it.

In arbitrary Governments, the constitution of the Ministry follows the constitution of the Legislature. Both the Law and the Magistrate are the creatures of Will. It must be so. Nothing, indeed, will appear more certain, on any tolerable consideration of this matter, than that *every sort of Government ought to have its Administration correspondent to its Legislature.* If it should be otherwise, things must fall into an hideous disorder. The people of a free Commonwealth, who have taken such care that their laws should be the result of general consent, cannot be so senseless as to suffer their executory system to be composed of persons on whom they have no dependence, and whom no proofs of the public love and confidence have recommended to those powers, upon the use of which the very being of the State depends.

Thoughts on the Present Discontents

The popular election of magistrates, and popular disposition of rewards and honours, is one of the first advantages of a free State. Without it, or something equivalent to it, perhaps the people cannot long enjoy the substance of freedom; certainly none of the vivifying energy of good Government. The frame of our Commonwealth did not admit of such an actual election: but it provided as well, and (while the spirit of the constitution is preserved) better, for all the effects of it, than by the method of suffrage in any democratic State whatsoever. It had always, until of late, been held the first duty of Parliament, *to refuse to support Government, until power was in the hands of persons who were acceptable to the people, or while factions predominated in the Court in which the nation had no confidence.* Thus all the good effects of popular [35] election were supposed to be secured to us, without the mischiefs attending on perpetual intrigue, and a distinct canvass for every particular office throughout the body of the people. This was the most noble and refined part of our constitution. The people, by their representatives and grandees, were intrusted with a deliberative power in making laws; the King with the controul of his negative. The King was intrusted with the deliberative choice and the election to office; the people had the negative in a Parliamentary refusal to support. Formerly this power of controul was what kept Ministers in awe of Parliaments, and Parliaments in reverence with the people. If the use of this power of controul on the system and persons of Administration is gone, everything is lost, Parliament and all. We may assure ourselves, that if Parliament will tamely see evil men take possession of all the strong-holds of their country, and allow them time and means to fortify themselves, under a pretence of giving them a fair trial, and upon a hope of discovering, whether they will not be reformed by power, and whether their measures will not be better than their morals; such a Parliament will give countenance to their measures also, whatever that Parliament may pretend, and whatever those measures may be.

Every good political institution must have a preventive operation as well as a remedial. It ought to have a natural tendency to exclude bad men from Government, and not to trust for the safety of the State to subsequent punishment alone: punishment, which has ever been tardy and uncertain; and which, when power is suffered in bad hands, may chance to fall rather on the injured than the criminal.

Before men are put forward into the great trusts of the State, they ought by their conduct to have obtained such a degree of estimation in their country, as may be some sort of pledge and security to the publick, that they will not abuse [36] those trusts. It is no mean security for a proper use of power, that a man has shown by the general tenor of his actions, that the affection, the good opinion, the confidence, of his fellow-citizens have been among the principal objects of his life; and that he has owed none of the gradations of his power or fortune to a settled contempt, or occasional forfeiture of their esteem.

That man who before he comes into power has no friends, or who coming into power is obliged to desert his friends, or who losing it has no friends to sympathize with him; he who has no sway among any part of the landed or commercial interest, but whose whole importance has begun with his office, and is sure to end with it; is a person who ought never to be suffered by a controuling Parliament to continue in any of those situations which confer the lead and direction of all our public affairs; because such a man *has no connexion with the interest of the people*.

Those knots or cabals of men who have got together, avowedly without any public principle, in order to sell their conjunct iniquity at the higher rate, and are therefore universally odious, ought never to be suffered to domineer in the State; because they have *no connexion with the sentiments and opinions of the people*.

These are considerations which in my opinion enforce the

necessity of having some better reason, in a free country, and a free Parliament, for supporting the Ministers of the Crown, than that short one, *That the King has thought proper to appoint them.* There is something very courtly in this. But it is a principle pregnant with all sorts of mischief, in a constitution like ours, to turn the views of active men from the country to the Court. Whatever be the road to power, that is the road which will be trod. If the opinion of the country be of no use as a means of power or consideration, the qualities which usually procure that opinion will be no longer [37] cultivated. And whether it will be right, in a State so popular in its constitution as ours, to leave ambition without popular motives, and to trust all to the operation of pure virtue in the minds of Kings and Ministers, and public men, must be submitted to the judgement and good sense of the people of England.

Cunning men are here apt to break in, and, without directly controverting the principle, to raise objections from the difficulty under which the Sovereign labours, to distinguish the genuine voice and sentiments of his people, from the clamour of a faction, by which it is so easily counterfeited. The nation, they say, is generally divided into parties, with views and passions utterly irreconcileable. If the King should put his affairs into the hands of any one of them, he is sure to disgust the rest; if he select particular men from among them all, it is an hazard that he disgusts them all. Those who are left out, however divided before, will soon run into a body of opposition; which, being a collection of many discontents into one focus, will without doubt be hot and violent enough. Faction will make its cries resound through the nation, as if the whole were in an uproar, when by far the majority, and much the better part, will seem for awhile as it were annihilated by the quiet in which their virtue and moderation incline them to enjoy the blessings of Government. Besides that, the opinion of the meer vulgar is a miserable rule even with regard to themselves, on account of their violence and instability. So that if you were to gratify them in their humour to-day, that very gratification would be a ground of their dissatisfaction on the next. Now as all these rules of public opinion are to be collected with great difficulty, and to be applied with equal uncertainty as to the effect, what better can a King of England do, than to employ such men as he finds to have views and inclinations most conformable [38] to his own; who are least infected with pride and self-will; and who are least moved by such popular humours as are perpetually traversing his designs, and disturbing his service; trusting that when he means no ill to his people, he will be supported in his appointments, whether he chooses to keep or to change, as his private judgment or his pleasure leads him? He will find a sure resource in the real weight and influence of the Crown, when it is not suffered to become an instrument in the hands of a faction.

I will not pretend to say that there is nothing at all in this mode of reasoning; because I will not assert, that there is no difficulty in the art of Government. Undoubtedly the very best Administration must encounter a great deal of opposition; and the very worst will find more support than it deserves. Sufficient appearances will never be wanting to those who have a mind to deceive themselves. It is a fallacy in constant use with those who would level all things, and confound right with wrong, to insist upon the inconveniences which are attached to every choice, without taking into consideration the different weight and consequence of those inconveniences. The question is not concerning *absolute* discontent or *perfect* satisfaction in Government; neither of which can be pure and unmixed at any time, or upon any system. The controversy is about that degree of good-humour in the people, which may possibly be attained, and ought certainly to be looked for. While some politicians may be waiting to know whether the sense of every individual be against them, accurately distinguishing the vulgar from the better sort, drawing lines between the enterprizes of a faction and the efforts of a people, they may chance to see the Government, which they are so nicely weighing, and dividing, and distinguishing, tumble to the ground in the midst of their wise deliberation. Prudent men, when so great an object as the security of Government, or even its [39] peace, is at stake, will not run the risque of a decision which may be fatal to it. They who can read the political sky will see an hurricane in a cloud no bigger than an hand at the very edge of the horizon, and will run into the first harbour. No lines can be laid down for civil or political wisdom. They are a matter incapable of exact definition. But, though no man can draw a stroke between the confines of day and night, yet light and darkness are upon the whole tolerably distinguishable. Nor will it be impossible for a Prince to find out such a mode of Government, and such persons to administer it, as will give a great degree of content to his people; without any curious and anxious research for that abstract, universal, perfect harmony, which while he is seeking, he abandons those means of ordinary tranquillity which are in his power without any research at all.

It is not more the duty than it is the interest of a Prince, to aim at giving tranquillity to his Government. But those who advise him may have an interest in disorder and confusion. If the opinion of the people is against them, they will naturally wish that it should have no prevalence. Here it is that the people must on their part show themselves sensible of their own value. Their whole importance, in the first instance, and afterwards their whole freedom, is at stake. Their freedom cannot long survive their importance. Here it is that the natural strength of the kingdom, the great peers, the leading landed gentlemen, the opulent merchants and manufacturers, the substantial yeomanry, must interpose, to rescue their Prince, themselves, and their posterity.

We are at present at issue upon this point. We are in the

great crisis of this contention; and the part which men take, one way or other, will serve to discriminate their characters and their principles. Until the matter is decided, the country will remain in its present confusion. For while a system of Administration is attempted, entirely repugnant to [40] the genius of the people, and not conformable to the plan of their Government, everything must necessarily be disordered for a time, until this system destroys the constitution, or the constitution gets the better of this system.

THERE IS, IN MY OPINION, a peculiar venom and malignity in this political distemper beyond any that I have heard or read of. In former times the projectors of arbitrary Government attacked only the liberties of their country; a design surely mischievous enough to have satisfied a mind of the most unruly ambition. But a system unfavourable to freedom may be so formed, as considerably to exalt the grandeur of the State; and men may find in the pride and splendor of that prosperity some sort of consolation for the loss of their solid privileges. Indeed the increase of the power of the State has often been urged by artful men, as a pretext for some abridgement of the public liberty. But the scheme of the junto under consideration, not only strikes a palsy into every nerve of our free constitution, but in the same degree benumbs and stupifies the whole executive power: rendering Government in all its grand operations languid, uncertain, ineffective; making Ministers fearful of attempting, and incapable of executing, any useful plan of domestic arrangement, or of foreign politicks. It tends to produce neither the security of a free Government, nor the energy of a Monarchy that is absolute. Accordingly, the Crown has dwindled away, in proportion to the unnatural and turgid growth of this excrescence on the Court.

The interior Ministry are sensible, that war is a situation which sets in its full light the value of the hearts of a people;

and they well know, that the beginning of the importance of the people must be the end of theirs. For this reason they discover upon all occasions the utmost fear of every thing, which by possibility may lead to such an event. I do not [41] mean that they manifest any of that pious fear which is backward to commit the safety of the country to the dubious experiment of war. Such a fear, being the tender sensation of virtue, excited, as it is regulated, by reason, frequently shows itself in a seasonable boldness, which keeps danger at a distance, by seeming to despise it. Their fear betrays to the first glance of the eye, its true cause, and its real object. Foreign powers, confident in the knowledge of their character, have not scrupled to violate the most solemn treaties; and, in defiance of them, to make conquests in the midst of a general peace, and in the heart of Europe. Such was the conquest of Corsica, by the professed enemies of the freedom of mankind, in defiance of those who were formerly its professed defenders. We have had just claims upon the same powers; rights which ought to have been sacred to them as well as to us, as they had their origin in our lenity and generosity towards France and Spain in the day of their great humiliation. Such I call the ransom of Manilla, and the demand on France for the East India prisoners. But these powers put a just confidence in their resource of the *double Cabinet.* These demands (one of them at least) are hastening fast towards an acquittal by prescription. Oblivion begins to spread her cobwebs over all our spirited remonstrances. Some of the most valuable branches of our trade are also on the point of perishing from the same cause. I do not mean those branches which bear without the hand of the vine-dresser; I mean those which the policy of treaties had formerly secured to us; I mean to mark and distinguish the trade of Portugal, the loss of which, and the power of the Cabal, have one and the same aera.

If, by any chance, the Ministers who stand before the

curtain possess or affect any spirit, it makes little or no impression. Foreign Courts and Ministers, who were among the first to discover and to profit by this invention of the [42] *double Cabinet,* attended very little to their remonstrances. They know that those shadows of Ministers have nothing to do in the ultimate disposal of things. Jealousies and animosities are sedulously nourished in the outward Administration, and have been even considered as a *causa sine qua non* in its constitution: thence foreign Courts have a certainty, that nothing can be done by common counsel in this nation. If one of those Ministers officially takes up a business with spirit, it serves only the better to signalize the meanness of the rest, and the discord of them all. His collegues in office are in haste to shake him off, and to disclaim the whole of his proceedings. Of this nature was that astonishing transaction, in which Lord Rochford, our Ambassador at Paris, remonstrated against the attempt upon Corsica, in consequence of a direct authority from Lord Shelburne. This remonstrance the French Minister treated with the contempt that was natural; as he was assured, from the Ambassador of his Court to ours, that these orders of Lord Shelburne were not supported by the rest of the (I had like to have said British) Administration. Lord Rochford, a man of spirit, could not endure this situation. The consequences were, however, curious. He returns from Paris, and comes home full of anger. Lord Shelburne, who gave the orders, is obliged to give up the seals. Lord Rochford, who obeyed these orders, receives them. He goes, however, into another department of the same office, that he might not be obliged officially to acquiesce, in one situation, under what he had officially remonstrated against, in another. At Paris, the Duke of Choiseul considered this office arrangement as a compliment to him: here it was spoke of as an attention to the delicacy of Lord Rochford. But whether the compliment was to one or both, to this nation it was the same. By this transaction the condition of our Court lay exposed in all its nakedness. [43] Our office correspondence has lost all pretence to authenticity; British policy is brought into derision in those nations, that a while ago trembled at the power of our arms, whilst they looked up with confidence to the equity, firmness, and candour, which shone in all our negociations. I represent this matter exactly in the light in which it has been universally received.

SUCH HAS BEEN THE ASPECT of our foreign politicks, under the influence of a *double Cabinet*. With such an arrangement at Court, it is impossible it should have been otherwise. Nor is it possible that this scheme should have a better effect upon the government of our dependencies, the first, the dearest, and most delicate objects, of the interior policy of this empire. The Colonies know, that Administration is separated from the Court, divided within itself, and detested by the nation. The *double Cabinet* has, in both the parts of it, shown the most malignant dispositions towards them, without being able to do them the smallest mischief.

They are convinced, by sufficient experience, that no plan, either of lenity or rigour, can be pursued with uniformity and perseverance. Therefore they turn their eyes entirely from Great Britain, where they have neither dependence on friendship, nor apprehension from enmity. They look to themselves, and their own arrangements. They grow every day into alienation from this country; and whilst they are becoming disconnected with our Government, we have not the consolation to find, that they are even friendly in their new independence. Nothing can equal the futility, the weakness, the rashness, the timidity, the perpetual contradiction, in the management of our affairs in that part of the world. A volume might be written on this melancholy subject; but it were better to leave it entirely to the reflexions [44] of the reader himself, than not to treat it in the extent it deserves.

THOUGHTS ON THE PRESENT DISCONTENTS

IN WHAT MANNER our domestic oeconomy is affected by this system, it is needless to explain. It is the perpetual subject of their own complaints.

The Court Party resolve the whole into faction. Having said something before upon this subject, I shall only observe here, that, when they give this account of the prevalence of faction, they present no very favourable aspect of the confidence of the people in their own Government. They may be assured, that however they amuse themselves with a variety of projects for substituting something else in the place of that great and only foundation of Government, the confidence of the people, every attempt will but make their condition worse. When men imagine that their food is only a cover for poison, and when they neither love nor trust the hand that serves it, it is not the name of the roast beef of Old England, that will persuade them to sit down to the table that is spread for them. When the people conceive that laws, and tribunals, and even popular assemblies, are perverted from the ends of their institution, they find in those names of degenerated establishments only new motives to discontent. Those bodies, which, when full of life and beauty, lay in their arms and were their joy and comfort, when dead and putrid, become but the more loathsome from remembrance of former endearments. A sullen gloom, and furious disorder, prevail by fits: the nation loses its relish for peace and prosperity, as it did in that season of fullness which opened our troubles in the time of Charles the First. A species of men to whom a state of order would become a sentence of obscurity, are nourished into a dangerous magnitude by the heat of intestine disturbances; and it is no wonder that, by a sort of sinister piety, they cherish, in their turn, the disorders which are the [45] parents of all their consequence. Superficial observers consider such persons as the cause of the public uneasiness, when, in truth, they are nothing more than the effect of it. Good men look upon this distracted scene with sorrow and indignation. Their hands are tied behind them. They are despoiled of all the power which might enable them to reconcile the strength of Government with the rights of the people. They stand in a most distressing alternative. But in the election among evils they hope better things from temporary confusion, than from established servitude. In the mean time, the voice of law is not to be heard. Fierce licentiousness begets violent restraints. The military arm is the sole reliance; and then, call your constitution what you please, it is the sword that governs. The civil power, like every other that calls in the aid of an ally stronger than itself, perishes by the assistance it receives. But the contrivers of this scheme of Government will not trust solely to the military power; because they are cunning men. Their restless and crooked spirit drives them to rake in the dirt of every kind of expedient. Unable to rule the multitude, they endeavour to raise divisions amongst them. One mob is hired to destroy another; a procedure which at once encourages the boldness of the populace, and justly increases their discontent. Men become pensioners of state on account of their abilities in the array of riot, and the discipline of confusion. Government is put under the disgraceful necessity of protecting from the severity of the laws that very licentiousness, which the laws had been before violated to repress. Everything partakes of the original disorder. Anarchy predominates without freedom, and servitude without submission or subordination. These are the consequences inevitable to our public peace, from the scheme of rendering the executory Government at once odious and feeble; of freeing Administration from the constitutional and salutary controul of [46] Parliament, and inventing for it a *new controul,* unknown to the constitution, an *interior Cabinet;* which brings the whole body of Government into confusion and contempt.

AFTER HAVING STATED, as shortly as I am able, the effects of this system on our foreign affairs, on the policy of our

Government with regard to our dependencies, and on the interior oeconomy of the Commonwealth; there remains only, in this part of my design, to say something of the grand principle which first recommended this system at Court. The pretence was, to prevent the King from being enslaved by a faction, and made a prisoner in his closet. This scheme might have been expected to answer at least its own end, and to indemnify the King, in his personal capacity, for all the confusion into which it has thrown his Government. But has it in reality answered this purpose? I am sure, if it had, every affectionate subject would have one motive for enduring with patience all the evils which attend it.

In order to come at the truth in this matter, it may not be amiss to consider it somewhat in detail. I speak here of the King, and not of the Crown; the interests of which we have already touched. Independent of that greatness which a King possesses merely by being a representative of the national dignity, the things in which he may have an individual interest seem to be these: wealth accumulated; wealth spent in magnificence, pleasure, or beneficence; personal respect and attention; and above all, private ease and repose of mind. These compose the inventory of prosperous circumstances, whether they regard a Prince or a subject; their enjoyments differing only in the scale upon which they are formed.

Suppose then we were to ask, whether the King has been richer than his predecessors in accumulated wealth, since the establishment of the plan of Favouritism? I believe it will [47] be found that the picture of royal indigence which our Court has presented until this year, has been truly humiliating. Nor has it been relieved from this unseemly distress, but by means which have hazarded the affection of the people, and shaken their confidence in Parliament. If the public treasures had been exhausted in magnificence and splendour, this distress would have been accounted for, and in some measure justified. Nothing would be more unworthy of this nation, than with a mean and mechanical rule, to mete out the splendour of the Crown. Indeed I have found very few persons disposed to so ungenerous a procedure. But the generality of people, it must be confessed, do feel a good deal mortified, when they compare the wants of the Court with its expences. They do not behold the cause of this distress in any part of the apparatus of Royal magnificence. In all this, they see nothing but the operations of parsimony, attended with all the consequences of profusion. Nothing expended, nothing saved. Their wonder is increased by their knowledge, that besides the revenue settled on his Majesty's Civil List to the amount of 800,000*l.* a year, he has a farther aid, from a large pension list, near 90,000*l.* a year, in Ireland; from the produce of the Dutchy of Lancaster (which we are told has been greatly improved); from the revenue of the Dutchy of Cornwall; from the American quit-rents; from the four and a half *per cent.* duty in the Leeward Islands; this last worth to be sure considerably more than 40,000*l.* a year. The whole is certainly not much short of a million annually.

These are revenues within the knowledge and cognizance of our national Councils. We have no direct right to examine into the receipts from his Majesty's German Dominions, and the Bishoprick of Osnabrug. This is unquestionably true. But that which is not within the province of Parliament, is yet within the sphere of every man's own reflexion. If a foreign Prince resided amongst us, the state of his revenues [48] could not fail of becoming the subject of our speculation. Filled with an anxious concern for whatever regards the welfare of our Sovereign, it is impossible, in considering the miserable circumstances into which he has been brought, that this obvious topick should be entirely passed over. There is an opinion universal, that these revenues produce something not inconsiderable, clear of all charges and establishments. This produce the people do not believe to be hoarded, nor perceive to be spent. It is accounted for in the only manner

it can, by supposing that it is drawn away, for the support of
that Court Faction, which, whilst it distresses the nation, im-
poverishes the Prince in every one of his resources. I once
more caution the reader, that I do not urge this consideration
concerning the foreign revenue, as if I supposed we had a direct right to examine into the expenditure of any part of it;
but solely for the purpose of showing how little this system of
Favouritism has been advantageous to the Monarch himself;
which, without magnificence, has sunk him into a state of
unnatural poverty; at the same time that he possessed every
means of affluence, from ample revenues, both in this country, and in other parts of his dominions.

Has this system provided better for the treatment becoming his high and sacred character, and secured the King
from those disgusts attached to the necessity of employing
men who are not personally agreeable? This is a topick upon
which for many reasons I could wish to be silent; but the
pretence of securing against such causes of uneasiness, is the
corner-stone of the Court Party. It has however so happened,
that if I were to fix upon any one point, in which this system
has been more particularly and shamefully blameable, the
effects which it has produced would justify me in choosing
for that point its tendency to degrade the personal dignity
of the Sovereign, and to expose him to a thousand contradictions and mortifications. It is but too evident in what [49]
manner these projectors of Royal greatness have fulfilled all
their magnificent promises. Without recapitulating all the circumstances of the reign, every one of which is more or less a
melancholy proof of the truth of what I have advanced, let us
consider the language of the Court but a few years ago, concerning most of the persons now in the external Administration: let me ask, whether any enemy to the personal feelings
of the Sovereign, could possibly contrive a keener instrument
of mortification, and degradation of all dignity, than almost
every part and member of the present arrangement? Nor, in

the whole course of our history, has any compliance with the will of the people ever been known to extort from any Prince a greater contradiction to all his own declared affections and dislikes, than that which is now adopted, in direct opposition to every thing the people approve and desire.

An opinion prevails, that greatness has been more than once advised to submit to certain condescensions towards individuals, which have been denied to the entreaties of a nation. For the meanest and most dependent instrument of this system knows, that there are hours when its existence may depend upon his adherence to it; and he takes his advantage accordingly. Indeed it is a law of nature, that whoever is necessary to what we have made our object, is sure, in some way, or in some time or other, to become our master. All this however is submitted to, in order to avoid that monstrous evil of governing in concurrence with the opinion of the people. For it seems to be laid down as a maxim, that a King has some sort of interest in giving uneasiness to his subjects: that all who are pleasing to them, are to be of course disagreeable to him: that as soon as the persons who are odious at Court are known to be odious to the people, it is snatched at as a lucky occasion of showering down upon them all kinds of emoluments and honours. [50] None are considered as well-wishers to the Crown, but those who advised to some unpopular course of action; none capable of serving it, but those who are obliged to call at every instant upon all its power for the safety of their lives. None are supposed to be fit priests in the temple of Government, but the persons who are compelled to fly into it for sanctuary. Such is the effect of this refined project; such is ever the result of all the contrivances which are used to free men from the servitude of their reason, and from the necessity of ordering their affairs according to their evident interests. These contrivances oblige them to run into a real and ruinous servitude, in order to avoid a supposed restraint that might be attended with advantage.

If therefore this system has so ill answered its own grand pretence of saving the King from the necessity of employing persons disagreeable to him, has it given more peace and tranquillity to his Majesty's private hours? No, most certainly. The father of his people cannot possibly enjoy repose, while his family is in such a state of distraction. Then what has the Crown or the King profited by all this fine-wrought scheme? Is he more rich, or more splendid, or more powerful, or more at his ease, by so many labours and contrivances? Have they not beggared his Exchequer, tarnished the splendor of his Court, sunk his dignity, galled his feelings, discomposed the whole order and happiness of his private life?

It will be very hard, I believe, to state in what respect the King has profited by that Faction which presumptuously choose to call themselves *his friends*.

If particular men had grown into an attachment, by the distinguished honour of the society of their Sovereign; and, by being the partakers of his amusements, came sometimes to prefer the gratification of his personal inclinations to the support of his high character, the thing would be very [51] natural, and it would be excusable enough. But the pleasant part of the story is, that these *King's friends* have no more ground for usurping such a title, than a resident freeholder in Cumberland or in Cornwall. They are only known to their Sovereign by kissing his hand, for the offices, pensions, and grants, into which they have deceived his benignity. May no storm ever come, which will put the firmness of their attachment to the proof; and which, in the midst of confusions, and terrors, and sufferings, may demonstrate the eternal difference between a true and severe friend to the Monarchy, and a slippery sycophant of the Court; *Quantum infido scurrae distabit amicus!*

So FAR I HAVE CONSIDERED the effect of the Court system, chiefly as it operates upon the executive Government, on the temper of the people, and on the happiness of the Sovereign. It remains that we should consider, with a little attention, its operation upon Parliament.

Parliament was indeed the great object of all these politicks, the end at which they aimed, as well as the instrument by which they were to operate. But, before Parliament could be made subservient to a system, by which it was to be degraded from the dignity of a national council, into a mere member of the Court, it must be greatly changed from its original character.

In speaking of this body, I have my eye chiefly on the House of Commons. I hope I shall be indulged in a few observations on the nature and character of that assembly; not with regard to its *legal form and power,* but to its *spirit,* and to the purposes it is meant to answer in the constitution.

The House of Commons was supposed originally to be *no part of the standing Government of this country.* It was considered as a *controul,* issuing *immediately* from the people, [52] and speedily to be resolved into the mass from whence it arose. In this respect it was in the higher part of Government what juries are in the lower. The capacity of a magistrate being transitory, and that of a citizen permanent, the latter capacity it was hoped would of course preponderate in all discussions, not only between the people and the standing authority of the Crown, but between the people and the fleeting authority of the House of Commons itself. It was hoped that, being of a middle nature between subject and Government, they would feel with a more tender and a nearer interest everything that concerned the people, than the other remoter and more permanent parts of Legislature.

Whatever alterations time and the necessary accommodation of business may have introduced, this character can never be sustained, unless the House of Commons shall be made to bear some stamp of the actual disposition of the people at large. It would (among public misfortunes) be an evil more natural and tolerable, that the House of Commons should be infected with every epidemical phrensy of the people, as this would indicate some consanguinity, some sympathy of nature with their constituents, than that they should in all cases be wholly untouched by the opinions and feelings of the people out of doors. By this want of sympathy they would cease to be an House of Commons. For it is not the derivation of the power of that House from the people, which makes it in a distinct sense their representative. The King is the representative of the people; so are the Lords; so are the Judges. They all are trustees for the people, as well as the Commons; because no power is given for the sole sake of the holder; and although Government certainly is an institution of Divine authority, yet its forms, and the persons who administer it, all originate from the people.

A popular origin cannot therefore be the characteristical [53] distinction of a popular representative. This belongs equally to all parts of Government, and in all forms. The virtue, spirit, and essence of an House of Commons consists in its being the express image of the feelings of the nation. It was not instituted to be a controul *upon* the people, as of late it has been taught, by a doctrine of the most pernicious tendency. It was designed as a controul *for* the people. Other institutions have been formed for the purpose of checking popular excesses; and they are, I apprehend, fully adequate to their object. If not, they ought to be made so. The House of Commons, as it was never intended for the support of peace and subordination, is miserably appointed for that service; having no stronger weapon than its Mace, and no better officer than its Serjeant at Arms, which it can command of its own proper authority. A vigilant and jealous eye over executory and judicial magistracy; an anxious care of public money, an openness, approaching towards facility, to public complaint: these seem to be the true characteristics of an House of Commons. But an addressing House of Commons, and a petitioning nation; an House of Commons full of confidence, when the nation is plunged in despair; in the utmost harmony with Ministers, whom the people regard with the utmost abhorrence; who vote thanks, when the public opinion calls upon them for impeachments; who are eager to grant, when the general voice demands account; who, in all disputes between the people and Administration, presume against the people; who punish their disorders, but refuse even to inquire into the provocations to them; this is an unnatural, a monstrous state of things in this constitution. Such an Assembly may be a great, wise, aweful senate; but it is not, to any popular purpose, an House of Commons. This change from an immediate state of procuration and delegation to a course of acting as from original power, is the way in which all the [54] popular magistracies in the world have been perverted from their purposes. It is indeed their greatest and sometimes their incurable corruption. For there is a material distinction between that corruption by which particular points are carried against reason, (this is a thing which cannot be prevented by human wisdom, and is of less consequence,) and the corruption of the principle itself. For then the evil is not accidental, but settled. The distemper becomes the natural habit.

For my part, I shall be compelled to conclude the principle of Parliament to be totally corrupted, and therefore its ends entirely defeated, when I see two symptoms: first, a rule of indiscriminate support to all Ministers; because this destroys the very end of Parliament as a controul, and is a general previous sanction to misgovernment; and secondly, the setting up any claims adverse to the right of free election; for this tends to subvert the legal authority by which the House of Commons sits.

I know that, since the Revolution, along with many dangerous, many useful powers of Government have been weakened. It is absolutely necessary to have frequent recourse to the Legislature. Parliaments must therefore sit every year, and for great part of the year. The dreadful disorders of frequent elections have also necessitated a septennial instead of a triennial duration. These circumstances, I mean the constant habit of authority, and the unfrequency of elections, have tended very much to draw the House of Commons towards the character of a standing Senate. It is a disorder which has arisen from the cure of greater disorders; it has arisen from the extreme difficulty of reconciling liberty under a monarchical Government, with external strength and with internal tranquillity.

It is very clear that we cannot free ourselves entirely from this great inconvenience; but I would not increase an evil, [55] because I was not able to remove it; and because it was not in my power to keep the House of Commons religiously true to its first principles, I would not argue for carrying it to a total oblivion of them. This has been the great scheme of power in our time. They who will not conform their conduct to the public good, and cannot support it by the prerogative of the Crown, have adopted a new plan. They have totally abandoned the shattered and old-fashioned fortress of prerogative, and made a lodgement in the strong-hold of Parliament itself. If they have any evil design to which there is no ordinary legal power commensurate, they bring it into Parliament. In Parliament the whole is executed from the beginning to the end. In Parliament the power of obtaining their object is absolute; and the safety in the proceeding perfect: no rules to confine, no after reckonings to terrify. Parliament cannot with any great propriety punish others, for things in which they themselves have been accomplices. Thus the controul of Parliament upon the executory power is lost; because Parliament is made to partake in every considerable act of Government. *Impeachment, that great guardian of the purity of the Constitution, is in danger of being lost, even to the idea of it.*

By this plan several important ends are answered to the

Cabal. If the authority of Parliament supports itself, the credit of every act of Government, which they contrive, is saved: but if the act be so very odious that the whole strength of Parliament is insufficient to recommend it, then Parliament is itself discredited; and this discredit increases more and more that indifference to the constitution, which it is the constant aim of its enemies, by their abuse of Parliamentary powers, to render general among the people. Whenever Parliament is persuaded to assume the offices of executive Government, it will lose all the confidence, love, and veneration, which it has ever enjoyed whilst it was [56] supposed the *corrective and controul* of the acting powers of the State. This would be the event, though its conduct in such a perversion of its functions should be tolerably just and moderate; but if it should be iniquitous, violent, full of passion, and full of faction, it would be considered as the most intolerable of all the modes of tyranny.

For a considerable time this separation of the representatives from their constituents went on with a silent progress; and had those, who conducted the plan for their total separation, been persons of temper and abilities any way equal to the magnitude of their design, the success would have been infallible: but by their precipitancy they have laid it open in all its nakedness; the nation is alarmed at it: and the event may not be pleasant to the contrivers of the scheme. In the last session, the corps called the *King's friends* made an hardy attempt all at once, *to alter the right of election itself;* to put it into the power of the House of Commons to disable any person disagreeable to them from sitting in Parliament, without any other rule than their own pleasure; to make incapacities, either general for descriptions of men, or particular for individuals; and to take into their body, persons who avowedly had never been chosen by the majority of legal electors, nor agreeably to any known rule of law.

The arguments upon which this claim was founded and

combated, are not my business here. Never has a subject been more amply and more learnedly handled, nor upon one side, in my opinion, more satisfactorily; they who are not convinced by what is already written would not receive conviction *though one arose from the dead.*

I too have thought on this subject: but my purpose here, is only to consider it as a part of the favourite project of Government; to observe on the motives which led to it; and to trace its political consequences.

[57] A violent rage for the punishment of Mr. Wilkes was the pretence of the whole. This gentleman, by setting himself strongly in opposition to the Court Cabal, had become at once an object of their persecution, and of the popular favour. The hatred of the Court Party pursuing, and the countenance of the people protecting him, it very soon became not at all a question on the man, but a trial of strength between the two parties. The advantage of the victory in this particular contest was the present, but not the only, nor by any means, the principal, object. Its operation upon the character of the House of Commons was the great point in view. The point to be gained by the Cabal was this: that a precedent should be established, tending to show, *That the favour of the People was not so sure a road as the favour of the Court even to popular honours and popular trusts.* A strenuous resistance to every appearance of lawless power; a spirit of independence carried to some degree of enthusiasm; an inquisitive character to discover, and a bold one to display, every corruption and every error of Government; these are the qualities which recommend a man to a seat in the House of Commons, in open and merely popular elections. An indolent and submissive disposition; a disposition to think charitably of all the actions of men in power, and to live in a mutual intercourse of favours with them; an inclination rather to countenance a strong use of authority, than to bear any sort of licentiousness on the part of the people; these are unfavourable qualities in an open election for Members of Parliament.

The instinct which carries the people towards the choice of the former, is justified by reason; because a man of such a character, even in its exorbitancies, does not directly contradict the purposes of a trust, the end of which is a controul on power. The latter character, even when it is not in its extreme, will execute this trust but very imperfectly; and, if [58] deviating to the least excess, will certainly frustrate instead of forwarding the purposes of a controul on Government. But when the House of Commons was to be new modelled, this principle was not only to be changed, but reversed. Whilst any errours committed in support of power were left to the law, with every advantage of favourable construction, of mitigation, and finally of pardon; all excesses on the side of liberty, or in pursuit of popular favour, or in defence of popular rights and privileges, were not only to be punished by the rigour of the known law, but by a *discretionary* proceeding, which brought on *the loss of the popular object itself.* Popularity was to be rendered, if not directly penal, at least highly dangerous. The favour of the people might lead even to a disqualification of representing them. Their odium might become, strained through the medium of two or three constructions, the means of sitting as the trustee of all that was dear to them. This is punishing the offence in the offending part. Until this time, the opinion of the people, through the power of an Assembly, still in some sort popular, led to the greatest honours and emoluments in the gift of the Crown. Now the principle is reversed; and the favour of the Court is the only sure way of obtaining and holding those honours which ought to be in the disposal of the people.

It signifies very little how this matter may be quibbled away. Example, the only argument of effect in civil life, demonstrates the truth of my proposition. Nothing can alter my opinion concerning the pernicious tendency of this example, until I see some man for his indiscretion in the support of power, for his violent and intemperate servility, rendered incapable of sitting in parliament. For as it now stands, the fault of overstraining popular qualities, and, irregularly if you please, asserting popular privileges, has led to disqualification; the opposite fault never has produced [59] the slightest punishment. Resistance to power has shut the door of the House of Commons to one man; obsequiousness and servility, to none.

Not that I would encourage popular disorder, or any disorder. But I would leave such offences to the law, to be punished in measure and proportion. The laws of this country are for the most part constituted, and wisely so, for the general ends of Government, rather than for the preservation of our particular liberties. Whatever therefore is done in support of liberty, by persons not in public trust, or not acting merely in that trust, is liable to be more or less out of the ordinary course of the law; and the law itself is sufficient to animadvert upon it with great severity. Nothing indeed can hinder that severe letter from crushing us, except the temperaments it may receive from a trial by jury. But if the habit prevails of *going beyond the law,* and superseding this judicature, of carrying offences, real or supposed, into the legislative bodies, who shall establish themselves into *courts of criminal equity,* (so *the Star Chamber* has been called by Lord Bacon,) all the evils of the *Star Chamber* are revived. A large and liberal construction in ascertaining offences, and a discretionary power in punishing them, is the idea of *criminal equity;* which is in truth a monster in Jurisprudence. It signifies nothing whether a court for this purpose be a Committee of Council, or an House of Commons, or an House of Lords; the liberty of the subject will be equally subverted by it. The true end and purpose of that House of Parliament which entertains such a jurisdiction will be destroyed by it.

I will not believe, what no other man living believes, that Mr. Wilkes was punished for the indecency of his publications, or the impiety of his ransacked closet. If he had fallen in a common slaughter of libellers and blasphemers, I could well believe that nothing more was meant than was [60] pretended. But when I see, that, for years together, full as impious, and perhaps more dangerous writings to religion, and virtue, and order, have not been punished, nor their authors discountenanced; that the most audacious libels on Royal Majesty have passed without notice; that the most treasonable invectives against the laws, liberties, and constitution of the country, have not met with the slightest animadversion; I must consider this as a shocking and shameless pretence. Never did an envenomed scurrility against everything sacred and civil, public and private, rage through the kingdom with such a furious and unbridled licence. All this while the peace of the nation must be shaken, to ruin one libeller, and to tear from the populace a single favourite.

Nor is it that vice merely skulks in an obscure and contemptible impunity. Does not the public behold with indignation, persons not only generally scandalous in their lives, but the identical persons who, by their society, their instruction, their example, their encouragement, have drawn this man into the very faults which have furnished the Cabal with a pretence for his persecution, loaded with every kind of favour, honour, and distinction, which a Court can bestow? Add but the crime of servility (the *foedum crimen servitutis*) to every other crime, and the whole mass is immediately transmuted into virtue, and becomes the just subject of reward and honour. When therefore I reflect upon this method pursued by the Cabal in distributing rewards and punishments, I must conclude that Mr. Wilkes is the object of persecution, not on account of what he has done in common with others who are the objects of reward, but for that in which he differs from many of them: that he is pursued for the spirited dispositions which are blended with his vices; for his unconquerable firmness, for his resolute, indefatigable, strenuous resistance against oppression.

[61] In this case, therefore, it was not the man that was

to be punished, nor his faults that were to be discountenanced. Opposition to acts of power was to be marked by a kind of civil proscription. The popularity which should arise from such an opposition was to be shown unable to protect it. The qualities by which court is made to the people, were to render every fault inexpiable, and every error irretrievable. The qualities by which court is made to power, were to cover and to sanctify everything. He that will have a sure and honourable seat in the House of Commons, must take care how he adventures to cultivate popular qualities; otherwise he may remember the old maxim, *Breves et infaustos populi Romani amores.* If, therefore, a pursuit of popularity expose a man to greater dangers than a disposition to servility, the principle which is the life and soul of popular elections will perish out of the Constitution.

It behoves the people of England to consider how the House of Commons under the operation of these examples must of necessity be constituted. On the side of the Court will be, all honours, offices, emoluments; every sort of personal gratification to avarice or vanity; and, what is of more moment to most gentlemen, the means of growing, by innumerable petty services to individuals, into a spreading interest in their country. On the other hand, let us suppose a person unconnected with the Court, and in opposition to its system. For his own person, no office, or emolument, or title; no promotion ecclesiastical, or civil, or military, or naval, for children, or brothers, or kindred. In vain an expiring interest in a borough calls for offices, or small livings, for the children of mayors, and aldermen, and capital burgesses. His court rival has them all. He can do an infinite number of acts of generosity and kindness, and even of public spirit. He can procure indemnity from quarters. He can procure advantages in trade. He [62] can get pardons for offences. He can obtain a thousand favours, and avert a thousand evils. He may, while he betrays every valuable interest of the kingdom, be a benefactor, a patron, a father, a guardian angel, to his borough. The unfortunate independent member has nothing to offer, but harsh refusal, or pitiful excuse, or despondent representation of an hopeless interest. Except from his private fortune, in which he may be equalled, perhaps exceeded, by his Court competitor, he has no way of showing any one good quality, or of making a single friend. In the House, he votes for ever in a dispirited minority. If he speaks, the doors are locked. A body of loquacious placemen go out to tell the world, that all he aims at, is to get into office. If he has not the talent of elocution, which is the case of many as wise and knowing men as any in the House, he is liable to all these inconveniencies, without the eclat which attends upon any tolerably successful exertion of eloquence. Can we conceive a more discouraging post of duty than this? Strip it of the poor reward of popularity; suffer even the excesses committed in defence of the popular interest to become a ground for the majority of that House to form a disqualification out of the line of the law, and at their pleasure, attended not only with the loss of the franchise, but with every kind of personal disgrace; if this shall happen, the people of this kingdom may be assured that they cannot be firmly or faithfully served by any man. It is out of the nature of men and things that they should; and their presumption will be equal to their folly, if they expect it. The power of the people, within the laws, must show itself sufficient to protect every representative in the animated performance of his duty, or that duty cannot be performed. The House of Commons can never be a controul on other parts of Government, unless they are controuled themselves by their constituents; and unless these constituents possess [63] some right in the choice of that House, which it is not in the power of that House to take away. If they suffer this power of arbitrary incapacitation to stand, they have utterly perverted every other power of the House of Commons. The late proceeding, I will not say, *is* contrary to law; it *must* be so; for the power which is claimed cannot, by any possibility, be a legal power in any limited member of Government.

The power which they claim, of declaring incapacities, would not be above the just claims of a final judicature, if they had not laid it down as a leading principle, that they had no rule in the exercise of this claim, but their own *discretion*. Not one of their abettors has ever undertaken to assign the principle of unfitness, the species or degree of delinquency, on which the House of Commons will expel, nor the mode of proceeding upon it, nor the evidence upon which it is established. The direct consequence of which is, that the first franchise of an Englishman, and that on which all the rest vitally depend, is to be forfeited for some offence which no man knows, and which is to be proved by no known rule whatsoever of legal evidence. This is so anomalous to our whole constitution, that I will venture to say, the most trivial right, which the subject claims, never was, nor can be, forfeited in such a manner.

The whole of their usurpation is established upon this method of arguing. We do not *make* laws. No; we do not contend for this power. We only *declare* law; and, as we are a tribunal both competent and supreme, what we declare to be law becomes law, although it should not have been so before. Thus the circumstance of having no *appeal* from their jurisdiction is made to imply that they have no *rule* in the exercise of it: the judgement does not derive its validity from its conformity to the law; but preposterously the law is made to attend on the judgement; and the rule of the [64] judgement is no other than the *occasional will of the House.* An arbitrary discretion leads, legality follows; which is just the very nature and description of a legislative act.

This claim in their hands was no barren theory. It was pursued into its utmost consequences; and a dangerous principle has begot a correspondent practice. A systematic spirit has been shown upon both sides. The electors of Middlesex chose a person whom the House of Commons had voted incapable; and the House of Commons has taken in a member whom the electors of Middlesex had not chosen. By a construction on that legislative power which had been assumed, they declared that the true legal sense of the country was contained in the minority, on that occasion; and might, on a resistance to a vote of incapacity, be contained in any minority.

When any construction of law goes against the spirit of the privilege it was meant to support, it is a vicious construction. It is material to us to be represented really and *bona fide*, and not in forms, in types, and shadows, and fictions of law. The right of election was not established merely as a *matter of form*, to satisfy some method and rule of technical reasoning; it was not a principle which might substitute a *Titius* or a *Maevius*, a *John Doe* or *Richard Roe*, in the place of a man specially chosen; not a principle which was just as well satisfied with one man as with another. It is a right, the effect of which is to give to the people that man, and *that man only*, whom, by their voices, actually, not constructively given, they declare that they know, esteem, love, and trust. This right is a matter within their own power of judging and feeling; not an *ens rationis* and creature of law: nor can those devices, by which anything else is substituted in the place of such an actual choice, answer in the least degree the end of representation.

I know that the courts of law have made as strained constructions [65] in other cases. Such is the construction in common recoveries. The method of construction which in that case gives to the persons in remainder, for their security and representative, the door-keeper, cryer, or sweeper of the Court, or some other shadowy being without substance or effect, is a fiction of a very coarse texture. This was however suffered, by the acquiescence of the whole kingdom, for ages; because the evasion of the old Statute of Westminster, which authorized perpetuities, had more sense and utility than the law which was evaded. But an attempt to turn the right of election into such a farce and mockery as a fictitious fine and recovery, will, I hope, have another fate; because the laws which give it are infinitely dear to us, and the evasion is infinitely contemptible.

The people indeed have been told, that this power of discretionary disqualification is vested in hands that they may trust, and who will be sure not to abuse it to their prejudice. Until I find something in this argument differing from that on which every mode of despotism has been defended, I shall not be inclined to pay it any great compliment. The people are satisfied to trust themselves with the exercise of their own privileges, and do not desire this kind intervention of the House of Commons to free them from the burthen. They are certainly in the right. They ought not to trust the House of Commons with a power over their franchises; because the constitution, which placed two other co-ordinate powers to controul it, reposed no such confidence in that body. It were a folly well deserving servitude for its punishment, to be full of confidence where the laws are full of distrust; and to give to an House of Commons, arrogating to its sole resolution the most harsh and odious part of legislative authority, that degree of submission which is due only to the Legislature itself.

When the House of Commons, in an endeavour to obtain [66] new advantages at the expence of the other orders of the State, for the benefits of the *Commons at large,* have pursued strong measures; if it were not just, it was at least natural, that the constituents should connive at all their proceedings; because we were ourselves ultimately to profit. But when this submission is urged to us, in a contest between the representatives and ourselves, and where nothing can be put into their scale which is not taken from ours, they fancy us to be children when they tell us they are our representatives, our own flesh and blood, and that all the stripes they give us are for our good. The very desire of that body to have such a trust contrary to law reposed in them, shews that they are not worthy of it. They certainly will abuse it; because all men possessed of an uncontrouled discretionary power leading to the aggrandisement and profit of their own body have always abused it: and I see no particular sanctity in our times, that is at all likely, by a miraculous operation, to overrule the course of nature.

But we must purposely shut our eyes, if we consider this matter merely as a contest between the House of Commons and the Electors. The true contest is between the Electors of the Kingdom and the Crown; the Crown acting by an instrumental House of Commons. It is precisely the same, whether the Ministers of the Crown can disqualify by a dependent House of Commons, or by a dependent court of *Star Chamber,* or by a dependent court of King's Bench. If once Members of Parliament can be practically convinced that they do not depend on the affection or opinion of the people for their political being, they will give themselves over, without even an appearance of reserve, to the influence of the Court.

Indeed, a Parliament unconnected with the people, is essential to a Ministry unconnected with the people; and therefore those who saw through what mighty difficulties the interior Ministry waded, and the exterior were dragged, in [67] this business, will conceive of what prodigious importance, the new corps of *King's men* held this principle of occasional and personal incapacitation, to the whole body of their design.

When the House of Commons was thus made to consider itself as the master of its constituents, there wanted but one thing to secure that House against all possible future deviation towards popularity; an *unlimited* fund of money to be laid out according to the pleasure of the Court.

To COMPLEAT THE SCHEME of bringing our Court to a resemblance to the neighbouring Monarchies, it was necessary, in effect, to destroy those appropriations of revenue, which seem to limit the property, as the other laws had done the powers, of the Crown. An opportunity for this purpose was taken, upon an application to Parliament for payment of the debts of the Civil List; which in 1769 had amounted to 513,000*l.* Such application had been made upon former occasions; but to do it in the former manner would by no means answer the present purpose.

Whenever the Crown had come to the Commons to desire a supply for the discharging of debts due on the Civil List; it was always asked and granted with one of the three following qualifications; sometimes with all of them. Either it was stated, that the revenue had been diverted from its purposes by Parliament: or that those duties had fallen short of the sum for which they were given by Parliament, and that the intention of the Legislature had not been fulfilled: or that the money required to discharge the Civil List debt was to be raised chargeable on the Civil List duties. In the reign of Queen Anne, the Crown was found in debt. The lessening and granting away some part of her revenue by Parliament was alleged as the cause of that debt, and pleaded as an equitable ground, (such it certainly was,) for discharging it. [68] It does not appear that the duties which were then applied to the ordinary Government produced clear above 580,000*l.* a year; because, when they were afterwards granted to George the First, 120,000*l.* was added, to complete the whole to 700,000*l.* a year. Indeed it was then asserted, and, I have no doubt, truly, that for many years the nett produce did not amount to above 550,000*l.* The Queen's extraordinary charges were besides very considerable; equal, at least, to any we have known in our time. The application to Parliament was not for an absolute grant of money; but to empower the Queen to raise it by borrowing upon the Civil List funds.

The Civil List debt was twice paid in the reign of George the First. The money was granted upon the same plan which had been followed in the reign of Queen Anne. The Civil List revenues were then mortgaged for the sum to be raised, and stood charged with the ransom of their own deliverance.

George the Second received an addition to his Civil List. Duties were granted for the purpose of raising 800,000*l.* a year. It was not until he had reigned nineteen years, and after the last rebellion, that he called upon Parliament for a discharge of the Civil List debt. The extraordinary charges brought on by the rebellion, account fully for the necessities of the Crown. However, the extraordinary charges of Government were not thought a ground fit to be relied on. A deficiency of the Civil List duties for several years before was stated as the principal, if not the sole, ground on which an application to Parliament could be justified. About this time the produce of these duties had fallen pretty low; and even upon an average of the whole reign they never produced 800,000*l.* a year clear to the Treasury.

That Prince reigned fourteen years afterwards: not only no new demands were made; but with so much good order [69] were his revenues and expenses regulated, that, although many parts of the establishment of the Court were upon a larger and more liberal scale than they have been since, there was a considerable sum in hand, on his decease, amounting to about 170,000*l.*, applicable to the service of the Civil List of his present Majesty. So that, if this Reign commenced with a greater charge than usual, there was enough, and more than enough, abundantly to supply all the extraordinary expence. That the Civil List should have been exceeded in the two former reigns, especially in the reign of George the First, was not at all surprizing. His revenue was but 700,000*l.* annually; if it ever produced so much clear. The prodigious and dangerous disaffection to the very being of the establishment, and the cause of a Pretender then powerfully abetted from abroad, produced many demands of an extraordinary nature both abroad and at home.

Much management and great expenses were necessary. But the throne of no Prince has stood upon more unshaken foundations than that of his present Majesty.

To have exceeded the sum given for the Civil List, and to have incurred a debt without special authority of Parliament, was, *prima facie,* a criminal act: as such, Ministers ought naturally rather to have withdrawn it from the inspection, than to have exposed it to the scrutiny, of Parliament. Certainly they ought, of themselves, officially to have come armed with every sort of argument, which, by explaining, could excuse a matter in itself of presumptive guilt. But the terrors of the House of Commons are no longer for Ministers.

On the other hand, the peculiar character of the House of Commons, as trustee of the public purse, would have led them to call with a punctilious solicitude for every public account, and to have examined into them with the most rigorous accuracy.

[70] The capital use of an account is, that the reality of the charge, the reason of incurring it, and the justice and necessity of discharging it, should all appear antecedent to the payment. No man ever pays first, and calls for his account afterwards; because he would thereby let out of his hands the principal, and indeed only effectual, means of compelling a full and fair one. But, in national business, there is an additional reason for a previous production of every account. It is a check, perhaps the only one, upon a corrupt and prodigal use of public money. An account after payment is to no rational purpose an account. However, the House of Commons thought all these to be antiquated principles; they were of opinion, that the most Parliamentary way of proceeding was, to pay first what the Court thought proper to demand, and to take its chance for an examination into accounts at some time of greater leisure.

The nation had settled 800,000*l.* a year on the Crown, as sufficient for the purpose of its dignity, upon the estimate of its own Ministers. When Ministers came to Parliament, and said that this allowance had not been sufficient for the purpose, and that they had incurred a debt of 500,000*l.*, would it not have been natural for Parliament first to have asked, how, and by what means, their appropriated allowance came to be insufficient? Would it not have savoured of some attention to justice, to have seen in what periods of Administration this debt had been originally incurred; that they might discover, and if need were, animadvert on the persons who were found the most culpable? To put their hands upon such articles of expenditure as they thought improper or excessive, and to secure, in future, against such misapplication or exceeding? Accounts for any other purposes are but a matter of curiosity, and no genuine Parliamentary object. All the accounts which could answer any Parliamentary end were refused, or postponed by previous questions. [71] Every idea of prevention was rejected, as conveying an improper suspicion of the Ministers of the Crown.

When every leading account had been refused, many others were granted with sufficient facility.

But with great candour also, the House was informed, that hardly any of them could be ready until the next session; some of them perhaps not so soon. But, in order firmly to establish the precedent of *payment previous to account,* and to form it into a settled rule of the House, the god in the machine was brought down, nothing less than the wonder-working *Law of Parliament.* It was alledged, that it is the law of Parliament, when any demand comes from the Crown, that the House must go immediately into the Committee of Supply; in which Committee it was allowed, that the production and examination of accounts would be quite proper and regular. It was therefore carried, that they should go into the Committee without delay, and without accounts, in order to examine with great order and regularity things that could not possibly come before them. After this stroke of orderly and Parliamentary wit and humour, they went into the Committee; and very generously voted the payment.

There was a circumstance in that debate too remarkable to be overlooked. This debt of the Civil List was all along argued upon the same footing as a debt of the State, contracted upon national authority. Its payment was urged as equally pressing upon the public faith and honour; and when the whole year's account was stated, in what is called *The Budget,* the Ministry valued themselves on the payment of so much public debt, just as if they had discharged 500,000*l.* of navy or exchequer bills. Though, in truth, their payment, from the Sinking Fund, of debt which was never contracted by Parliamentary authority, was, to all intents and purposes, so much debt incurred. But such is the present [72] notion of public credit, and payment of debt. No wonder that it produces such effects.

Nor was the House at all more attentive to a provident security against future, than it had been to a vindictive retrospect to past, mismanagements. I should have thought indeed that a Ministerial promise, during their own continuance in office, might have been given, though this would have been but a poor security for the publick. Mr. Pelham gave such an assurance, and he kept his word. But nothing was capable of extorting from our Ministers anything which had the least resemblance to a promise of confining the expences of the Civil List within the limits which had been settled by Parliament. This reserve of theirs I look upon to be equivalent to the clearest declaration, that they were resolved upon a contrary course.

However, to put the matter beyond all doubt, in the Speech from the Throne, after thanking Parliament for the relief so liberally granted, the Ministers inform the two Houses, that they will *endeavour* to confine the expences of the Civil Government—within what limits, think you? those which the law had prescribed? Not in the least—"such limits as the *honour of the Crown* can possibly admit."

Thus they established an *arbitrary* standard for that dignity which Parliament had defined and limited to a *legal* standard. They gave themselves, under the lax and indeterminate idea of the *honour of the Crown*, a full loose for all manner of dissipation, and all manner of corruption. This arbitrary standard they were not afraid to hold out to both Houses; while an idle and unoperative Act of Parliament, estimating the dignity of the Crown at 800,000*l.*, and confining it to that sum, adds to the number of obsolete statutes which load the shelves of libraries without any sort of advantage to the people.

After this proceeding, I suppose that no man can be so [73] weak as to think that the Crown is limited to any settled allowance whatsoever. For if the Ministry has 800,000*l.* a year by the law of the land; and if by the law of Parliament all the debts which exceed it are to be paid previous to the production of any account; I presume that this is equivalent to an income with no other limits than the abilities of the subject and the moderation of the Court; that is to say, it is such an income as is possessed by every absolute Monarch in Europe. It amounts, as a person of great ability said in the debate, to an unlimited power of drawing upon the Sinking Fund. Its effect on the public credit of this kingdom must be obvious; for in vain is the Sinking Fund the great buttress of all the rest, if it be in the power of the Ministry to resort to it for the payment of any debts which they may choose to incur, under the name of the Civil List, and through the medium of a Committee, which thinks itself obliged by law to vote supplies without any other account than that of the mere existence of the debt.

Five hundred thousand pounds is a serious sum. But it is nothing to the prolific principle upon which the sum was voted; a principle that may be well called, *the fruitful mother of an hundred more.* Neither is the damage to public credit of very great consequence, when compared with that which results to public morals and to the safety of the constitution, from the exhaustless mine of corruption opened by the precedent, and to be wrought by the principle of the late payment of the debts of the Civil List. The power of discretionary disqualification by one law of Parliament, and the necessity of paying every debt of the Civil List by another law of Parliament, if suffered to pass unnoticed, must establish such a fund of rewards and terrors as will make Parliament the best appendage and support of arbitrary power that ever was invented by the wit of man. This is felt. The quarrel [74] is begun between the Representatives and the People. The Court Faction have at length committed them.

In such a strait the wisest may well be perplexed, and the boldest staggered. The circumstances are in a great measure new. We have hardly any land-marks from the wisdom of our ancestors, to guide us. At best we can only follow the spirit of their proceeding in other cases. I know the diligence with which my observations on our public disorders have been made; I am very sure of the integrity of the motives on which they are published: I cannot be equally confident in any plan for the absolute cure of those disorders, or for their certain future prevention. My aim is to bring this matter into more public discussion. Let the sagacity of others work upon it. It is not uncommon for medical writers to describe histories of diseases very accurately, on whose cure they can say but very little.

THE FIRST IDEAS which generally suggest themselves, for the cure of Parliamentary disorders, are, to shorten the duration of Parliaments; and to disqualify all, or a great number of placemen, from a seat in the House of Commons. Whatever efficacy there may be in those remedies, I am sure in the present state of things it is impossible to apply them. A restoration of the right of free election is a preliminary indispensable to every other reformation. What alterations ought afterwards to be made in the constitution, is a matter of deep and difficult research.

Thoughts on the Present Discontents

If I wrote merely to please the popular palate, it would indeed be as little troublesome to me as to another, to extol these remedies, so famous in speculation, but to which their greatest admirers have never attempted seriously to resort in practice. I confess then, that I have no sort of reliance upon either a Triennial Parliament, or a Place-bill. With regard to the former, perhaps, it might rather serve to counteract, than [75] to promote, the ends that are proposed by it. To say nothing of the horrible disorders among the people attending frequent elections, I should be fearful of committing, every three years, the independent gentlemen of the country into a contest with the Treasury. It is easy to see which of the contending parties would be ruined first. Whoever has taken a careful view of public proceedings, so as to endeavour to ground his speculations on his experience, must have observed how prodigiously greater the power of Ministry is in the first and last session of a Parliament, than it is in the intermediate periods, when Members sit a little firm on their seats. The persons of the greatest Parliamentary experience, with whom I have conversed, did constantly, in canvassing the fate of questions, allow something to the Court side, upon account of the elections depending or imminent. The evil complained of, if it exists in the present state of things, would hardly be removed by a triennial Parliament: for, unless the influence of Government in elections can be entirely taken away, the more frequently they return, the more they will harass private independence; the more generally men will be compelled to fly to the settled systematic interest of Government, and to the resources of a boundless Civil List. Certainly something may be done, and ought to be done, towards lessening that influence in elections; and this will be necessary upon a plan either of longer or shorter duration of Parliament. But nothing can so perfectly remove the evil, as not to render such contentions, too frequently repeated, utterly ruinous, first to independence of fortune, and then to independence of spirit. As I am only giving an opinion on this point, and not at all debating it in an adverse line, I hope I may be excused in another observation. With great truth I may aver, that I never remember to have talked on this subject with any man much conversant with public business, who considered short Parliaments as a real improvement of [76] the constitution. Gentlemen, warm in a popular cause, are ready enough to attribute all the declarations of such persons to corrupt motives. But the habit of affairs, if, on one hand, it tends to corrupt the mind, furnishes it, on the other, with the means of better information. The authority of such persons will always have some weight. It may stand upon a par with the speculations of those who are less practised in business; and who, with perhaps purer intentions, have not so effectual means of judging. It is besides an effect of vulgar and puerile malignity to imagine, that every Statesman is of course corrupt; and that his opinion, upon every constitutional point, is solely formed upon some sinister interest.

The next favourite remedy is a Place-bill. The same principle guides in both; I mean, the opinion which is entertained by many, of the infallibility of laws and regulations, in the cure of public distempers. Without being as unreasonably doubtful as many are unwisely confident, I will only say, that this also is a matter very well worthy of serious and mature reflexion. It is not easy to foresee, what the effect would be of disconnecting with Parliament, the greatest part of those who hold civil employments, and of such mighty and important bodies as the military and naval establishments. It were better, perhaps, that they should have a corrupt interest in the forms of the constitution, than that they should have none at all. This is a question altogether different from the disqualification of a particular description of Revenue Officers from seats in Parliament; or, perhaps, of all the lower sorts of them from votes in elections. In the former case, only the few are affected; in the latter, only the inconsiderable.

But a great official, a great professional, a great military and naval interest, all necessarily comprehending many people of the first weight, ability, wealth, and spirit, has been gradually formed in the kingdom. These new interests must be let into a share of representation, [77] else possibly they may be inclined to destroy those institutions of which they are not permitted to partake. This is not a thing to be trifled with; nor is it every well-meaning man that is fit to put his hands to it. Many other serious considerations occur. I do not open them here, because they are not directly to my purpose; proposing only to give the reader some taste of the difficulties that attend all capital changes in the constitution; just to hint the uncertainty, to say no worse, of being able to prevent the Court, as long as it has the means of influence abundantly in its power, from applying that influence to Parliament; and perhaps, if the public method were precluded, of doing it in some worse and more dangerous method. Underhand and oblique ways would be studied. The science of evasion, already tolerably understood, would then be brought to the greatest perfection. It is no inconsiderable part of wisdom, to know how much of an evil ought to be tolerated; lest, by attempting a degree of purity impracticable in degenerate times and manners, instead of cutting off the subsisting ill practices, new corruptions might be produced for the concealment and security of the old. It were better, undoubtedly, that no influence at all could affect the mind of a Member of Parliament. But of all modes of influence, in my opinion, a place under the Government is the least disgraceful to the man who holds it, and by far the most safe to the country. I would not shut out that sort of influence which is open and visible, which is connected with the dignity and the service of the State, when it is not in my power to prevent the influence of contracts, of subscriptions, of direct bribery, and those innumerable methods of clandestine corruption, which are abundantly in the hands of the Court, and which will be applied as long

as these means of corruption, and the disposition to be corrupted, have existence amongst us. Our Constitution stands
on a nice equipoise, with steep precipices and deep waters
upon all sides [78] of it. In removing it from a dangerous
leaning towards one side, there may be a risque of oversetting
it on the other. Every project of a material change in a Government so complicated as ours, combined at the same time
with external circumstances still more complicated, is a matter full of difficulties; in which a considerate man will not be
too ready to decide; a prudent man too ready to undertake;
or an honest man too ready to promise. They do not respect
the publick nor themselves, who engage for more than they
are sure that they ought to attempt, or that they are able to
perform. These are my sentiments, weak perhaps, but honest and unbiassed; and submitted entirely to the opinion of
grave men, well affected to the constitution of their country,
and of experience in what may best promote or hurt it.

Indeed, in the situation in which we stand, with an immense revenue, an enormous debt, mighty establishments,
Government itself a great banker and a great merchant, I see
no other way for the preservation of a decent attention to
public interest in the Representatives, but *the interposition of
the body of the people itself,* whenever it shall appear, by some
flagrant and notorious act, by some capital innovation, that
these Representatives are going to over-leap the fences of the
law, and to introduce an arbitrary power. This interposition
is a most unpleasant remedy. But, if it be a legal remedy, it is
intended on some occasion to be used; to be used then only,
when it is evident that nothing else can hold the constitution
to its true principles.

THE DISTEMPERS OF MONARCHY were the great subjects
of apprehension and redress, in the last century; in this, the
distempers of Parliament. It is not in Parliament alone that
the remedy for Parliamentary disorders can be compleated;

hardly indeed can it begin there. Until a confidence in Government is re-established, the people ought to be excited [79] to a more strict and detailed attention to the conduct of their Representatives. Standards, for judging more systematically upon their conduct, ought to be settled in the meetings of counties and corporations. Frequent and correct lists of the voters in all important questions ought to be procured.

By such means something may be done. By such means it may appear who those are, that, by an indiscriminate support of all Administrations, have totally banished all integrity and confidence out of public proceedings; have confounded the best men with the worst; and weakened and dissolved, instead of strengthening and compacting, the general frame of Government. If any person is more concerned for government and order, than for the liberties of his country, even he is equally concerned to put an end to this course of indiscriminate support. It is this blind and undistinguishing support, that feeds the spring of those very disorders, by which he is frighted into the arms of the faction which contains in itself the source of all disorders, by enfeebling all the visible and regular authority of the State. The distemper is increased by his injudicious and preposterous endeavours, or pretences, for the cure of it.

An exterior Administration, chosen for its impotency, or after it is chosen purposely rendered impotent, in order to be rendered subservient, will not be obeyed. The laws themselves will not be respected, when those who execute them are despised: and they will be despised, when their power is not immediate from the Crown, or natural in the kingdom. Never were Ministers better supported in Parliament. Parliamentary support comes and goes with office, totally regardless of the man, or the merit. Is Government strengthened? It grows weaker and weaker. The popular torrent gains upon it every hour. Let us learn from our experience. It is not support that is wanting to Government, [80] but reformation. When Ministry rests upon public opinion, it is not indeed built upon a rock of adamant; it has, however, some stability. But when it stands upon private humour, its structure is of stubble, and its foundation is on quicksand. I repeat it again—He that supports every Administration, subverts all Government. The reason is this. The whole business in which a Court usually takes an interest goes on at present equally well, in whatever hands, whether high or low, wise or foolish, scandalous or reputable; there is nothing therefore to hold it firm to any one body of men, or to any one consistent scheme of politicks. Nothing interposes, to prevent the full operation of all the caprices and all the passions of a Court upon the servants of the publick. The system of Administration is open to continual shocks and changes, upon the principles of the meanest cabal, and the most contemptible intrigue. Nothing can be solid and permanent. All good men at length fly with horrour from such a service. Men of rank and ability, with the spirit which ought to animate such men in a free state, while they decline the jurisdiction of dark cabal on their actions and their fortunes, will, for both, chearfully put themselves upon their country. They will trust an inquisitive and distinguishing Parliament; because it does enquire, and does distinguish. If they act well, they know that, in such a Parliament, they will be supported against any intrigue; if they act ill, they know that no intrigue can protect them. This situation, however aweful, is honourable. But in one hour, and in the self-same Assembly, without any assigned or assignable cause, to be precipitated from the highest authority to the most marked neglect, possibly into the greatest peril of life and reputation, is a situation full of danger, and destitute of honour. It will be shunned equally by every man of prudence, and every man of spirit.

[81] Such are the consequences of the division of Court from the Administration; and of the division of public men among themselves. By the former of these, lawful Govern-

ment is undone; by the latter, all opposition to lawless power is rendered impotent. Government may in a great measure be restored, if any considerable bodies of men have honesty and resolution enough never to accept Administration, unless this garrison of *King's men,* which is stationed, as in a citadel, to controul and enslave it, be entirely broken and disbanded, and every work they have thrown up be levelled with the ground. The disposition of public men to keep this corps together, and to act under it, or to co-operate with it, is a touch-stone by which every Administration ought in future to be tried. There has not been one which has not sufficiently experienced the utter incompatibility of that Faction with the public peace, and with all the ends of good Government: since, if they opposed it, they soon lost every power of serving the Crown; if they submitted to it, they lost all the esteem of their country. Until Ministers give to the publick a full proof of their entire alienation from that system, however plausible their pretences, we may be sure they are more intent on the emoluments than the duties of office. If they refuse to give this proof, we know of what stuff they are made. In this particular, it ought to be the electors' business to look to their Representatives. The electors ought to esteem it no less culpable in their Member to give a single vote in Parliament to such an Administration, than to take an office under it; to endure it, than to act in it. The notorious infidelity and versatility of Members of Parliament, in their opinions of men and things, ought in a particular manner to be considered by the electors in the enquiry which is recommended to them. This is one of the principal holdings of that destructive system, which has endeavoured to unhinge all the virtuous, honourable, and useful connexions in the kingdom.

[82] THIS CABAL HAS, with great success, propagated a doctrine which serves for a colour to those acts of treachery; and whilst it receives any degree of countenance, it will be

utterly senseless to look for a vigorous opposition to the Court Party. The doctrine is this: That all political connexions are in their nature factious, and as such ought to be dissipated and destroyed; and that the rule for forming Administrations is mere personal ability, rated by the judgment of this Cabal upon it, and taken by draughts from every division and denomination of public men. This decree was solemnly promulgated by the head of the Court corps, the Earl of Bute himself, in a speech which he made, in the year 1766, against the then Administration, the only Administration which he has ever been known directly and publicly to oppose.

It is indeed in no way wonderful, that such persons should make such declarations. That connexion and Faction are equivalent terms, is an opinion which has been carefully inculcated at all times by unconstitutional Statesmen. The reason is evident. Whilst men are linked together, they easily and speedily communicate the alarm of an evil design. They are enabled to fathom it with common counsel, and to oppose it with united strength. Whereas, when they lie dispersed, without concert, order, or discipline, communication is uncertain, counsel difficult, and resistance impracticable. Where men are not acquainted with each other's principles, nor experienced in each other's talents, nor at all practised in their mutual habitudes and dispositions by joint efforts in business; no personal confidence, no friendship, no common interest, subsisting among them; it is evidently impossible that they can act a public part with uniformity, perseverance, or efficacy. In a connexion, the most inconsiderable man, by adding to the weight of the whole, has his value, and his use; out of it, the greatest talents are wholly unserviceable to the public. No man, who is not inflamed by vain-glory [83] into enthusiasm, can flatter himself that his single, unsupported, desultory, unsystematic endeavours, are of power to defeat the subtle designs and united Cabals of ambitious citizens. When bad men combine, the good must associate; else they will fall, one by one, an unpitied sacrifice in a contemptible struggle.

THOUGHTS ON THE PRESENT DISCONTENTS

It is not enough in a situation of trust in the common-wealth, that a man means well to his country; it is not enough that in his single person he never did an evil act, but always voted according to his conscience, and even harangued against every design which he apprehended to be prejudicial to the interests of his country. This innoxious and ineffectual character, that seems formed upon a plan of apology and disculpation, falls miserably short of the mark of public duty. That duty demands and requires, that what is right should not only be made known, but made prevalent; that what is evil should not only be detected, but defeated. When the public man omits to put himself in a situation of doing his duty with effect, it is an omission that frustrates the purposes of his trust almost as much as if he had formally betrayed it. It is surely no very rational account of a man's life, that he has always acted right; but has taken special care to act in such a manner that his endeavours could not possibly be productive of any consequence.

I do not wonder that the behaviour of many parties should have made persons of tender and scrupulous virtue somewhat out of humour with all sorts of connexion in politicks. I admit that people frequently acquire in such confederacies a narrow, bigotted, and proscriptive spirit; that they are apt to sink the idea of the general good in this circumscribed and partial interest. But, where duty renders a critical situation a necessary one, it is our business to keep free from the evils attendant upon it; and not to fly from the situation itself. If a fortress is seated in an unwholesome air, an [84] officer of the garrison is obliged to be attentive to his health, but he must not desert his station. Every profession, not excepting the glorious one of a soldier, or the sacred one of a priest, is liable to its own particular vices; which, however, form no argument against those ways of life; nor are the vices themselves inevitable to every individual in those professions. Of such a nature are connexions in politicks; essentially necessary for the full performance of our public duty, accidentally liable to degenerate into faction. Commonwealths are made of families, free commonwealths of parties also; and we may as well affirm, that our natural regards and ties of blood tend inevitably to make men bad citizens, as that the bonds of our party weaken those by which we are held to our country.

Some legislators went so far as to make neutrality in party a crime against the State. I do not know whether this might not have been rather to overstrain the principle. Certain it is, the best patriots in the greatest commonwealths have always commended and promoted such connexions. *Idem sentire de republica,* was with them a principal ground of friendship and attachment; nor do I know any other capable of forming firmer, dearer, more pleasing, more honourable, and more virtuous habitudes. The Romans carried this principle a great way. Even the holding of offices together, the disposition of which arose from chance, not selection, gave rise to a relation which continued for life. It was called *necessitudo sortis;* and it was looked upon with a sacred reverence. Breaches of any of these kinds of civil relation were considered as acts of the most distinguished turpitude. The whole people was distributed into political societies, in which they acted in support of such interests in the State as they severally affected. For it was then thought no crime, to endeavour by every honest means to advance to superiority and power those of your own [85] sentiments and opinions. This wise people was far from imagining that those connexions had no tie, and obliged to no duty; but that men might quit them without shame, upon every call of interest. They believed private honour to be the great foundation of public trust; that friendship was no mean step towards patriotism; that he who, in the common intercourse of life, shewed he regarded somebody besides himself, when he came to act in a public situation, might probably consult some other interest than his own. Never may we become *plus sages que les sages,* as the French comedian has happily expressed it—wiser than all the wise and good men who have lived before us. It was their wish, to see public and private virtues, not dissonant and jarring, and mutually destructive, but harmoniously combined, growing out of one another in a noble and orderly gradation, reciprocally supporting and supported. In one of the most fortunate periods of our history this country was governed by a *connexion;* I mean the great connexion of Whigs in the reign of Queen Anne. They were complimented upon the principle of this connexion by a poet who was in high esteem with them. Addison, who knew their sentiments, could not praise them for what they considered as no proper subject of commendation. As a poet who knew his business, he could not applaud them for a thing which in general estimation was not highly reputable. Addressing himself to Britain,

Thy favourites grow not up by fortune's sport,
Or from the crimes or follies of a Court;
On the firm basis of desert they rise,
From long-try'd faith, and friendship's holy ties.

The Whigs of those days believed that the only proper method of rising into power was through hard essays of practised friendship and experimented fidelity. At that time it was not imagined, that patriotism was a bloody idol, which [86] required the sacrifice of children and parents, or dearest connexions in private life, and of all the virtues that rise from those relations. They were not of that ingenious paradoxical morality to imagine that a spirit of moderation was properly shown in patiently bearing the sufferings of your friends; or that disinterestedness was clearly manifested at the expence of other people's fortune. They believed that no men could act with effect, who did not act in concert; that no men could act in concert, who did not act with confidence; that no men could act with confidence, who were not bound together by common opinions, common affections, and common interests.

These wise men, for such I must call Lord Sunderland, Lord Godolphin, Lord Somers, and Lord Marlborough, were too well principled in these maxims upon which the whole fabrick of public strength is built, to be blown off their ground by the breath of every childish talker. They were not afraid that they should be called an ambitious Junto; or that their resolution to stand or fall together should, by place-men, be interpreted into a scuffle for places.

Party is a body of men united, for promoting by their joint endeavours the national interest, upon some particular principle in which they are all agreed. For my part, I find it impossible to conceive, that any one believes in his own politicks, or thinks them to be of any weight, who refuses to adopt the means of having them reduced into practice. It is the business of the speculative philosopher to mark the proper ends of Government. It is the business of the politician, who is the philosopher in action, to find out proper means towards those ends, and to employ them with effect. Therefore every honourable connexion will avow it as their first purpose, to pursue every just method to put the men who hold their opinions into such a condition as may enable them to carry their common plans into execution, with all [87] the power and authority of the State. As this power is attached to certain situations, it is their duty to contend for these situations. Without a proscription of others, they are bound to give to their own party the preference in all things; and by no means, for private considerations, to accept any offers of power in which the whole body is not included; nor to suffer themselves to be led, or to be controuled, or to be over-balanced, in office or in council, by those who contradict the very fundamental principles on which their party is formed, and even those upon which every fair connexion must stand. Such a generous contention for power, on such manly and honourable maxims, will easily be distinguished from the mean and interested struggle for place and emolument. The very stile of such persons will serve to discriminate them from those numberless impostors, who have deluded the ignorant with professions incompatible with human practice, and have afterwards incensed them by practices below the level of vulgar rectitude.

It is an advantage to all narrow wisdom and narrow morals, that their maxims have a plausible air; and, on a cursory view, appear equal to first principles. They are light and portable. They are as current as copper coin; and about as valuable. They serve equally the first capacities and the lowest; and they are, at least, as useful to the worst men as the best. Of this stamp is the cant of *Not men but measures;* a sort of charm, by which many people get loose from every honourable engagement. When I see a man acting this desultory and disconnected part, with as much detriment to his own fortune as prejudice to the cause of any party, I am not persuaded that he is right; but I am ready to believe he is in earnest. I respect virtue in all its situations; even when it is found in the unsuitable company of weakness. I lament to see qualities, rare and valuable, squandered away without any public utility. But when a [88] gentleman with great visible emoluments abandons the party in which he has long acted, and tells you, it is because he proceeds upon his own judgement; that he acts on the merits of the several measures as they arise; and that he is obliged to follow his own conscience, and not that of others; he gives reasons which it is impossible to controvert, and discovers a character which it is impossible to mistake. What shall we think of him who never differed from a certain set of men until the moment they lost their power, and who never agreed with them in a single instance afterwards? Would not such a coincidence of interest and opinion be rather fortunate? Would it not be an extraordinary cast upon the dice, that a man's connexions should degenerate into faction, precisely at the critical moment when they lose their power, or he accepts a place? When people desert their connexions, the desertion is a manifest *fact,* upon which a direct simple issue lies, triable by plain men. Whether a *measure* of government be right or wrong, is *no matter of fact,* but a mere affair of opinion, on which men may, as they do, dispute and wrangle without end. But whether the individual *thinks* the measure right or wrong, is a point at still a greater distance from the reach of all human decision. It is therefore very convenient to politicians, not to put the judgement of their conduct on overt-acts, cognizable in any ordinary court, but upon such a matter as can be triable only in that secret tribunal, where they are sure of being heard with favour, or where at worst the sentence will be only private whipping.

I believe the reader would wish to find no substance in a doctrine which has a tendency to destroy all test of character as deduced from conduct. He will therefore excuse my adding something more, towards the further clearing up a point, which the great convenience of obscurity to dishonesty has been able to cover with some degree of darkness and doubt.

[89] In order to throw an odium on political connexion, these politicians suppose it a necessary incident to it, that you are blindly to follow the opinions of your party, when in direct opposition to your own clear ideas; a degree of servitude that no worthy man could bear the thought of submitting to; and such as, I believe, no connexions (except some Court Factions) ever could be so senselessly tyrannical as to impose. Men thinking freely, will, in particular instances, think differently. But still as the greater part of the measures which arise in the course of public business are related to, or dependent on, some great *leading general principles in Government,* a man must be peculiarly unfortunate in the choice of his political company if he does not agree with them at least nine times in ten. If he does not concur in these general principles upon which the party is founded, and which necessarily draw on a concurrence in their application, he ought from the beginning to have chosen some other, more conformable to his opinions. When the question is in its nature doubtful, or not

very material, the modesty which becomes an individual, and (in spite of our Court moralists) that partiality which becomes a well-chosen friendship, will frequently bring on an acquiescence in the general sentiment. Thus the disagreement will naturally be rare; it will be only enough to indulge freedom, without violating concord, or disturbing arrangement. And this is all that ever was required for a character of the greatest uniformity and steadiness in connexion. How men can proceed without any connexion at all, is to me utterly incomprehensible. Of what sort of materials must that man be made, how must he be tempered and put together, who can sit whole years in Parliament, with five hundred and fifty of his fellow-citizens, amidst the storm of such tempestuous passions, in the sharp conflict of so many wits, and tempers, and characters, in the agitation of such mighty questions, in the discussion of such [90] vast and ponderous interests, without seeing any one sort of men, whose character, conduct, or disposition, would lead him to associate himself with them, to aid and be aided, in any one system of public utility?

I remember an old scholastic aphorism, which says that "the man who lives wholly detached from others, must be either an angel or a devil." When I see in any of these detached gentlemen of our times the angelic purity, power, and beneficence, I shall admit them to be angels. In the mean time we are born only to be men. We shall do enough if we form ourselves to be good ones. It is therefore our business carefully to cultivate in our minds, to rear to the most perfect vigour and maturity, every sort of generous and honest feeling that belongs to our nature. To bring the dispositions that are lovely in private life into the service and conduct of the commonwealth; so to be patriots, as not to forget we are gentlemen. To cultivate friendships, and to incur enmities. To have both strong, but both selected: in the one, to be placable; in the other, immoveable. To model our principles to our duties and our situation. To be fully persuaded, that all virtue which is impracticable is spurious; and rather to run the risque of falling into faults in a course which leads us to act with effect and energy, than to loiter out our days without blame, and without use. Public life is a situation of power and energy; he trespasses against his duty who sleeps upon his watch, as well as he that goes over to the enemy.

There is, however, a time for all things. It is not every conjuncture which calls with equal force upon the activity of honest men; but critical exigences now and then arise; and I am mistaken, if this be not one of them. Men will see the necessity of honest combination; but they may see it when it is too late. They may embody, when it will be ruinous to themselves, and of no advantage to the country; [91] when, for want of such a timely union as may enable them to oppose in favour of the laws, with the laws on their side, they may at length find themselves under the necessity of conspiring, instead of consulting. The law, for which they stand, may become a weapon in the hands of its bitterest enemies; and they will be cast, at length, into that miserable alternative, between slavery and civil confusion, which no good man can look upon without horror; an alternative in which it is impossible he should take either part, with a conscience perfectly at repose. To keep that situation of guilt and remorse at the utmost distance is, therefore, our first obligation. Early activity may prevent late and fruitless violence. As yet we work in the light. The scheme of the enemies of public tranquillity has disarranged, it has not destroyed us.

If the reader believes that there really exists such a Faction as I have described; a Faction ruling by the private inclinations of a Court, against the general sense of the people; and that this Faction, whilst it pursues a scheme for undermining all the foundations of our freedom, weakens (for the present at least) all the powers of executory Government, rendering us abroad contemptible, and at home distracted; he will believe also, that nothing but a firm combination of public men against this body, and that, too, supported by the hearty concurrence of the people at large, can possibly get the better of it. The people will see the necessity of restoring public men to an attention to the public opinion, and of restoring the constitution to its original principles. Above all, they will endeavour to keep the House of Commons from assuming a character which does not belong to it. They will endeavour to keep that House, for its existence, for its powers, and its privileges, as independent of every other, and as dependent upon themselves, as possible. This servitude is to an House of Commons (like obedience to the Divine [92] law,) "perfect freedom." For if they once quit this natural, rational, and liberal obedience, having deserted the only proper foundation of their power, they must seek a support in an abject and unnatural dependence somewhere else. When, through the medium of this just connexion with their constituents, the genuine dignity of the House of Commons is restored, it will begin to think of casting from it, with scorn, as badges of servility, all the false ornaments of illegal power, with which it has been, for some time, disgraced. It will begin to think of its old office of CONTROUL. It will not suffer that last of evils to predominate in the country; men without popular confidence, public opinion, natural connexion, or natural trust, invested with all the powers of Government.

When they have learned this lesson themselves, they will be willing and able to teach the Court, that it is the true interest of the Prince to have but one Administration; and that one composed of those who recommend themselves to their Sovereign through the opinion of their country, and not by their obsequiousness to a favourite. Such men will serve their Sovereign with affection and fidelity; because his choice of them, upon such principles, is a compliment to their virtue. They will be able to serve him effectually; because they will add the weight of the country to the force of the executory power. They will be able to serve their King with dignity; because they will never abuse his name to the gratification of their private spleen or avarice. This, with allowances for human frailty, may probably be the general character of a Ministry, which thinks itself accountable to the House of Commons, when the House of Commons thinks itself accountable to its constituents. If other ideas should prevail, things must remain in their present confusion; until they are hurried into all the rage of civil violence; or until they sink into the dead repose of despotism.

Speech of Edmund Burke, Esq.,

on American Taxation

April 19, 1774

[Second Edition. Dodsley, 1775.]

PREFACE

The following Speech has been much the subject of conversation; and the desire of having it printed was last summer very general. The means of gratifying the public curiosity were obligingly furnished from the notes of some gentlemen, Members of the last Parliament.

THE TWO SPEECHES IN AMERICA

[94] This piece has been for some months ready for the press. But a delicacy, possibly overscrupulous, has delayed the publication to this time. The friends of administration have been used to attribute a great deal of the opposition to their measures in America to the writings published in England. The Editor of this Speech kept it back, until all the measures of Government have had their full operation, and can be no longer affected, if ever they could have been affected, by any publication.

Most Readers will recollect the uncommon pains taken at the beginning of the last session of the last Parliament, and indeed during the whole course of it, to asperse the characters, and decry the measures, of those who were supposed to be friends to America; in order to weaken the effect of their opposition to the acts of rigour then preparing against the Colonies. This Speech contains a full refutation of the charges against that party with which Mr. Burke has all along acted. In doing this, he has taken a review of the effects of all the schemes which have been successively adopted in the government of the Plantations. The subject is interesting; the matters of information various, and important; and the publication at this time, the Editor hopes, will not be thought unseasonable.

SPEECH, &C.

During the last Session of the last Parliament, on the 19th of April, 1774, Mr. Rose Fuller, Member for Rye, made the following motion; That an Act made in the seventh year of the reign of his present Majesty, intituled, "An Act for granting certain duties in the British Colonies and Plantations in America; for allowing a drawback of the duties of Customs upon the exportation from this Kingdom of Coffee and Cocoa Nuts, of the produce of the said Colonies or Plantations; for discontinuing the drawbacks payable on China earthen ware exported to America; and for more effectually preventing the clandestine running of goods in the said Colonies and Plantations"; might be read.

And the same being read accordingly; He moved, "That this House will, upon this day sevennight, resolve itself into a Committee of the whole House, to take into consideration the duty of 3 *d. per* pound weight upon tea, payable in all his [95] Majesty's Dominions in America, imposed by the said Act; and also the appropriation of the said duty."

On this latter motion a warm and interesting debate arose, in which Mr. Burke spoke as follows:

S<small>IR</small>,

I AGREE WITH the Honourable Gentleman who spoke last, that this subject is not new in this House. Very disagreeably to this House, very unfortunately to this Nation, and to the peace and prosperity of this whole Empire, no topic has been more familiar to us. For nine long years, session after session, we have been lashed round and round this miserable circle of occasional arguments and temporary expedients. I am sure our heads must turn, and our stomachs nauseate with them. We have had them in every shape; we have looked at them in every point of view. Invention is exhausted; reason is fatigued; experience has given judgement; but obstinacy is not yet conquered.

The Honourable Gentleman has made one endeavour more to diversify the form of this disgusting argument. He has thrown out a speech composed almost entirely of challenges. Challenges are serious things; and as he is a man of prudence as well as resolution, I dare say he has very well weighed those challenges before he delivered them. I had long the happiness to sit at the same side of the House, and to agree with the Honourable Gentleman on all the American questions. My sentiments, I am sure, are well known to him; and I thought I had been perfectly acquainted with his. Though I find myself mistaken, he will still permit me to use the privilege of an old friendship; he will permit me to apply myself to the House under the sanction of his authority; and, on the various grounds he has measured out, to submit to you the poor opinions which I have formed upon a matter of importance enough to demand the fullest consideration I could bestow upon it.

[96] He has stated to the House two grounds of deliberation; one narrow and simple, and merely confined to the question on your paper: the other more large and more complicated; comprehending the whole series of the Parliamentary proceedings with regard to America, their causes, and their consequences. With regard to the latter ground, he states it as useless, and thinks it may be even dangerous, to enter into so extensive a field of enquiry. Yet, to my surprise, he had hardly laid down this restrictive proposition, to which his authority would have given so much weight, when directly, and with the same authority, he condemns it; and declares it absolutely necessary to enter into the most ample historical detail. His zeal has thrown him a little out of his usual accuracy. In this perplexity what shall we do, Sir, who are willing to submit to the law he gives us? He has reprobated in one part of his Speech the rule he had laid down for debate in the other; and, after narrowing the ground for all those who are to speak after him, he takes an excursion himself, as unbounded as the subject and the extent of his great abilities.

Sir, When I cannot obey all his laws, I will do the best I can. I will endeavour to obey such of them as have the sanction of his example; and to stick to that rule, which, though not consistent with the other, is the most rational. He was certainly in the right when he took the matter largely. I cannot prevail on myself to agree with him in his censure of his own conduct. It is not, he will give me leave to say, either use-less or dangerous. He asserts, that retrospect is not wise; and the proper, the only proper, subject of enquiry, is "not how we got into this difficulty, but how we are to get out of it." In other words, we are, according to him, to consult our in-vention, and to reject our experience. The mode of delibera-tion he recommends is diametrically opposite to every rule of reason and every principle of good [97] sense established amongst mankind. For that sense and that reason I have always understood absolutely to prescribe, whenever we are involved in difficulties from the measures we have pursued, that we should take a strict review of those measures, in order to correct our errors, if they should be corrigible; or at least to avoid a dull uniformity in mischief, and the unpitied ca-lamity of being repeatedly caught in the same snare.

Sir, I will freely follow the Honourable Gentleman in his historical discussion, without the least management for men or measures, further than as they shall seem to me to deserve it. But before I go into that large consideration, because I would omit nothing that can give the House satisfaction, I wish to tread the narrow ground to which alone the Hon-ourable Gentleman, in one part of his Speech, has so strictly confined us.

HE DESIRES TO KNOW, whether, if we were to repeal this tax, agreeably to the proposition of the Honourable Gentle-man who made the motion, the Americans would not take post on this concession, in order to make a new attack on the next body of taxes; and whether they would not call for a repeal of the duty on wine as loudly as they do now for the repeal of the duty on tea? Sir, I can give no security on this subject. But I will do all that I can, and all that can be fairly demanded. To the *experience* which the Honourable Gentle-man reprobates in one instant, and reverts to in the next; to that experience, without the least wavering or hesitation on my part, I steadily appeal; and would to God there was no other arbiter to decide on the vote with which the House is to conclude this day!

When Parliament repealed the Stamp Act in the year 1766, I affirm, first, that the Americans did *not* in consequence of this measure call upon you to give up the former Parliamentary [98] revenue which subsisted in that country; or even any one of the articles which compose it. I affirm also, that when, departing from the maxims of that repeal, you revived the scheme of taxation, and thereby filled the minds of the Colonists with new jealousy, and all sorts of apprehensions, then it was that they quarrelled with the old taxes, as well as the new; then it was, and not till then, that they questioned all the parts of your legislative power; and by the battery of such questions have shaken the solid structure of this Empire to its deepest foundations.

Of those two propositions I shall, before I have done, give such convincing, such damning proof, that however the contrary may be whispered in circles, or bawled in newspapers, they never more will dare to raise their voices in this House. I speak with great confidence. I have reason for it. The Ministers are with me. *They* at least are convinced that the repeal of the Stamp Act had not, and that no repeal can have, the consequences which the Honourable Gentleman who defends their measures is so much alarmed at. To their conduct I refer him for a conclusive answer to his objection. I carry my proof irresistibly into the very body of both Ministry and Parliament; not on any general reasoning growing out of collateral matter, but on the conduct of the Honourable Gentleman's Ministerial friends on the new revenue itself.

The Act of 1767, which grants this Tea duty, sets forth in its preamble, that it was expedient to raise a revenue in America, for the support of the civil government there, as well as for purposes still more extensive. To this support the Act assigns six branches of duties. About two years after this Act passed, the Ministry, I mean the present Ministry, thought it expedient to repeal five of the duties and to leave (for reasons best known to themselves) only the sixth standing. Suppose any person, at the time of that [99] repeal, had thus addressed the Minister: "Condemning, as you do, the Repeal of the Stamp Act, Why do you venture to repeal the duties upon glass, paper, and painters' colours? Let your pretence for the Repeal be what it will, are you not thoroughly convinced, that your concessions will produce, not satisfaction, but insolence, in the Americans; and that the giving up these taxes will necessitate the giving up of all the rest?" This objection was as palpable then as it is now; and it was as good for preserving the five duties as for retaining the sixth. Besides, the Minister will recollect, that the Repeal of the Stamp Act had but just preceded his Repeal; and the ill policy of that measure, (had it been so impolitic as it has been represented,) and the mischiefs it produced, were quite recent. Upon the principles therefore of the Honourable Gentleman, upon the principles of the Minister himself, the Minister has nothing at all to answer. He stands condemned by himself, and by all his associates old and new, as a destroyer, in the first trust of finance, of the revenues; and in the first rank of honour, as a betrayer of the dignity of his Country.

Most men, especially great men, do not always know their well-wishers. I come to rescue that Noble Lord out of the hands of those he calls his friends; and even out of his own. I will do him the justice he is denied at home. He has not been this wicked or imprudent man. He knew that a repeal had no tendency to produce the mischiefs which give so much alarm to his Honourable friend. His work was not bad in its principle, but imperfect in its execution; and the motion on your paper presses him only to compleat a proper plan, which, by some unfortunate and unaccountable error, he had left unfinished.

I hope, Sir, the Honourable Gentleman who spoke last,

is thoroughly satisfied, and satisfied out of the proceedings of Ministry on their own favourite Act, that his fears from a [100] repeal are groundless. If he is not, I leave him, and the Noble Lord who sits by him, to settle the matter, as well as they can, together; for if the repeal of American taxes destroys all our government in America—He is the man!—and he is the worst of all the repealers, because he is the last.

BUT I HEAR IT RUNG continually in my ears, now and formerly—"the Preamble! what will become of the Preamble, if you repeal this Tax?"—I am sorry to be compelled so often to expose the calamities and disgraces of Parliament. The preamble of this law, standing as it now stands, has the lie direct given to it by the provisionary part of the Act; if that can be called provisionary which makes no provision. I should be afraid to express myself in this manner, especially in the face of such a formidable array of ability as is now drawn up before me, composed of the antient household troops of that side of the House, and the new recruits from this, if the matter were not clear and indisputable. Nothing but truth could give me this firmness; but plain truth and clear evidence can be beat down by no ability. The Clerk will be so good as to turn to the Act, and to read this favourite Preamble:

Whereas it is *expedient* that a revenue should be raised in your Majesty's Dominions in America, for making a more *certain* and *adequate* provision for defraying the charge of the *administration of justice and support of civil government,* in such Provinces where it shall be found necessary; and towards *further defraying* the expenses *of defending, protecting, and securing the said Dominions.*

You have heard this pompous performance. Now where is the revenue which is to do all these mighty things? Five-sixths repealed—abandoned—sunk—gone—lost for ever. [101] Does the poor solitary Tea duty support the purposes of this preamble? Is not the supply there stated as effectually abandoned as if the Tea duty had perished in the general wreck? Here, Mr. Speaker, is a precious mockery—a preamble without an act—taxes granted in order to be repealed—and the reasons of the grant still carefully kept up! This is raising a revenue in America! This is preserving dignity in England! If you repeal this tax in compliance with the motion, I readily admit that you lose this fair preamble. Estimate your loss in it. The object of the Act is gone already; and all you suffer is the purging the Statute-book of the opprobrium of an empty, absurd, and false recital.

It has been said again and again, that the five Taxes were repealed on commercial principles. It is so said in the paper in my hand; a paper which I constantly carry about; which I have often used, and shall often use again. What is got by this paltry pretence of commercial principles I know not: for if your government in America is destroyed by the *repeal of Taxes,* it is of no consequence upon what ideas the repeal is grounded. Repeal this Tax too upon commercial principles if you please. These principles will serve as well now as they did formerly. But you know that, either your objection to a repeal from these supposed consequences has no validity, or that this pretence never could remove it. This commercial motive never was believed by any man, either in America, which this letter is meant to soothe, or in England, which it is meant to deceive. It was impossible it should. Because every man, in the least acquainted with the detail of Commerce, must know, that several of the articles on which the Tax was repealed, were fitter objects of Duties than almost any other articles that could possibly be chosen; without comparison more so, than the Tea that was left taxed; as infinitely less liable to be eluded by contraband. [102] The Tax upon Red and White Lead was of this nature. You have, in this kingdom, an advantage in Lead, that amounts to a monopoly. When you find yourself in this situation of advantage, you sometimes venture to tax even your own export. You did so soon after the last war; when, upon this principle, you ventured to impose a duty on Coals. In all the articles of American contraband trade, who ever heard of the smuggling of Red Lead and White Lead? You might, therefore, well enough, without danger of contraband, and without injury to Commerce, (if this were the whole consideration,) have taxed these commodities. The same may be said of Glass. Besides, some of the things taxed were so trivial, that the loss of the objects themselves, and their utter annihilation out of American Commerce, would have been comparatively as nothing. But is the article of Tea such an object in the Trade of England, as not to be felt, or felt but slightly, like White Lead and Red Lead, and Painters' Colours? Tea is an object of far other importance. Tea is perhaps the most important object, taking it with its necessary connections, of any in the mighty circle of our Commerce. If commercial principles had been the true motives to the Repeal, or had they been at all attended to, Tea would have been the last article we should have left taxed for a subject of controversy.

Sir, It is not a pleasant consideration; but nothing in the world can read so awful and so instructive a lesson, as the conduct of Ministry in this business, upon the mischief of not having large and liberal ideas in the management of great affairs. Never have the servants of the state looked at the whole of your complicated interests in one connected view. They have taken things by bits and scraps, some at one time and one pretence, and some at another, just as they pressed, without any sort of regard to their relations or dependencies. They never had any kind of system, right or [103] wrong; but only invented occasionally some miserable tale for the day, in order meanly to sneak out of difficulties, into which they had proudly strutted. And they were put to all these shifts and devices, full of meanness and full of mischief, in order to pilfer piece-meal a repeal of an Act, which they had not the generous courage, when they found and felt their error, honourably and fairly to disclaim. By such management, by the irresistible operation of feeble counsels, so paltry a sum as Three-pence in the eyes of a financier, so insignificant an article as Tea in the eyes of a philosopher, have shaken the pillars of a Commercial Empire that circled the whole globe.

Do you forget that, in the very last year, you stood on the precipice of general bankruptcy? Your danger was indeed great. You were distressed in the affairs of the East India Company; and you well know what sort of things are involved in the comprehensive energy of that significant appellation. I am not called upon to enlarge to you on that danger, which you thought proper yourselves to aggravate, and to display to the world with all the parade of indiscreet declamation. The monopoly of the most lucrative trades, and the possession of imperial revenues, had brought you to the verge of beggary and ruin. Such was your representation—such, in some measure, was your case. The vent of Ten Millions of pounds of this commodity, now locked up by the operation of an injudicious Tax, and rotting in the warehouses of the Company, would have prevented all this distress, and all that series of desperate measures which you thought yourselves obliged to take in consequence of it. America would have furnished that vent, which no other part of the world can furnish but America; where Tea is next to a necessary of life; and where the demand grows upon the supply. I hope our dear-bought East India Committees have done us at least so much good, as to let us know, that, [104] without a more extensive sale of that article, our East India revenues and acquisitions can have no certain connection with this country. It is through the American trade of Tea that your East India conquests are to be prevented from crushing you with their burthen. They are ponderous indeed: and they must have that great country to lean upon, or they tumble upon your head. It is the same folly that has lost you at once the benefit of the West and of the East. This folly has thrown open folding-doors to contraband; and will be the means of giving the profits of the trade of your Colonies to every nation but yourselves. Never did a people suffer so much for the empty words of a preamble. It must be given up. For on what principles does it stand? This famous revenue stands, at this hour, on all the debate, as a description of revenue not as yet known in all the comprehensive (but too comprehensive!) vocabulary of finance — *a preambulary tax.* It is indeed a tax of sophistry, a tax of pedantry, a tax of disputation, a tax of war and rebellion, a tax for anything but benefit to the imposers, or satisfaction to the subject.

Well! but whatever it is, gentlemen will force the Colonists to take the Teas. You will force them? Has seven years' struggle yet been able to force them? O but it seems, "We are in the right. The Tax is trifling — in fact it is rather an exoneration than an imposition; three-fourths of the duty formerly payable on teas exported to America is taken off; the place of collection is only shifted; instead of the retention of a shilling from the Draw-back here, it is three-pence Custom paid in America." All this, Sir, is very true. But this is the very folly and mischief of the Act. Incredible as it may seem, you know that you have deliberately thrown away a large duty which you held secure and quiet in your hands, for the vain hope of getting one three-fourths less, through every hazard, through certain litigation, and possibly through war.

[105] The manner of proceeding in the duties on paper and glass, imposed by the same Act, was exactly in the same spirit. There are heavy excises on those articles when used in England. On export, these excises are drawn back. But instead of withholding the Draw-back, which might have been done, with ease, without charge, without possibility of smuggling; and instead of applying the money (money already in your hands) according to your pleasure, you began your operations in finance by flinging away your revenue; you allowed the whole Draw-back on export, and then you charged the duty, (which you had before discharged,) pay-

able in the Colonies; where it was certain the collection would devour it to the bone; if any revenue were ever suffered to be collected at all. One spirit pervades and animates the whole mass.

Could anything be a subject of more just alarm to America, than to see you go out of the plain high road of finance, and give up your most certain revenues and your clearest interests, merely for the sake of insulting your Colonies? No man ever doubted that the commodity of Tea could bear an imposition of three-pence. But no commodity will bear three-pence, or will bear a penny, when the general feelings of men are irritated, and two millions of people are resolved not to pay. The feelings of the Colonies were formerly the feelings of Great Britain. Theirs were formerly the feelings of Mr. Hampden when called upon for the payment of twenty shillings. Would twenty shillings have ruined Mr. Hampden's fortune? No! but the payment of half twenty shillings, on the principle it was demanded, would have made him a slave. It is the weight of that preamble, of which you are so fond, and not the weight of the duty, that the Americans are unable and unwilling to bear.

It is then, Sir, upon the *principle* of this measure, and nothing else, that we are at issue. It is a principle of political [106] expediency. Your Act of 1767 asserts, that it is expedient to raise a revenue in America; your Act of 1769, which takes away that revenue, contradicts the Act of 1767; and, by something much stronger than words, asserts, that it is not expedient. It is a reflexion upon your wisdom to persist in a solemn Parliamentary declaration of the expediency of any object, for which, at the same time, you make no sort of provision. And pray, Sir, let not this circumstance escape you; it is very material; that the preamble of this Act, which we wish to repeal, is not *declaratory of a right,* as some gentlemen seem to argue it; it is only a recital of the *expediency* of a certain exercise of a right supposed already to have been asserted;

an exercise you are now contending for by ways and means, which you confess, though they were obeyed, to be utterly insufficient for their purpose. You are therefore at this moment in the aukward situation of fighting for a phantom; a quiddity; a thing that wants, not only a substance, but even a name; for a thing, which is neither abstract right, nor profitable enjoyment.

They tell you, Sir, that your dignity is tied to it. I know not how it happens, but this dignity of yours is a terrible incumbrance to you; for it has of late been ever at war with your interest, your equity, and every idea of your policy. Shew the thing you contend for to be reason; shew it to be common sense; shew it to be the means of attaining some useful end; and then I am content to allow it what dignity you please. But what dignity is derived from the perseverance in absurdity, is more than ever I could discern. The Honourable Gentleman has said well—indeed, in most of his *general* observations I agree with him—he says, that this subject does not stand as it did formerly. Oh, certainly not! Every hour you continue on this ill-chosen ground, your difficulties thicken on you; and therefore my conclusion is, remove from a bad position as quickly as you can. The [107] disgrace, and the necessity, of yielding, both of them, grow upon you every hour of your delay.

But will you repeal the Act, says the Honourable Gentleman, at this instant, when America is in open resistance to your authority, and that you have just revived your system of taxation? He thinks he has driven us into a corner. But thus pent up, I am content to meet him; because I enter the lists supported by my old authority, his new friends, the Ministers themselves. The Honourable Gentleman remembers, that about five years ago as great disturbances as the present prevailed in America on account of the new taxes. The Ministers represented these disturbances as treasonable;

and this House thought proper, on that representation, to make a famous address for a revival, and for a new application, of a statute of Henry the Eighth. We besought the King, in that well-considered address, to inquire into treasons, and to bring the supposed traytors from America to Great Britain for trial. His Majesty was pleased graciously to promise a compliance with our request. All the attempts from this side of the House to resist these violences, and to bring about a repeal, were treated with the utmost scorn. An apprehension of the very consequences now stated by the Honourable Gentleman, was then given as a reason for shutting the door against all hope of such an alteration. And so strong was the spirit for supporting the new taxes, that the Session concluded with the following remarkable declaration. After stating the vigorous measures which had been pursued, the Speech from the Throne proceeds:

You have assured me of your *firm* support in the *prosecution* of them. Nothing, in my opinion, could be more likely to enable the well-disposed among my subjects in that part of the world, effectually to discourage and defeat the designs of the factious and [108] seditious, than the hearty concurrence of every branch of the Legislature, in *maintaining the execution of the laws* in *every* part of my Dominions.

After this no man dreamt that a repeal under this Ministry could possibly take place. The Honourable Gentleman knows as well as I, that the idea was utterly exploded by those who sway the House. This speech was made on the ninth day of May, 1769. Five days after this speech, that is, on the 13th of the same month, the public Circular Letter, a part of which I am going to read to you, was written by Lord Hillsborough, Secretary of State for the Colonies. After reciting the substance of the King's Speech, he goes on thus:

I can take upon me to assure you, notwithstanding insinuations to the contrary, from men with *factious and seditious views,* that his Majesty's *present Administration have at no time entertained a design to propose to Par-*

liament to lay any further taxes upon America for the purpose of RAISING A REVENUE; and that it is at present their intention to propose, the next Session of Parliament, to take off the duties upon glass, paper, and colours, upon consideration of such duties *having been laid contrary to the true principles of Commerce.*

These have *always* been, and *still are,* the sentiments of his *Majesty's present servants;* and by which *their conduct in respect to America has been governed.* And *his Majesty* relies upon your prudence and fidelity for such an explanation of *his* measures, as may tend to remove the prejudices which have been excited by the misrepresentations of those who are enemies to the peace and prosperity of Great Britain and her Colonies; and to re-establish that mutual *confidence and affection,* upon which the glory and safety of the British Empire depend.

Here, Sir, is a canonical book of ministerial scripture; the General Epistle to the Americans. What does the gentleman say to it? Here a repeal is promised; promised without [109] condition; and while your authority was actually resisted. I pass by the public promise of a Peer relative to the repeal of taxes by this House. I pass by the use of the King's name in a matter of supply, that sacred and reserved right of the Commons. I conceal the ridiculous figure of Parliament, hurling its thunders at the gigantic rebellion of America; and then, five days after, prostrate at the feet of those assemblies we affected to despise; begging them, by the intervention of our ministerial sureties, to receive our submission, and heartily promising amendment. These might have been serious matters formerly; but we are grown wiser than our fathers. Passing, therefore, from the constitutional consideration to the mere policy, does not this Letter imply, that the idea of taxing America for the purpose of revenue is an abominable project; when the Ministry suppose that none but *factious* men, and with seditious views, could charge them with it? does not this Letter adopt and sanctify the American distinction of *taxing for a revenue?* does it not formally reject all future taxation on that principle? does it not state the ministerial rejection of such principle of taxation, not as the occasional, but the constant, opinion of the King's servants? does it not say, I care not how consistently—but does it not say, that their conduct with regard to America has been *always* governed by this policy? It goes a great deal further. These excellent and trusty servants of the King, justly fearful lest they themselves should have lost all credit with the world, bring out the image of their gracious Sovereign from the inmost and most sacred shrine, and they pawn him as a security for their promises— "*His Majesty* relies on your prudence and fidelity for such an explanation of *his* measures." These sentiments of the Minister, and these measures of his Majesty, can only relate to the principle and practice of taxing for a revenue; and accordingly Lord Botetourt, stating it as such, did, with great propriety, and in the exact spirit of his instructions, [110] endeavour to remove the fears of the Virginian assembly, lest the sentiments, which it seems (unknown to the world) had *always* been those of the Ministers, and by which *their conduct in respect to America had been governed,* should by some possible revolution, favourable to wicked American taxers, be hereafter counteracted. He addresses them in this manner:

It may possibly be objected, that, as his Majesty's present administration are *not immortal,* their successors may be inclined to attempt to undo what the present Ministers shall have attempted to perform; and to that objection I can give but this answer; that it is my firm opinion, that the plan I have stated to you will certainly take place; and that it will never be departed from; and so determined am I for ever to abide by it, that I will be content to be declared infamous, if I do not, to the last hour of my life, at all times, in all places, and upon all occasions, exert every power with which I either am or ever shall be legally invested, in order to obtain and *maintain* for the Continent of America that *satisfaction* which I have been authorized to promise this day, by the *confidential* servants of our gracious Sovereign, who to my certain knowledge rates his honour so high, *that he would rather part with his crown, than preserve it by deceit.*

A glorious and true character! which (since we suffer his Ministers with impunity to answer for his ideas of taxation) we ought to make it our business to enable his Majesty to pre-serve in all its lustre. Let him have character, since ours is no more! Let some part of government be kept in respect!

This Epistle was not the letter of Lord Hillsborough solely; though he held the official pen. It was the letter of the Noble Lord upon the floor, and of all the King's then Min-isters, who (with I think the exception of two only) are his Ministers at this hour. The very first news that a British [111] Parliament heard of what it was to do with the duties which it had given and granted to the King, was by the publication of the votes of American assemblies. It was in America that your resolutions were pre-declared. It was from thence that we knew to a certainty, how much exactly, and not a scruple more or less, we were to repeal. We were unworthy to be let into the secret of our own conduct. The assemblies had *confidential* communications from his Majesty's *confidential* servants. We were nothing but instruments. Do you, after this, wonder that you have no weight and no respect in the Colonies? After this, are you surprised, that Parliament is every day and every-where losing (I feel it with sorrow, I utter it with reluctance) that reverential affection, which so endearing a name of au-thority ought ever to carry with it; that you are obeyed solely from respect to the bayonet; and that this House, the ground and pillar of freedom, is itself held up only by the treacher-ous under-pinning and clumsy buttresses of arbitrary power?

If this dignity, which is to stand in the place of just policy and common sense, had been consulted, there was a time for preserving it, and for reconciling it with any concession. If in the Session of 1768, that Session of idle terror and empty menaces, you had, as you were often pressed to do, repealed these taxes; then your strong operations would have come justified and enforced, in case your concessions had been returned by outrages. But, preposterously, you began with violence; and before terrors could have any effect, either good or bad, your Ministers immediately begged pardon, and promised that repeal to the obstinate Americans, which they had refused in an easy, good-natured, complying British Parliament. The assemblies which had been publicly and avowedly dissolved for *their* contumacy, are called together to receive *your* submission. Your ministerial directors blustered like tragic tyrants here; and then went mumping with [112] a sore leg in America, canting and whining, and complaining of faction, which represented them as friends to a revenue from the Colonies. I hope nobody in this House will hereafter have the impudence to defend American taxes in the name of Ministry. The moment they do, with this letter of attorney in my hand, I will tell them, in the authorized terms, they are wretches, "with factious and seditious views; enemies to the peace and prosperity of the Mother Country and the Colonies," and subverters "of the mutual affection and confidence on which the glory and safety of the British Empire depend."

After this letter, the question is no more on propriety or dignity. They are gone already. The faith of your Sovereign is pledged for the political principle. The general declaration in the Letter goes to the whole of it. You must therefore either abandon the scheme of taxing; or you must send the Ministers tarred and feathered to America, who dared to hold out the Royal Faith for a renunciation of all taxes for revenue. Them you must punish, or this faith you must preserve. The preservation of this faith is of more consequence than the duties on *red lead,* or *white lead,* or on broken *glass,* or *atlas-ordinary,* or *demi-fine,* or *blue royal,* or *bastard,* or *fool's-cap,* which you have given up; or the Three-pence on tea which you retained. The Letter went stampt with the public authority of this Kingdom. The instructions for the Colony Government go under no other sanction; and America cannot believe, and will not obey you, if you do not preserve this channel of communication sacred. You are now punishing the Colonies for acting on distinctions, held out by that very Ministry which is here shining in riches, in favour, and in power; and urging the punishment of the very offence to which they had themselves been the tempters.

Sir, If reasons respecting simply your own commerce, [113] which is your own convenience, were the sole grounds of the repeal of the five duties; why does Lord Hillsborough, in disclaiming in the name of the King and Ministry their ever having had an intent to tax for revenue, mention it as the means "of re-establishing the confidence and affection of the Colonies?" Is it a way of soothing *others,* to assure them that you will take good care of *yourself?* The medium, the only medium, for regaining their affection and confidence, is, that you will take off something oppressive to their minds. Sir, the Letter strongly enforces that idea: for though the repeal of the taxes is promised on commercial principles, yet the means of counteracting "the insinuations of men with factious and seditious views," is, by a disclaimer of the intention of taxing for revenue, as a constant invariable sentiment and rule of conduct in the government of America.

I remember that the noble Lord on the floor, not in a former debate to be sure, (it would be disorderly to refer to it, I suppose I read it somewhere,) but the noble Lord was pleased to say, that he did not conceive how it could enter into the head of man to impose such taxes as those of 1767; I mean those taxes which he voted for imposing, and voted for repealing; as being taxes contrary to all the principles of commerce, laid on *British Manufactures.*

I dare say the noble Lord is perfectly well read, because the duty of his particular office requires he should be so, in all our revenue laws; and in the policy which is to be collected out of them. Now, Sir, when he had read this Act of American revenue, and a little recovered from his astonishment, I suppose he made one step retrograde (it is but one) and looked at the Act which stands just before in the Statute Book. The American Revenue Act is the forty-fifth chapter; the other to which I refer is the forty-fourth of the same session. These two Acts are both to the same purpose; [114] both Revenue Acts; both taxing out of the Kingdom; and both taxing British manufactures exported. As the 45th is an Act for raising a revenue in America, the 44th is an Act for raising a revenue in the Isle of Man. The two Acts perfectly agree in all respects, except one. In the Act for taxing the Isle of Man, the noble Lord will find (not, as in the American Act, four or five articles) but almost the *whole body* of British manufactures, taxed from two and a half to fifteen *per cent.*, and some articles, such as that of spirits, a great deal higher. You did not think it uncommercial to tax the whole mass of your manufactures, and, let me add, your agriculture too; for, I now recollect, British corn is there also taxed up to ten *per cent.*, and this too in the very head quarters, the very citadel of smuggling, the Isle of Man. Now will the noble Lord condescend to tell me why he repealed the taxes on the manufactures sent out to America, and not the taxes on the manufactures exported to the Isle of Man? The principle was exactly the same, the objects charged infinitely more extensive, the duties without comparison higher. Why? Why, notwithstanding all his childish pretexts, because the taxes were quietly submitted to in the Isle of Man; and because they raised a flame in America. Your reasons were political, not commercial. The repeal was made, as Lord Hillsborough's Letter well expresses it, to regain "the confidence and affection of the Colonies, on which the glory and safety of the British Empire depend." A wise and just motive surely, if ever there was such. But the mischief and dishonour is, that you have not done what you had given the Colonies just cause to expect, when your Ministers disclaimed the idea of taxes for a revenue. There is nothing simple, nothing manly, nothing ingenuous, open, decisive, or steady, in the proceeding, with regard either to the continuance or the repeal of the taxes. The whole has an air of littleness and fraud. The article of tea is [115] slurred over in the Circular Letter, as it were by accident—nothing is said of a resolution either to keep that tax, or to give it up. There is no fair dealing in any part of the transaction.

If you mean to follow your true motive and your public faith, give up your tax on tea for raising a revenue, the principle of which has, in effect, been disclaimed in your name; and which produces you no advantage; no, not a penny. Or, if you choose to go on with a poor pretence instead of a solid reason, and will still adhere to your cant of commerce, you have ten thousand times more strong commercial reasons for giving up this duty on tea, than for abandoning the five others that you have already renounced.

The American consumption of teas is annually, I believe, worth 300,000*l.* at the least farthing. If you urge the American violence as a justification of your perseverance in enforcing this tax, you know that you can never answer this plain question—Why did you repeal the others given in the same Act, whilst the very same violence subsisted? But you did not find the violence cease upon that concession. No! because the concession was far short of satisfying the principle which Lord Hillsborough had abjured; or even the pretence on which the repeal of the other taxes was announced; and because, by enabling the East India Company to open a shop for defeating the American resolution not to pay that specific tax, you manifestly shewed a hankering after the principle of the Act which you formerly had renounced. Whatever road you take leads to a compliance with this motion. It opens to you at the end of every visto. Your commerce, your policy, your promises, your reasons, your pretences, your consistency, your inconsistency—all jointly oblige you to this repeal.

But still it sticks in our throats—"If we go so far, the Americans will go farther." We do not know that. We [116] ought, from experience, rather to presume the contrary. Do we not know for certain that the Americans are going on as fast as possible, whilst we refuse to gratify them? Can they do more, or can they do worse, if we yield this point? I think this concession will rather fix a turn-pike to prevent their further progress. It is impossible to answer for bodies of men. But I am sure the natural effect of fidelity, clemency, kindness in governors, is peace, good-will, order, and esteem on the part of the governed. I would certainly, at least, give these fair principles a fair trial; which, since the making of this act to this hour, they never have had.

SIR, THE HONOURABLE GENTLEMAN having spoken what he thought necessary upon the narrow part of the subject, I have given him, I hope, a satisfactory answer. He next presses me by a variety of direct challenges and oblique reflexions to say something on the historical part. I shall, therefore, Sir, open myself fully on that important and delicate subject; not for the sake of telling you a long story, (which I know, Mr. Speaker, you are not particularly fond of,) but for the sake of the weighty instruction that, I flatter myself, will necessarily result from it. I shall not be longer, if I can help it, than so serious a matter requires.

Permit me then, Sir, to lead your attention very far back; back to the Act of Navigation; the corner-stone of the policy of this country with regard to its Colonies. Sir, that policy was, from the beginning, purely commercial; and the commercial system was wholly restrictive. It was the system of a monopoly. No trade was let loose from that constraint, but merely to enable the Colonists to dispose of what, in the course of your trade, you could not take; or to enable them to dispose of such articles as we forced upon them, and for which, without some degree of liberty, they could not pay. Hence all your specific and detailed enumerations: hence [117] the innumerable checks and counterchecks: hence that infinite variety of paper chains by which you bind together this complicated

system of the Colonies. This principle of commercial monopoly runs through no less than twenty-nine Acts of Parliament, from the year 1660 to the unfortunate period of 1764.

In all those acts the system of commerce is established,
as that from whence alone you proposed to make the Colonies contribute (I mean directly and by the operation of your
superintending legislative power,) to the strength of the Empire. I venture to say, that during that whole period, a Parliamentary revenue from thence was never once in contemplation. Accordingly, in all the number of laws passed with
regard to the Plantations, the words which distinguish revenue laws, specifically as such, were, I think, premeditately
avoided. I do not say, Sir, that a form of words alters the
nature of the law, or abridges the power of the lawgiver. It
certainly does not. However, titles and formal preambles are
not always idle words; and the lawyers frequently argue from
them. I state these facts to shew, not what was your right,
but what has been your settled policy. Our revenue laws have
usually a *title,* purporting their being *grants;* and the words
give and grant usually precede the enacting parts. Although
duties were imposed on America in Acts of King Charles the
Second, and in Acts of King William, no one title of giving
"an aid to His Majesty," or any other of the usual titles to
Revenue Acts, was to be found in any of them till 1764; nor
were the words "give and grant" in any preamble until the
Sixth of George the Second. However, the title of this Act of
George the Second, notwithstanding the words of donation,
considers it merely as a regulation of trade—"An Act for the
better securing of the trade of His Majesty's Sugar Colonies
in America." This Act was made on a compromise of all, and
at the express [118] desire of a part, of the Colonies themselves. It was therefore in some measure with their consent;
and having a title directly purporting only a *commercial regulation,* and being in truth nothing more, the words were passed
by, at a time when no jealousy was entertained, and things

were little scrutinized. Even Governor Bernard, in his second printed letter, dated in 1763, gives it as his opinion, that "it was an Act of *prohibition,* not of revenue." This is certainly true, that no Act avowedly for the purpose of revenue, and with the ordinary title and recital taken together, is found in the Statute Book until the year 1764. All before this period stood on commercial regulation and restraint. The scheme of a Colony revenue by British authority appeared therefore to the Americans in the light of a great innovation. The words of Governor Bernard's ninth letter, written in Nov. 1765, state this idea very strongly. "It must," says he, "have been supposed, *such an innovation as a Parliamentary taxation* would cause a great *alarm,* and meet with much *opposition* in most parts of America; it was *quite new* to the people, and had no *visible bounds* set to it." After stating the weakness of government there, he says; "Was this a time to introduce *so great a novelty* as a Parliamentary inland taxation in America?" Whatever the right might have been, this mode of using it was absolutely new in policy and practice.

Sir, they who are friends to the schemes of American revenue say, that the commercial restraint is full as hard a law for America to live under. I think so too. I think it, if uncompensated, to be a condition of as rigorous servitude as men can be subject to. But America bore it from the fundamental Act of Navigation until 1764. Why? Because men do bear the inevitable constitution of their original nature with all its infirmities. The Act of Navigation attended the Colonies from their infancy; grew with their [119] growth and strengthened with their strength. They were confirmed in obedience to it, even more by usage than by law. They scarcely had remembered a time when they were not subject to such restraint. Besides, they were indemnified for it by a pecuniary compensation. Their monopolist happened to be one of the richest men in the world. By his immense capital, primarily employed, not for their benefit, but his own, they were enabled to proceed with their fisheries, their agriculture, their ship-building, (and their trade too, within the limits,) in such a manner as got far the start of the slow languid operations of unassisted nature. This capital was a hot-bed to them. Nothing in the history of mankind is like their progress. For my part, I never cast an eye on their flourishing commerce, and their cultivated and commodious life, but they seem to me rather antient nations grown to perfection through a long series of fortunate events, and a train of successful industry, accumulating wealth in many centuries, than the Colonies of yesterday; than a set of miserable outcasts, a few years ago not so much sent as thrown out, on the bleak and barren shore of a desolate wilderness three thousand miles from all civilized intercourse.

All this was done by England, whilst England pursued trade, and forgot revenue. You not only acquired commerce, but you actually created the very objects of trade in America; and by that creation you raised the trade of this kingdom at least four-fold. America had the compensation of your capital, which made her bear her servitude. She had another compensation, which you are now going to take away from her. She had, except the commercial restraint, every characteristic mark of a free people in all her internal concerns. She had the image of the British Constitution. She had the substance. She was taxed by her own representatives. She chose most of her own magistrates. She [120] paid them all. She had in effect the sole disposal of her own internal government. This whole state of commercial servitude and civil liberty, taken together, is certainly not perfect freedom; but comparing it with the ordinary circumstances of human nature, it was a happy and a liberal condition.

I know, Sir, that great and not unsuccessful pains have been taken to inflame our minds by an outcry, in this House and out of it, that in America the Act of Navigation neither is, nor ever was, obeyed. But if you take the Colonies through,

I affirm, that its authority never was disputed; that it was no-where disputed for any length of time; and, on the whole, that it was well observed. Wherever the Act pressed hard, many individuals indeed evaded it. This is nothing. These scattered individuals never denied the law, and never obeyed it. Just as it happens whenever the laws of trade, whenever the laws of revenue, press hard upon the people in England; in that case all your shores are full of contraband. Your right to give a mo-nopoly to the East India Company, your right to lay immense duties on French brandy, are not disputed in England. You do not make this charge on any man. But you know that there is not a creek from Pentland Frith to the Isle of Wight, in which they do not smuggle immense quantities of teas, East India goods, and brandies. I take it for granted, that the authority of Governor Bernard in this point is indisputable. Speaking of these laws as they regarded that part of America now in so unhappy a condition, he says, "I believe they are nowhere better supported than in this Province; I do not pretend that it is entirely free from a breach of these laws; but that such a breach, if discovered, is justly punished." What more can you say of the obedience to any laws in any Country? An obedi-ence to these laws formed the acknowledgment, instituted by yourselves, for your [121] superiority; and was the payment you originally imposed for your protection.

Whether you were right or wrong in establishing the Colonies on the principles of commercial monopoly, rather than on that of revenue, is at this day a problem of mere speculation. You cannot have both by the same authority. To join together the restraints of an universal internal and exter-nal monopoly, with an universal internal and external taxa-tion, is an unnatural union; perfect uncompensated slavery. You have long since decided for yourself and them; and you and they have prospered exceedingly under that decision.

This nation, Sir, never thought of departing from that choice until the period immediately on the close of the last war. Then a scheme of government new in many things seemed to have been adopted. I saw, or I thought I saw, several symptoms of a great change, whilst I sat in your gallery, a good while before I had the honour of a seat in this House. At that period the necessity was established of keeping up no less than twenty new regiments, with twenty colonels capable of seats in this House. This scheme was adopted with very general applause from all sides, at the very time that, by your conquests in America, your danger from foreign attempts in that part of the world was much lessened, or indeed rather quite over. When this huge encrease of military establishment was resolved on, a revenue was to be found to support so great a burthen. Country gentlemen, the great patrons of oeconomy, and the great resisters of a standing armed force, would not have entered with much alacrity into the vote for so large and so expensive an army, if they had been very sure that they were to continue to pay for it. But hopes of another kind were held out to them; and in particular, I well remember, that Mr. Townshend, in a brilliant harangue on this subject, did dazzle [122] them, by playing before their eyes the image of a revenue to be raised in America.

Here began to dawn the first glimmerings of this new Colony system. It appeared more distinctly afterwards, when it was devolved upon a person to whom, on other accounts, this country owes very great obligations. I do believe, that he had a very serious desire to benefit the public. But with no small study of the detail, he did not seem to have his view, at least equally, carried to the total circuit of our affairs. He generally considered his objects in lights that were rather too detached. Whether the business of an American revenue was imposed upon him altogether; whether it was entirely the result of his own speculation; or, what is more probable, that his own ideas rather coincided with the instructions he had received; certain it is, that, with the best intentions in the world, he first brought this fatal scheme into form, and established it by Act of Parliament.

No man can believe, that at this time of day I mean to lean on the venerable memory of a great man, whose loss we deplore in common. Our little party-differences have been long ago composed; and I have acted more with him, and certainly with more pleasure with him, than ever I acted against him. Undoubtedly Mr. Grenville was a first-rate figure in this country. With a masculine understanding, and a stout and resolute heart, he had an application undissipated and unwearied. He took public business, not as a duty which he was to fulfil, but as a pleasure he was to enjoy; and he seemed to have no delight out of this House, except in such things as some way related to the business that was to be done within it. If he was ambitious, I will say this for him, his ambition was of a noble and generous strain. It was to raise himself, not by the low, pimping politicks of a Court, but to win his way to power, through the laborious gradations of public service; and to secure to himself a well-earned [123] rank in Parliament, by a thorough knowledge of its constitution, and a perfect practice in all its business.

Sir, if such a man fell into errors, it must be from defects not intrinsic; they must be rather sought in the particular habits of his life; which, though they do not alter the groundwork of character, yet tinge it with their own hue. He was bred in a profession. He was bred to the law, which is, in my opinion, one of the first and noblest of human sciences; a science which does more to quicken and invigorate the understanding, than all the other kinds of learning put together; but it is not apt, except in persons very happily born, to open and to liberalize the mind exactly in the same proportion. Passing from that study he did not go very largely into the world; but plunged into business; I mean into the business of office; and the limited and fixed methods and forms established there. Much knowledge is to be had undoubtedly in that line; and there is no knowledge which is not valuable. But it may be truly said, that men too much conversant with office are rarely minds of remarkable enlargement. Their habits of office are apt to give them a turn to think the substance of business not to be much more important than the forms in which it is conducted. These forms are adapted to ordinary occasions; and therefore persons who are nurtured in office do admirably well as long as things go on in their common order; but when the high roads are broken up, and the waters out, when a new and troubled scene is opened, and the file affords no precedent, then it is that a greater knowledge of mankind, and a far more extensive comprehension of things, is requisite, than ever office gave, or than office can ever give. Mr. Grenville thought better of the wisdom and power of human legislation than in truth it deserves. He conceived, and many conceived along with him, that the flourishing trade of this country was greatly owing to law and institution, and not quite so much [124] to liberty; for but too many are apt to believe regulation to be commerce, and taxes to be revenue. Among regulations, that which stood first in reputation was his idol. I mean the Act of Navigation. He has often professed it to be so. The policy of that Act is, I readily admit, in many respects, well understood. But I do say, that if the Act be suffered to run the full length of its principle, and is not changed and modified according to the change of times and the fluctuation of circumstances, it must do great mischief, and frequently even defeat its own purpose.

After the war, and in the last years of it, the trade of America had encreased far beyond the speculations of the most sanguine imaginations. It swelled out on every side. It filled all its proper channels to the brim. It overflowed with a rich redundance, and breaking its banks on the right and on the left, it spread out upon some places where it was indeed improper, upon others where it was only irregular.

It is the nature of all greatness not to be exact; and great trade will always be attended with considerable abuses. The contraband will always keep pace in some measure with the fair trade. It should stand as a fundamental maxim, that no vulgar precaution ought to be employed in the cure of evils, which are closely connected with the cause of our prosperity. Perhaps this great person turned his eyes somewhat less than was just towards the incredible increase of the fair trade; and looked with something of too exquisite a jealousy towards the contraband. He certainly felt a singular degree of anxiety on the subject; and even began to act from that passion earlier than is commonly imagined. For whilst he was First Lord of the Admiralty, though not strictly called upon in his official line, he presented a very strong memorial to the Lords of the Treasury, (my Lord Bute was then at the head of the board,) heavily complaining of the growth of the illicit commerce in America. Some mischief happened even [125] at that time from this over-earnest zeal. Much greater happened afterwards, when it operated with greater power in the highest department of the finances. The bonds of the Act of Navigation were straitened so much, that America was on the point of having no trade, either contraband or legitimate. They found, under the construction and execution so used, the Act no longer tying, but actually strangling them. All this coming with new enumerations of commodities; with regulations which in a manner put a stop to the mutual coasting intercourse of the Colonies: with the appointment of Courts of Admiralty under various improper circumstances; with a sudden extinction of the paper currencies; with a compulsory provision for the quartering of soldiers; the people of America thought themselves proceeded against as delinquents, or, at best, as people under suspicion of delinquency; and in such a manner as, they imagined, their recent services in the war did not at all merit. Any of these innumerable regulations, perhaps, would not have alarmed alone; some might be thought reasonable; the multitude struck them with terror.

BUT THE GRAND MANOEUVRE in that business of new regulating the Colonies, was the 15th Act of the Fourth of George the Third; which, besides containing several of the matters to which I have just alluded, opened a new principle; and here properly began the second period of the policy of this country with regard to the colonies; by which the scheme of a regular Plantation Parliamentary revenue was adopted in theory, and settled in practice. A revenue not substituted in the place of, but superadded to, a monopoly; which monopoly was enforced at the same time with additional strictness, and the execution put into military hands.

This Act, Sir, had for the first time the title of "granting duties in the Colonies and Plantations of America"; and for [126] the first time it was asserted in the preamble, "that it was *just* and *necessary*, that a revenue should be raised there." Then came the technical words of "giving and granting"; and thus a complete American Revenue Act was made in all the forms, and with a full avowal of the right, equity, policy, and even necessity of taxing the Colonies, without any formal consent of theirs. There are contained also in the preamble to that Act these very remarkable words—the Commons, &c.—"being desirous to make *some* provision in the *present* session of Parliament *towards* raising the said revenue." By these words it appeared to the Colonies, that this Act was but a beginning of sorrows; that every session was to produce something of the same kind; that we were to go on, from day to day, in charging them with such taxes as we pleased, for such a military force as we should think proper. Had this plan been pursued, it was evident that the provincial assemblies, in which the Americans felt all their portion of importance, and beheld their sole image of freedom, were *ipso facto* annihilated. This ill prospect before them seemed to be boundless in extent, and endless in duration. Sir, they were not mistaken. The Ministry valued themselves when this Act passed, and when they give notice of the Stamp Act, that both of the duties came very short of their ideas of American taxation. Great was the applause of this measure here. In England we cried out for new taxes on America, whilst they cried out that they were nearly crushed with those which the war and their own grants had brought upon them.

Sir, it has been said in the debate, that when the first American Revenue Act (the Act in 1764, imposing the port duties) passed, the Americans did not object to the principle. It is true they touched it but very tenderly. It was not a direct attack. They were, it is true, as yet novices; as yet unaccustomed to direct attacks upon any of the rights of [127] Parliament. The duties were port duties, like those they had been accustomed to bear; with this difference, that the title was not the same, the preamble not the same, and the spirit altogether unlike. But of what service is this observation to the cause of those that make it? It is a full refutation of the pretence for their present cruelty to America; for it shews, out of their own mouths, that our Colonies were backward to enter into the present vexatious and ruinous controversy.

There is also another circulation abroad, (spread with a malignant intention, which I cannot attribute to those who say the same thing in this House,) that Mr. Grenville gave the Colony agents an option for their assemblies to tax themselves, which they had refused. I find that much stress is laid on this, as a fact. However, it happens neither to be true nor possible. I will observe first, that Mr. Grenville never thought fit to make this apology for himself in the innumerable debates that were had upon the subject. He might have proposed to the Colony agents, that they should agree in some mode of taxation as the ground of an Act of Parliament. But he never could have proposed that they should tax themselves on requisition, which is the assertion of the day. Indeed, Mr. Grenville well knew, that the Colony agents could have no general powers to consent to it; and they had no time to consult their assemblies for particular powers, before he passed his first Revenue Act. If you compare dates, you will find it impossible. Burthened as the agents knew the colonies were at that time, they could not give the least hope of such grants. His own favourite governour was of opinion that the Americans were not then taxable objects.

Nor was the time less favourable to the *equity* of such a taxation. I don't mean to dispute the reasonableness of America contributing to the charges of Great Britain [128] *when she is able;* nor, I believe, would the Americans themselves have disputed it, at a *proper time and season.* But it should be considered that the American governments themselves have, in the prosecution of the late war, contracted very large debts; which it will take some years to pay off, and in the mean time occasion very *burdensome taxes for that purpose* only. For instance, this government, which is as much before-hand as any, raises every year 37,500*l.* sterling for sinking their debt, and must continue it for four years longer at least before it will be clear.

These are the words of Governor Bernard's letter to a member of the old Ministry, and which he has since printed. Mr. Grenville could not have made this proposition to the agents, for another reason. He was of opinion, which he has declared in this House an hundred times, that the Colonies could not legally grant any revenue to the Crown; and that infinite mischiefs would be the consequence of such a power. When Mr. Grenville had passed the first Revenue Act, and in the same session had made this House come to a resolution for laying a stamp-duty on America, between that time and the passing the Stamp Act into a law, he told a considerable and most respectable merchant, a member of this House, whom I am truly sorry I do not now see in his place, when he represented against this proceeding, that if the stamp-duty was disliked, he was willing to exchange it for any other

Speech on American Taxation

equally productive; but that, if he objected to the Americans being taxed by Parliament, he might save himself the trouble of the discussion, as he was determined on the measure. This is the fact, and, if you please, I will mention a very unquestionable authority for it.

Thus, Sir, I have disposed of this falsehood. But falsehood has a perennial spring. It is said, that no conjecture could be made of the dislike of the Colonies to the principle. This is as untrue as the other. After the resolution of the [129] House, and before the passing of the Stamp Act, the Colonies of Massachuset's Bay and New York did send remonstrances, objecting to this mode of Parliamentary taxation. What was the consequence? They were suppressed; they were put under the table, notwithstanding an Order of Council to the contrary, by the Ministry which composed the very Council that had made the Order: and thus the House proceeded to its business of taxing without the least regular knowledge of the objections which were made to it. But to give that House its due, it was not over-desirous to receive information, or to hear remonstrance. On the 15th of February, 1765, whilst the Stamp Act was under deliberation, they refused with scorn even so much as to receive four petitions presented from so respectable Colonies as Connecticut, Rhode Island, Virginia, and Carolina; besides one from the traders of Jamaica. As to the Colonies, they had no alternative left to them, but to disobey; or to pay the taxes imposed by that Parliament which was not suffered, or did not suffer itself, even to hear them remonstrate upon the subject.

THIS WAS THE STATE OF THE COLONIES before his Majesty thought fit to change his Ministers. It stands upon no authority of mine. It is proved by uncontrovertible records. The Honourable Gentleman has desired some of us to lay our hands upon our hearts, and answer to his queries upon the historical part of this consideration; and by his manner (as well as my eyes could discern it) he seemed to address himself to me.

Sir, I will answer him as clearly as I am able, and with great openness; I have nothing to conceal. In the year sixty-five, being in a very private station, far enough from any line of business, and not having the honour of a seat in this House, it was my fortune, unknowing and unknown to the then Ministry, by the intervention of a common friend, [130] to become connected with a very noble person, and at the head of the Treasury department. It was indeed in a situation of little rank and no consequence, suitable to the mediocrity of my talents and pretensions. But a situation near enough to enable me to see, as well as others, what was going on; and I did see in that noble person such sound principles, such an enlargement of mind, such clear and sagacious sense, and such unshaken fortitude, as have bound me, as well as others much better than me, by an inviolable attachment to him from that time forward. Sir, Lord Rockingham very early in that summer received a strong representation from many weighty English merchants and manufacturers, from governors of provinces and commanders of men of war, against almost the whole of the American commercial regulations: and particularly with regard to the total ruin which was threatened to the Spanish trade. I believe, Sir, the noble Lord soon saw his way in this business. But he did not rashly determine against Acts which it might be supposed were the result of much deliberation. However, Sir, he scarcely began to open the ground, when the whole veteran body of office took the alarm. A violent out-cry of all (except those who knew and felt the mischief) was raised against any alteration. On one hand, his attempt was a direct violation of treaties and public law; on the other, the Act of Navigation and all the corps of trade laws were drawn up in array against it.

The first step the noble Lord took, was to have the opinion of his excellent, learned, and ever lamented friend the late Mr. Yorke, then Attorney-General, on the point of law. When he knew that formally and officially, which in substance he had known before, he immediately dispatched orders to redress the grievance. But I will say it for the then minister, he is of that constitution of mind, that I know he would have issued, on the same critical occasion, the very [131] same orders, if the Acts of Trade had been, as they were not, directly against him; and would have chearfully submitted to the equity of Parliament for his indemnity.

On the conclusion of this business of the Spanish trade, the news of the troubles on account of the Stamp Act arrived in England. It was not until the end of October that these accounts were received. No sooner had the sound of that mighty tempest reached us in England, than the whole of the then opposition, instead of feeling humbled by the unhappy issue of their measures, seemed to be infinitely elated, and cried out, that the Ministry, from envy to the glory of their predecessors, were prepared to repeal the Stamp Act. Near nine years after, the Honourable Gentleman takes quite opposite ground, and now challenges me to put my hand to my heart, and say, whether the Ministry had resolved on the repeal till a considerable time after the meeting of Parliament. Though I do not very well know what the Honourable Gentleman wishes to infer from the admission, or from the denial, of this fact, on which he so earnestly adjures me; I do put my hand on my heart, and assure him, that they did *not* come to a resolution directly to repeal. They weighed this matter as its difficulty and importance required. They considered maturely among themselves. They consulted with all who could give advice or information. It was not determined until a little before the meeting of Parliament; but it was determined, and the main lines of their own plan marked out, before that meeting. Two questions arose—(I hope I am not going into a narrative troublesome to the House—)

[A cry of, "Go on, go on."]

The first of the two considerations was, whether the repeal should be total, or whether only partial; taking out everything burthensome and productive, and reserving only an empty acknowledgement, such as a stamp on cards or dice. [132] The other question was, on what principle the Act should be repealed? On this head also two principles were started. One, that the legislative rights of this country, with regard to America, were not entire, but had certain restrictions and limitations. The other principle was, that taxes of this kind were contrary to the fundamental principles of commerce on which the Colonies were founded; and contrary to every idea of political equity; by which equity we are bound, as much as possible, to extend the spirit and benefit of the British constitution to every part of the British dominions. The option, both of the measure, and of the principle of repeal, was made before the session; and I wonder how any one can read the King's speech at the opening of that session, without seeing in that speech both the repeal and the Declaratory Act very sufficiently crayoned out. Those who cannot see this can see nothing.

Surely the Honourable Gentleman will not think that a great deal less time than was then employed ought to have been spent in deliberation, when he considers that the news of the troubles did not arrive till towards the end of October. The Parliament sat to fill the vacancies on the 14th day of December, and on business the 14th of the following January.

Sir, a partial repeal, or, as the *bon ton* of the court then was, a *modification,* would have satisfied a timid, unsystematic, procrastinating Ministry, as such a measure has since done such a Ministry. A modification is the constant resource of weak, undeciding minds. To repeal by the denial of our right to tax in the preamble, (and this too did not want advisers,) would have cut, in the heroic style, the Gordian knot with a sword. Either measure would have cost no more than a day's debate. But when the total repeal was adopted; and adopted on principles of policy, of equity, and of commerce; this plan made it necessary to enter into [133] many and difficult measures. It became necessary to open a very large field of evidence commensurate to these extensive views. But then this labour did knight's service. It opened the eyes of several to the true state of the American affairs; it enlarged their ideas; it removed prejudices; and it conciliated the opinions and affections of men. The noble Lord, who then took the lead in administration, my Honourable Friend under me, and a Right Honourable Gentleman, (if he will not reject his share, and it was a large one, of this business,) exerted the most laudable industry in bringing before you the fullest, most impartial, and least garbled body of evidence that was ever produced to this House. I think the inquiry lasted in the committee for six weeks; and, at its conclusion, this House, by an independent, noble, spirited, and unexpected majority; by a majority that will redeem all the acts ever done by majorities in Parliament; in the teeth of all the old mercenary Swiss of state, in despite of all the speculators and augurs of political events, in defiance of the whole embattled legion of veteran pensioners and practised instruments of a Court, gave a total repeal to the Stamp Act, and (if it had been so permitted) a lasting peace to this whole Empire.

I state, Sir, these particulars, because this act of spirit and fortitude has lately been, in the circulation of the season, and in some hazarded declamations in this House, attributed to timidity. If, Sir, the conduct of Ministry, in proposing the Repeal, had arisen from timidity with regard to themselves, it would have been greatly to be condemned. Interested timidity disgraces as much in the Cabinet, as personal timidity does in the field. But timidity, with regard to the well-being of our country, is heroic virtue. The noble Lord who then conducted affairs, and his worthy collegues, whilst they trembled at the prospect of such distresses as you have since brought upon yourselves, were not afraid steadily to look in [134] the face that glaring and dazzling influence at which the eyes of eagles have blenched. He looked in the face one of the ablest, and, let me say, not the most scrupulous, oppositions, that perhaps ever was in this House; and withstood it, unaided by even one of the usual supports of administration. He did this when he repealed the Stamp Act. He looked in the face a person he had long respected and regarded, and whose aid was then particularly wanting; I mean Lord Chatham. He did this when he passed the Declaratory Act.

It is now given out for the usual purposes by the usual emissaries, that Lord Rockingham did not consent to the repeal of this Act until he was bullied into it by Lord Chatham; and the reporters have gone so far as publicly to assert, in an hundred companies, that the Honourable Gentleman under the gallery, who proposed the repeal in the American Committee, had another sett of resolutions in his pocket directly the reverse of those he moved. These artifices of a desperate cause are at this time spread abroad, with incredible care, in every part of the town, from the highest to the lowest companies; as if the industry of the circulation were to make amends for the absurdity of the report.

Sir, whether the noble Lord is of a complexion to be bullied by Lord Chatham, or by any man, I must submit to those who know him. I confess, when I look back to that time, I consider him as placed in one of the most trying situations in which, perhaps, any man ever stood. In the House of Peers there were very few of the Ministry, out of the noble Lord's own particular connexion, (except Lord Egmont, who acted, as far as I could discern, an honourable and manly part,) that did not look to some other future arrangement, which warped his politicks. There were in both Houses new and menacing appearances, that might very naturally drive any [135] other, than a most resolute minister, from his measure or from his station. The household troops openly revolted.

The allies of Ministry, (those, I mean, who supported some of their measures, but refused responsibility for any,) endeavoured to undermine their credit, and to take ground that must be fatal to the success of the very cause which they would be thought to countenance. The question of the repeal was brought on by Ministry in the Committee of this House, in the very instant when it was known that more than one Court negotiation was carrying on with the heads of the Opposition. Everything, upon every side, was full of traps and mines. Earth below shook; heaven above menaced; all the elements of Ministerial safety were dissolved. It was in the midst of this chaos of plots and counter-plots; it was in the midst of this complicated warfare against public opposition and private treachery, that the firmness of that noble Person was put to the proof. He never stirred from his ground; no, not an inch. He remained fixed and determined, in principle, in measure, and in conduct. He practised no managements. He secured no retreat. He sought no apology.

I will likewise do justice, I ought to do it, to the Honourable Gentleman who led us in this House. Far from the duplicity wickedly charged on him, he acted his part with alacrity and resolution. We all felt inspired by the example he gave us, down even to myself, the weakest in that phalanx. I declare for one, I knew well enough (it could not be concealed from anybody) the true state of things; but, in my life, I never came with so much spirits into this House. It was a time for a *man* to act in. We had powerful enemies; but we had faithful and determined friends; and a glorious cause. We had a great battle to fight; but we had the means of fighting; not as now, when our arms are tied behind us. We did fight that day, and conquer.

[136] I remember, Sir, with a melancholy pleasure, the situation of the Honourable Gentleman who made the motion for the repeal; in that crisis, when the whole trading interest of this Empire, crammed into your lobbies, with a

trembling and anxious expectation, waited, almost to a winter's return of light, their fate from your resolutions. When, at length, you had determined in their favour, and your doors, thrown open, showed them the figure of their deliverer in the well-earned triumph of his important victory, from the whole of that grave multitude there arose an involuntary burst of gratitude and transport. They jumped upon him like children on a long absent father. They clung about him as captives about their redeemer. All England, all America, joined to his applause. Nor did he seem insensible to the best of all earthly rewards, the love and admiration of his fellow-citizens. *Hope elevated and joy brightened his crest.* I stood near him; and his face, to use the expression of the Scripture of the first martyr—his face was as if it had been the face of an angel. I do not know how others feel; but if I had stood in that situation, I never would have exchanged it for all that kings in their profusion could bestow. I did hope that that day's danger and honour would have been a bond to hold us all together for ever. But, alas! that, with other pleasing visions, is long since vanished.

Sir, this act of supreme magnanimity has been represented, as if it had been a measure of an Administration, that having no scheme of their own, took a middle line, pilfered a bit from one side and a bit from the other. Sir, they took *no* middle lines. They differed fundamentally from the schemes of both parties; but they preserved the objects of both. They preserved the authority of Great Britain. They preserved the equity of Great Britain. They made the Declaratory Act; they repealed the Stamp Act. They did both *fully;* because the Declaratory Act was *without qualification;* [137] and the repeal of the Stamp Act *total.* This they did in the situation I have described.

Now, Sir, what will the adversary say to both these Acts? If the principle of the Declaratory Act was not good, the principle we are contending for this day is monstrous. If the principle of the Repeal was not good, why are we not at war for a real, substantial, effective revenue? If both were bad, why has this Ministry incurred all the inconveniencies of both and of all schemes? Why have they enacted, repealed, enforced, yielded, and now attempt to enforce again?

SIR, I THINK I MAY as well now, as at any other time, speak to a certain matter of fact, not wholly unrelated to the question under your consideration. We, who would persuade you to revert to the antient policy of this Kingdom, labour under the effect of this short current phrase, which the Court leaders have given out to all their corps, in order to take away the credit of those who would prevent you from that frantic war you are going to wage upon your Colonies. Their cant is this; "All the disturbances in America have been created by the Repeal of the Stamp Act." I suppress for a moment my indignation at the falsehood, baseness, and absurdity of this most audacious assertion. Instead of remarking on the motives and character of those who have issued it for circulation, I will clearly lay before you the state of America, antecedently to that Repeal; after the Repeal; and since the renewal of the schemes of American taxation.

It is said, that the disturbances, if there were any, before the Repeal, were slight; and without difficulty or inconvenience might have been suppressed. For an answer to this assertion I will send you to the great author and patron of the Stamp Act, who certainly meaning well to the authority of this Country, and fully apprized of the state of that, made, [138] before a Repeal was so much as agitated in this House, the motion which is on your Journals; and which, to save the Clerk the trouble of turning to it, I will now read to you. It was for an amendment to the Address of the 17th of December, 1765:

"To express our just resentment and indignation at the *outrages, tumults, and insurrections* which have been excited and carried on in North America; and at the resistance given, by *open* and *rebellious* force, to the execution of the laws in that part of His Majesty's Dominions. And to assure His Majesty, that his faithful Commons, animated with the warmest duty and attachment to his Royal Person and Government, will firmly and effectually support His Majesty in all such measures as shall be necessary for preserving and supporting the legal dependence of the Colonies on the Mother Country," &c., &c.

Here was certainly a disturbance preceding the Repeal; such a disturbance as Mr. Grenville thought necessary to qualify by the name of an *insurrection,* and the epithet of a *rebellious* force: terms much stronger than any by which those, who then supported his motion, have ever since thought proper to distinguish the subsequent disturbances in America. They were disturbances which seemed to him and his friends to justify as strong a promise of support, as hath been usual to give in the beginning of a war with the most powerful and declared enemies. When the accounts of the American Governors came before the House, they appeared stronger even than the warmth of public imagination had painted them; so much stronger, that the papers on your table bear me out in saying, that all the late disturbances, which have been at one time the Minister's motives for the repeal of five out of six of the new Court taxes, and are now his pretences for refusing to repeal that sixth, did not amount—why do I compare them?—no, not [139] to a tenth part of the tumults and violence which prevailed long before the Repeal of that Act.

Ministry cannot refuse the authority of the Commander-in-chief, General Gage, who, in his letter of the 4th of November, from New York, thus represents the state of things:

It is difficult to say, from the *highest to the lowest,* who has not been *accessary* to this *insurrection,* either by writing or *mutual agreements,* to oppose the Act, by what they are pleased to term all legal opposition to it. Nothing effectual has been proposed, either to prevent or quell the tumult. *The rest of the Provinces are in the same situation* as to a positive refusal to take the stamps; and threatening those who shall take them, *to plunder and murder them;* and this affair stands *in all the Provinces,* that unless the Act, from its own nature, enforce itself, nothing but a *very* considerable military force can do it.

It is remarkable, Sir, that the persons who formerly trumpeted forth the most loudly, the violent resolutions of assemblies; the universal insurrections; the seizing and burning the stamped papers; the forcing stamp officers to resign their commissions under the gallows; the rifling and pulling down of the houses of magistrates; and the expulsion from their country of all who dared to write or speak a single word in defence of the powers of Parliament; these very trumpeters are now the men that represent the whole as a mere trifle; and choose to date all the disturbances from the Repeal of the Stamp Act, which put an end to them. Hear your officers abroad, and let them refute this shameless falsehood, who, in all their correspondence, state the disturbances as owing to their true causes, the discontent of the people, from the taxes. You have this evidence in your own archives—and it will give you compleat satisfaction; if you are not so far lost to all Parliamentary ideas of [140] information, as rather to credit the lye of the day, than the records of your own House.

Sir, this vermin of Court reporters, when they are forced into day upon one point, are sure to burrow in another; but they shall have no refuge; I will make them bolt out of all their holes. Conscious that they must be baffled, when they attribute a precedent disturbance to a subsequent measure, they take other ground, almost as absurd, but very common in modern practice, and very wicked; which is, to attribute the ill effect of ill-judged conduct to the arguments which had been used to dissuade us from it. They say, that the opposition made in Parliament to the Stamp Act at the time of its passing, encouraged the Americans to their resistance. This has even formally appeared in print in a regular volume, from an advocate of that faction, a Dr. Tucker. This Dr. Tucker is already a dean, and his earnest labours in this vineyard will, I suppose, raise him to a bishoprick. But this assertion too, just like the rest, is false. In all the papers which have loaded your table; in all the vast crowd of verbal witnesses that appeared at your bar, witnesses which were indiscriminately produced from both sides of the House; not the least hint of such a cause of disturbance has ever appeared. As to the fact of a strenuous opposition to the Stamp Act, I sat as a stranger in your gallery when the Act was under consideration. Far from anything inflammatory, I never heard a more languid debate in this House. No more than two or three gentlemen, as I remember, spoke against the Act, and that with great reserve, and remarkable temper. There was but one division in the whole progress of the Bill; and the minority did not reach to more than 39 or 40. In the House of Lords I do not recollect that there was any debate or division at all. I am sure there was no protest. In fact, the affair passed with so very, very little noise, that in town they scarcely knew the nature of what you were doing. [141] The opposition to the Bill in England never could have done this mischief, because there scarcely ever was less of opposition to a bill of consequence.

Sir, the agents and distributors of falsehoods have, with their usual industry, circulated another lye of the same nature with the former. It is this, that the disturbances arose from the account which had been received in America of the change in the Ministry. No longer awed, it seems, with the spirit of the former rulers, they thought themselves a match for what our calumniators chose to qualify by the name of so feeble a Ministry as succeeded. Feeble in one sense these men certainly may be called; for, with all their efforts, and they have made many, they have not been able to resist the distempered vigour, and insane alacrity, with which you are rushing to your ruin. But it does so happen, that the falsity of this circulation is (like the rest) demonstrated by indisputable dates and records.

So little was the change known in America, that the letters of your Governors, giving an account of these disturbances long after they had arrived at their highest pitch, were all directed to the *Old Ministry,* and particularly to the *Earl of Halifax,* the Secretary of State corresponding with the Colonies, without once in the smallest degree intimating the slightest suspicion of any Ministerial revolution whatsoever. The Ministry was not changed in England until the 10th day of July, 1765. On the 14th of the preceding June, Governor Fauquier from Virginia writes thus; and writes thus to the Earl of Halifax:

Government is set at *defiance,* not having strength enough in her hands to enforce obedience to the laws of the community.—The private distress, which every man feels, increases the *general dissatisfaction* at the duties laid by the *Stamp Act,* which breaks out and shows itself upon every trifling occasion.

[142] The general dissatisfaction had produced some time before, that is, on the 29th of May, several strong public resolves against the Stamp Act; and those resolves are assigned by Governor Bernard, as the cause of the *insurrections* in Massachuset's Bay, in his letter of the 15th of August, still addressed to the Earl of Halifax; and he continued to address such accounts to that Minister quite to the 7th of September of the same year. Similar accounts, and of as late a date, were sent from other governors, and all directed to Lord Halifax. Not one of these letters indicates the slightest idea of a change, either known, or even apprehended.

Thus are blown away the insect race of courtly falsehoods! thus perish the miserable inventions of the wretched runners for a wretched cause, which they have fly-blown into every weak and rotten part of the country, in vain hopes that when their maggots had taken wing, their importunate buzzing might sound something like the public voice!

Sir, I have troubled you sufficiently with the state of America before the Repeal. Now I turn to the Honourable Gentleman who so stoutly challenges us to tell, whether, after the Repeal, the Provinces were quiet? This is coming home to the point. Here I meet him directly; and answer most readily, *They were quiet.* And I, in my turn, challenge him to prove when, and where, and by whom, and in what numbers, and with what violence, the other laws of trade, as gentlemen assert, were violated in consequence of your concession? or that even your other revenue laws were attacked? But I quit the vantage-ground on which I stand, and where I might leave the burthen of the proof upon him: I walk down upon the open plain, and undertake to show, that they were not only quiet, but showed many unequivocal marks of acknowledgement and gratitude. And to give him every advantage, I select the obnoxious Colony of Massachuset's Bay, [143] which at this time (but without hearing her) is so heavily a culprit before Parliament—I will select their proceedings even under circumstances of no small irritation. For, a little imprudently, I must say, Governor Bernard mixed in the administration of the lenitive of the Repeal no small acrimony arising from matters of a separate nature. Yet see, Sir, the effect of that lenitive, though mixed with these bitter ingredients; and how this rugged people can express themselves on a measure of concession.

"If it is not in our power," (say they in their address to Governor Bernard,) "in so full a manner as will be expected, to show our respectful gratitude to the Mother Country, or to make a dutiful and affectionate return to the indulgence of the King and Parliament, it shall be no fault of ours; for this we intend, and hope we shall be able fully to effect."

Speech on American Taxation

Would to God that this temper had been cultivated, managed, and set in action! other effects than those which we have since felt would have resulted from it. On the requisition for compensation to those who had suffered from the violence of the populace, in the same address they say,

The recommendation enjoined by Mr. Secretary Conway's letter, and in consequence thereof made to us, we will embrace the first convenient opportunity to consider and act upon.

They did consider; they did act upon it. They obeyed the requisition. I know the mode has been chicaned upon; but it was substantially obeyed; and much better obeyed than I fear the Parliamentary requisition of this session will be, though enforced by all your rigour, and backed with all your power. In a word, the damages of popular fury were compensated by legislative gravity. Almost every other part of America in various ways demonstrated their gratitude. I am bold to say, that so sudden a calm recovered after so violent [144] a storm is without parallel in history. To say that no other disturbance should happen from any other cause, is folly. But as far as appearances went, by the judicious sacrifice of one law, you procured an acquiescence in all that remained. After this experience, nobody shall persuade me, when a whole people are concerned, that acts of lenity are not means of conciliation.

I hope the Honourable Gentleman has received a fair and full answer to his question.

I HAVE DONE WITH THE THIRD PERIOD of your policy; that of your Repeal; and the return of your ancient system, and your antient tranquillity and concord. Sir, this period was not as long as it was happy. Another scene was opened, and other actors appeared on the stage. The state, in the condition I have described it, was delivered into the hands of Lord Chatham—a great and celebrated name; a name that keeps the name of this country respectable in every other on the globe. It may be truly called—

Clarum et venerabile nomen
Gentibus, et multum nostrae quod proderat urbi.

Sir, the venerable age of this great man, his merited rank, his superior eloquence, his splendid qualities, his eminent services, the vast space he fills in the eye of mankind; and, more than all the rest, his fall from power, which, like death, canonizes and sanctifies a great character, will not suffer me to censure any part of his conduct. I am afraid to flatter him; I am sure I am not disposed to blame him. Let those, who have betrayed him by their adulation, insult him with their malevolence. But what I do not presume to censure, I may have leave to lament. For a wise man, he seemed to me at that time to be governed too much by general maxims. I speak with the freedom of history, and I hope without offence. One or two of these maxims, flowing from an opinion not [145] the most indulgent to our unhappy species, and surely a little too general, led him into measures that were greatly mischievous to himself; and for that reason, among others, perhaps fatal to his country; measures, the effects of which, I am afraid, are for ever incurable. He made an administration, so checkered and speckled; he put together a piece of joinery, so crossly indented and whimsically dove-tailed; a cabinet so variously inlaid; such a piece of diversified Mosaic; such a tesselated pavement without cement; here a bit of black stone, and there a bit of white; patriots and courtiers; King's friends and republicans; whigs and tories; treacherous friends and open enemies; that it was indeed a very curious shew; but utterly unsafe to touch, and unsure to stand on. The colleagues whom he had assorted at the same boards, stared at each other, and were obliged to ask, "Sir, your name?"—"Sir, you have the advantage of me"—"Mr. Such-a-one"—"I beg a thousand pardons—" I venture to say, it did so happen, that persons had a single office divided between them, who had never spoke to each other in their lives, until they found themselves, they knew not how, pigging together, heads and points, in the same truckle-bed.

Sir, in consequence of this arrangement, having put so much the larger part of his enemies and opposers into power, the confusion was such, that his own principles could not possibly have any effect or influence in the conduct of affairs. If ever he fell into a fit of the gout, or if any other cause withdrew him from public cares, principles directly the contrary were sure to predominate. When he had executed his plan, he had not an inch of ground to stand upon. When he had accomplished his scheme of administration, he was no longer a minister.

When his face was hid but for a moment, his whole system was on a wide sea, without chart or compass. The gentlemen, his particular friends, who, with the names of various [146] departments of ministry, were admitted to seem as if they acted a part under him, with a modesty that becomes all men, and with a confidence in him, which was justified, even in its extravagance, by his superior abilities, had never, in any instance, presumed upon any opinion of their own. Deprived of his guiding influence, they were whirled about, the sport of every gust, and easily driven into any port; and as those who joined with them in manning the vessel were the most directly opposite to his opinions, measures, and character, and far the most artful and most powerful of the set, they easily prevailed, so as to seize upon the vacant, unoccupied, and derelict minds of his friends; and instantly they turned the vessel wholly out of the course of his policy. As if it were to insult as well as to betray him, even long before the close of the first session of his administration, when everything was publicly transacted, and with great parade, in his name, they made an Act, declaring it highly just and expedient to raise a revenue in America. For even then, Sir, even before this splendid orb was entirely set, and while the Western horizon was in a blaze with his descending glory, on the opposite quarter of the heavens arose another luminary, and, for his hour, became lord of the ascendant.

This light too is passed and set for ever. You understand, to be sure, that I speak of Charles Townshend, officially the re-producer of this fatal scheme; whom I cannot even now remember without some degree of sensibility. In truth, Sir, he was the delight and ornament of this House, and the charm of every private society which he honoured with his presence. Perhaps there never arose in this country, nor in any country, a man of a more pointed and finished wit; and (where his passions were not concerned) of a more refined, exquisite, and penetrating judgement. If he had not so great a stock, as some have had who flourished formerly, [147] of knowledge long treasured up, he knew better by far, than any man I ever was acquainted with, how to bring together, within a short time, all that was necessary to establish, to illustrate, and to decorate that side of the question he supported. He stated his matter skilfully and powerfully. He particularly excelled in a most luminous explanation and display of his subject. His style of argument was neither trite and vulgar, nor subtle and abstruse. He hit the House just between wind and water. And not being troubled with too anxious a zeal for any matter in question, he was never more tedious, or more earnest, than the pre-conceived opinions and present temper of his hearers required; to whom he was always in perfect unison. He conformed exactly to the temper of the House; and he seemed to guide, because he was always sure to follow it.

I beg pardon, Sir, if, when I speak of this and of other great men, I appear to digress in saying something of their characters. In this eventful history of the revolutions of America, the characters of such men are of much importance. Great men are the guide-posts and land-marks in the state. The credit of such men at court, or in the nation, is the sole cause of all the public measures. It would be an invidious thing (most foreign, I trust, to what you think my disposition) to remark the errors into which the authority of great names has brought the nation, without doing justice, at the same time, to the great qualities whence that authority arose. The subject is instructive to those who wish to form themselves on whatever of excellence has gone before them. There are many young members in the House (such of late has been the rapid succession of public men) who never saw that prodigy, Charles Townshend; nor of course know what a ferment he was able to excite in everything by the violent ebullition of his mixed virtues and failings. For failings he had undoubtedly— many of us remember them; we are this [148] day considering the effect of them. But he had no failings which were not owing to a noble cause; to an ardent, generous, perhaps an immoderate, passion for fame; a passion which is the instinct of all great souls. He worshipped that goddess wheresoever she appeared; but he paid his particular devotions to her in her favourite habitation, in her chosen temple, the House of Commons. Besides the characters of the individuals that compose our body, it is impossible, Mr. Speaker, not to observe that this House has a collective character of its own. That character too, however imperfect, is not unamiable. Like all great public collections of men, you possess a marked love of virtue, and an abhorrence of vice. But among vices, there is none which the House abhors in the same degree with *obstinacy*. Obstinacy, Sir, is certainly a great vice; and in the changeful state of political affairs it is frequently the cause of great mischief. It happens, however, very unfortunately, that almost the whole line of the great and masculine virtues, constancy, gravity, magnanimity, fortitude, fidelity, and firmness, are closely allied to this disagreeable quality, of which you have so just an abhorrence; and, in their excess, all these virtues very easily fall into it. He, who paid such a punctilious attention to all your feelings, certainly took care not to shock them by that vice which is the most disgustful to you.

That fear of displeasing those who ought most to be

pleased, betrayed him sometimes into the other extreme. He had voted, and, in the year 1765, had been an advocate, for the Stamp Act. Things and the disposition of men's minds were changed. In short, the Stamp Act began to be no favourite in this House. He therefore attended at the private meeting, in which the resolutions moved by a Right Honourable Gentleman were settled; resolutions leading to the Repeal. The next day he voted for that Repeal; and [149] he would have spoken for it too, if an illness, (not, as was then given out, a political, but to my knowledge, a very real illness,) had not prevented it.

The very next session, as the fashion of this world passeth away, the Repeal began to be in as bad an odour in this House as the Stamp Act had been in the session before. To conform to the temper which began to prevail, and to prevail most amongst those most in power, he declared, very early in the winter, that a revenue must be had out of America. Instantly he was tied down to his engagements by some, who had no objection to such experiments, when made at the cost of persons for whom they had no particular regard. The whole body of courtiers drove him onward. They always talked as if the King stood in a sort of humiliated state, until something of the kind should be done.

Here this extraordinary man, then Chancellor of the Exchequer, found himself in great straits. To please universally was the object of his life; but to tax and to please, no more than to love and to be wise, is not given to men. However, he attempted it. To render the tax palatable to the partizans of American revenue, he made a preamble stating the necessity of such a revenue. To close with the American distinction, this revenue was *external* or port-duty; but again, to soften it to the other party, it was a duty of *supply*. To gratify the *Colonists*, it was laid on British manufactures; to satisfy the *merchants of Britain*, the duty was trivial, and (except that on tea, which touched only the devoted East India Company) on none of the grand objects of commerce. To counterwork the American contraband, the duty on tea was reduced from a shilling to three-pence. But to secure the favour of those who would tax America, the scene of collection was changed, and, with the rest, it was levied in the Colonies. What need I say more? This fine-spun scheme had the usual fate of all exquisite policy. [150] But the original plan of the duties, and the mode of executing that plan, both arose singly and solely from a love of our applause. He was truly the child of the House. He never thought, did, or said anything, but with a view to you. He every day adapted himself to your disposition; and adjusted himself before it, as at a looking-glass.

He had observed (indeed it could not escape him) that several persons, infinitely his inferiors in all respects, had formerly rendered themselves considerable in this House by one method alone. They were a race of men (I hope in God the species is extinct) who, when they rose in their place, no man living could divine, from any known adherence to parties, to opinions, or to principles; from any order or system in their politicks; or from any sequel or connexion in their ideas, what part they were going to take in any debate. It is astonishing how much this uncertainty, especially at critical times, called the attention of all parties on such men. All eyes were fixed on them, all ears open to hear them; each party gaped, and looked alternately for their vote, almost to the end of their speeches. While the House hung in this uncertainty, now the *Hear-hims* rose from this side—now they rebellowed from the other; and that party, to whom they fell at length from their tremulous and dancing balance, always received them in a tempest of applause. The fortune of such men was a temptation too great to be resisted by one, to whom a single whiff of incense withheld gave much greater pain, than he received delight in the clouds of it, which daily rose about him from the prodigal superstition of innumerable admirers. He was a candidate for contradictory honours; and his great aim was to make those agree in admiration of him who never agreed in anything else.

Hence arose this unfortunate Act, the subject of this day's debate; from a disposition which, after making an American revenue to please one, repealed it to please others, and again [151] revived it in hopes of pleasing a third, and of catching something in the ideas of all.

THIS REVENUE ACT of 1767 formed the fourth period of American policy. How we have fared since then—what woeful variety of schemes have been adopted; what enforcing, and what repealing; what bullying, and what submitting; what doing, and undoing; what straining, and what relaxing; what assemblies dissolved for not obeying, and called again without obedience; what troops sent out to quell resistance, and on meeting that resistance, recalled; what shiftings, and changings, and jumblings of all kinds of men at home, which left no possibility of order, consistency, vigour, or even so much as a decent unity of colour in any one public measure— It is a tedious, irksome task. My duty may call me to open it out some other time; on a former occasion I tried your temper on a part of it; for the present I shall forbear.

After all these changes and agitations, your immediate situation upon the question on your paper is at length brought to this. You have an Act of Parliament, stating, that "it is *expedient* to raise a revenue in America." By a partial repeal you annihilated the greatest part of that revenue, which this preamble declares to be so expedient. You have substituted no other in the place of it. A Secretary of State has disclaimed, in the King's name, all thoughts of such a substitution in future. The principle of this disclaimer goes to what has been left, as well as what has been repealed. The tax which lingers after its companions (under a preamble declaring an American revenue expedient, and for the sole purpose of supporting the theory of that preamble) militates with the assurance authentically conveyed to the Colonies; and is an exhaustless source of jealousy and animosity. On this state, which I take to be a fair one; [152] not being able to discern any grounds of honour, advantage, peace, or power, for adhering, either to the Act or to the preamble, I shall vote for the question which leads to the repeal of both.

If you do not fall in with this motion, then secure something to fight for, consistent in theory and valuable in practice. If you must employ your strength, employ it to uphold you in some honourable right, or some profitable wrong. If you are apprehensive that the concession recommended to you, though proper, should be a means of drawing on you further but unreasonable claims, why then employ your force in supporting that reasonable conception against those unreasonable demands. You will employ it with more grace; with better effect; and with great probable concurrence of all the quiet and rational people in the provinces; who are now united with, and hurried away by, the violent; having indeed different dispositions, but a common interest. If you apprehend that on a concession you shall be pushed by metaphysical process to the extreme lines, and argued out of your whole authority, my advice is this; when you have recovered your old, your strong, your tenable position, then face about—stop short—do nothing more—reason not at all—oppose the antient policy and practice of the Empire, as a rampart against the speculations of innovators on both sides of the question; and you will stand on great, manly, and sure ground. On this solid basis fix your machines, and they will draw worlds towards you.

Your Ministers, in their own and his Majesty's name, have already adopted the American distinction of internal and external duties. It is a distinction, whatever merit it may have, that was originally moved by the Americans themselves; and I think they will acquiesce in it, if they are not pushed with too much logick and too little sense, in all the consequences.

That is, if external taxation be understood, [153] as they and you understand it, when you please, to be not a distinction of geography, but of policy; that it is a power for regulating trade, and not for supporting establishments. The distinction, which is as nothing with regard to right, is of most weighty consideration in practice. Recover your old ground, and your old tranquillity—try it—I am persuaded the Americans will compromise with you. When confidence is once restored, the odious and suspicious *summum jus* will perish of course. The spirit of practicability, of moderation, and mutual convenience, will never call in geometrical exactness as the arbitrator of an amicable settlement. Consult and follow your experience. Let not the long story, with which I have exercised your patience, prove fruitless to your interests.

For my part, I should choose (if I could have my wish) that the proposition of the Honourable Gentleman for the Repeal could go to America without the attendance of the penal Bills. Alone I could almost answer for its success. I cannot be certain of its reception in the bad company it may keep. In such heterogeneous assortments, the most innocent person will lose the effect of his innocency. Though you should send out this angel of peace, yet you are sending out a destroying angel too: and what would be the effect of the conflict of these two adverse spirits, or which would predominate in the end, is what I dare not say: whether the lenient measures would cause American passion to subside, or the severe would increase its fury. All this is in the hand of Providence. Yet now, even now, I should confide in the prevailing virtue and efficacious operation of lenity, though working in darkness, and in chaos, in the midst of all this unnatural and turbid combination: I should hope it might produce order and beauty in the end.

Let us, Sir, embrace some system or other before we end this Session. Do you mean to tax America, and to draw a [154] productive revenue from thence? If you do, speak out; name, fix, ascertain this revenue; settle its quantity; define its objects; provide for its collection; and then fight when you have something to fight for. If you murder—rob! if you kill—take possession! and do not appear in the character of madmen, as well as assassins, violent, vindictive, bloody, and tyrannical, without an object. But may better counsels guide you!

Again, and again, revert to your own principles—*Seek Peace, and ensue it*—leave America, if she has taxable matter in her, to tax herself. I am not here going into the distinctions of rights, not attempting to mark their boundaries. I do not enter into these metaphysical distinctions; I hate the very sound of them. Leave the Americans as they antiently stood, and these distinctions, born of our unhappy contest, will die along with it. They and we, and their and our ancestors, have been happy under that system. Let the memory of all actions, in contradiction to that good old mode, on both sides, be extinguished for ever. Be content to bind America by laws of trade; you have always done it. Let this be your reason for binding their trade. Do not burthen them by taxes; you were not used to do so from the beginning. Let this be your reason for not taxing. These are the arguments of states and kingdoms. Leave the rest to the schools; for there only they may be discussed with safety. But, if intemperately, unwisely, fatally, you sophisticate and poison the very source of government, by urging subtle deductions, and consequences odious to those you govern, from the unlimited and illimitable nature of supreme sovereignty, you will teach them by these means to call that sovereignty itself in question. When you drive him hard, the boar will surely turn upon the hunters. If that sovereignty and their freedom cannot be reconciled, which will they take? They will cast your sovereignty in your face. [155] No-body will be argued into slavery. Sir, let the gentlemen on the other side call forth all their ability; let the best of them get up, and tell me, what one character of liberty the Americans have, and what one brand of slavery they are free from, if they are bound in their property and industry, by all the restraints you can imagine on commerce, and at the same time are made pack-horses of every tax you choose to impose, without the least share in granting them. When they bear the burthens of unlimited monopoly, will you bring them to bear the burthens of unlimited revenue too? The Englishman in America will feel that this is slavery—that it is *legal* slavery, will be no compensation, either to his feelings or his understanding.

A Noble Lord, who spoke some time ago, is full of the fire of ingenuous youth; and when he has modelled the ideas of a lively imagination by further experience, he will be an ornament to his country in either House. He has said, that the Americans are our children, and how can they revolt against their parent? He says, that if they are not free in their present state, England is not free; because Manchester, and other considerable places, are not represented. So then, because some towns in England are not represented, America is to have no representative at all. They *are* our children; but when children ask for bread, we are not to give a stone. Is it because the natural resistance of things, and the various mutations of time, hinder our government, or any scheme of government, from being any more than a sort of approximation to the right—is it therefore that the Colonies are to recede from it infinitely? When this child of ours wishes to assimilate to its parent, and to reflect with a true filial resemblance the beauteous countenance of British liberty; are we to turn to them the shameful parts of our Constitution? are we to give them our weakness for their strength? our opprobrium for their glory? [156] and the slough of slavery, which we are not able to work off, to serve them for their freedom?

If this be the case, ask yourselves this question, Will they be content in such a state of slavery? If not, look to the consequences. Reflect how you are to govern a people, who think they ought to be free, and think they are not. Your scheme yields no revenue; it yields nothing but discontent, disorder, disobedience; and such is the state of America, that after wading up to your eyes in blood, you could only end just where you begun; that is, to tax where no revenue is to be found, to—my voice fails me; my inclination indeed carries me no farther—all is confusion beyond it.

Well, Sir, I have recovered a little, and before I sit down I must say something to another point with which gentlemen urge us. What is to become of the Declaratory Act asserting the entireness of British legislative authority, if we abandon the practice of taxation?

For my part I look upon the rights stated in that Act, exactly in the manner in which I viewed them on its very first proposition, and which I have often taken the liberty, with great humility, to lay before you. I look, I say, on the imperial rights of Great Britain, and the privileges which the Colonists ought to enjoy under these rights, to be just the most reconcilable things in the world. The Parliament of Great Britain sits at the head of her extensive Empire in two capacities: one as the local legislature of this island, providing for all things at home, immediately, and by no other instrument than the executive power. The other, and I think her nobler capacity, is what I call her *imperial character;* in which, as from the throne of heaven, she superintends all the several inferior legislatures, and guides and controuls them all, without annihilating any. As all these provincial legislatures are only co-ordinate with each other, they ought all to be subordinate to her; else they can [157] neither preserve mutual peace, nor hope for mutual justice, nor effectually afford mutual assistance. It is necessary to coerce the negligent, to restrain the violent, and to aid the weak and deficient, by the over-ruling plenitude of her power. She is never to intrude into the place of the others, whilst they are equal to the common ends of their institution. But in order to enable Parliament to answer all these ends of provident and beneficent superintendence, her powers must be boundless. The gentlemen who think the powers of Parliament limited, may please themselves to talk of requisitions. But suppose the requisitions are not obeyed? What! Shall there be no reserved power in the Empire, to supply a deficiency which may weaken, divide, and dissipate the whole? We are engaged in war—the Secretary of State calls upon the Colonies to contribute—some would do it, I think most would chearfully furnish whatever is demanded—one or two, suppose, hang back, and, easing themselves, let the stress of the draft lie on the others—surely it is proper, that some authority might legally say—"Tax yourselves for the common supply, or Parliament will do it for you." This backwardness was, as I am told, actually the case of Pennsylvania for some short time towards the beginning of the last war, owing to some internal dissensions in the Colony. But whether the fact were so, or otherwise, the case is equally to be provided for by a competent sovereign power. But then this ought to be no ordinary power; nor ever used in the first instance. This is what I meant, when I have said at various times, that I consider the power of taxing in Parliament as an instrument of empire, and not as a means of supply.

Such, Sir, is my idea of the Constitution of the British Empire, as distinguished from the Constitution of Britain; and on these grounds I think subordination and liberty may be sufficiently reconciled through the whole; whether [158] to serve a refining speculatist, or a factious demagogue, I know not; but enough surely for the ease and happiness of man.

Sir, whilst we held this happy course, we drew more from the Colonies than all the impotent violence of despotism ever could extort from them. We did this abundantly in the last war. It has never been once denied: and what reason have we to imagine that the Colonies would not have proceeded in supplying government as liberally, if you had not stepped in and hindered them from contributing, by interrupting the channel in which their liberality flowed with so strong a course; by attempting to take, instead of being satisfied to receive? Sir William Temple says, that Holland has loaded itself with ten times the impositions, which it revolted from Spain, rather than submit to. He says true. Tyranny is a poor provider. It knows neither how to accumulate, nor how to extract.

I charge therefore to this new and unfortunate system the loss not only of peace, of union, and of commerce, but even of revenue, which its friends are contending for. It is morally certain, that we have lost at least a million of free grants since the peace. I think we have lost a great deal more; and that those, who look for a revenue from the provinces, never could have pursued, even in that light, a course more directly repugnant to their purposes.

Now, Sir, I trust I have shown, first on that narrow ground which the Honourable Gentleman measured, that you are likely to lose nothing by complying with the motion, except what you have lost already. I have shown afterwards, that in time of peace you flourished in commerce, and, when war required it, had sufficient aid from the Colonies, while you pursued your antient policy; that you threw everything into confusion when you made the Stamp Act; and that you restored everything to peace and order when [159] you repealed it. I have shown that the revival of the system of taxation has produced the very worst effects; and that the partial repeal has produced, not partial good, but universal evil. Let these considerations, founded on facts, not one of which can be denied, bring us back to our reason by the road of our experience.

I cannot, as I have said, answer for mixed measures: but surely this mixture of lenity would give the whole a better chance of success. When you once regain confidence, the way will be clear before you. Then you may enforce the Act of Navigation when it ought to be enforced. You will yourselves open it where it ought still further to be opened. Proceed in what you do, whatever you do, from policy, and not from rancour. Let us act like men—let us act like statesmen. Let us hold some sort of consistent conduct. It is agreed that a revenue is not to be had in America. If we lose the profit, let us get rid of the odium.

On this business of America, I confess I am serious, even to sadness. I have had but one opinion concerning it since I sat, and before I sat, in Parliament. The noble Lord will, as usual, probably attribute the part taken by me and my friends in this business, to a desire of getting his places. Let him enjoy this happy and original idea. If I deprived him of it, I should take away most of his wit, and all his argument. But I had rather bear the brunt of all his wit, and indeed blows much heavier, than stand answerable to God for embracing a system that tends to the destruction of some of the very best and fairest of his works. But I know the map of England, as well as the noble Lord, or as any other person; and I know that the way I take is not the road to preferment. My excellent and honourable friend under me on the floor has trod that road with great toil for upwards of twenty years together. He is not yet arrived at the noble Lord's destination. However, the tracks of my worthy friend [160] are those I have ever wished to follow; because I know they lead to honour. Long may we tread the same road together; whoever may accompany us, or whoever may laugh at us on our journey! I honestly and solemnly declare, I have in all seasons adhered to the system of 1766, for no other reason, than that I think it laid deep in your truest interests; and that, by limiting the exercise, it fixes, on the firmest foundations, a real, consistent, well-grounded authority in Parliament. Until you come back to that system, there will be no peace for England.

FINIS

Speech of Edmund Burke, Esq.,

on Moving His Resolutions for

Conciliation with the Colonies

MARCH 22, 1775
[Second Edition, Dodsley, 1775.]

I HOPE, SIR, that notwithstanding the austerity of the
Chair, your good nature will incline you to some degree of

indulgence [162] towards human frailty. You will not think it unnatural, that those who have an object depending, which strongly engages their hopes and fears, should be somewhat inclined to superstition. As I came into the House full of anxiety about the event of my motion, I found, to my infinite surprise, that the grand penal Bill, by which we had passed sentence on the trade and sustenance of America, is to be returned to us from the other House. I do confess, I could not help looking on this event as a fortunate omen. I look upon it as a sort of providential favour; by which we are put once more in possession of our deliberative capacity, upon a business so very questionable in its nature, so very uncertain in its issue. By the return of this Bill, which seemed to have taken its flight for ever, we are at this very instant nearly as free to chuse a plan for our American Government as we were on the first day of the Session. If, Sir, we incline to the side of conciliation, we are not at all embarrassed (unless we please to make ourselves so) by any incongruous mixture of coercion and restraint. We are therefore called upon, as it were by a superior warning voice, again to attend to America; to attend to the whole of it together; and to review the subject with an unusual degree of care and calmness.

Surely it is an awful subject; or there is none so on this side of the grave. When I first had the honour of a seat in this House, the affairs of that Continent pressed themselves upon us, as the most important and most delicate object of Parliamentary attention. My little share in this great deliberation oppressed me. I found myself a partaker in a very high trust; and having no sort of reason to rely on the strength of my natural abilities for the proper execution of that trust, I was obliged to take more than common pains to instruct myself in everything which relates to our Colonies. I was not less under the necessity of forming some fixed ideas [163] concerning the general policy of the British Empire. Something of this sort seemed to be indispensable; in order, amidst so vast a fluctuation of passions and opinions, to concenter my thoughts; to ballast my conduct; to preserve me from being blown about by every wind of fashionable doctrine. I really did not think it safe, or manly, to have fresh principles to seek upon every fresh mail which should arrive from America.

At that period I had the fortune to find myself in perfect concurrence with a large majority in this House. Bowing under that high authority, and penetrated with the sharpness and strength of that early impression, I have continued ever since, without the least deviation, in my original sentiments. Whether this be owing to an obstinate perseverance in error, or to a religious adherence to what appears to me truth and reason, it is in your equity to judge.

Sir, Parliament having an enlarged view of objects, made, during this interval, more frequent changes in their sentiments and their conduct, than could be justified in a particular person upon the contracted scale of private information. But though I do not hazard anything approaching to a censure on the motives of former Parliaments to all those alterations, one fact is undoubted, that under them the state of America has been kept in continual agitation. Everything administered as remedy to the public complaint, if it did not produce, was at least followed by, an heightening of the distemper; until, by a variety of experiments, that important Country has been brought into her present situation; a situation which I will not miscall, which I dare not name; which I scarcely know how to comprehend in the terms of any description.

In this posture, Sir, things stood at the beginning of the Session. About that time, a worthy Member of great Parliamentary [164] experience, who, in the year 1766, filled the chair of the American Committee with much ability, took me aside; and, lamenting the present aspect of our politicks, told me, things were come to such a pass, that our former methods of proceeding in the House would be no longer tolerated. That the public tribunal (never too indulgent to a long and unsuccessful opposition) would now scrutinize our conduct with unusual severity. That the very vicissitudes and shiftings of Ministerial measures, instead of convicting their authours of inconstancy and want of system, would be taken as an occasion of charging us with a predetermined discontent, which nothing could satisfy; whilst we accused every measure of vigour as cruel, and every proposal of lenity as weak and irresolute. The publick, he said, would not have patience to see us play the game out with our adversaries: we must produce our hand. It would be expected, that those who for many years had been active in such affairs should show, that they had formed some clear and decided idea of the principles of Colony Government; and were capable of drawing out something like a platform of the ground which might be laid for future and permanent tranquillity.

I felt the truth of what my Honourable Friend represented; but I felt my situation too. His application might have been made with far greater propriety to many other gentlemen. No man was indeed ever better disposed, or worse qualified, for such an undertaking, than myself. Though I gave so far into his opinion, that I immediately threw my thoughts into a sort of Parliamentary form, I was by no means equally ready to produce them. It generally argues some degree of natural impotence of mind, or some want of knowledge of the world, to hazard Plans of Government, except from a seat of Authority. Propositions are made, not only ineffectually, but somewhat disreputably, when the minds of men are [165] not properly disposed for their reception; and for my part, I am not ambitious of ridicule; not absolutely a candidate for disgrace.

Besides, Sir, to speak the plain truth, I have in general no very exalted opinion of the virtue of Paper Government; nor of any Politicks, in which the plan is to be wholly separated from the execution. But when I saw that anger and violence prevailed every day more and more; and that things were hastening towards an incurable alienation of our Colonies; I confess my caution gave way. I felt this, as one of those few moments in which decorum yields to a higher duty. Public calamity is a mighty leveller; and there are occasions when any, even the slightest, chance of doing good, must be laid hold on, even by the most inconsiderable person.

To restore order and repose to an Empire so great and so distracted as ours, is, merely in the attempt, an undertaking that would ennoble the flights of the highest genius, and obtain pardon for the efforts of the meanest understanding. Struggling a good while with these thoughts, by degrees I felt myself more firm. I derived, at length, some confidence from what in other circumstances usually produces timidity. I grew less anxious, even from the idea of my own insignificance. For, judging of what you are, by what you ought to be, I persuaded myself that you would not reject a reasonable proposition, because it had nothing but its reason to recommend it. On the other hand, being totally destitute of all shadow of influence, natural or adventitious, I was very sure, that, if my proposition were futile or dangerous; if it were weakly conceived, or improperly timed, there was nothing exterior to it, of power to awe, dazzle, or delude you. You will see it just as it is; and you will treat it just as it deserves.

The proposition is Peace. Not Peace through the medium [166] of War; not Peace to be hunted through the labyrinth of intricate and endless negociations; not Peace to arise out of universal discord, fomented, from principle, in all parts of the Empire; not Peace to depend on the Juridical Determination of perplexing questions; or the precise marking the shadowy boundaries of a complex Government. It is simple Peace; sought in its natural course, and in its ordinary haunts. It is Peace sought in the Spirit of Peace; and laid in principles purely pacific. I propose, by removing the Ground of the difference, and by restoring the *former unsuspecting confi-*

dence of the Colonies in the Mother Country, to give permanent satisfaction to your people; and (far from a scheme of ruling by discord) to reconcile them to each other in the same act, and by the bond of the very same interest which reconciles them to British Government.

My idea is nothing more. Refined policy ever has been the parent of confusion; and ever will be so, as long as the world endures. Plain good intention, which is as easily discovered at the first view, as fraud is surely detected at last, is, let me say, of no mean force in the Government of Mankind. Genuine Simplicity of heart is an healing and cementing principle. My Plan, therefore, being formed upon the most simple grounds imaginable, may disappoint some people, when they hear it. It has nothing to recommend it to the pruriency of curious ears. There is nothing at all new and captivating in it. It has nothing of the Splendor of the Project which has been lately laid upon your Table by the Noble Lord in the Blue Ribband. It does not propose to fill your lobby with squabbling Colony Agents, who will require the interposition of your Mace, at every instant, to keep the peace amongst them. It does not institute a magnificent Auction of Finance, where captivated provinces come to general ransom by bidding against each other, until you knock down the hammer, and determine a proportion of [167] payments beyond all the powers of Algebra to equalize and settle.

The plan which I shall presume to suggest, derives, however, one great advantage from the proposition and registry of that Noble Lord's Project. The idea of conciliation is admissible. First, the House, in accepting the resolution moved by the Noble Lord, has admitted, notwithstanding the menacing front of our Address, notwithstanding our heavy Bills of Pains and Penalties—that we do not think ourselves precluded from all ideas of free Grace and Bounty.

The House has gone farther; it has declared conciliation admissible, *previous* to any submission on the part of America.

It has even shot a good deal beyond that mark, and has admitted, that the complaints of our former mode of exerting the Right of Taxation were not wholly unfounded. That right thus exerted is allowed to have something reprehensible in it; something unwise, or something grievous; since, in the midst of our heat and resentment, we, of ourselves, have proposed a capital alteration; and, in order to get rid of what seemed so very exceptionable, have instituted a mode that is altogether new; one that is, indeed, wholly alien from all the ancient methods and forms of Parliament.

The *principle* of this proceeding is large enough for my purpose. The means proposed by the Noble Lord for carrying his ideas into execution, I think, indeed, are very indifferently suited to the end; and this I shall endeavour to show you before I sit down. But, for the present, I take my ground on the admitted principle. I mean to give peace. Peace implies reconciliation; and, where there has been a material dispute, reconciliation does in a manner always imply concession on the one part or on the other. In this state of things I make no difficulty in affirming that the proposal ought to originate from us. Great and acknowledged [168] force is not impaired, either in effect or in opinion, by an unwillingness to exert itself. The superior power may offer peace with honour and with safety. Such an offer from such a power will be attributed to magnanimity. But the concessions of the weak are the concessions of fear. When such a one is disarmed, he is wholly at the mercy of his superior; and he loses for ever that time and those chances, which, as they happen to all men, are the strength and resources of all inferior power.

The capital leading questions on which you must this day decide are these two: First, whether you ought to concede; and secondly, what your concession ought to be. On the first of these questions we have gained (as I have just taken the liberty of observing to you) some ground. But I am sensible that a good deal more is still to be done. Indeed, Sir, to enable us to determine both on the one and the other of these great questions with a firm and precise judgement, I think it may be necessary to consider distinctly the true nature and the peculiar circumstances of the object which we have before us. Because after all our struggle, whether we will or not, we must govern America, according to that nature, and to those circumstances; and not according to our own imaginations; nor according to abstract ideas of right; by no means according to mere general theories of government, the resort to which appears to me, in our present situation, no better than arrant trifling. I shall therefore endeavour, with your leave, to lay before you some of the most material of these circumstances in as full and as clear a manner as I am able to state them.

THE FIRST THING that we have to consider with regard to the nature of the object is—the number of people in the Colonies. I have taken for some years a good deal of pains on that point. I can by no calculation justify myself in [169] placing the number below Two Millions of inhabitants of our own European blood and colour; besides at least 500,000 others, who form no inconsiderable part of the strength and opulence of the whole. This, Sir, is, I believe, about the true number. There is no occasion to exaggerate, where plain truth is of so much weight and importance. But whether I put the present numbers too high or too low, is a matter of little moment. Such is the strength with which population shoots in that part of the world, that, state the numbers as high as we will, whilst the dispute continues, the exaggeration ends. Whilst we are discussing any given magnitude, they are grown to it. Whilst we spend our time in deliberating on the mode of governing Two Millions, we shall find we have Millions more to manage. Your children do not grow faster from infancy to manhood, than they spread from families to communities, and from villages to nations.

I put this consideration of the present and the growing

numbers in the front of our deliberation; because, Sir, this consideration will make it evident to a blunter discernment than yours, that no partial, narrow, contracted, pinched, occasional system will be at all suitable to such an object. It will show you that it is not to be considered as one of those *Minima* which are out of the eye and consideration of the law; not a paltry excrescence of the state; not a mean dependant, who may be neglected with little damage, and provoked with little danger. It will prove that some degree of care and caution is required in the handling such an object; it will show that you ought not, in reason, to trifle with so large a mass of the interests and feelings of the human race. You could at no time do so without guilt; and be assured you will not be able to do it long with impunity.

BUT THE POPULATION of this country, the great and growing [170] population, though a very important consideration, will lose much of its weight, if not combined with other circumstances. The commerce of your Colonies is out of all proportion beyond the numbers of the people. This ground of their commerce indeed has been trod some days ago, and with great ability, by a distinguished person, at your bar. This gentleman, after Thirty-five years—it is so long since he first appeared at the same place to plead for the commerce of Great Britain—has come again before you to plead the same cause, without any other effect of time, than, that to the fire of imagination and extent of erudition, which even then marked him as one of the first literary characters of his age, he has added a consummate knowledge in the commercial interest of his country, formed by a long course of enlightened and discriminating experience.

Sir, I should be inexcusable in coming after such a person with any detail; if a great part of the members who now fill the House had not the misfortune to be absent when he appeared at your bar. Besides, Sir, I propose to take the matter at periods of time somewhat different from his. There is, if I mistake not, a point of view, from whence if you will look at the subject, it is impossible that it should not make an impression upon you.

I have in my hand two accounts; one a comparative state of the export trade of England to its Colonies, as it stood in the year 1704, and as it stood in the year 1772. The other a state of the export trade of this country to its Colonies alone, as it stood in 1772, compared with the whole trade of England to all parts of the world (the Colonies included) in the year 1704. They are from good vouchers; the latter period from the accounts on your table, the earlier from an original manuscript of Davenant, who first established the Inspector-General's office, which has been ever since his time so abundant a source of Parliamentary information.

[171] The export trade to the Colonies consists of three great branches. The African, which, terminating almost wholly in the Colonies, must be put to the account of their commerce; the West Indian; and the North American. All these are so interwoven, that the attempt to separate them, would tear to pieces the contexture of the whole; and if not entirely destroy, would very much depreciate the value of all the parts. I therefore consider these three denominations to be, what in effect they are, one trade.

The trade to the Colonies, taken on the export side, at the beginning of this century, that is, in the year 1704, stood thus:

Exports to North America, and the West Indies	£483,265
To Africa	86,665
	£569,930

In the year 1772, which I take as a middle year between the highest and lowest of those lately laid on your table, the account was as follows:

To North America, and the West Indies	£4,791,734
To Africa	866,398
To which if you add the export trade from Scotland, which had in 1704 no existence	364,000
	£6,022,132

From Five Hundred and odd Thousand, it has grown to Six Millions. It has increased no less than twelve-fold. This is the state of the Colony trade, as compared with itself at these two periods, within this century; and this is matter for meditation. But this is not all. Examine my second account. See how the export trade to the Colonies alone in [172] 1772 stood in the other point of view, that is, as compared to the whole trade of England in 1704.

The whole export trade of England, including that to the Colonies, in 1704	£6,509,000
Export to the Colonies alone, in 1772	6,024,000
Difference,	£485,000

The trade with America alone is now within less than 500,000*l.* of being equal to what this great commercial nation, England, carried on at the beginning of this century with the whole world! If I had taken the largest year of those on your table, it would rather have exceeded. But, it will be said, is not this American trade an unnatural protuberance, that has drawn the juices from the rest of the body? The reverse. It is the very food that has nourished every other part into its present magnitude. Our general trade has been greatly augmented; and augmented more or less in almost every part to which it ever extended; but with this material difference, that of the Six Millions which in the beginning of the century constituted the whole mass of our export commerce, the Colony trade was but one twelfth part; it is now (as a part of Sixteen Millions) considerably more than a third of the whole. This is the relative proportion of the importance of the Colonies at these two periods: and all reasoning concerning our mode of treating them must have this proportion as its basis; or it is a reasoning weak, rotten, and sophistical.

Mr. Speaker, I cannot prevail on myself to hurry over this great consideration. *It is good for us to be here.* We stand where we have an immense view of what is, and what is past. Clouds, indeed, and darkness rest upon the future. Let us, however, before we descend from this noble eminence, reflect that this growth of our national prosperity has happened [173] within the short period of the life of man. It has happened within Sixty-eight years. There are those alive whose memory might touch the two extremities. For instance, my Lord Bathurst might remember all the stages of the progress. He was in 1704 of an age at least to be made to comprehend such things. He was then old enough *acta parentum jam legere, et quae sit potuit cognoscere virtus.* Suppose, Sir, that the angel of this auspicious youth, foreseeing the many virtues, which made him one of the most amiable, as he is one of the most fortunate, men of his age, had opened to him in vision, that when, in the fourth generation the third Prince of the House of Brunswick had sat Twelve years on the throne of that nation, which (by the happy issue of moderate and healing counsels) was to be made Great Britain, he should see his son, Lord Chancellor of England, turn back the current of hereditary dignity to its fountain, and raise him to a higher rank of Peerage, whilst he enriched the family with a new one—if amidst these bright and happy scenes of domestic honour and prosperity, that angel should have drawn up the curtain, and unfolded the rising glories of his country, and, whilst he was gazing with admiration on the then commercial grandeur of England, the Genius should point out to him a little speck, scarcely visible in the mass of the national interest, a small seminal principle, rather than a formed body, and should tell him—

"Young man, there is America—which at this day serves for little more than to amuse you with stories of savage men, and uncouth manners; yet shall, before you taste of death, show itself equal to the whole of that commerce which now attracts the envy of the world. Whatever England has been growing to by a progressive increase of improvement, brought in by varieties of people, by succession of civilizing conquests and civilizing settlements in a series of Seventeen Hundred years, you shall see as much [174] added to her by America in the course of a single life!" If this state of his country had been foretold to him, would it not require all the sanguine credulity of youth, and all the fervid glow of enthusiasm, to make him believe it? Fortunate man, he has lived to see it! Fortunate indeed, if he lives to see nothing that shall vary the prospect, and cloud the setting of his day!

Excuse me, Sir, if turning from such thoughts I resume this comparative view once more. You have seen it on a large scale; look at it on a small one. I will point out to your attention a particular instance of it in the single province of Pennsylvania. In the year 1704, that province called for 11,459*l.* in value of your commodities, native and foreign. This was the whole. What did it demand in 1772? Why, nearly Fifty times as much; for in that year the export to Pennsylvania was 507,909*l.*, nearly equal to the export to all the Colonies together in the first period.

I choose, Sir, to enter into these minute and particular details; because generalities, which in all other cases are apt to heighten and raise the subject, have here a tendency to sink it. When we speak of the commerce with our Colonies, fiction lags after truth; invention is unfruitful, and imagination cold and barren.

So far, Sir, as to the importance of the object, in view of its commerce, as concerned in the exports from England. If I were to detail the imports, I could show how many enjoyments they procure, which deceive the burthen of life; how

many materials which invigorate the springs of national industry, and extend and animate every part of our foreign and
domestic commerce. This would be a curious subject indeed:
but I must prescribe bounds to myself in a matter so vast and
various.

I PASS THEREFORE to the Colonies in another point of
view, [175] their agriculture. This they have prosecuted with
such a spirit, that, besides feeding plentifully their own growing multitude, their annual export of grain, comprehending
rice, has some years ago exceeded a million in value. Of their
last harvest, I am persuaded they will export much more. At
the beginning of the century some of these colonies imported
corn from the mother country. For some time past, the Old
World has been fed from the New. The scarcity which you
have felt would have been a desolating famine, if this child
of your old age, with a true filial piety, with a Roman charity,
had not put the full breast of its youthful exuberance to the
mouth of its exhausted parent.

AS TO THE WEALTH which the Colonies have drawn from
the sea by their fisheries, you had all that matter fully opened
at your bar. You surely thought those acquisitions of value,
for they seemed even to excite your envy; and yet the spirit
by which that enterprising employment has been exercised,
ought rather, in my opinion, to have raised your esteem and
admiration. And pray, Sir, what in the world is equal to it?
Pass by the other parts, and look at the manner in which the
people of New England have of late carried on the Whale
Fishery. Whilst we follow them among the tumbling mountains of ice, and behold them penetrating into the deepest
frozen recesses of Hudson's Bay and Davis's Streights, whilst
we are looking for them beneath the Arctic Circle, we hear
that they have pierced into the opposite region of polar
cold, that they are at the antipodes, and engaged under the

frozen Serpent of the south. Falkland Island, which seemed too remote and romantic an object for the grasp of national ambition, is but a stage and resting-place in the progress of their victorious industry. Nor is the equinoctial heat more discouraging to them, than the accumulated winter of both the poles. We know that whilst some of them draw the line [176] and strike the harpoon on the coast of Africa, others run the longitude, and pursue their gigantic game along the coast of Brazil. No sea but what is vexed by their fisheries. No climate that is not witness to their toils. Neither the perseverance of Holland, nor the activity of France, nor the dexterous and firm sagacity of English enterprize, ever carried this most perilous mode of hardy industry to the extent to which it has been pushed by this recent people; a people who are still, as it were, but in the gristle, and not yet hardened into the bone of manhood. When I contemplate these things; when I know that the Colonies in general owe little or nothing to any care of ours, and that they are not squeezed into this happy form by the constraints of watchful and suspicious government, but that, through a wise and salutary neglect, a generous nature has been suffered to take her own way to perfection; when I reflect upon these effects, when I see how profitable they have been to us, I feel all the pride of power sink, and all presumption in the wisdom of human contrivances melt and die away within me. My rigour relents. I pardon something to the spirit of liberty.

I AM SENSIBLE, SIR, that all which I have asserted in my detail, is admitted in the gross; but that quite a different conclusion is drawn from it. America, Gentlemen say, is a noble object. It is an object well worth fighting for. Certainly it is, if fighting a people be the best way of gaining them. Gentlemen in this respect will be led to their choice of means by their complexions and their habits. Those who understand the military art, will of course have some predilection for it.

Those who wield the thunder of the state, may have more confidence in the efficacy of arms. But I confess, possibly for want of this knowledge, my opinion is much more in favour of prudent management, than of force; considering force not as an odious, but a feeble instrument, [177] for preserving a people so numerous, so active, so growing, so spirited as this, in a profitable and subordinate connexion with us.

First, Sir, permit me to observe, that the use of force alone is but *temporary*. It may subdue for a moment; but it does not remove the necessity of subduing again: and a nation is not governed, which is perpetually to be conquered.

My next objection is its *uncertainty*. Terror is not always the effect of force; and an armament is not a victory. If you do not succeed, you are without resource; for, conciliation failing, force remains; but, force failing, no further hope of reconciliation is left. Power and authority are sometimes bought by kindness; but they can never be begged as alms by an impoverished and defeated violence.

A further objection to force is, that you *impair the object* by your very endeavours to preserve it. The thing you fought for is not the thing which you recover; but depreciated, sunk, wasted, and consumed in the contest. Nothing less will content me, than *whole America*. I do not choose to consume its strength along with our own; because in all parts it is the British strength that I consume. I do not choose to be caught by a foreign enemy at the end of this exhausting conflict; and still less in the midst of it. I may escape; but I can make no insurance against such an event. Let me add, that I do not choose wholly to break the American spirit; because it is the spirit that has made the country.

Lastly, we have no sort of *experience* in favour of force as an instrument in the rule of our Colonies. Their growth and their utility has been owing to methods altogether different. Our ancient indulgence has been said to be pursued to a fault. It may be so. But we know, if feeling is evidence, that our fault was more tolerable than our attempt [178] to mend it; and our sin far more salutary than our penitence.

THESE, SIR, ARE MY REASONS for not entertaining that high opinion of untried force, by which many Gentlemen, for whose sentiments in other particulars I have great respect, seem to be so greatly captivated. But there is still behind a third consideration concerning this object, which serves to determine my opinion on the sort of policy which ought to be pursued in the management of America, even more than its population and its commerce, I mean its *Temper and Character.*

In this Character of the Americans, a love of Freedom is the predominating feature which marks and distinguishes the whole: and as an ardent is always a jealous affection, your Colonies become suspicious, restive, and untractable, whenever they see the least attempt to wrest from them by force, or shuffle from them by chicane, what they think the only advantage worth living for. This fierce spirit of Liberty is stronger in the English Colonies probably than in any other people of the earth; and this from a great variety of powerful causes; which, to understand the true temper of their minds, and the direction which this spirit takes, it will not be amiss to lay open somewhat more largely.

First, the people of the Colonies are descendants of Englishmen. England, Sir, is a nation, which still I hope respects, and formerly adored, her freedom. The Colonists emigrated from you when this part of your character was most predominant; and they took this bias and direction the moment they parted from your hands. They are therefore not only devoted to Liberty, but to Liberty according to English ideas, and on English principles. Abstract Liberty, like other mere abstractions, is not to be found. Liberty inheres in some sensible object; and every nation [179] has formed to itself some favourite point, which by way of eminence becomes the criterion of their happiness. It happened, you know, Sir, that the great contests for freedom in this country were from the earliest times chiefly upon the question of Taxing. Most of the contests in the ancient commonwealths turned primarily on the right of election of magistrates; or on the balance among the several orders of the state. The question of money was not with them so immediate. But in England it was otherwise. On this point of Taxes the ablest pens, and most eloquent tongues, have been exercised; the greatest spirits have acted and suffered. In order to give the fullest satisfaction concerning the importance of this point, it was not only necessary for those who in argument defended the excellence of the English Constitution, to insist on this privilege of granting money as a dry point of fact, and to prove, that the right had been acknowledged in ancient parchments, and blind usages, to reside in a certain body called an House of Commons. They went much farther; they attempted to prove, and they succeeded, that in theory it ought to be so, from the particular nature of an House of Commons, as an immediate representative of the people; whether the old records had delivered this oracle or not. They took infinite pains to inculcate, as a fundamental principle, that in all monarchies the people must in effect themselves, mediately or immediately, possess the power of granting their own money, or no shadow of liberty can subsist. The Colonies draw from you, as with their life-blood, these ideas and principles. Their love of liberty, as with you, fixed and attached on this specific point of taxing. Liberty might be safe, or might be endangered, in twenty other particulars, without their being much pleased or alarmed. Here they felt its pulse; and as they found that beat, they thought themselves sick or sound. I do not say whether they were [180] right or wrong in applying your general arguments to their own case. It is not easy indeed to make a monopoly of theorems and corollaries. The fact is, that they did thus apply those general arguments; and your mode of governing them, whether through lenity or indolence, through wisdom or mistake, confirmed them in the imagination, that they, as well as you, had an interest in these common principles.

They were further confirmed in this pleasing error by the form of their provincial legislative assemblies. Their governments are popular in an high degree; some are merely popular; in all, the popular representative is the most weighty; and this share of the people in their ordinary government never fails to inspire them with lofty sentiments, and with a strong aversion from whatever tends to deprive them of their chief importance.

If anything were wanting to this necessary operation of the form of government, religion would have given it a complete effect. Religion, always a principle of energy, in this new people is no way worn out or impaired; and their mode of professing it is also one main cause of this free spirit. The people are protestants; and of that kind which is the most adverse to all implicit submission of mind and opinion. This is a persuasion not only favourable to liberty, but built upon it. I do not think, Sir, that the reason of this averseness in the dissenting churches, from all that looks like absolute government, is so much to be sought in their religious tenets, as in their history. Every one knows that the Roman Catholick religion is at least coeval with most of the governments where it prevails; that it has generally gone hand in hand with them, and received great favour and every kind of support from authority. The Church of England too was formed from her cradle under the nursing care of regular government. But the dissenting interests have sprung up in direct opposition to all the ordinary powers of the world; [181] and could justify that opposition only on a strong claim to natural liberty. Their very existence depended on the powerful and unremitted assertion of that claim. All protestantism, even the most cold and passive, is a sort of dissent. But the religion most prevalent in our Northern Colonies is a refinement on the principle of resistance; it is the dissidence of dissent, and the protestantism of the protestant religion. This religion, under a variety of denominations agreeing in nothing but in the communion of the spirit of liberty, is predominant in most of the Northern provinces; where the Church of England, notwithstanding its legal rights, is in reality no more than a sort of private sect, not composing most probably the tenth of the people. The Colonists left England when this spirit was high, and in the emigrants was the highest of all; and even that stream of foreigners, which has been constantly flowing into these Colonies, has, for the greatest part, been composed of dissenters from the establishments of their several countries, and have brought with them a temper and character far from alien to that of the people with whom they mixed.

Sir, I can perceive by their manner, that some Gentlemen object to the latitude of this description; because in the Southern Colonies the Church of England forms a large body, and has a regular establishment. It is certainly true. There is, however, a circumstance attending these Colonies, which, in my opinion, fully counterbalances this difference, and makes the spirit of liberty still more high and haughty than in those to the North-ward. It is, that in Virginia and the Carolinas they have a vast multitude of slaves. Where this is the case in any part of the world, those who are free, are by far the most proud and jealous of their freedom. Freedom is to them not only an enjoyment, but a kind of rank and privilege. Not seeing there, that freedom, as in countries where it is a common blessing, and as broad and general [182] as the air, may be united with much abject toil, with great misery, with all the exterior of servitude, liberty looks, amongst them, like something that is more noble and liberal. I do not mean, Sir, to commend the superior morality of this sentiment, which has at least as much pride as virtue in it; but I cannot alter the nature of man. The fact is so; and these people of the Southern Colonies are much more strongly, and with an higher and more stubborn spirit, attached to liberty, than those to the North-ward. Such were all the ancient commonwealths; such were our Gothick ancestors; such in our days were the Poles; and such will be all masters of slaves, who are not slaves themselves. In such a people, the haughtiness of domination combines with the spirit of freedom, fortifies it, and renders it invincible.

Permit me, Sir, to add another circumstance in our Colonies, which contributes no mean part towards the growth and effect of this untractable spirit. I mean their education. In no country perhaps in the world is the law so general a study. The profession itself is numerous and powerful; and in most provinces it takes the lead. The greater number of the Deputies sent to the Congress were Lawyers. But all who read, (and most do read,) endeavour to obtain some smattering in that science. I have been told by an eminent Bookseller, that in no branch of his business, after tracts of popular devotion, were so many books as those on the Law exported to the Plantations. The Colonists have now fallen into the way of printing them for their own use. I hear that they have sold nearly as many of Blackstone's Commentaries in America as in England. General Gage marks out this disposition very particularly in a letter on your table. He states, that all the people in his government are lawyers, or smatterers in law; and that in Boston they have been enabled, by successful chicane, wholly to evade many parts of one of your capital penal constitutions. The smartness of debate [183] will say, that this knowledge ought to teach them more clearly the rights of legislature, their obligations to obedience, and the penalties of rebellion. All this is mighty well. But my Honourable and Learned Friend on the floor, who condescends to mark what I say for animadversion, will disdain that ground. He has heard, as well as I, that when great honours and great emoluments do not win over this knowledge to the service of the state, it is a formidable adversary to government. If the spirit be not tamed and broken by these happy methods, it is stubborn and litigious. *Abeunt studia in mores.* This study renders men acute, inquisitive, dexterous, prompt in attack, ready in defence, full of resources. In other countries, the people, more simple, and of a less mercurial cast, judge of an ill principle in government only by an actual grievance; here they anticipate the evil, and judge of the pressure of the grievance by the badness of the principle. They augur mis-government at a distance; and snuff the approach of tyranny in every tainted breeze.

The last cause of this disobedient spirit in the Colonies is hardly less powerful than the rest, as it is not merely moral, but laid deep in the natural constitution of things. Three thousand miles of ocean lie between you and them. No contrivance can prevent the effect of this distance in weakening government. Seas roll, and months pass, between the order and the execution; and the want of a speedy explanation of a single point is enough to defeat a whole system. You have, indeed, winged ministers of vengeance, who carry your bolts in their pounces to the remotest verge of the sea. But there a power steps in, that limits the arrogance of raging passions and furious elements, and says, *So far shalt thou go, and no farther.* Who are you, that you should fret and rage, and bite the chains of Nature? Nothing worse happens to you than does to all nations who have extensive Empire; and it happens in all the forms into which Empire can be [184] thrown. In large bodies, the circulation of power must be less vigorous at the extremities. Nature has said it. The Turk cannot govern Aegypt, and Arabia, and Curdistan, as he governs Thrace; nor has he the same dominion in Crimea and Algiers, which he has at Brusa and Smyrna. Despotism itself is obliged to truck and huckster. The Sultan gets such obedience as he can. He governs with a loose rein, that he may govern at all; and the whole of the force and vigour of his authority in his centre is derived from a prudent relaxation in all his borders. Spain, in her provinces, is, perhaps, not so well obeyed as you are in yours. She complies too; she submits; she watches times. This is the immutable condition, the eternal Law, of extensive and detached Empire.

Then, Sir, from these six capital sources; of Descent; of Form of Government; of Religion in the Northern Provinces; of Manners in the Southern; of Education; of the Remoteness of Situation from the First Mover of Government; from all these causes a fierce Spirit of Liberty has grown up. It has grown with the growth of the people in your Colonies, and increased with the increase of their wealth; a Spirit, that unhappily meeting with an exercise of Power in England, which, however lawful, is not reconcileable to any ideas of Liberty, much less with theirs, has kindled this flame that is ready to consume us.

I DO NOT MEAN TO COMMEND either the Spirit in this excess, or the moral causes which produce it. Perhaps a more smooth and accommodating Spirit of Freedom in them would be more acceptable to us. Perhaps ideas of Liberty might be desired, more reconcileable with an arbitrary and boundless authority. Perhaps we might wish the Colonists to be persuaded, that their Liberty is more secure when held in trust for them by us, as their guardians during a perpetual [185] minority, than with any part of it in their own hands. The question is, not whether their spirit deserves praise or blame; but—what, in the name of God, shall we do with it? You have before you the object, such as it is, with all its glories, with all its imperfections on its head. You see the magnitude; the importance; the temper; the habits; the disorders. By all these considerations we are strongly urged to determine something concerning it. We are called upon to fix some rule and line for our future conduct, which may give a little stability to our politicks, and prevent the return of such unhappy deliberations as the present. Every such return will bring the matter before us in a still more untractable form. For, what astonishing and incredible things have we not seen already! What monsters have not been generated from this unnatural contention! Whilst every principle of authority and resistance has been pushed, upon both sides, as far as it would go, there is nothing so solid and certain, either in reasoning or in practice, that has not been shaken. Until very lately, all authority in America seemed to be nothing but an emanation from yours. Even the popular part of the Colony Constitution derived all its activity, and its first vital movement, from the pleasure of the Crown. We thought, Sir, that the utmost which the discontented Colonists could do, was to disturb authority; we never dreamt they could of themselves supply it; knowing in general what an operose business it is, to establish a Government absolutely new. But having, for our purposes, in this contention, resolved, that none but an obedient Assembly should sit; the humours of the people there, finding all passage through the legal channel stopped, with great violence broke out another way. Some provinces have tried their experiment, as we have tried ours; and theirs has succeeded. They have formed a Government sufficient for its purposes, without the bustle of a Revolution, or the troublesome formality of an Election. [186] Evident necessity, and tacit consent, have done the business in an instant. So well they have done it, that Lord Dunmore (the account is among the fragments on your table) tells you, that the new institution is infinitely better obeyed than the antient Government ever was in its most fortunate periods. Obedience is what makes Government, and not the names by which it is called; not the name of Governor, as formerly, or Committee, as at present. This new Government has originated directly from the people; and was not transmitted through any of the ordinary artificial media of a positive constitution. It was not a manufacture ready formed, and transmitted to them in that condition from England. The evil arising from hence is this; that the Colonists having once found the possibility of enjoying the advantages of order in the midst of a struggle for Liberty, such struggles will not henceforward seem so terrible to the settled and sober part of mankind as they had appeared before the trial.

Pursuing the same plan of punishing by the denial of the exercise of Government to still greater lengths, we wholly abrogated the antient Government of Massachuset. We were confident that the first feeling, if not the very prospect of anarchy, would instantly enforce a compleat submission. The experiment was tried. A new, strange, unexpected face of things appeared. Anarchy is found tolerable. A vast province has now subsisted, and subsisted in a considerable degree of health and vigour, for near a twelvemonth, without Governor, without public Council, without Judges, without executive Magistrates. How long it will continue in this state, or what may arise out of this unheard-of situation, how can the wisest of us conjecture? Our late experience has taught us that many of those fundamental principles, formerly believed infallible, are either not of the importance they were imagined to be; or that we have not at all adverted to some other far more important and far more powerful [187] principles, which entirely overrule those we had considered as omnipotent. I am much against any further experiments, which tend to put to the proof any more of these allowed opinions, which contribute so much to the public tranquillity. In effect, we suffer as much at home by this loosening of all ties, and this concussion of all established opinions, as we do abroad. For, in order to prove that the Americans have no right to their Liberties, we are every day endeavouring to subvert the maxims, which preserve the whole Spirit of our own. To prove that the Americans ought not to be free, we are obliged to depreciate the value of Freedom itself; and we never seem to gain a paltry advantage over them in debate, without attacking some of those principles, or deriding some of those feelings, for which our ancestors have shed their blood.

But, Sir, in wishing to put an end to pernicious experiments, I do not mean to preclude the fullest enquiry. Far from it. Far from deciding on a sudden or partial view, I would patiently go round and round the subject, and survey it minutely in every possible aspect. Sir, if I were capable of engaging you to an equal attention, I would state, that, as far as I am capable of discerning, there are but three ways of proceeding relative to this stubborn Spirit, which prevails in your Colonies, and disturbs your Government. These are—To change that Spirit, as inconvenient, by removing the Causes. To prosecute it as criminal. Or, to comply with it as necessary. I would not be guilty of an imperfect enumeration; I can think of but these three. Another has indeed been started, that of giving up the Colonies; but it met so slight a reception, that I do not think myself obliged to dwell a great while upon it. It is nothing but a little sally of anger; like the frowardness of peevish children; who, when they cannot get all they would have, are resolved to take nothing.

[188] THE FIRST OF THESE PLANS, to change the Spirit as inconvenient, by removing the causes, I think is the most like a systematick proceeding. It is radical in its principle; but it is attended with great difficulties, some of them little short, as I conceive, of impossibilities. This will appear by examining into the Plans which have been proposed.

As the growing population in the Colonies is evidently one cause of their resistance, it was last session mentioned in both Houses, by men of weight, and received not without applause, that in order to check this evil, it would be proper for the Crown to make no further grants of land. But to this scheme there are two objections. The first, that there is already so much unsettled land in private hands, as to afford room for an immense future population, although the Crown not only withheld its grants, but annihilated its soil. If this be the case, then the only effect of this avarice of desolation, this hoarding of a royal wilderness, would be to raise the value of the possessions in the hands of the great private monopolists, without any adequate check to the growing and alarming mischief of population.

But if you stopped your grants, what would be the consequence? The people would occupy without grants. They have already so occupied in many places. You cannot station garrisons in every part of these deserts. If you drive the people from one place, they will carry on their annual Tillage, and remove with their flocks and herds to another. Many of the people in the back settlements are already little attached to particular situations. Already they have topped the Appalachian mountains. From thence they behold before them an immense plain, one vast, rich, level meadow; a square of five hundred miles. Over this they would wander without a possibility of restraint; they would change their manners with the habits of their life; would soon forget a government by which they were disowned; would become Hordes of [189] English Tartars; and pouring down upon your unfortified frontiers a fierce and irresistible cavalry, become masters of your Governors and your Counsellors, your collectors, and comptrollers, and of all the Slaves that adhered to them. Such would, and, in no long time, must be, the effect of attempting to forbid as a crime, and to suppress as an evil, the Command and Blessing of Providence, *Encrease and Multiply*. Such would be the happy result of the endeavour to keep as a lair of wild beasts, that earth, which God, by an express Charter, has *given to the children of men*. Far different, and surely much wiser, has been our policy hitherto. Hitherto we have invited our people, by every kind of bounty, to fixed establishments. We have invited the husbandman to look to authority for his title. We have taught him piously to believe in the mysterious virtue of wax and parchment. We have thrown each tract of land, as it was peopled, into districts; that the ruling power should never be wholly out of sight. We have settled all we could; and we have carefully attended every settlement with government.

Adhering, Sir, as I do, to this policy, as well as for the reasons I have just given, I think this new project of hedging-in population to be neither prudent nor practicable.

To impoverish the Colonies in general, and in particular to arrest the noble course of their marine enterprizes, would be a more easy task. I freely confess it. We have shown a disposition to a system of this kind; a disposition even to continue the restraint after the offence; looking on ourselves as rivals to our Colonies, and persuaded that of course we must gain all that they shall lose. Much mischief we may certainly do. The power inadequate to all other things is often more than sufficient for this. I do not look on the direct and immediate power of the Colonies to resist our violence as very formidable. In this, however, I may be mistaken. But when I consider, that we have Colonies for [190] no purpose but to be serviceable to us, it seems to my poor understanding a little preposterous, to make them unserviceable, in order to keep them obedient. It is, in truth, nothing more than the old, and, as I thought, exploded problem of tyranny, which proposes to beggar its subjects into submission. But remember, when you have completed your system of impoverishment, that nature still proceeds in her ordinary course; that discontent will encrease with misery; and that there are critical moments in the fortune of all states, when they who are too weak to contribute to your prosperity, may be strong enough to complete your ruin. *Spoliatis arma supersunt.*

The temper and character which prevail in our Colonies, are, I am afraid, unalterable by any human art. We cannot, I fear, falsify the pedigree of this fierce people, and persuade them that they are not sprung from a nation in whose veins the blood of freedom circulates. The language in which they would hear you tell them this tale would detect the imposition; your speech would betray you. An Englishman is the unfittest person on earth, to argue another Englishman into slavery.

I think it is nearly as little in our power to change their republican Religion, as their free descent; or to substitute the Roman Catholick, as a penalty; or the Church of England, as an improvement. The mode of inquisition and dragooning is going out of fashion in the Old World; and I should not confide much to their efficacy in the New. The education of the Americans is also on the same unalterable bottom with their religion. You cannot persuade them to burn their books of curious science; to banish their lawyers from their courts of laws; or to quench the lights of their assemblies, by refusing to choose those persons who are best read in their privileges. It would be no less impracticable to think of wholly annihilating the popular [191] assemblies, in which these lawyers sit. The army, by which we must govern in their place, would be far more chargeable to us; not quite so effectual; and perhaps, in the end, full as difficult to be kept in obedience.

With regard to the high aristocratick spirit of Virginia and the Southern Colonies, it has been proposed, I know, to reduce it, by declaring a general enfranchisement of their slaves. This project has had its advocates and panegyrists; yet I never could argue myself into any opinion of it. Slaves are often much attached to their masters. A general wild offer of liberty would not always be accepted. History furnishes few instances of it. It is sometimes as hard to persuade slaves to be free, as it is to compel freemen to be slaves; and in this auspicious scheme, we should have both these pleasing tasks on our hands at once. But when we talk of enfranchisement, do we not perceive that the American master may enfranchise too; and arm servile hands in defence of freedom? A measure to which other people have had recourse more than once, and not without success, in a desperate situation of their affairs.

Slaves as these unfortunate black people are, and dull as all men are from slavery, must they not a little suspect the offer of freedom from that very nation which has sold them to their present masters? from that nation, one of whose causes of quarrel with those masters is their refusal to deal any more in that inhuman traffick? An offer of freedom from England would come rather oddly, shipped to them in an African vessel, which is refused an entry into the ports of Virginia or Carolina, with a cargo of three hundred Angola negroes. It would be curious to see the Guinea captain attempting at the same instant to publish his proclamation of liberty, and to advertise his sale of slaves.

But let us suppose all these moral difficulties got over. The Ocean remains. You cannot pump this dry; and as [192] long as it continues in its present bed, so long all the causes which weaken authority by distance will continue. "*Ye gods, annihilate but space and time, And make two lovers happy!*" was a pious and passionate prayer; but just as reasonable, as many of the serious wishes of very grave and solemn politicians.

IF THEN, SIR, it seems almost desperate to think of any alterative course, for changing the moral causes, and not quite easy to remove the natural, which produce prejudices irreconcileable to the late exercise of our authority; but that the spirit infallibly will continue; and, continuing, will produce such effects as now embarrass us; the second mode under consideration is, to prosecute that spirit in its overt acts, as *criminal.*

At this proposition I must pause a moment. The thing seems a great deal too big for my ideas of jurisprudence. It should seem to my way of conceiving such matters, that there is a very wide difference in reason and policy, between the mode of proceeding on the irregular conduct of scattered individuals, or even of bands of men, who disturb order within the state, and the civil dissensions which may, from time to time, on great questions, agitate the several communities which compose a great Empire. It looks to me to be narrow and pedantic, to apply the ordinary ideas of criminal justice to this great public contest. I do not know the method of drawing up an indictment against a whole people. I cannot insult and ridicule the feelings of Millions of my fellow-creatures, as Sir Edward Coke insulted one excellent individual (Sir Walter Rawleigh) at the bar. I hope I am not ripe to pass sentence on the gravest public bodies, intrusted with magistracies of great authority and dignity, and charged with the safety of their fellow-citizens, upon the very same title that I am. I really think, that for [193] wise men, this is not judicious; for sober men, not decent; for minds tinctured with humanity, not mild and merciful.

Perhaps, Sir, I am mistaken in my idea of an Empire, as distinguished from a single State or Kingdom. But my idea of it is this; that an Empire is the aggregate of many States under one common head; whether this head be a monarch, or a presiding republick. It does, in such constitutions, frequently happen (and nothing but the dismal, cold, dead uniformity of servitude can prevent its happening) that the subordinate parts have many local privileges and immunities. Between these privileges and the supreme common authority the line may be extremely nice. Of course disputes, often, too, very bitter disputes, and much ill blood, will arise. But though every privilege is an exemption (in the case) from the ordinary exercise of the supreme authority, it is no denial of it. The claim of a privilege seems rather, *ex vi termini,* to imply a superior power. For to talk of the privileges of a State, or of a person, who has no superior, is hardly any better than speaking nonsense. Now, in such unfortunate quarrels among the component parts of a great political union of communities, I can scarcely conceive anything more compleatly imprudent, than for the Head of the Empire to insist, that, if any privilege is pleaded against his will, or his acts, his whole authority is denied; instantly to proclaim rebellion, to beat to arms, and to put the offending provinces under the ban. Will not this, Sir, very soon teach the provinces to make no distinctions on their part? Will it not teach them that the Government, against which a claim of Liberty is tantamount to high-treason, is a Government to which submission is equivalent to slavery? It may not always be quite convenient to impress dependent communities with such an idea.

We are indeed, in all disputes with the Colonies, by the necessity of things, the judge. It is true, Sir. But I confess, [194] that the character of judge in my own cause is a thing that frightens me. Instead of filling me with pride, I am exceedingly humbled by it. I cannot proceed with a stern, assured, judicial confidence, until I find myself in something more like a judicial character. I must have these hesitations as long as I am compelled to recollect, that, in my little reading upon such contests as these, the sense of mankind has, at least, as often decided against the superior as the subordinate power. Sir, let me add too, that the opinion of my having some abstract right in my favour, would not put me much at my ease in passing sentence; unless I could be sure, that there were no rights which, in their exercise under certain circumstances, were not the most odious of all wrongs, and the most vexatious of all injustice. Sir, these considerations have great weight with me, when I find things so circumstanced, that I see the same party, at once a civil litigant against me in point of right; and a culprit before me, while I sit as a criminal judge, on acts of his, whose moral quality is to be decided upon the merits of that very litigation. Men are every now and then put, by the complexity of human affairs, into strange situations; but Justice is the same, let the Judge be in what situation he will.

There is, Sir, also a circumstance which convinces me, that this mode of criminal proceeding is not (at least in the present stage of our contest) altogether expedient; which is nothing less than the conduct of those very persons who have seemed to adopt that mode, by lately declaring a rebellion in Massachuset's Bay, as they had formerly addressed to have

Traitors brought hither, under an Act of Henry the Eighth, for Trial. For though rebellion is declared, it is not proceeded against as such; nor have any steps been taken towards the apprehension or conviction of any individual offender, either on our late or our former Address; but modes of public coercion have been adopted, and such as have much [195] more resemblance to a sort of qualified hostility towards an independent power than the punishment of rebellious subjects. All this seems rather inconsistent; but it shows how difficult it is to apply these juridical ideas to our present case.

In this situation, let us seriously and coolly ponder. What is it we have got by all our menaces, which have been many and ferocious? What advantage have we derived from the penal laws we have passed, and which, for the time, have been severe and numerous? What advances have we made towards our object, by the sending of a force, which, by land and sea, is no contemptible strength? Has the disorder abated? Nothing less. When I see things in this situation, after such confident hopes, bold promises, and active exertions, I cannot, for my life, avoid a suspicion, that the plan itself is not correctly right.

IF THEN THE REMOVAL of the causes of this Spirit of American Liberty be, for the greater part, or rather entirely, impracticable; if the ideas of Criminal Process be inapplicable, or if applicable, are in the highest degree inexpedient; what way yet remains? No way is open, but the third and last—to comply with the American Spirit as necessary; or, if you please, to submit to it as a necessary Evil.

If we adopt this mode; if we mean to conciliate and concede; let us see of what nature the concession ought to be: to ascertain the nature of our concession, we must look at their complaint. The Colonies complain, that they have not the characteristic Mark and Seal of British Freedom. They complain, that they are taxed in a Parliament, in which they are not represented. If you mean to satisfy them at all, you must satisfy them with regard to this complaint. If you mean to please any people, you must give them the boon which they ask; not what you may think better for them, [196] but of a kind totally different. Such an act may be a wise regulation, but it is no concession: whereas our present theme is the mode of giving satisfaction.

SIR, I THINK YOU MUST PERCEIVE, that I am resolved this day to have nothing at all to do with the question of the right of taxation. Some gentlemen startle—but it is true; I put it totally out of the question. It is less than nothing in my consideration. I do not indeed wonder, nor will you, Sir, that gentlemen of profound learning are fond of displaying it on this profound subject. But my consideration is narrow, confined, and wholly limited to the Policy of the question. I do not examine, whether the giving away a man's money be a power excepted and reserved out of the general trust of government; and how far all mankind, in all forms of Polity, are entitled to an exercise of that Right by the Charter of Nature. Or whether, on the contrary, a Right of Taxation is necessarily involved in the general principle of Legislation, and inseparable from the ordinary Supreme Power. These are deep questions, where great names militate against each other; where reason is perplexed; and an appeal to authorities only thickens the confusion. For high and reverend authorities lift up their heads on both sides; and there is no sure footing in the middle. This point is the *great Serbonian bog, Betwixt Damiata and Mount Casius old, Where armies whole have sunk.* I do not intend to be overwhelmed in that bog, though in such respectable company. The question with me is, not whether you have a right to render your people miserable; but whether it is not your interest to make them happy. It is not, what a lawyer tells me I *may* do; but what humanity, reason, and justice tell me I *ought* to do. Is a politic act the worse for being a generous one? Is no concession proper, but that which is made from your want of right to keep what you grant? Or does it lessen the [197] grace or dignity of relaxing in the exercise of an odious claim, because you have your evidence-room full of Titles, and your magazines stuffed with arms to enforce them? What signify all those titles, and all those arms? Of what avail are they, when the reason of the thing tells me, that the assertion of my title is the loss of my suit; and that I could do nothing but wound myself by the use of my own weapons?

Such is stedfastly my opinion of the absolute necessity of keeping up the concord of this Empire by an unity of spirit, though in a diversity of operations, that, if I were sure the colonists had, at their leaving this country, sealed a regular compact of servitude; that they had solemnly abjured all the rights of citizens; that they had made a vow to renounce all Ideas of Liberty for them and their posterity to all generations; yet I should hold myself obliged to conform to the temper I found universally prevalent in my own day, and to govern two million of men, impatient of Servitude, on the principles of Freedom. I am not determining a point of law; I am restoring tranquillity; and the general character and situation of a people must determine what sort of government is fitted for them. That point nothing else can or ought to determine.

My idea, therefore, without considering whether we yield as matter of right, or grant as matter of favour, is *to admit the people of our Colonies into an interest in the Constitution;* and, by recording that admission in the Journals of Parliament, to give them as strong an assurance as the nature of the thing will admit, that we mean for ever to adhere to that solemn declaration of systematic indulgence.

Some years ago, the Repeal of a Revenue Act, upon its understood principle, might have served to show, that we intended an unconditional abatement of the exercise of a Taxing Power. Such a measure was then sufficient to [198] remove all suspicion, and to give perfect content. But unfortunate events, since that time, may make something further necessary; and not more necessary for the satisfaction of the Colonies, than for the dignity and consistency of our own future proceedings.

I HAVE TAKEN a very incorrect measure of the disposition of the House, if this proposal in itself would be received with dislike. I think, Sir, we have few American Financiers. But our misfortune is, we are too acute; we are too exquisite in our conjectures of the future, for men oppressed with such great and present evils. The more moderate among the opposers of Parliamentary Concession freely confess, that they hope no good from Taxation; but they apprehend the Colonists have further views; and if this point were conceded, they would instantly attack the Trade Laws. These Gentlemen are convinced, that this was the intention from the beginning; and the quarrel of the Americans with Taxation was no more than a cloak and cover to this design. Such has been the language even of a Gentleman of real moderation, and of a natural temper well adjusted to fair and equal Government. I am, however, Sir, not a little surprized at this kind of discourse, whenever I hear it; and I am the more surprized, on account of the arguments which I constantly find in company with it, and which are often urged from the same mouths, and on the same day.

For instance, when we alledge, that it is against reason to tax a people under so many restraints in trade as the Americans, the Noble Lord in the blue ribband shall tell you, that the restraints on trade are futile and useless; of no advantage to us, and of no burthen to those on whom they are imposed; that the trade to America is not secured by the Acts of Navigation, but by the natural and irresistible advantage of a commercial preference.

[199] Such is the merit of the Trade Laws in this pos-

ture of the debate. But when strong internal circumstances are urged against the taxes; when the scheme is dissected; when experience and the nature of things are brought to prove, and do prove, the utter impossibility of obtaining an effective revenue from the Colonies; when these things are pressed, or rather press themselves, so as to drive the advocates of Colony Taxes to a clear admission of the futility of the scheme; then, Sir, the sleeping Trade Laws revive from their trance; and this useless taxation is to be kept sacred, not for its own sake, but as a counter-guard and security of the laws of trade.

Then, Sir, you keep up Revenue Laws which are mischievous, in order to preserve Trade Laws that are useless. Such is the wisdom of our plan in both its members. They are separately given up as of no value; and yet one is always to be defended for the sake of the other. But I cannot agree with the Noble Lord, nor with the pamphlet from whence he seems to have borrowed these ideas, concerning the inutility of the Trade Laws. For, without idolizing them, I am sure they are still, in many ways, of great use to us: and in former times they have been of the greatest. They do confine, and they do greatly narrow, the market for the Americans. But my perfect conviction of this does not help me in the least to discern how the Revenue Laws form any security whatsoever to the commercial regulations; or that these commercial regulations are the true ground of the quarrel; or that the giving way, in any one instance of authority, is to lose all that may remain unconceded.

One fact is clear and indisputable. The public and avowed origin of this quarrel was on taxation. This quarrel has indeed brought on new disputes on new questions; but certainly the least bitter, and the fewest of all, on the Trade Laws. To judge which of the two be the real, radical cause [200] of quarrel, we have to see whether the commercial dispute did, in order of time, precede the dispute on taxation? There is not a shadow of evidence for it. Next, to enable us to judge whether at this moment a dislike to the Trade Laws be the real cause of quarrel, it is absolutely necessary to put the taxes out of the question by a repeal. See how the Americans act in this position, and then you will be able to discern correctly what is the true object of the controversy, or whether any controversy at all will remain. Unless you consent to remove this cause of difference, it is impossible, with decency, to assert that the dispute is not upon what it is avowed to be. And I would, Sir, recommend to your serious consideration, whether it be prudent to form a rule for punishing people, not on their own acts, but on your conjectures? Surely it is preposterous at the very best. It is not justifying your anger, by their misconduct; but it is converting your ill-will into their delinquency.

But the Colonies will go further. Alas! alas! when will this speculation against fact and reason end? What will quiet these panic fears which we entertain of the hostile effect of a conciliatory conduct? Is it true, that no case can exist, in which it is proper for the Sovereign to accede to the desires of his discontented subjects? Is there anything peculiar in this case, to make a rule for itself? Is all authority of course lost, when it is not pushed to the extreme? Is it a certain maxim, that the fewer causes of dissatisfaction are left by government, the more the subject will be inclined to resist and rebel?

All these objections being in fact no more than suspicions, conjectures, divinations; formed in defiance of fact and experience; they did not, Sir, discourage me from entertaining the idea of a conciliatory concession, founded on the principles which I have just stated.

[201] IN FORMING A PLAN for this purpose, I endeavoured to put myself in that frame of mind which was the most natural, and the most reasonable; and which was certainly the most probable means of securing me from all error. I set out with a perfect distrust of my own abilities; a total renun-

ciation of every speculation of my own; and with a profound reverence for the wisdom of our ancestors, who have left us the inheritance of so happy a constitution, and so flourishing an empire, and what is a thousand times more valuable, the treasury of the maxims and principles which formed the one, and obtained the other.

During the reigns of the kings of Spain of the Austrian family, whenever they were at a loss in the Spanish councils, it was common for their statesmen to say, that they ought to consult the genius of Philip the Second. The genius of Philip the Second might mislead them; and the issue of their affairs showed, that they had not chosen the most perfect standard. But, Sir, I am sure that I shall not be misled, when in a case of constitutional difficulty, I consult the genius of the English Constitution. Consulting at that oracle (it was with all due humility and piety) I found four capital examples in a similar case before me; those of Ireland, Wales, Chester, and Durham.

Ireland, before the English conquest, though never governed by a despotick power, had no Parliament. How far the English Parliament itself was at that time modelled according to the present form, is disputed among antiquaries. But we have all the reason in the world to be assured that a form of Parliament, such as England then enjoyed, she instantly communicated to Ireland; and we are equally sure that almost every successive improvement in constitutional liberty, as fast as it was made here, was transmitted thither. The feudal Baronage, and the feudal Knighthood, the roots of our primitive Constitution, were early [202] transplanted into that soil; and grew and flourished there. Magna Charta, if it did not give us originally the House of Commons, gave us at least a House of Commons of weight and consequence. But your ancestors did not churlishly sit down alone to the feast of Magna Charta. Ireland was made immediately a partaker. This benefit of English laws and liberties, I confess, was not at first extended to *all* Ireland. Mark the consequence. English authority and English liberties had exactly the same boundaries. Your standard could never be advanced an inch before your privileges. Sir John Davis shows beyond a doubt, that the refusal of a general communication of these rights was the true cause why Ireland was five hundred years in subduing; and after the vain projects of a Military Government, attempted in the reign of Queen Elizabeth, it was soon discovered, that nothing could make that country English, in civility and allegiance, but your laws and your forms of legislature. It was not English arms, but the English Constitution, that conquered Ireland. From that time, Ireland has ever had a general Parliament, as she had before a partial Parliament. You changed the people; you altered the religion; but you never touched the form or the vital substance of free government in that Kingdom. You deposed kings; you restored them; you altered the succession to theirs, as well as to your own Crown; but you never altered their Constitution; the principle of which was respected by usurpation; restored with the restoration of Monarchy, and established, I trust, for ever, by the glorious Revolution. This has made Ireland the great and flourishing Kingdom that it is; and from a disgrace and a burthen intolerable to this nation, has rendered her a principal part of our strength and ornament. This country cannot be said to have ever formally taxed her. The irregular things done in the confusion of mighty troubles, and on the hinge of [203] great revolutions, even if all were done that is said to have been done, form no example. If they have any effect in argument, they make an exception to prove the rule. None of your own liberties could stand a moment if the casual deviations from them, at such times, were suffered to be used as proofs of their nullity. By the lucrative amount of such casual breaches in the constitution, judge what the stated and fixed rule of supply has been in that Kingdom. Your Irish pensioners would starve if they had no other fund to live on than taxes granted by English authority. Turn your eyes to those popular grants from whence all your great supplies are come; and learn to respect that only source of public wealth in the British Empire.

My next example is Wales. This country was said to be reduced by Henry the Third. It was said more truly to be so by Edward the First. But though then conquered, it was not looked upon as any part of the Realm of England. Its old Constitution, whatever that might have been, was destroyed; and no good one was substituted in its place. The care of that tract was put into the hands of Lords Marchers—a form of government of a very singular kind; a strange heterogeneous monster, something between Hostility and Government; perhaps it has a sort of resemblance, according to the modes of those terms, to that of Commander-in-chief at present, to whom all civil power is granted as secondary. The manners of the Welsh nation followed the Genius of the Government; the people were ferocious, restive, savage, and uncultivated; sometimes composed, never pacified. Wales, within itself, was in perpetual disorder; and it kept the frontier of England in perpetual alarm. Benefits from it to the state, there were none. Wales was only known to England by incursion and invasion.

Sir, during that state of things, Parliament was not idle. [204] They attempted to subdue the fierce spirit of the Welsh by all sorts of rigorous laws. They prohibited by statute the sending all sorts of arms into Wales, as you prohibit by proclamation (with something more of doubt on the legality) the sending arms to America. They disarmed the Welsh by statute, as you attempted (but still with more question on the legality) to disarm New England by an instruction. They made an Act to drag offenders from Wales into England for trial, as you have done (but with more hardship) with regard to America. By another Act, where one of the parties was an Englishman, they ordained, that his trial should be always by English. They made Acts to restrain trade, as you do; and they prevented the Welsh from the use of fairs and markets, as you do the Americans from fisheries and foreign ports. In short, when the Statute Book was not quite so much swelled as it is now, you find no less than fifteen acts of penal regulation on the subject of Wales.

Here we rub our hands—A fine body of precedents for the authority of Parliament and the use of it!—I admit it fully; and pray add likewise to these precedents, that all the while, Wales rid this Kingdom like an *incubus;* that it was an unprofitable and oppressive burthen; and that an Englishman travelling in that country could not go six yards from the high road without being murdered.

The march of the human mind is slow. Sir, it was not, until after Two Hundred years, discovered, that, by an eternal law, Providence had decreed vexation to violence; and poverty to rapine. Your ancestors did however at length open their eyes to the ill husbandry of injustice. They found that the tyranny of a free people could of all tyrannies the least be endured; and that laws made against a whole nation were not the most effectual methods of securing its obedience. Accordingly, in the Twenty-seventh year of Henry [205] the Eighth, the course was entirely altered. With a preamble stating the entire and perfect rights of the Crown of England, it gave to the Welsh all the rights and privileges of English subjects. A political order was established; the military power gave way to the civil; the Marches were turned into Counties. But that a nation should have a right to English liberties, and yet no share at all in the fundamental security of these liberties—the grant of their own property—seemed a thing so incongruous; that, Eight years after, that is, in the Thirty-fifth of that reign, a complete and not ill proportioned representation by counties and boroughs was bestowed upon Wales, by Act of Parliament. From that moment, as by a charm, the tumults subsided; obedience was restored; peace, order, and civilization followed in the train of liberty. When the day-star of the English Constitution had arisen in their hearts, all was harmony within and without

—simul alba nautis
   Stella refulsit,
Defluit saxis agitatus humor;
Concidunt venti, fugiuntque nubes,
Et minax (quod sic voluere) ponto
   Unda recumbit.

The very same year the County Palatine of Chester received the same relief from its oppressions, and the same remedy to its disorders. Before this time Chester was little less distempered than Wales. The inhabitants, without rights themselves, were the fittest to destroy the rights of others; and from thence Richard the Second drew the standing army of Archers, with which for a time he oppressed England. The people of Chester applied to Parliament in a petition penned as I shall read to you:

To the King our Sovereign Lord, in most humble wise shewen unto your Excellent Majesty the inhabitants of your Grace's County Palatine of Chester; (1.) That [206] where the said County Palatine of Chester is and hath been always hitherto exempt, excluded and separated out and from your High Court of Parliament, to have any Knights and Burgesses within the said Court; by reason whereof the said inhabitants have hitherto sustained manifold disherisons, losses, and damages, as well in their lands, goods, and bodies, as in the good, civil, and politic governance and maintenance of the commonwealth of their said country: (2.) And forasmuch as the said inhabitants have always hitherto been bound by the Acts and Statutes made and ordained by your said Highness, and your most noble progenitors, by authority of the said Court, as far forth as other counties, cities, and boroughs have been, that have had their Knights and Burgesses within your said Court of Parliament, and yet have had neither Knight ne Burgess there for the said County Palatine; the said inhabitants, for lack thereof, have been oftentimes touched and grieved with Acts and Statutes made within the said Court, as well derogatory unto the most ancient jurisdictions, liberties, and privileges of your said County Palatine, as prejudicial unto the commonwealth, quietness, rest, and peace of your Grace's most bounden subjects inhabiting within the same.

What did Parliament with this audacious address?—Reject it as a libel? Treat it as an affront to Government? Spurn it as a derogation from the rights of legislature? Did they toss it over the table? Did they burn it by the hands of the common hangman?—They took the petition of grievance, all rugged as it was, without softening or temperament, unpurged of the original bitterness and indignation of complaint; they made it the very preamble to their Act of redress; and consecrated its principle to all ages in the sanctuary of legislation.

Here is my third example. It was attended with the success of the two former. Chester, civilized as well as Wales, has demonstrated that freedom, and not servitude, is the cure [207] of anarchy; as religion, and not atheism, is the true remedy for superstition. Sir, this pattern of Chester was followed in the reign of Charles the Second, with regard to the County Palatine of Durham, which is my fourth example. This county had long lain out of the pale of free legislation. So scrupulously was the example of Chester followed, that the style of the preamble is nearly the same with that of the Chester Act; and, without affecting the abstract extent of the authority of Parliament, it recognises the equity of not suffering any considerable district, in which the British subjects may act as a body, to be taxed without their own voice in the grant.

NOW IF THE DOCTRINES of policy contained in these preambles, and the force of these examples in the Acts of Parliaments, avail anything, what can be said against applying them with regard to America? Are not the people of America as much Englishmen as the Welsh? The preamble of the Act of Henry the Eighth says, the Welsh speak a language no way resembling that of his Majesty's English subjects. Are the Americans not as numerous? If we may trust the learned and accurate Judge Barrington's account of North Wales, and take that as a standard to measure the rest, there is no comparison. The people cannot amount to above 200,000; not a tenth part of the number in the Colonies. Is America in rebellion? Wales was hardly ever free from it. Have you attempted to govern America by penal statutes? You made Fifteen for Wales. But your legislative authority is perfect with regard to America.—Was it less perfect in Wales, Chester, and Durham? But America is virtually represented.—What! does the electric force of virtual representation more easily pass over the Atlantic, than pervade Wales, which lies in your neighbourhood; or than Chester and Durham, surrounded [208] by abundance of representation that is actual and palpable? But, Sir, your ancestors thought this sort of virtual representation, however ample, to be totally insufficient for the freedom of the inhabitants of territories that are so near, and comparatively so inconsiderable. How then can I think it sufficient for those which are infinitely greater, and infinitely more remote?

You will now, Sir, perhaps imagine, that I am on the point of proposing to you a scheme for a representation of the Colonies in Parliament. Perhaps I might be inclined to entertain some such thought; but a great flood stops me in my course. *Opposuit natura*—I cannot remove the eternal barriers of the creation. The thing, in that mode, I do not know to be possible. As I meddle with no theory, I do not absolutely assert the impracticability of such a representation. But I do not see my way to it; and those who have been more confident have not been more successful. However, the arm of public benevolence is not shortened; and there are often several means to the same end. What nature has disjoined in one way, wisdom may unite in another. When we cannot give the benefit as we would wish, let us not refuse it altogether. If we cannot give the principal, let us find a substitute. But how? Where? What substitute?

Fortunately I am not obliged for the ways and means of this substitute to tax my own unproductive invention. I am not even obliged to go to the rich treasury of the fertile framers of imaginary commonwealths; not to the Republick of Plato; not to the Utopia of More; not to the Oceana of Harrington. It is before me—it is at my feet, *and the rude swain Treads daily on it with his clouted shoon.* I only wish you to recognise, for the theory, the ancient Constitutional policy of this Kingdom with regard to representation, as that policy has been declared in Acts of Parliament; and, as to [209] the practice, to return to that mode which an uniform experience has marked out to you, as best; and in which you walked with security, advantage, and honour, until the year 1763.

My Resolutions therefore mean to establish the equity and justice of a taxation of America by *grant,* and not by *imposition.* To mark the *legal competency* of the Colony Assemblies for the support of their government in peace, and for public aids in time of war. To acknowledge that this legal competency has had *a dutiful and beneficial exercise;* and that experience has shown the *benefit of their grants,* and the *futility of Parliamentary taxation as a method of supply.*

THESE SOLID TRUTHS compose six fundamental propositions. There are three more Resolutions corollary to these. If you admit the first set, you can hardly reject the others. But if you admit the first, I shall be far from sollicitous whether you accept or refuse the last. I think these six massive pillars will be of strength sufficient to support the temple of British concord. I have no more doubt than I entertain of my existence, that, if you admitted these, you would command an immediate peace; and, with but tolerable future management, a lasting obedience in America. I am not arrogant in this confident assurance. The propositions are all mere matters of fact; and if they are such facts as draw irresistible conclusions even in the stating, this is the power of truth, and not any management of mine.

SPEECH ON CONCILIATION WITH THE COLONIES

Sir, I shall open the whole plan to you, together with such observations on the motions as may tend to illustrate them where they may want explanation. The first is a Resolution—

That the Colonies and Plantations of Great Britain in North America, consisting of Fourteen separate Governments, and containing Two Millions and upwards of [210] free inhabitants, have not had the liberty and privilege of electing and sending any Knights and Burgesses, or others, to represent them in the High Court of Parliament.

This is a plain matter of fact, necessary to be laid down, and (excepting the description) it is laid down in the language of the Constitution; it is taken nearly *verbatim* from Acts of Parliament.

The second is like unto the first—

That the said Colonies and Plantations have been liable to, and bounden by, several subsidies, payments, rates, and taxes, given and granted by Parliament, though the said Colonies and Plantations have not their Knights and Burgesses, in the said High Court of Parliament, of their own election, to represent the condition of their country; by lack whereof they have been oftentimes touched and grieved by subsidies given, granted, and assented to, in the said Court, in a manner prejudicial to the commonwealth, quietness, rest, and peace of the subjects inhabiting within the same.

Is this description too hot, or too cold, too strong, or too weak? Does it arrogate too much to the supreme legislature? Does it lean too much to the claims of the people? If it runs into any of these errors, the fault is not mine. It is the language of your own ancient Acts of Parliament.

Non meus hic sermo, sed quae praecepit Ofellus,
Rusticus, abnormis sapiens.

It is the genuine produce of the antient, rustic, manly, home-bred sense of this country—I did not dare to rub off a particle of the venerable rust that rather adorns and preserves, than destroys, the metal. It would be a profanation to touch with a tool the stones which construct the sacred altar of peace. I would not violate with modern polish the ingenuous and noble roughness of these truly Constitutional materials. [211] Above all things, I was resolved not to be guilty of tampering: the odious vice of restless and unstable minds. I put my foot in the tracks of our forefathers; where I can neither wander nor stumble. Determining to fix articles of peace, I was resolved not to be wise beyond what was written; I was resolved to use nothing else than the form of sound words; to let others abound in their own sense; and carefully to abstain from all expressions of my own. What the Law has said, I say. In all things else I am silent. I have no organ but for her words. This, if it be not ingenious, I am sure is safe.

There are indeed words expressive of grievance in this second Resolution, which those who are resolved always to be in the right will deny to contain matter of fact, as applied to the present case; although Parliament thought them true, with regard to the Counties of Chester and Durham. They will deny that the Americans were ever "touched and grieved" with the taxes. If they consider nothing in taxes but their weight as pecuniary impositions, there might be some pretence for this denial. But men may be sorely touched and deeply grieved in their privileges, as well as in their purses. Men may lose little in property by the act which takes away all their freedom. When a man is robbed of a trifle on the highway, it is not the Two-pence lost that constitutes the capital outrage. This is not confined to privileges. Even antient indulgences withdrawn, without offence on the part of those who enjoyed such favours, operate as grievances. But were the Americans then not touched and grieved by the taxes, in some measure, merely as taxes? If so, why were they almost all either wholly repealed, or exceedingly reduced? Were they not touched and grieved even by the regulating Duties of the Sixth of George the Second? Else why were the duties first reduced to one Third in 1764, and afterwards to a Third of that Third in the year 1766? Were they not [212] touched and grieved by the Stamp Act? I shall say they were, until that tax is revived. Were they not touched and grieved by the duties of 1767, which were likewise repealed, and which Lord Hillsborough tells you (for the Ministry) were laid contrary to the true principle of commerce? Is not the assurance given by that noble person to the Colonies of a resolution to lay no more taxes on them, an admission that taxes would touch and grieve them? Is not the Resolution of the Noble Lord in the blue ribband, now standing on your Journals, the strongest of all proofs that Parliamentary subsidies really touched and grieved them? Else why all these changes, modifications, repeals, assurances, and Resolutions?

The next proposition is—

That, from the distance of the said Colonies, and from other circumstances, no method hath hitherto been devised for procuring a representation in Parliament for the said Colonies.

This is an assertion of a fact. I go no further on the paper; though, in my private judgement, an useful representation is impossible; I am sure it is not desired by them; nor ought it perhaps by us; but I abstain from opinions.

The fourth Resolution is—

That each of the said Colonies hath within itself a body, chosen in part, or in the whole, by the freemen, freeholders, or other free inhabitants thereof, commonly called the General Assembly, or General Court; with powers legally to raise, levy, and assess, according to the several usage of such Colonies, duties and taxes towards defraying all sorts of public services.

This competence in the Colony Assemblies is certain. It is proved by the whole tenour of their Acts of Supply in all the Assemblies, in which the constant style of granting is, "an aid to his Majesty"; and Acts granting to the Crown [213] have regularly for near a century passed the public offices without dispute. Those who have been pleased paradoxically to deny this right, holding that none but the British Parliament can grant to the Crown, are wished to look to what is done, not only in the Colonies, but in Ireland, in one uniform unbroken tenour every session. Sir, I am surprised that this doctrine should come from some of the law servants of the Crown. I say, that if the Crown could be responsible, his Majesty—but certainly the Ministers, and even these law officers themselves, through whose hands the Acts pass, biennially in Ireland, or annually in the Colonies, are in an habitual course of committing impeachable offences. What habitual offenders have been all Presidents of the Council, all Secretaries of State, all First Lords of Trade, all Attornies and all Solicitors General! However, they are safe; as no one impeaches them; and there is no ground of charge against them, except in their own unfounded theories.

The fifth Resolution is also a Resolution of fact—

That the said General Assemblies, General Courts, or other bodies legally qualified as aforesaid, have at sundry times freely granted several large subsidies and public aids for his Majesty's service, according to their abilities, when required thereto by letter from one of his Majesty's principal Secretaries of State; and that their right to grant the same, and their chearfulness and sufficiency in the said grants, have been at sundry times acknowledged by Parliament.

To say nothing of their great expenses in the Indian wars; and not to take their exertion in foreign ones, so high as the supplies in the year 1695; not to go back to their public contributions in the year 1710; I shall begin to travel only where the Journals give me light; resolving to deal in nothing but fact, authenticated by Parliamentary record; and to build myself wholly on that solid basis.

[214] On the 4th of April, 1748, a Committee of this House came to the following Resolution:

Speech on Conciliation with the Colonies

Resolved,

That it is the opinion of this Committee, That it is just and reasonable that the several Provinces and Colonies of Massachuset's Bay, New Hampshire, Connecticut, and Rhode Island, be reimbursed the expenses they have been at in taking and securing to the Crown of Great Britain the Island of Cape Breton and its dependencies.

The expenses were immense for such Colonies. They were above 200,000*l*. sterling; money first raised and advanced on their public credit.

On the 28th of January, 1756, a Message from the King came to us, to this effect;

His Majesty, being sensible of the zeal and vigour with which his faithful subjects of certain Colonies in North America have exerted themselves in defence of his Majesty's just rights and possessions, recommends it to this House to take the same into their consideration, and to enable his Majesty to give them such assistance as may be *a proper reward and encouragement.*

On the 3rd of February, 1756, the House came to a suitable Resolution, expressed in words nearly the same as those of the Message: but with the further addition, that the money then voted was as an *encouragement* to the Colonies to exert themselves with vigour. It will not be necessary to go through all the testimonies which your own records have given to the truth of my Resolutions. I will only refer you to the places in the Journals:

Vol. xxvii.—16th and 19th May, 1757.

Vol. xxviii.—June 1st, 1758—April 26th and 30th, 1759—March 26th and 31st, and April 28th, 1760—Jan. 9th and 20th, 1761.

Vol. xxix.—Jan. 22nd and 26th, 1762—March 14th and 17th, 1763.

[215] Sir, here is the repeated acknowledgment of Parliament, that the Colonies not only gave, but gave to satiety. This nation has formally acknowledged two things; first, that the

Colonies had gone beyond their abilities, Parliament having thought it necessary to reimburse them; secondly, that they had acted legally and laudably in their grants of money, and their maintenance of troops, since the compensation is expressly given as reward and encouragement. Reward is not bestowed for acts that are unlawful; and encouragement is not held out to things that deserve reprehension. My Resolution therefore does nothing more than collect into one proposition, what is scattered through your Journals. I give you nothing but your own; and you cannot refuse in the gross, what you have so often acknowledged in detail. The admission of this, which will be so honourable to them and to you, will, indeed, be mortal to all the miserable stories, by which the passions of the misguided people have been engaged in an unhappy system. The people heard, indeed, from the beginning of these disputes, one thing continually dinned in their ears, that reason and justice demanded, that the Americans, who paid no Taxes, should be compelled to contribute. How did that fact, of their paying nothing, stand, when the Taxing System began? When Mr. Grenville began to form his system of American Revenue, he stated in this House, that the Colonies were then in debt two millions six hundred thousand pounds sterling money; and was of opinion they would discharge that debt in four years. On this state, those untaxed people were actually subject to the payment of taxes to the amount of six hundred and fifty thousand a year. In fact, however, Mr. Grenville was mistaken. The funds given for sinking the debt did not prove quite so ample as both the Colonies and he expected. The calculation was too sanguine; the reduction was not completed till some years after, and at different times in different Colonies. However, the [216] Taxes after the war continued too great to bear any addition, with prudence or propriety; and when the burthens imposed in consequence of former requisitions were discharged, our tone became too high to resort again to requisition. No Colony, since that time, ever has had any requisition whatsoever made to it.

We see the sense of the Crown, and the sense of Parliament, on the productive nature of a *Revenue by Grant*. Now search the same Journals for the produce of the *Revenue by Imposition*. Where is it? Let us know the volume and the page. What is the gross, what is the nett produce? To what service is it applied? How have you appropriated its surplus? What, can none of the many skilful Index-makers that we are now employing, find any trace of it? Well, let them and that rest together. But are the Journals, which say nothing of the Revenue, as silent on the discontent? Oh no! a child may find it. It is the melancholy burthen and blot of every page.

I think then I am, from those Journals, justified in the sixth and last Resolution, which is—

That it hath been found by experience, that the manner of granting the said supplies and aids, by the said General Assemblies, hath been more agreeable to the said Colonies, and more beneficial, and conducive to the public service, than the mode of giving and granting aids in Parliament, to be raised and paid in the said Colonies.

This makes the whole of the fundamental part of the plan. The conclusion is irresistible. You cannot say, that you were driven by any necessity to an exercise of the utmost Rights of Legislature. You cannot assert, that you took on yourselves the task of imposing Colony Taxes, from the want of another legal body, that is competent to the purpose of supplying the exigencies of the State without wounding [217] the prejudices of the people. Neither is it true that the body so qualified, and having that competence, had neglected the duty.

The question now, on all this accumulated matter, is; whether you will choose to abide by a profitable experience, or a mischievous theory; whether you choose to build on imagination, or fact; whether you prefer enjoyment or hope; satisfaction in your subjects, or discontent?

If these propositions are accepted, everything which has been made to enforce a contrary system, must, I take it for granted, fall along with it. On that ground, I have drawn the following Resolution, which, when it comes to be moved, will naturally be divided in a proper manner:

That it may be proper to repeal an Act, made in the seventh year of the reign of his present Majesty, intituled, An Act for granting certain duties in the British Colonies and Plantations in America; for allowing a drawback of the duties of Customs upon the exportation from this Kingdom, of coffee and cocoa-nuts of the produce of the said Colonies or Plantations; for discontinuing the drawbacks payable on China earthenware exported to America; and for more effectually preventing the clandestine running of goods in the said Colonies and Plantations.—And that it may be proper to repeal an Act, made in the fourteenth year of the reign of his present Majesty, intituled, An Act to discontinue, in such manner, and for such time, as are therein mentioned, the landing and discharging, lading or shipping, of goods, wares, and merchandise, at the town and within the harbour of Boston, in the province of Massachuset's Bay, in North America.—And that it may be proper to repeal an Act, made in the fourteenth year of the reign of his present Majesty, intituled, An Act for the impartial administration of justice, in the cases of persons questioned for any acts done by them, in the execution of the law, or for the suppression of riots and tumults, in the province of Massachuset's Bay, in New England.—And that it may [218] be proper to repeal an Act, made in the fourteenth year of the reign of his present Majesty, intituled, An Act for the better regulating of the Government of the province of the Massachuset's Bay, in New England.—And, also, that it may be proper to explain and amend an Act, made in the thirty-fifth year of the reign of King Henry the Eighth, intituled, An Act for the Trial of Treasons committed out of the King's Dominions.

I wish, Sir, to repeal the Boston Port Bill, because (independently of the dangerous precedent of suspending the rights of the subject during the King's pleasure) it was passed, as I apprehend, with less regularity, and on more partial principles, than it ought. The corporation of Boston was not heard before it was condemned. Other towns, full as guilty as she was, have not had their ports blocked up. Even the Restraining Bill of the present Session does not go to the length of the Boston Port Act. The same ideas of prudence, which induced you not to extend equal punishment to equal guilt, even when you were punishing, induced me, who mean not to chastise, but to reconcile, to be satisfied with the punishment already partially inflicted.

Ideas of prudence and accommodation to circumstances, prevent you from taking away the Charters of Connecticut and Rhode Island, as you have taken away that of Massachuset's Colony, though the Crown has far less power in the two former provinces than it enjoyed in the latter; and though the abuses have been full as great, and as flagrant, in the exempted as in the punished. The same reasons of prudence and accommodation have weight with me in restoring the Charter of Massachuset's Bay. Besides, Sir, the act which changes the Charter of Massachuset's is in many particulars so exceptionable, that if I did not wish absolutely to repeal, I would by all means desire to alter it; as several of its provisions tend to the subversion of all [219] public and private justice. Such, among others, is the power in the Governor to change the sheriff at his pleasure; and to make a new returning officer for every special cause. It is shameful to behold such a regulation standing among English Laws.

The Act for bringing persons accused of committing murder under the orders of Government to England for Trial is but temporary. That Act has calculated the probable duration of our quarrel with the Colonies; and is accommodated to that supposed duration. I would hasten the happy moment of reconciliation; and therefore must, on my principle, get rid of that most justly obnoxious Act.

The Act of Henry the Eighth, for the Trial of Treasons, I do not mean to take away, but to confine it to its proper bounds and original intention; to make it expressly for Trial of Treasons (and the greatest Treasons may be committed) in places where the jurisdiction of the Crown does not extend.

Having guarded the privileges of Local Legislature, I would next secure to the Colonies a fair and unbiassed Judicature; for which purpose, Sir, I propose the following Resolution:

That, from the time when the General Assembly or General Court of any Colony or Plantation in North America, shall have appointed by Act of Assembly, duly confirmed, a settled salary to the offices of the Chief Justice and other Judges of the Superior Court, it may be proper that the said Chief Justice and other Judges of the Superior Courts of such Colony, shall hold his and their office and offices during their good behaviour; and shall not be removed therefrom, but when the said removal shall be adjudged by his Majesty in Council, upon a hearing on complaint from the General Assembly, or on a complaint from the Governor, or Council, or the House of Representatives severally, or of the Colony in which the said Chief Justice and other Judges have exercised the said offices.

[220] The next Resolution relates to the Courts of Admiralty.

It is this:

That it may be proper to regulate the Courts of Admiralty, or Vice-Admiralty, authorized by the fifteenth Chapter of the Fourth of George the Third, in such a manner as to make the same more commodious to those who sue, or are sued, in the said Courts, and to provide for the more decent maintenance of the Judges in the same.

These Courts I do not wish to take away; they are in themselves proper establishments. This Court is one of the capital securities of the Act of Navigation. The extent of its jurisdiction, indeed, has been encreased; but this is altogether as proper, and is indeed on many accounts more eligible, where new powers were wanted, than a Court absolutely new. But Courts incommodiously situated, in effect, deny justice; and a Court, partaking in the fruits of its own condemnation, is a robber. The Congress complain, and complain justly, of this grievance.

These are the three consequential propositions. I have thought of two or three more; but they come rather too near detail, and to the province of executive Government; which I wish Parliament always to superintend, never to assume. If the first six are granted, congruity will carry the latter three. If not, the things that remain unrepealed will be, I hope, rather unseemly incumbrances on the building, than very materially detrimental to its strength and stability.

HERE, SIR, I SHOULD CLOSE; but I plainly perceive some objections remain, which I ought, if possible, to remove. The first will be, that, in resorting to the doctrine of our ancestors, as contained in the preamble to the Chester Act, I prove too much; that the grievance from a want of representation, stated in that preamble, goes to the whole of [221] Legislation as well as to Taxation. And that the Colonies, grounding themselves upon that doctrine, will apply it to all parts of Legislative Authority.

To this objection, with all possible deference and humility, and wishing as little as any man living to impair the smallest particle of our supreme authority, I answer, that *the words are the words of Parliament, and not mine;* and, that all false and inconclusive inferences, drawn from them, are not mine; for I heartily disclaim any such inference. I have chosen the words of an Act of Parliament, which Mr. Grenville, surely a tolerably zealous and very judicious advocate for the sovereignty of Parliament, formerly moved to have read at your table in confirmation of his tenets. It is true, that Lord Chatham considered these preambles as declaring strongly in favour of his opinions. He was a no less powerful advocate for the privileges of the Americans. Ought I not from hence to presume, that these preambles are as favourable as possible to both, when properly understood; favourable both to the rights of Parliament, and to the privilege of the dependencies of this Crown? But, Sir, the object of grievance in my resolution I have not taken from the Chester, but from the Durham Act, which confines the hardship of want of representation to the case of subsidies; and which therefore falls in exactly with the case of the Colonies. But whether the unrepresented counties were *de jure*, or *de facto*, bound, the preambles do not accurately distinguish; nor indeed was it necessary; for, whether *de jure*, or *de facto*, the Legislature thought the exercise of the power of taxing, as of right, or as of fact without right, equally a grievance, and equally oppressive.

I do not know that the Colonies have, in any general way, or in any cool hour, gone much beyond the demand of humanity in relation to taxes. It is not fair to judge of the temper or dispositions of any man, or any set of men, when [222] they are composed and at rest, from their conduct, or their expressions, in a state of disturbance and irritation. It is besides a very great mistake to imagine, that mankind follow up practically any speculative principle, either of government or of freedom, as far as it will go in argument and logical illation. We Englishmen stop very short of the principles upon which we support any given part of our Constitution; or even the whole of it together. I could easily, if I had not already tired you, give you very striking and convincing instances of it. This is nothing but what is natural and proper. All government, indeed every human benefit and enjoyment, every virtue, and every prudent act, is founded on compromise and barter. We balance inconveniences; we give and take; we remit some rights, that we may enjoy others; and we choose rather to be happy citizens, than subtle disputants. As we must give away some natural liberty, to enjoy civil advantages; so we must sacrifice some civil liberties, for the advantages to be derived from the communion and fellowship of a great empire. But, in all fair dealings, the thing bought must bear some proportion to the purchase paid. None will barter away *the immediate jewel of his soul.* Though a great house is apt to make slaves haughty, yet it is purchasing a part of the artificial importance of a great empire too dear, to pay for it all essential rights, and all the intrinsic dignity of human nature. None of us who would not risque his life rather than fall under a government purely arbitrary. But although there are some amongst us who think our Constitution wants many improvements, to make it a complete system of liberty; perhaps none who are of that opinion would think it right to aim at such improvement, by disturbing his country, and risquing everything that is dear to him. In every arduous enterprize, we consider what we are to lose, as well as what we are to gain; and the more and better stake of liberty [223] every people possess, the less they will hazard in a vain attempt to make it more. These are *the cords of man.* Man acts from adequate motives relative to his interest; and not on metaphysical speculations. Aristotle, the great master of reasoning, cautions us, and with great weight and propriety, against this species of delusive geometrical accuracy in moral arguments, as the most fallacious of all sophistry.

The Americans will have no interest contrary to the grandeur and glory of England, when they are not oppressed by the weight of it; and they will rather be inclined to respect the acts of a superintending legislature; when they see them the acts of that power, which is itself the security, not the rival, of their secondary importance. In this assurance, my mind most perfectly acquiesces: and I confess I feel not the least alarm from the discontents which are to arise from putting people at their ease; nor do I apprehend the destruction of this Empire, from giving, by an act of free grace and indulgence, to two millions of my fellow-citizens some share of those rights, upon which I have always been taught to value myself.

It is said, indeed, that this power of granting, vested in American Assemblies, would dissolve the unity of the

Empire; which was preserved entire, although Wales, and Chester, and Durham were added to it. Truly, Mr. Speaker, I do not know what this unity means; nor has it ever been heard of, that I know, in the constitutional policy of this country. The very idea of subordination of parts, excludes this notion of simple and undivided unity. England is the head; but she is not the head and the members too. Ireland has ever had from the beginning a separate, but not an independent, legislature; which, far from distracting, promoted the union of the whole. Everything was sweetly and harmoniously disposed through both islands for the conservation of English dominion, and the communication of English [224] liberties. I do not see that the same principles might not be carried into twenty islands, and with the same good effect. This is my model with regard to America, as far as the internal circumstances of the two countries are the same. I know no other unity of this Empire, than I can draw from its example during these periods, when it seemed to my poor understanding more united than it is now, or than it is likely to be by the present methods.

BUT SINCE I SPEAK of these methods, I recollect, Mr. Speaker, almost too late, that I promised, before I finished, to say something of the proposition of the Noble Lord on the floor, which has been so lately received, and stands on your Journals. I must be deeply concerned, whenever it is my misfortune to continue a difference with the majority of this House. But as the reasons for that difference are my apology for thus troubling you, suffer me to state them in a very few words. I shall compress them into as small a body as I possibly can, having already debated that matter at large, when the question was before the Committee.

First, then, I cannot admit that proposition of a ransom by auction; because it is a meer project. It is a thing new; unheard of; supported by no experience; justified by

---

no analogy; without example of our ancestors, or root in the Constitution. It is neither regular Parliamentary taxation, nor Colony grant. *Experimentum in corpore vili*, is a good rule, which will ever make me adverse to any trial of experiments on what is certainly the most valuable of all subjects, the peace of this Empire.

Secondly, it is an experiment which must be fatal in the end to our Constitution. For what is it but a scheme for taxing the Colonies in the anti-chamber of the Noble Lord and his successours? To settle the quotas and proportions in this House, is clearly impossible. You, Sir, may flatter [225] yourself you shall sit a State auctioneer, with your hammer in your hand, and knock down to each Colony as it bids. But to settle (on the plan laid down by the Noble Lord) the true proportional payment for four or five and twenty governments, according to the absolute and the relative wealth of each, and according to the British proportion of wealth and burthen, is a wild and chimerical notion. This new taxation must therefore come in by the back door of the Constitution. Each quota must be brought to this House ready formed; you can neither add nor alter. You must register it. You can do nothing further. For on what grounds can you deliberate either before or after the proposition? You cannot hear the counsel for all these provinces, quarrelling each on its own quantity of payment, and its proportion to others. If you should attempt it, the Committee of Provincial Ways and Means, or by whatever other name it will delight to be called, must swallow up all the time of Parliament.

Thirdly, it does not give satisfaction to the complaint of the Colonies. They complain, that they are taxed without their consent; you answer, that you will fix the sum at which they shall be taxed. That is, you give them the very grievance for the remedy. You tell them indeed, that you will leave the mode to themselves. I really beg pardon: it gives me pain to mention it; but you must be sensible that you will not perform this part of the compact. For, suppose the Colonies were to lay the duties, which furnished their Contingent, upon the importation of your manufactures; you know you would never suffer such a tax to be laid. You know, too, that you would not suffer many other modes of taxation. So that, when you come to explain yourself, it will be found, that you will neither leave to themselves the quantum nor the mode; nor indeed anything. The whole is delusion from one end to the other.

Fourthly, this method of ransom by auction, unless it be [226] *universally* accepted, will plunge you into great and inextricable difficulties. In what year of our Lord are the proportions of payments to be settled? To say nothing of the impossibility that Colony agents should have general powers of taxing the Colonies at their discretion; consider, I implore you, that the communication by special messages, and orders between these agents and their constituents on each variation of the case, when the parties come to contend together, and to dispute on their relative proportions, will be a matter of delay, perplexity, and confusion that never can have an end.

If all the Colonies do not appear at the outcry, what is the condition of those assemblies, who offer by themselves or their agents, to tax themselves up to your ideas of their proportion? The refractory Colonies, who refuse all composition, will remain taxed only to your old impositions, which, however grievous in principle, are trifling as to production. The obedient Colonies in this scheme are heavily taxed; the refractory remain unburthened. What will you do? Will you lay new and heavier taxes by Parliament on the disobedient? Pray consider in what way you can do it. You are perfectly convinced, that, in the way of taxing, you can do nothing but at the ports. Now suppose it is Virginia that refuses to appear at your auction, while Maryland and North Carolina bid handsomely for their ransom, and are taxed to your quota, how will you put these Colonies on a par? Will you tax the tobacco of Virginia? If you do, you give its death-wound to your English revenue at home, and to one of the very greatest articles of your own foreign trade. If you tax the import of that rebellious Colony, what do you tax but your own manufactures, or the goods of some other obedient and already well-taxed Colony? Who has said one word on this labyrinth of detail, which bewilders you more and more as you enter into it? Who has presented, who can present you with a clue, to lead you out of it? I think, Sir, [227] it is impossible, that you should not recollect that the Colony bounds are so implicated in one another, (you know it by your other experiments in the Bill for prohibiting the New England Fishery,) that you can lay no possible restraints on almost any of them which may not be presently eluded, if you do not confound the innocent with the guilty, and burthen those whom, upon every principle, you ought to exonerate. He must be grossly ignorant of America, who thinks that, without falling into this confusion of all rules of equity and policy, you can restrain any single Colony, especially Virginia and Maryland, the central and most important of them all.

Let it also be considered, that, either in the present confusion you settle a permanent contingent, which will and must be trifling; and then you have no effectual revenue: or you change the quota at every exigency; and then on every new repartition you will have a new quarrel.

Reflect besides, that when you have fixed a quota for every Colony, you have not provided for prompt and punctual payment. Suppose one, two, five, ten years' arrears. You cannot issue a Treasury Extent against the failing Colony. You must make new Boston Port Bills, new restraining laws, new Acts for dragging men to England for trial. You must send out new fleets, new armies. All is to begin again. From this day forward the Empire is never to know an hour's tranquillity. An intestine fire will be kept alive in the bowels of the Colonies, which one time or other must consume this whole

Empire. I allow indeed that the empire of Germany raises her revenue and her troops by quotas and contingents; but the revenue of the empire, and the army of the empire, is the worst revenue, and the worst army, in the world.

Instead of a standing revenue, you will therefore have a perpetual quarrel. Indeed the noble Lord, who proposed [228] this project of a ransom by auction, seemed himself to be of that opinion. His project was rather designed for breaking the union of the Colonies, than for establishing a revenue. He confessed, he apprehended that his proposal would not be to *their taste*. I say, this scheme of disunion seems to be at the bottom of the project; for I will not suspect that the noble Lord meant nothing but merely to delude the nation by an airy phantom which he never intended to realize. But whatever his views may be; as I propose the peace and union of the Colonies as the very foundation of my plan, it cannot accord with one whose foundation is perpetual discord.

COMPARE THE TWO. This I offer to give you is plain and simple. The other full of perplexed and intricate mazes. This is mild; that harsh. This is found by experience effectual for its purposes; the other is a new project. This is universal; the other calculated for certain Colonies only. This is immediate in its conciliatory operation; the other remote, contingent, full of hazard. Mine is what becomes the dignity of a ruling people, gratuitous, unconditional, and not held out as a matter of bargain and sale. I have done my duty in proposing it to you. I have indeed tired you by a long discourse; but this is the misfortune of those to whose influence nothing will be conceded, and who must win every inch of their ground by argument. You have heard me with goodness. May you decide with wisdom! For my part, I feel my mind greatly disburthened by what I have done to-day. I have been the less fearful of trying your patience, because on this subject I mean to spare it altogether in future. I have this comfort, that in every stage of the American affairs, I have steadily opposed the measures that have produced the confusion, and may bring on the destruction, of this empire. I now go so far as to risque a [229] proposal of my own. If I cannot give peace to my country; I give it to my conscience.

But what (says the Financier) is peace to us without money? Your plan gives us no Revenue. No! But it does—For it secures to the subject the power of REFUSAL; the first of all Revenues. Experience is a cheat, and fact a liar, if this power in the subject of proportioning his grant, or of not granting at all, has not been found the richest mine of Revenue ever discovered by the skill or by the fortune of man. It does not indeed vote you £152,750: II: 2¾ths, nor any other paltry limited sum. But it gives the strong box itself, the fund, the bank, from whence only revenues can arise amongst a people sensible of freedom: *Posita luditur arca.* Cannot you, in England; cannot you, at this time of day; cannot you, a House of Commons, trust to the principle which has raised so mighty a revenue, and accumulated a debt of near 140 millions in this country? Is this principle to be true in England, and false everywhere else? Is it not true in Ireland? Has it not hitherto been true in the Colonies? Why should you presume, that, in any country, a body duly constituted for any function, will neglect to perform its duty, and abdicate its trust? Such a presumption would go against all governments in all modes. But, in truth, this dread of penury of supply, from a free assembly, has no foundation in nature. For first observe, that, besides the desire which all men have naturally of supporting the honour of their own government, that sense of dignity, and that security to property, which ever attends freedom, has a tendency to increase the stock of the free community. Most may be taken where most is accumulated. And what is the soil or climate where experience has not uniformly proved, that the voluntary flow of heaped-up plenty, bursting from the weight of its own rich luxuriance, has ever run with a more copious stream of revenue, than [230] could be squeezed from the dry husks of oppressed indigence, by the straining of all the politic machinery in the world?

Next we know, that parties must ever exist in a free country. We know too, that the emulations of such parties, their contradictions, their reciprocal necessities, their hopes, and their fears, must send them all in their turns to him that holds the balance of the state. The parties are the Gamesters; but Government keeps the table, and is sure to be the winner in the end. When this game is played, I really think it is more to be feared that the people will be exhausted, than that Government will not be supplied. Whereas, whatever is got by acts of absolute power ill obeyed, because odious, or by contracts ill kept, because constrained, will be narrow, feeble, uncertain, and precarious. "*Ease would retract Vows made in pain, as violent and void.*"

I, for one, protest against compounding our demands: I declare against compounding for a poor limited sum, the immense, ever-growing, eternal Debt, which is due to generous Government from protected freedom. And so may I speed in the great object I propose to you, as I think it would not only be an act of injustice, but would be the worst oeconomy in the world, to compel the Colonies to a sum certain, either in the way of ransom, or in the way of compulsory compact.

But to clear up my ideas on this subject—a revenue from America transmitted hither—do not delude yourselves—you never can receive it—No, not a shilling. We have experience that from remote countries it is not to be expected. If, when you attempted to extract revenue from Bengal, you were obliged to return in loan what you had taken in imposition; what can you expect from North America? For certainly, if ever there was a country qualified to produce [231] wealth, it is India; or an institution fit for the transmission, it is the East India Company. America has none of these aptitudes. If America gives you taxable objects, on which you lay your duties here, and gives you, at the same time, a surplus by a foreign sale of her commodities to pay the duties on these objects, which you tax at home, she has performed her part to the British revenue. But with regard to her own internal establishments; she may, I doubt not she will, contribute in moderation. I say in moderation; for she ought not to be permitted to exhaust herself. She ought to be reserved to a war; the weight of which, with the enemies that we are most likely to have, must be considerable in her quarter of the globe. There she may serve you, and serve you essentially.

For that service, for all service, whether of revenue, trade, or empire, my trust is in her interest in the British Constitution. My hold of the Colonies is in the close affection which grows from common names, from kindred blood, from similar privileges, and equal protection. These are ties, which, though light as air, are as strong as links of iron. Let the Colonists always keep the idea of their civil rights associated with your Government—they will cling and grapple to you; and no force under heaven will be of power to tear them from their allegiance. But let it be once understood, that your government may be one thing, and their Privileges another; that these two things may exist without any mutual relation—the cement is gone; the cohesion is loosened; and everything hastens to decay and dissolution. As long as you have the wisdom to keep the sovereign authority of this country as the sanctuary of liberty, the sacred temple consecrated to our common faith, wherever the chosen race and sons of England worship freedom, they will turn their faces towards you. The more they multiply, the more friends you will have; the more ardently they love [232] liberty, the more perfect will be their obedience. Slavery they can have anywhere. It is a weed that grows in every soil. They may have it from Spain, they may have it from Prussia. But, until you become lost to all feeling of your true interest and your natural dignity, freedom they can have from none but you. This is the commodity of price, of which you have the monopoly. This is the true Act of Navigation, which binds to you the commerce of the Colonies, and through them secures to you the wealth of the world. Deny them this participation of freedom, and you break that sole bond, which originally made, and must still preserve, the unity of the Empire. Do not entertain so weak an imagination, as that your registers and your bonds, your affidavits and your sufferances, your cockets and your clearances, are what form the great securities of your commerce. Do not dream that your letters of office, and your instructions, and your suspending clauses, are the things that hold together the great contexture of the mysterious whole. These things do not make your government. Dead instruments, passive tools as they are, it is the spirit of the English communion that gives all their life and efficacy to them. It is the spirit of the English Constitution, which, infused through the mighty mass, pervades, feeds, unites, invigorates, vivifies every part of the empire, even down to the minutest member.

Is it not the same virtue which does everything for us here in England? Do you imagine then, that it is the Land Tax Act which raises your revenue? that it is the annual vote in the Committee of Supply which gives you your army? or that it is the Mutiny Bill which inspires it with bravery and discipline? No! surely no! It is the love of the people; it is their attachment to their government, from the sense of the deep stake they have in such a glorious institution—which gives you your army and your navy, and infuses into both [233] that liberal obedience, without which your army would be a base rabble, and your navy nothing but rotten timber.

All this, I know well enough, will sound wild and chimerical to the profane herd of those vulgar and mechanical politicians, who have no place among us; a sort of people who think that nothing exists but what is gross and material; and who therefore, far from being qualified to be directors of the great movement of empire, are not fit to turn a wheel in the machine. But to men truly initiated and rightly taught, these ruling and master principles, which, in the opinion of such men as I have mentioned, have no substantial existence, are in truth every thing, and all in all. Magnanimity in politicks is not seldom the truest wisdom; and a great empire and little minds go ill together. If we are conscious of our station, and glow with zeal to fill our places as becomes our situation and ourselves, we ought to auspicate all our public proceedings on America with the old warning of the church, *Sursum corda!* We ought to elevate our minds to the greatness of that trust to which the order of Providence has called us. By adverting to the dignity of this high calling, our ancestors have turned a savage wilderness into a glorious empire; and have made the most extensive, and the only honourable conquests, not by destroying, but by promoting the wealth, the number, the happiness, of the human race. Let us get an American revenue as we have got an American empire. English privileges have made it all that it is; English privileges alone will make it all it can be.

In full confidence of this unalterable truth, I now (*quod felix faustumque sit*) lay the first stone of the Temple of peace; and I move you,

That the Colonies and Plantations of Great Britain in North America, consisting of Fourteen separate governments, and containing Two Millions and upwards of free inhabitants, have not had the liberty and privilege [234] of electing and sending any Knights and Burgesses, or others, to represent them in the High Court of Parliament.

[Upon this Resolution, the previous question was put, and carried; for the previous question 270, against it, 78.

The first four motions and the last had the previous question put on them. The others were negatived.]

THE END

NOTES

THOUGHTS ON THE CAUSE OF THE PRESENT DISCONTENTS

PAGE 69. *Hoc vero occultum, intestinum,* &c. Cic. in C. Verrem Act. Secunda, lib. i. cap. xv. sec. 39. Burke's original quotation is faulty, and has been corrected in the text. Translate *non existit,* "escapes observation." The allusion is to the treachery of Verres, when quaestor, to his praetor Cn. Carbo: the quaestor being bound to his praetor, according to the official policy of Rome, by a quasi-filial tie, known as *necessitudo sortis.* This tie is mentioned by Burke (p. 148) as an illustration of the party obligation in English politics. The introduction of the quotation at the commencement of this pamphlet points vaguely to similar treachery on the part of the Court and the House of Commons towards the English nation, and directly to the powerlessness of the nation to resist the poisonous influence of the Court Cabal. The passage was perhaps suggested by Lord Chatham's speech in the Lords, January 22, 1770: "The grand capital mischief is fixed at home. It corrupts the very foundation of our political existence, and preys upon the vitals of the state." This quotation almost foreshadows the accusation of Warren Hastings, between whom and Verres Burke always sought to establish a similarity, though it would have been easier to demonstrate a contrast.

P. 70, L. 1. *It is an undertaking,* &c. Burke understood thoroughly the art of the *preamble.* He never makes it so long as to fatigue the reader or hearer at the outset. If he introduces general observations, it is done in such a way as to prepare for the particular points which are to follow, and with strict reference to that object. Being the most philosophical, he is naturally the most sententious of orators; and the canon of the Roman rhetorician, *sententias interponi raro convenit, ut rei actores, non vivendi praeceptores esse* [236] *videamur* (Rhet. ad Herenn. iv. 17), is much relaxed in his practice. Introduced in its proper place, as a preparation for a *particular* consideration, the *sententia* stimulates the audience, and heightens the effect.

L. 5. come near to *persons of weight,* &c., i.e. so as to touch, ruffle them. Under the general mention of "persons of weight and consequence," Burke alludes to the King.

L. 8. *obliged to blame the favourites of the people,* i.e. the popular ex-minister Lord Chatham. The pamphlet in its earliest form contained a severe attack on Chatham, which was expunged previous to publication. Burke's Correspondence, vol. i. p. 200.

L. 10. *instrument of faction.* Cp. p. 110, l. 4. Among the members of his party Burke was anxious to have it understood that this pamphlet was a manifesto from the whole body (Correspondence, vol i. pp. 198, 199): but he repudiated the idea of being "a mere conduit for the conveyance of other people's sentiments or principles," in letters on the subject to his private friends (Correspondence, vol. i. p. 226).

L. 12. *our law has invested,* &c. "All persons, noblemen and others (except women, clergymen, persons decrepit, and infants under fifteen) are bound to attend the justices in suppressing a riot."—Blackstone. Compare his insisting on the *legal* nature of the "interposition of the body of the people itself," infra, p. 142, and the conclusion of the Letter to W. Elliot, Esq.: "Private persons may sometimes assume that magistracy which does not depend on the nomination of Kings," &c.

L. 14. *private people . . . stepping a little out of their ordinary sphere.* Burke was at this time an active member of Parliament. From this and other passages (see pp. 130–31) it is clear that he wrote in the character of a private citizen. This apology for the public expression of private opinion was a stock piece in English political writing down to the reign of George III. Political pamphlets, and series of pamphlets under a general name by the same author, grew rarer after this time, when anonymous writers could get their letters inserted in the newspapers.

L. 19. *reason upon them* liberally. A favourite epithet with Burke. Cp. "liberal obedience," p. 288.

L. 22. *rulers for the day . . . cause of Government.* Burke distinguishes between the essence of government, which is permanent and resides rather in the spirit of the governed than in anything outside of them, and the merely temporary external administration. Cp. Speech on the Econ. Reform, near beginning; "the settled, habitual systematick affection I bear to the *cause* and to the *principles of government.*" The present passage hints at the distinction between the interests of the King and those of his ministers.

L. 26. *Compose the minds of the* subject. Used collectively for *the people.*

L. 27. *abstract value of the voice of the people*—of which Burke had a low opinion. See p. 103 and note.

THOUGHTS ON THE PRESENT DISCONTENTS

L. 28. *reputation, the most precious possession of every individual*—alluding to the passage from "Othello," quoted at p. 279.

[237] **L. 32.** *Nations are not primarily ruled by laws; less by violence.* A commonplace of the politicians of ancient Rome. "So in human societies—however important force may be, it is not the ruling power; it does not govern the destinies; it is the ideas, the moral influences concealed under the accidental forms that force imposes, which regulate the course of societies." Guizot, Civilisation in Europe. See the doctrine fully developed, Lecture V.

P. 71, L. 11. *The temper of the people . . . ought to be the first study of a Statesman.* Instead of the temper of the House of Commons. Cp. the passage on C. Townshend, pp. 210–11. The maxim is an old commonplace. Tacitus, Ann. lib. 3: "Noscenda tibi natura vulgi est, et quibus modis temperanter habeatur." Martial:

Principis est virtus maxima nôsse suos.

L. 20. *levity of the vulgar.* "Multitudinis levitas" is an expression of Cicero, who often insists on the fact. "Vulgo nihil incertius," Pro Muraena. "In multitudine est varietas, et crebra tanquam tempestatum, sic sententiarum commutatio," Pro Domo.

L. 21. *all times have* not *been alike.* "I have read my friend Congreve's verses to Lord Cobham, which end with a vile and false moral, and I remember is not in Horace to Tibullus, which he imitates, 'that all times are equally virtuous and vicious,' wherein he differs from all Poets, Philosophers and Christians that ever writ." Swift to Bolingbroke, April 5, 1729. But Marcus Antoninus, Bacon, and Guicciardini, have expressed the contrary opinion. It is perhaps put most forcibly by Machiavelli, "giudico il mondo sempre esser stato ad un medesimo modo," &c. Discorsi sopra T. Livio, Lib. II, Introduction. The question on both sides is stated by Burke in his review of Brown's "Estimate of the Manners," &c., Annual Register, 1758, p. 444. Sir T. Browne says: "'Tis better to think that times past have been better than times present, than that times were always bad." Christian Morals, Part III, Sect. 3.

P. 72, L. 6. *disconnexion . . . in families*—alluding particularly to the Temple family. In general Lord Temple was a staunch opponent of the Court; his brother, George Grenville, a supporter of the Court, and his brother-in-law, Lord Chatham, politically separated from both. A reconciliation however had taken place before the publication of this pamphlet.

IB. *disconnexion in offices.* See infra p. 206, l. 32, &c., and note.

NOTES

L. 11. *great parties . . . . in a manner entirely dissolved.* An old commonplace. "These associations are broken; these distinct sets of ideas are shuffled out of their order; new combinations force themselves upon us. . . . The bulk of both parties are really united; united on principles of liberty, in opposition to an obscure remnant of one party, who disown those principles, and a mercenary detachment from the other, who betray them." Dissertation on Parties, Letter I, Bolingbroke's Works, 4to. edition, vol. ii. p. 32. The real distinction of Whig and Tory parties faded away after the Revolution: and [238] the names came to signify only particular political combinations based less on political principles than on personal attachments. Dissertation on Parties, Letter VII. Swift, in the Conduct of the Allies, regrets the necessity for using "those foolish terms." "Every opposition . . . assumed or obtained the title of the popular party. No distinction was made, in this respect, between Whig and Tory. Each party, when out of place, adopted the same principles." History of the Opposition, 1779, p. 3. In the passage before us Burke rightly mentions parties as a cause of disturbance: nor is he inconsistent in conceiving the remedy for the discontents to consist in restoring and maintaining party connexions (infra, p. 146 sq.). At this time the power of parties was at its lowest. When personal attachments were the basis of political connexion, and principles or intended measures counted for nothing, the royal influence judiciously used naturally prevailed against all opposition. But the instruments of this influence were Whigs, and the plan (Bolingbroke's) on which the whole of this misdirected policy proceeded, was Whiggish, if there is any meaning in words. (Cp. Lord Lyttelton's Letters from a Persian, No. 57.) Cp. the beginning of Swift's Letter to a Whig Lord, 1712: "The dispute between your Lordship and me has, I think, no manner of relation to what in the common style of these times, are called principles; wherein both parties seem well enough to agree, if we will but allow their professions. I can truly affirm that none of the reasonable sober Whigs I have conversed with, did ever avow any opinion concerning religion or government which I was not willing to subscribe; so that, according to my judgment, those terms of distinction ought to be dropped, and other terms introduced in their stead to denominate men as they are inclined to peace or war, to the last or the present ministry; for whoever thoroughly considers the matter will find these to be the only differences that divide the nation at present." On this subject read especially the Examiner, No. 44, by Swift.

L. 14. *at present . . . scheme of taxation.* There is an allusion to the attempted taxation of America, and to possible attempts of a like nature at home.

L. 16. *Nor are we engaged in unsuccessful war,* &c. "The last means (of averting popular discontents) consists in preventing dangers from abroad; for foreign dangers raise fears at home, and fears among the People raise jealousies of the Prince or State, and give them ill opinions either of their abilities or good intentions," &c. Sir William Temple on Popular Discontents.

L. 22. *those who administer our affairs.* The Duke of Grafton resigned while this pamphlet was in the press; but Lord North, his Chancellor of the Exchequer, succeeded him, and Onslow, Jenkinson, and Dyson, continued Junior Lords of the Treasury.

L. 23. *take notice . . . of their* speculation, i.e. theory.

L. 27. *immense wealth in the hands of some individuals.* A gloomy picture of the depravation of the country from these causes is drawn by [239] Dr. Brown, Estimate of the Manners and Principles of the Times, 1757–8. Chatham, Speech in the Lords, Jan. 22, 1770: "The riches of Asia have been poured in upon us, and have brought with them not only Asiatic luxury, but I fear, Asiatic principles of government," &c.

L. 31. *boldness of others from a guilty poverty.* On the frightful prevalence of crime at this time see Phillimore's Hist. of George III, p. 49.

P. 73, L. 5. *industry of some libellers*—especially of Junius, whose letters began January 21, 1769. Nearly forty of them had been published before Burke's pamphlet.

L. 17. *measures . . . persons*—the two political *categories.* Cp. infra. p. 151, l. 11.

L. 27. *to introduce poverty, as a constable,* &c. "He is an unskilful physician that cannot cure one disease without casting his patient into another: so he that can find no other way for correcting the errors of his people but by taking from them the conveniencies of life, shows that he knows not what it is to govern a free nation." Sir T. More's Utopia (Bp. Burnet's translation), Book I. Cp. inf. p. 248, "the exploded problem of tyranny, which proposes to beggar its subjects into submission."

L. 28. *If our dominions abroad are the roots which feed all this rank luxuriance of sedition.* "The *current price of boroughs*—for such is the corrupt state of the national representation in England, that this language is authorized by common use—was enormously raised by the rival plunderers of the East and of the West, who, by a new species of alchymy, had transmuted into English gold the *Blood of Africa* and the *Tears of Hindostan*. Many private fortunes were ruined, or materially impaired, by contests carried on with the utmost shamelessness of political depravity." Belsham, History of Great Britain, vol. v. p. 268 (Anno 1768).

P. 74, L. 5. *this untoward people*—"this untoward generation," Acts ii. 40.

IBID. *I hear it indeed sometimes asserted, &c.* "On the other hand, several of the Court party cried out for measures of severity. The authority of Parliament had been trampled upon. The K—— had been insulted on his throne. . . . . To support the ministers effectually it was not only necessary to adhere to their grand measure in the Middlesex election, as a perpetual rule of policy; but to punish the contraveners, who, otherwise, might continually keep alive that matter of complaint." Burke, Ann. Reg. 1770.

L. 29. *When popular discontents have been very prevalent, &c.* "Politicians may say what they please, but it is no hard thing for the meanest person to know whether he be well or ill governed," &c. Swift, Sermon V, on martyrdom of Charles I. See infra, p. 252.

L. 31. *something amiss in the conduct of Government.* "The disorders of the people, in the present time and in the present place, are owing to the usual and natural cause of such disorders at all times and in all places, when such have prevailed—the misconduct of government; they are owing to plans laid in error, pursued with obstinacy, and conducted without wisdom." Address to the King (1777).

[240] **L. 33.** *When they do wrong, it is their error.* "The errors and sufferings of the people are from their governors. . . . The people cannot see, but they can feel." Harrington's Political Aphorisms (1659).

P. 75, L. 1. *Les révolutions qui arrivent—impatience de souffrir.* Memoirs of Sully, tom. i. p. 133. (Burke.) But there follows (p. 97) a partial exculpation of the Earl of Bute, the only man who resembled the favourites of Henry III. The parallel of the discontents will not bear close examination, and it is due to Burke to add that not only is it none of his invention, but that in an earlier pamphlet he had taken some pains to expose its unsoundness. Grenville had introduced it in his pamphlet on the State of the Nation, with the foolish idea of exhibiting himself as the counterpart of Sully.

Thoughts on the Present Discontents

L. 3. *"Pour le populace,"* &c. *"General* rebellions and revolts of a whole people never were *encouraged,* now or at any time. They are always *provoked."* This is represented as the lesson of the "whole course of history" (Letter to the Sheriffs of Bristol).

L. 11. *trustees of power.* Cp. p. 118, "They are all Trustees for the people," &c., and note.

L. 32. *generality of people,* &c. Nothing is more striking than the general truth of Burke's aphorism that the majority of people are half a century behind-hand in their politics. It will scarcely be credited that in 1777 one Dr. Miles Newton preached a sermon at Oxford strenuously denying the doctrines of power derived from the people, and of the lawfulness of resistance. This effusion was provoked by the recent publication of Dr. Powell's Sermons. At the present day the Tories, of the two parties, are the least liable to the charge of hoarding worn-out ideas.

P. 76, L. 2. *in books everything is settled for them,* &c. History in the time of Burke had already begun to assume the philosophical tone, which assumes that the reader is either too dull or too indolent to draw an inference for himself. When this pamphlet was written, Robertson's chief works had been published, and Hume was in his fifth edition. On the difference between Burnet and modern historians, cp. Charles Lamb's letter to Manning, Works, p. 55.

L. 4. *Men are wise with but little reflection,* &c. "It is natural to mean well, when only abstracted ideas of virtue are proposed to the mind, and no particular passion turns us aside from rectitude: and so willing is every man to flatter himself, that the difference between approving laws and obeying them is frequently forgotten." Johnson, Rambler, No. 76. See the famous passage in vol. ii. p. 244.

L. 8. *the whole train of circumstances,* &c. "The examples which history presents to us, both of men and of events, are generally complete: the whole example is before us, &c." Bolingbroke, On the Study of History.

L. 11. *Whig on the business of an hundred years ago.* Alluding to the professed Whigs who had joined the Court party, and to ministers like George Grenville, Charles Townshend, Lord North, and Lord Mansfield, who boasted of the name of Whig, while leading the policy of would-be tyranny. [241] "He who has once been a Whig, let him act never so contrary to his principles, is nevertheless a Whig," &c. Lyttelton, Letters from a Persian, No. 57. The doggrel character of the Whig

member of Parliament, drawn by Soame Jenyns, himself a supporter
of Walpole, in his "Modern Fine Gentleman" (1746), will supply many
illustrations of this pamphlet:

> In parliament he purchases a seat,
> To make the accomplish'd gentleman complete:
> There, safe in self-sufficient impudence,
> Without experience, honesty, or sense,
> Unknowing in her interest, trade, or laws,
> He vainly undertakes his country's cause.
> Forth from his lips, prepared at all to rail,
> Torrents of nonsense burst, like bottled ale,
> Though shallow, muddy; brisk, though mighty dull;
> Fierce without strength; o'erflowing, yet not full;
> Now, quite a Frenchman in his garb and air,
> His neck yok'd down with bag and solitaire,
> The liberties of Britain he supports,
> And storms at placemen, ministers, and courts.

Next, we have him among his constituents:

> Now in cropt greasy hair, and leather breeches,
> He loudly bellows out his patriot speeches;
> King, lords, and commons ventures to abuse,
> Yet dares to show those ears he ought to lose.

The end of all is—

> He digs no longer in the exhausted mine,
> But seeks preferment, as the last resort,
> Cringes each morn at levées, bows at court,
> And, from the hand he hates, implores support;
> The minister, well pleas'd at small expence
> To silence so much rude impertinence,
> With squeeze and whisper yields to his demands,
> And on the venal list enrolled he stands;
> A ribband and a pension buy the slave;
> This bribes the fool about him, that the knave.
> And now, arriv'd at his meridian glory,
> He sinks apace, despis'd by Whig and Tory;
> Of independence now he talks no more,
> Nor shakes the senate with his patriot roar;
> But silent votes, and with court trappings hung,
> Eyes his own glittering star, and holds his tongue.

A contemporary observer writes: "Une très longue expérience prouve,
que dans la Grande Bretagne le *Patriotisme* de ceux, qui se montrent
opposés à la cour ou au parti du ministère, n'a pour objet que d'impor-

tuner le Souverain, de contrarier les actions de ses ministres, de renverser leurs projets les [242] plus sensés; uniquement, pour avoir part soi-même au ministère, c'est à dire, aux depouilles de la nation." Système Social, Part ii. ch. 6.

L. 13. *historical patriotism.* "You will be wise historically, a fool in practice." Vol. ii., ubi sup.

L. 16. *Many a stern republican,* &c. In Bubb Dodington's correspondence with the Duke of Newcastle, in reference to his preferment, which has been described as exhibiting the meanest sentiments that ever were trusted to paper, he declared that a peerage was "not worth the expense of new-painting his coach." Better men have assumed similar airs. "Halifax was in speculation a strong republican, and did not conceal it. He often made hereditary monarchy and aristocracy the subjects of his keen pleasantry, while he was fighting the battles of the Court, and obtaining for himself step after step in the peerage. In this way he tried to gratify at once his intellectual vanity, and his mere vulgar ambition." Macaulay, Essay on Sir William Temple. Cp. vol. ii. p. 155.

L. 18. *Our true Saxon constitution.* See Burke's interesting Fragment of an Essay on the History of English Law. "N. Bacon, in order to establish his republican system, has so distorted all the evidence he has produced, concealed so many things of consequence, and thrown such false colours upon the whole argument, that I know no book so likely to mislead the reader in antiquities, if yet it retains any authority. In reality, that ancient constitution, and those Saxon laws, made little or nothing for any of our modern parties. . . . Nothing has been a larger theme of panegyrick with all our writers on politicks and history, than the Anglo-Saxon government; and it is impossible not to conceive an high opinion of its laws, if we rather consider what is said of them, than what they visibly are," &c. (Bolingbroke had made large use of N. Bacon as an authority.) The figment of the Saxon constitution, however, long survived the ridicule of Burke. Cp. the once popular Lesson to a Young Prince, intended for Prince George, afterwards George IV, with its absurd copper-plate illustrations of different constitutions.

L. 19. *splendid bile.* Horace, Satires, ii. 3. 141.

L. 20. *coarsest* work—used like "job," *in malam partem:*

> You have made *good work,*
You and your apron men.
>
> Shakspeare, Coriolanus, iv. 6.

Cp. the common expression "what *work* was made of it," i.e. what a bungle.

L. 30. *alteration to the prejudice of our constitution.* It is a well-known maxim of Machiavelli that a free government must be perpetually making new regulations to secure its liberty. According to this doctrine, it is in the nature of things that some alterations should take place, and if they are not directed in one way they proceed, by a species of gravitation, in the other. Burke professes to enter thoroughly into that spirit of jealousy of government which prevailed for centuries among the English people. Bolingbroke writes in the Patriot King: "Men decline easily from virtue. There is a devil, too, in the political system—a constant tempter at hand."

[243] **L. 31.** *These attempts will naturally vary in their mode, according to times and circumstances.* "Seldom have two ages the same fashion in their pretexts and the same modes of mischief. Wickedness is a little more inventive. Whilst you are discussing fashion, the fashion is gone by. The very same vice assumes a new body. The spirit transmigrates; and far from losing its principle of life by the change of its appearance, it is renovated in its new organs with the fresh vigour of a juvenile activity." And so further in Burke's very best style, vol. ii. ubi sup.

P. 77, L. 1. *Furniture of ancient tyranny,* &c. "You will find nothing in their houses but the refuse of *Knave's* Acre: nothing but the rotten stuff, &c. &c. It is nearly two thousand years since it has been observed that these devices of ambition, avarice, and turbulence, were antiquated." Appeal from New to Old Whigs. "They have totally abandoned the shattered and old-fashioned fortress of Prerogative," &c., infra, p. 120.

L. 3. *to fall into the identical snare.* "The unpitied calamity of being repeatedly caught in the same snare," infra, p. 161.

> Oh, foolish *Israel!* never warned by ill!
> Still the same bait, and circumvented still!
> > Dryden, Absalom and Achitophel.

L. 7. *ship-money.* See Hallam, Constitutional History, ch. viii.

IBID. *An Extension of the Forest Laws.* As by Charles I. See Hallam, ibid; Macaulay, History of England, i. 195 (of Clarendon).

L. 11. *Exaction of two hundred pullets,* &c. "Uxor Hugonis de Nevill dat Domino Regi ducentas gallinas, eo quod possit jacere una nocte cum Domino suo Hugone de Nevill." Madox, Hist. Exch. c. xiii. p. 326. (Burke.)

THOUGHTS ON THE PRESENT DISCONTENTS

L. 13. *Every age has its own manners,* &c. Burke sums up, as usual with him, in a single sentence, the conclusions of the two preceding paragraphs.

L. 18. *Against the being of Parliament. . . . no designs have ever been entertained since the Revolution.* Burke might have gone back earlier. Lord Egmont was one of the first to draw attention to the exaggerated importance generally attached to the Revolution as an era of *civil* liberty. "The Revolution," says Mr. Hallam, "is justly entitled to honour as the era of religious in a far greater degree than civil liberty: the privileges of conscience having no earlier Magna Charta and Petition of Right whereto they could appeal against encroachment." Constitutional History, ch. xv.

L. 24. *However they may hire out the usufruct of their voices,* &c. This recalls the irony of Butler's Characters, published by Thyer in 1759 and noticed by Burke in the Annual Register for that year. Burke's pungent remark is copied by Macaulay in his essay on Sir William Temple.

L. 26. *Those who have been of the most known devotion,* &c. Dyson was especially forward in asserting it. See G. Grenville's Speech of February 2, 1769, Parliamentary History, xvi. 550.

P. 78, L. 1. *forms of a free . . . ends of an arbitrary Government.* The policy of Tiberius as described by Tacitus will at once suggest itself to the student. "A constitution may be lost, whilst all its forms are preserved," [244] Ann. Reg. 1763, p. 42. On the converse possibility, see Macaulay's essay on Lord Burleigh: "The government of the Tudors was a popular government under the forms of a despotism," &c.

L. 4. *The power of the Crown . . . Prerogative . . . Influence.*

> But let us grant excess of Tyranny
> Could scape the heavy hand of God and man;
> Yet by the natural variety
> Of frailties, reigning since the world began,
> Faint relaxations doubtless will ensue,
> And change force into craft, old times to new.
> Lord Brooke, Treat. of Monarchy, sect. 3.

"The formidable prerogatives of the Sovereign were, indeed, reduced within the bounds of a just executive authority, and limited by the strict letter of the laws. But the terror and jealousy of the people were quieted by this victory, and the mild and seducing dominion of influence stole upon us insensibly in its stead, bestowing a greater and more fatal authority than ever existed in the most arbitrary periods of the government. . . . The Crown, by appearing to act with the consent of the people through their representatives, though in fact by its own influence, is enabled to carry on a system which the most absolute prince could not have fastened upon England for centuries past." Erskine, Speech for Reform, May 26, 1797. He goes on to point out that Burke, "as he abhorred reform, must be supposed to have disclosed unwillingly the disgraces of Parliament." "The state of things has much altered in this country, since it was necessary to protect our representatives against the direct power of the Crown. We have nothing to apprehend from prerogative, but everything from undue influence." Junius, April 22, 1771.

L. 6. *Influence.* The name, and the thing itself, were alike borrowed from the great Whig lords. It might seem strange that the King should be the only English gentleman whose rightful possessions and lawful connexions entitled him to no political power or credit, but this doctrine was remorselessly urged by the Whigs.

L. 13. *moulded in its original stamina irresistible principles,* &c. A favourite image of Burke. "The heads of certain families should make it their business, by the whole course of their lives, principally by their example, to mould into the very vital stamina of their descendants, those principles which ought to be transmitted pure and unmixed to posterity." Letter to the Duke of Richmond, November 17, 1772.

L. 22. *the Court had drawn far less advantage.* This is partly to be explained by the predilections of the first two Georges. George the Third had an Englishman's passion for state business, and was naturally disposed to claim all the influence to which his active exertions might entitle him.

P. 79, L. 9. *confidence in their own strength . . . fear of offending their friends. Men of great natural interest — of great acquired consideration.* Alluding to Pitt on the one hand, and the great Whig leaders on the other.

L. 19. *returned again,* &c. The image of rain and the ocean was a favourite one with Burke. Readers of Cobbett will remember his attack on Burke for applying it to money raised by taxation and afterwards spent in [245] "refreshing showers" among the people by whom it was supplied. "Mortmain," a name given to the estate of bodies corporate, is synonymous with "inalienable domain."

L. 24. *nature of despotism to abhor power,* &c. It was the constant employment of the terms "despotism," "tyranny," "liberty," "the people,"

THOUGHTS ON THE PRESENT DISCONTENTS

&c., in this pamphlet, that so irritated those who called themselves *Supporters of the Bill of Rights* (Wilkes, Glynn, Sawbridge, &c.), of whom the "republican virago" (Correspondence i. 230), Mrs Macaulay, was the literary champion. That an aristocratic faction should lisp the Shibboleth of democracy seemed intolerable.

P. 80, L. 3. *A certain set of intriguing men . . . court of Frederick Prince of Wales.* See Introduction.

L. 9. *a person in rank indeed* respectable, &c. The Earl of Bute. "Respectable" is here used in the earlier and French sense = worthy of respect.

L. 10. *very ample in fortune.* This generously contradicts sinister remarks caused by the enormous amount (between 200,000*l.* and 300,000*l.*) expended by Lord Bute in purchasing an estate, laying out a park, and building houses, in 1763–1765, whilst his clear income was asserted to be only 5000*l.* per annum. Cp. Anti-Sejanus (Scott), Letter of August 3, 1765.

L. 16. *that idea was soon abandoned.* Bute resigned in April 1763.

L. 20. *the reformed plan,* &c. "The plan of Bute and George III," says Earl Russell, "was not so systematic, nor was the Whig government so beneficial as Burke has depicted: but the project was certainly formed of restoring to the Crown that absolute direction and control which Charles I and James II had been forced to relinquish, and from which George I and George II had quietly abstained." Bedford Corresp. vol. iii, Preface, p. xxix.

L. 27. executory *duties of government*—a legal word, employed by Burke in an unusual sense. He seems to have adopted it from the French phrase *puissance exécutrice* (Montesquieu). Swift and Addison said, as we do, *executive.*

P. 81, L. 2. *to bring Parliament to an acquiescence in this project.* The submission was not unprecedented. "The Parliament having resigned all their ecclesiastical liberties, proceeded to an entire surrender of their civil, and without any scruple or deliberation, they made by one act a total subversion of the English constitution." Hume, c. 37 (Henry VIII), alluding to 31 Hen. VIII. cap. 1, repealed by 1 Edw. VI. c. 12. Filangieri says of this occasion, "This part of the history of England may convince us that in mixed Governments of this nature, the prince may often succeed in his wishes, and even oppress the nation without any alteration in the form of the constitution, and without any risk to his personal safety, if he have only the address to corrupt the assembly which represents the sovereignty." Scienza della Legislazione, c. 10. Bolingbroke (Diss. on Parties, Letter [246] xvii.) takes exception to the maxim of Bacon, that England could never be undone, unless by parliaments: but the facts of history confirm the conclusion of the elder statesman. The maxim has been attributed to Lord Burleigh. Anecdotes of Lord Chatham, vol. ii. p. 216.

L. 21. *than in a Turkish army.* "As among the Turks, and most of the Eastern tyrannies, there is no nobility, and no man has any considerable advantage above the common people, unless by the immediate favour of the Prince; so in all the legal kingdoms of the North, the strength of the government has always been placed in the nobility; and no better defence has been found against the encroachments of ill Kings than by setting up an order of men, who, by holding large territories, and having great numbers of tenants and dependants, might be able to restrain the exorbitancies that either the Kings or the Commons, might run into." Sidney, Discourses Concerning Government, chap. iii. sec. 28.

L. 22. *might appoint one of his footmen.* Alluding to Lord Holland's saying "The King may make a page first minister." Walpole, Mem. iii. 66.

L. 25. *first name for rank or wisdom.* This distinction again alludes to the Duke of Newcastle and Pitt.

P. 82, L. 11. *Arguments not wholly unplausible.* The case is impartially stated by Burke in the Annual Register for 1763, chap. vii.

L. 12. *These opportunities and these arguments,* &c. A summary of the pamphlet. Cp. Argument, p. 69.

L. 26. *victorious in every part of the globe.* The earlier volumes of the Annual Register contain Burke's chronicle of these victories. See Macknight's Life of Burke, vol. i.

L. 28. *foreign habitudes.* As in the case of the two first Georges.

L. 31. *a large, but definite sum*—800,000*l.* See May's Const. Hist., ch. iv.

L. 32. *additions from conquest.* Canada and the Floridas, together with some possessions in the West Indies and in Africa.

P. 83, L. 3. *averseness from.* Better than the modern phrase "averse to."

L. 5. *reversionary hope.* Such as had existed when the return of the Pretender was still possible.

L. 6. *inspired his Majesty only with a more ardent desire to preserve unimpaired the spirit of that national freedom.* The pamphlet was intended to conciliate the monarch, while attacking his instruments. In his speeches and writings Burke always preserved a respectful tone towards the King. Among his friends he was not always so cautious. "One day he (Burke) came into the room (Reynolds's studio) when Goldsmith was there, full of ire and abuse against the late King (George III), and went on in such a torrent of unqualified invective that Goldsmith threatened to leave the room. The other, however, persisted; and Goldsmith went out, unable to bear it any longer." Hazlitt, Conversations of Northcote, p. 40. Another of these ebullitions occurred later on, when the King was seized by a fit of mental aberration, on which occasion he said publicly "that the Almighty had hurled him from his throne."

[247] **L. 14.** *natural influence . . . honourable service.* See note to p. 81, l. 25.

L. 17. *former bottom.* "Bottom" means here the keel of a ship.

L. 22. *gradually, but not slowly.* Notice the distinction.

L. 30. *under a forced coalition there rankled an incurable alienation,* &c. The formation of Pitt's first ministry in December 1756 was on a thoroughly popular basis. The refusal of Pitt, Temple, and Legge to support the unfortunate German expedition of the Duke of Cumberland, occasioned their removal: but the public will which had brought them in was strong enough to procure their recall. The second ministry was formed in June 1757, including Lord Anson, Sir R. Henley, and Mr. Fox, of the opposition. Fox was placed in the Pay Office, which Pitt had left: "a triumph," says his candid biographer, "too diminutive for the dignity of Mr. Pitt's mind. However, he enjoyed it: which shows the influence of little passions in men of the first abilities." Anecdotes of Lord Chatham, vol. i. p. 249.

L. 34. *endeavoured by various artifices to ruin his character.* Through fear lest the popular will, which had brought him back to power in 1757, might do so again. The hired press, in the hands of the Leicester House faction, branded him with the names of Pensioner, Apostate, Deserter, &c. A pamphlet of considerable size, says Adolphus, was formed by the republication of paragraphs which appeared against him in the newspapers on this single occasion. The barony of Chatham conferred on his wife at his resignation, and the annuity of 3000*l.* per. annum, furnished substantial grounds for unpopularity.

P. 84, L. 17. *Long possession,* &c. Burke was fond of recounting the historical merits of the Whig party. "If I have wandered," he writes in another place, "out of the paths of rectitude into those of an interested faction, it was in company with the Saviles, the Dowdeswells, the Wentworths, the Bentincks; with the Lenoxes, the Manchesters, the Keppels, the Saunderses; with the temperate, permanent, hereditary virtue of the whole house of Cavendish; names among which some have extended your fame and empire in arms, and all have fought the battle of your liberties in fields not less glorious."

L. 30. *The whole party was put under a proscription,* &c. A more severe political persecution never raged. See Walpole, Memoirs, vol. i. p. 233. "Numberless innocent families which had subsisted on salaries from 50*l.* to 100*l.* a year, turned out to misery and ruin." Speech of Lord Rockingham, Jan. 22, 1770. "A cruel and inhuman proscription at the Customhouse," Duke of Newcastle. Rockingham Memoirs, i. 235. Noblemen of the first consideration, like the Duke of Newcastle and Earl Temple were deprived of their county lieutenancies. The proscription was directed by Lord Holland.

P. 85, L. 9. *Here and there . . . a few individuals were left standing.* Lord Northington, Lord Granville, the Duke of Bedford, and Lord Halifax, besides Lord Holland (Fox), continued in office under Lord Bute.

L. 27. *a pamphlet which had all the appearance of a manifesto.* [248] "Sentiments of an honest man." (Burke.) The true title is "Seasonable Hints from an Honest Man on the present important crisis of a new Reign and a new Parliament." London, printed for A. Millar, 1761 (published March 16, 1761), p. 62. The author was Lord Bath (Pulteney), and the pamphlet is a curious link between two political generations, being the last effort of the great antagonist of Sir Robert Walpole (1725–1742). See Almon's Anecdotes of Lord Chatham, vol. ii. p. 219, and Walpole's Memoirs. Lord Bath was among Burke's earliest political acquaintances.

L. 31. *written with no small art and address.* The only remarkable passage in the pamphlet seems that which contains the aphorism borrowed from Defoe, "Party is the madness of the many for the gain of the few," p. 32. It is plainly written, and bears marks of declining power. Walpole says, "the author, and some of the doctrines it broached—not any merit in the composition—make it memorable." Mem. Geo. III. i. 54. "In general the language of the pamphlet was that of the Court, who conducted themselves by the advice bequeathed by Lord Bolingbroke, who had, and with truth, assured the late Prince of Wales that the Tories would be the heartiest in support of prerogative." Ibid. The reputation of the author as a wit, as well as a politician, was great. "How many Martials are in Pulteney lost!" Pope. "How can I Pult'ney, Chesterfield forget, While Roman spirit charms, and Attic wit?" Id. "All wit, about six years ago, came from L(ord) C(hesterfield): and nobody could say a clever thing that was not by the *vox populi* placed to his lordship's general account. For some time every Monitor, with very long sentences in it, was my friend Pitt's; every political pamphlet the E(arl) of B(ath)'s," &c. Ann. Register, 1760, p. 211.

P. 86, L. 4. *a perspective view of the Court,* i.e. a transparency, as in a puppet show.

L. 15. *those good souls, whose credulous morality,* &c. "Of all kinds of credulity, the most obstinate and wonderful is that of political zealots; of men, who, being numbered, they know not how nor why, in any of the parties that divide a State, resign the use of their own eyes and ears, and resolve to believe nothing that does not favour those whom they profess to follow." The Idler, Ann. Register, 1758. With such "good souls," arguments of a moral character, however misplaced, go a long way.

L. 21. *sure* constantly *to end,* i.e. without exception—not as now used = frequently. Cp. infra p. 150, and note.

L. 22. *talking prose all their lives without knowing anything of the matter.* "Mr. JORDAN: O' my conscience I have spoke Prose above these forty years, without knowing anything of the matter," &c. Molière, Bourgeois Gentilhomme (The Cit Turn'd Gentleman: Works French and English, 1755, vol. viii. p. 54). This stock-piece of humour was apparently introduced into English literature in "Martinus Scriblerus," ch. xii.

L. 29. *which had been infamously monopolized and huckstered.* "I have never deemed it reasonable that any confederacy of great names should monopolize to themselves the whole patronage and authority of the state: [249] should constitute themselves, as it were, into a corporation, a bank for circulating the favours of the Crown and the suffrages of the people, and distributing them only to their own adherents." Canning on the Whig doctrine of Party, Speech on Embassy to Lisbon, May 6, 1817.

L. 32. *Mettre le Roy hors de page.* A phrase applied by contemporary historians to Louis XI. Sidney, Discourses concerning Government, chap. ii. § 30: "For that reason (increasing the power of the crown) he is said by Mezeray and others 'to have brought those kings out of guardianship.' (D'avoir mis les roys hors de page)." It is also quoted by Bolingbroke, 6th "Letter on the Study of History."

L. 34. runners *of the Court*—those who did the lowest work, spies, messengers, &c. Burke's Correspondence, vol. ii. p. 205, "One of the runners of Government in the City—a tool of Harley." Infra, p. 203, "The wretched runners for a wretched cause."

P. 87, L. 10. *no concert, order, or effect,* &c. This, with many other topics, is repeated from the pamphlet on the State of the Nation. Cp. also p. 146, l. 20.

L. 30. *carried the glory, the power, the commerce of England,* &c. "That infernal chaos, into which he (Bute) from the first plunged affairs, at the time that through his cloudy imbecility it so soon thickened in the clear of the fairest horizon that ever tantalized a country with the promise of meridian splendor." Public Advertiser, August 30, 1776.

P. 88, L. 12. *condition of servility.* An impression of which George III always found it impossible to disabuse himself.

L. 19. *topicks . . . much employed by that political school.* See the political writings of the late Dr. Brown, and many others. (Burke.) Thoughts on Civil Liberty, Licentiousness, and Faction, Second Edition, 1765. This work is written somewhat in the spirit of Dr. Johnson, to attack Bolingbroke's views, based on the disavowal of natural religion, and Mandeville's, based on the alleged incurable depravity of human nature. Like Bolingbroke, however, he attacks the Whig doctrine of "men not measures," and aims "to unite all honest men of all parties," p. 124, and with Mandeville he maintains the unconditional necessity of corruption in all free governments, p. 142. The state of things which forced Pitt into power in 1757 is marked as the culminating point of the corruption of the age. He advocates "a general and prescribed improvement in the laws of Education" (p. 156) as a remedy for the disorders of the State ("a correspondent and adequate Code of Education inwrought into its first Essence," p. 159). A better work is the Estimate of the Manners and Principles of the Times, 2 vols. 1757–8 (reviewed in the Annual Register, 1758), an attack on the existing system of education, beginning with the universities, on effeminacy in manners, luxury in dress, &c.; the exorbitant advance of trade and wealth is adduced as a cause of depravity; and change is advocated on general moral grounds.

THOUGHTS ON THE PRESENT DISCONTENTS

L. 29. *lately appeared in the House of Lords a disposition to some attempts derogatory to the rights of the subject.* The allusion is to the Debates on the [250] Bill of Indemnity for those concerned in the Embargo on Wheat and Wheatflour going out of the Kingdom, 1766. This embargo was laid on by the King in Council previous to the meeting of Parliament. It was indignantly animadverted upon in both houses, on the ground that the assumption of a prerogative to dispense with an existing law, under any circumstances, was unconstitutional, and tended directly to establish an unlimited tyranny. But in the House of Lords especially, members and friends of the ministry who had set up as patrons and defenders of liberty, not only defended this exercise of prerogative under the peculiar circumstances which accompanied it (*Salus populi suprema lex,* "It is but forty days tyranny at the outside"), but supported as a matter of right such a dispensing power in the Crown. See Parliamentary History, vol. xvi. pp. 245–313.

P. 89, L. 8. *While they are men of property, it is impossible to prevent it . . . property is power.* The law that power follows the balance of property, first clearly laid down by Harrington, was thought by Adams to be a discovery comparable with Harvey's on the circulation of the blood. But Burke's Aristotelian views of the fallibility of general laws in politics, must be kept in mind. "That power goes with Property is not universally true, and the idea that the operation of it is certain and invariable may mislead us very fatally." Thoughts on French Affairs, December, 1791. The decline of the power of the crown after the Tudors was thought to be traceable to the alienation of the Crown Lands, which previously included about one fourth of the Kingdom. Bishop Burnet, with a view of reinstating the Crown in its former power, advised the House of Hanover to apply as much surplus revenue as possible (300,000*l.* or 400,000*l.* per annum) in repurchasing the Crown Lands. "This would purchase 15,000*l.* by the year of good land every year; which in about ten or fifteen years' time would be a good estate of its selfe, and may be so contrived as that the nation shall take but little notice in the doing it, &c." Memorial to Princess Sophia, p. 67.

L. 14. *any particular peers*—the Rockingham party.

L. 23. *a bad habit to moot cases,* &c. English political writers have always freely indulged in the habit.

L. 26. *that austere and insolent domination.* "The worst imaginable government, a feudal aristocracy," Burke's Abridgment of English Hist., Book iii. c. 8. Cp. the description of Poland under such a government, Ann. Reg. 1763. "Every new tribunal, erected for the decision of facts, without the interposition of a jury . . . is a step towards establishing aristocracy, the most oppressive of absolute governments." Id. 1768, p. 272.

L. 29. *influence of a Court, and of a Peerage, which . . . is the most imminent.* Pope thus describes the supposed paralysing influence of a Whig minister:

> Perhaps more high some daring son may soar,
> Proud to my list to add one monarch more;
> And nobly conscious princes are but things
> Born for First Ministers, as slaves for Kings.
> [251] Tyrant supreme! shall three Estates command,
> And make one mighty Dunciad of the land!
>
> Dunciad, iv. 599.

The opinion that England was like to end in despotism prevailed in many thinking minds from the time when Hume wrote the Essay on the British Government ("Absolute Monarchy—the true Euthanasia of the British Constitution") to the end of the reign of George III. "Despotism," wrote Bentham in 1817, "is advancing in seven-leagued boots." Works, iii. 486. On the anticipation of an absolute aristocracy, in the early part of that reign, cp. Churchill, The Farewell, Works, Fifth Edition, iii. 147, 148:

> Let not a Mob of Tyrants seize the helm,
> Nor titled upstarts league to rob the realm,
> Let not, whatever other ills assail,
> A damned ARISTOCRACY prevail.
> If, all too short, our course of Freedom run,
> 'Tis thy good pleasure we should be undone,
> Let us, some comfort in our griefs to bring,
> Be slaves to one, and be that one a King.

Cp. also Goldsmith, Traveller (1764);

> But when contending chiefs blockade the throne
> Contracting regal power to stretch their own,
> When I behold a factious band agree
> To call it freedom when themselves are free—
>
> .   .   .   .
>
> . . . half a patriot, half a coward grown,
> I fly from petty tyrants to the throne.

Dr. Primrose, in the Vicar of Wakefield (ch. xix), expresses a similar feeling. See also Cowper, Task, Book v. 485 sqq. The fear of the Whig nobles constantly haunted the brain of George the Third. He often declared his determination not to submit to be *shackled by those desperate men,* Correspondence with Lord North, passim. Burke was acute enough to see where the real weakness of the body of the Peers lay, and how few could leave below them what Grattan termed the "vulgar level of the great."

P. 90, L. 9. *back-stairs influence.* P. 81, l. 27.

L. 28. *Harrington's political club.* See next note.

P. 91, L. 20. *established a sort of Rota in the Court.* Harrington's club, called the Rota, had for its aim to bring the nation to adopt a scheme of aristocracy. The name is borrowed from the privy council of the Court of Rome. Sidrophel, in Hudibras, is described as being

> as full of tricks
As Rota-men of politics.

> Part II. Canto iii. 1107.

L. 21. *All sorts of parties . . . have been brought into Administration, . . . few have had the good fortune to escape without disgrace,* &c. Every statesman of the day, except Lord Temple, was in turn gulled by the King into accepting office, and then left to find out that he was expected to hold it by a tenure inconsistent alike with self-respect and constitutional traditions. [252] "Upon my word," writes Sir George Savile to Lord Rockingham, "I can see nothing before you, but cutting in again the other rubber with the trumps and strong suits still in one hand; who positively will let no one player so much as get through a game, much less have good cards or win. I am far from being politician enough to analyse or prove all I say, but I do say that it all goes exceedingly well to that tune. You know I always said, with many more, that you—the last set—were humbugged. Granting this, we have now three things which seem all to point one way. G. G. first, your set second, and Lord C—— last (which is precedence in matter of duping); all in turn made to believe that they should be supported; nay, in the last instance actually ostensibly supported, yet all by hook or by crook let down either by ineffectual support, or, as the case seems now, by admitting to a show of power on such previous conditions as shall sow the seeds of dissolution in the very establishment of a Ministry." Rockingham Memoirs, vol. ii. p. 41. Savile, a shrewd observer and clear speaker, was the first to predict the future greatness of Charles Fox.

P. 92, L. 7. *many rotten members belonging to the best connexions.* "That tail which draggles in the dirt, and which every party in every state *must* carry about it." Burke, Correspondence, vol. ii. p. 385. "Parties are like coin: which would never be fit for common use without some considerable alloy of the baser metals." Lord Stanhope, History of England, vol. v. p. 179. The image is borrowed from Bacon, Essay I.

L. 13. *the Junto* = cabal or faction. The opposite party applied the term to the Whigs; cp. "Seasonable Hints."

L. 14. *Retrenchment,* Fr. "retranchement" = intrenchment.

L. 24. *A minister of state.* The allusion is not to a Premier.

L. 25. *collegues,* Fr. "collégues," classical, and always used by Burke.

P. 93, L. 10. *some person of whom the party entertains an high opinion.* The allusion is to the young Duke of Grafton, who was one of the Secretaries in Lord Rockingham's ministry.

L. 17. *Afterwards they are sure to destroy him in his turn; by setting up in his place,* &c. The Duke of Grafton was displaced in January 1770, when Lord North became First Lord of the Treasury.

L. 24. *an attempt to strip a particular friend of his family estate.* Alluding to the scandalous attempt to deprive the Duke of Portland of Inglewood forest with the Manor and Castle of Carlisle, and extensive appurtenant election influence, by a grant to Sir James Lowther, the son-in-law of Lord Bute. These premises, though not specified in the grant from William III of the honour of Penrith to the Portland family, had been enjoyed by the family for several descents under that tenure. The grant was completed and sealed before the Duke had the opportunity of establishing his title, notwithstanding a caveat entered in the Exchequer, the Treasury relying on the antiquated prerogative maxim *nullum tempus occurrit regi.* Sir G. Savile's bill abolishing this maxim, though at first rejected, subsequently became law: and sixty years adverse possession now defeats the title of the Crown [253] to lands. In this way an attempted wrong on an individual, agreeably to the genius of English legislation, became the means of establishing the liberties of the community at large. On the share of the Duke of Grafton in the transaction alluded to by Burke, see Junius, Letter lxvii: "You hastened the grant, with an expedition unknown to the Treasury, that he might have it time enough to give a decisive turn to the election for the county." On this election the Duke and Sir James are supposed to have spent about 40,000*l.* apiece. May's Const. History, i. 354. Sir James Lowther, in one day, served four hundred ejectments on the tenants of three extensive domains: but was nonsuited in the Court of Exchequer.

Thoughts on the Present Discontents

P. 96, L. 1. *Like Janissaries, they derive a kind of freedom,* &c. Cp. "the ancient household troops of that side of the house." Infra, p. 164, &c. "In the teeth of all the old mercenary Swiss of state," p. 195, and p. 197. G. Grenville first applied the term to the King's men: "a set of Janissaries, who might at any time be ordered to put the bowstring around his neck." Bedford Correspondence, vol. iii.

L. 2. *the very condition of their servitude . . . people should be so desirous of adding themselves to that body.* Burke, in speaking of the Janissaries, perhaps has in mind the description in the letter of Lady M. W. Montagu to the Countess of Bristol, April 1, 1717. "This (offering to bring the head of the cadi who had neglected her orders) may give you some idea of the unlimited power of these fellows, who are all sworn brothers, and bound to revenge the injuries done to one another, whether at Cairo, Aleppo, or any part of the world. This inviolable league makes them so powerful, that the greatest man at Court never speaks to them but in a flattering tone; and in Asia, any man that is rich is forced to enrol himself a Janizary, to secure his estate."

L. 14. *invidious exclusion.* "The King of France," says Machiavelli, "suffers nobody to call himself of the King's party, because that would imply a party against him." "The King of England," pertinently remarks a critic of the day, "has no *enemies.*"

L. 23. *for eight years past.* The institution was supposed to have been set up after Lord Bute had been forced to resign, as a defence to the Crown against the Whig Ministries. See Butler's Reminiscences, vol. ii. p. 114.

P. 97, L. 1. *hid but for a moment.* Cp. infra, p. 207.

L. 5. *without any idea of proscription.* Referring to Lord Holland's proscription. See note to p. 84, l. 31.

L. 11. *abhorred and violently opposed by the Court Faction,* &c. But it was the inherent weakness of the Rockingham administration, and the unhappy schisms among the Whigs, rather than the opposition of the King's friends, which brought about its fall. This was notorious at the time. Cp. note to p. 196, l. 9.

L. 15. *I should say so little of the Earl of Bute,* &c. Burke wished rather to conciliate than to offend this nobleman. The democratic party were exceedingly enraged at his being treated so leniently.

[254] **L. 20.** *to* blacken *this nobleman.* This absolute use of the word is much better than the modern phrase, "to blacken his character." Cp.

NOTES

South, Serm. xxi.: "Do but paint an angel black, and that is enough to make him pass for a devil. 'Let us blacken him, let us blacken him what we can,' said that miscreant Harrison of the blessed King," &c. Cp. vol. ii. p. 210, l. 4.

L. 23. *a dangerous national quarrel*—alluding to the indecent attacks on the Scotch nation in the North Briton and other publications of that day.

L. 28. *indifference to the constitution.* By a natural reaction from the violent Whiggism of the early part of the century.

L. 30. *We should have been tried with it, if the Earl of Bute had never existed.* Burke here corrects the views of the author of the History of the Minority, p. 10.

L. 33. *firmly to* embody—now seldom used intransitively. Cp. infra, p. 154, l. 12.

IB. *to rail—to embody.* The idiom is French.

P. 98, L. 2. *He communicates very little in a direct manner,* &c. After 1764 Bute never seems to have directly communicated with the King, much less with Ministers. His visits, however, to Carlton House, on his return from abroad, were as frequent as ever, and were especially remarked during the month preceding the establishment of the Chatham Ministry in 1766.

L. 8. *whoever becomes a party to an Administration,* &c. The attack on Lord Chatham which the pamphlet in an earlier shape contained, and which was afterwards expunged, perhaps followed this paragraph.

IB. *But whoever,* &c. The sentence is negligently constructed.

L. 23. *System of Favouritism.* Unnatural perhaps, but not uncommon in similar circumstances. Bacon extols a system of Favouritism as the best remedy against the ambitious great. Essay of Ambition.

L. 32. *bitter waters,* Numbers v. 14. The rhetorical phrases and images borrowed from the Holy Scriptures, which always suggested themselves to Burke when rising above the common level of his argument, are naturally less thickly sown in this pamphlet than in his speeches. See pp. 105, 118, 122, 144.

L. 33. *drunk until we are ready to burst.* Pope, Moral Essays, Epistle iii. "Men and dogs shall drink him till they burst." "Largely drink, e'en till their bowels burst." Churchill, Gotham, Book ii. 3.

Thoughts on the Present Discontents

L. 35. *abused by bad or weak men*—and by the King himself, though Burke could only hint this. Yet without an unusually low standard of morality among public men, the King would have been unable to abuse his discretionary power.

P. 99, L. 3. *A plan of Favouritism, &c.—better of this system.* These pages demand attentive study; and the student will beware of taking for aphorisms which can be detached the frequent maxims which form the successive landing-places of the reasoning. Burke here assumes a concealed influence on the part of Lord Bute, though the existence of such an influence at this [255] time has been doubted on good authority. Chatham, Grafton, and North were no favourites.

L. 19. *The laws reach but a very little way.* Vide supra, p. 70.

L. 25. *scheme upon paper*—cp. "paper government," p. 224.

P. 100, L. 3. *We are no-ways concerned,* &c., i.e. the people.

L. 9. *security of* ideots—the old spelling, derived from the low Latin of the law.

L. 23. *In arbitrary Governments,* &c. . . . *Both the Law and the Magistrates are the creatures of Will.* All legislative power is in the strict sense arbitrary. "If it be objected that I am a defender of arbitrary powers, I confess I cannot comprehend how any society can be established or subsist without them; for the establishment of government is an arbitrary act, wholly depending on the will of men. . . . Magna Charta, which comprehends our antient laws, and all the subsequent statutes, were not sent from heaven, but made according to the will of men. . . . The difference between good and ill governments is not, that those of one sort have an arbitrary power which the others have not: for they all have it: but that those that are well constituted, place this power so as it may be beneficial to the people, and set such rules as are hardly to be transgressed, &c." Sidney, ch. iii. s. 45.

L. 27. *every sort of government,* &c. Cp. the principle of Montesquieu, that legislation should be relative to the principle as well as to the organisation of each Government. Raleigh, in his Maxims of State, has a remark very similar to that of Burke.

L. 30. *free Commonwealth.* Burke boldly points out the real character of the English constitution, and shows that the only alternative is a government practically arbitrary.

P. 101, L. 1. *The popular election of magistrates,* &c. The analogy of England with a republic like that of ancient Rome is firmly traced.

NOTES

L. 6. *did not admit of such an actual election,* &c. Burke's observations on this point are confirmed by a comparison of the democratic institutions which have been set up in different parts of the world, since they were penned, with the English political system. On the weakness of looking more to the form than to the working of an institution, cp. Aristotle, Pol., Book v.

L. 20. *the King with the controul of his negative.* "The circumstance that in England the royal veto has practically not been exercised for a century and a half, whilst the President of the United States (Tyler) has lately made frequent and energetic use of it, is often adduced as a proof of the powerlessness of the British Crown, whereas it is really of itself a great proof of the advancement of the English Constitution, and its wealth in preventive remedies (*Vorbeugungsmitteln*)." Dahlmann, Politik, Th. 1. cap. 5. Cp. vol. ii.: "All the struggle, all the dissension, arose afterwards upon the preference of a despotic democracy to a government of reciprocal controul. The triumph of a victorious party was over the principles of a British constitution."

P. 102, L. 1. *Every good political institution,* &c. The practical doctrines of the [256] English political system are here admirably laid down. Hallam evidently had Burke's expressions in mind in the following passage: "He has learned in a very different school from myself, who denies to Parliament at the present day a preventive as well as a vindictive control over the administration of affairs; a right of resisting, by those means which lie within its sphere, the appointment of unfit ministers. These means are now indirect; they need not to be the less effectual, and they are certainly more salutary on that account." Middle Ages, ch. viii. part 3.

L. 8. *Before men are put forward,* &c. England indeed now possesses a far greater security for the excellence of her chief ruler than any other country has ever had. He must be chosen, as it were, by a triple election. A constituency must return him, public opinion and Parliament must accept him as a leader, and the Sovereign must send for him.

L. 19. *that man,* &c. The allusion is to "independent" politicians like Lord Shelburne.

L. 29. *Those knots or cabals,* &c. The allusion is to the Bedford Whigs.

P. 103, L. 7. *Whatever be the road to power,* &c. A favourite image with Burke. Cp. infra, p. 220. "Men will not look to Acts of Parliament, to regulations, to declarations, to votes, and resolutions. No, they are not such fools. They will ask, what is the road to power, credit, wealth, and honour," &c. Speech on East India Bill.

L. 13. *operation of pure virtue.* The cant of the "Patriot King."

L. 16. *Cunning men,* &c. Burke states at length the case which he intends to refute.

L. 34. *opinion of the meer vulgar is a miserable rule.* Cp. p. 71, "ignorance and levity of the vulgar." It has been reserved for our own generation to put forth the monstrous paradox of the inherent wisdom of the mass of a people. The political philosophers of the period of the Commonwealth knew nothing of it. See Milton, and Baxter's Holy Commonwealth. chap. viii. Dryden is hardly more severe, Absalom and Achitophel;

Nor shall the rascal rabble here have place,
Whom kings no titles gave, and God no grace.

P. 104, L. 4. *public opinion . . . . collected with great difficulty.* The chief source was the city of London, where George III encountered the most uncompromising resistance on the Wilkes question and others. It was owing to this limitation of area that productions like the letters of Junius appeared to have so enormous an influence on public opinion. Johnson speaks of this author as working on "the cits of London and the boors of Middlesex." Owing to well-known circumstances the opinions of the city of London no longer possess this peculiar significance.

L. 24. *It is a fallacy,* &c. Remark the ease with which Burke mounts from a particular case to the widest general principles, and the strength of thought which in this process never lets go the special consideration. In this, as well as in the way of framing and applying his general principles, he resembles Aristotle.

[257] **L. 25.** *level all things.*

He levelled all, as one who had intent,
To clear the vile, and spot the innocent.
Crabbe, "The Maid's Story."

P. 105, L. 9. *a cloud no bigger than an hand.* 1 Kings xviii. 44.

L. 11. *no lines can be laid down,* &c. The student of Aristotle will be struck with the frequency with which the inestimable axioms of the Greek politician are employed, in an enriched form, by Burke. Not only is this true of detached sayings, but the Aristotelian political method was constantly present to him as a whole. Compare the following: "Nothing universal can be rationally affirmed on any moral or any political subject. Pure metaphysical abstraction does not belong to these matters. The lines of morality are not like ideal lines of mathematicks. They are broad and deep as well as long. They admit of exceptions; they demand modifications. These exceptions and modifications are not made by the process of logick, but by the rules of prudence. Prudence is not only the first in rank of the virtues political and moral, but she is the director, the regulator, the standard of them all. Metaphysicks cannot live without definition; but prudence is careful how she defines." Appeal from New to Old Whigs. "The state of civil society is a state of nature. Man is by nature reasonable. Art is man's nature. (Dahlmann commences his *Politik* with this aphorism.) Men qualified in the manner I have just described, form in nature as she operates on the common modification of society, the leading, guiding, and governing part. It is the soul to the body, without which the man does not exist." Doctrine of Natural Aristocracy, *ib.* "The vice of the ancient democracies, and one cause of their ruin was, that they ruled as you do, by occasional decrees, *psephismata.*" Vol. ii. p. 319. "But as human affairs and human actions are not of a metaphysical nature, but the subject is concrete, complex, and moral, they cannot be subjected (without exceptions which reduce it almost to nothing) to any certain rule." Report of Committee on Lords' Journals. "Civil freedom is not, as many have endeavoured to persuade you, a thing that lies hid in the depth of abtruse science. It is a blessing and a benefit, not an abstract speculation; and all the just reasoning that can be upon it is of so coarse a texture as perfectly to suit the ordinary capacities of those who are to enjoy, and of those who are to defend it, &c." Letter to Sheriffs of Bristol. See also infra, p. 254, &c., the Second Letter on a Regicide Peace, and many other of Burke's writings.

L. 13. *though no man can draw a stroke between the confines of day and night,* &c.

> If white and black blend, soften, and unite
> A thousand ways, is there no black or white?
>
> Pope, Essay on Man, il.

These lines are quoted by Burke in the "Sublime and Beautiful," and often alluded to in his later works.

[258] Black steals unheeded from the neighbouring white.

Dryden, Astraea Redux.

They set each other off, like light and shade,
And, as by stealth, with so much softness blend,
'Tis hard to say, where they begin, or end.
Churchill, Gotham, Book ii.

"The principles of right and wrong so intermix in centuries of human dealing, as to become inseparable, like light and shade: but does it follow that there is no such thing as light or shade; no such thing as right or wrong?" Grattan, Speech against the Union, Feb. 5, 1800.

L. 23. *those who advise him may have an interest in disorder and confusion.* "The interest of the present Royal family was to succeed without opposition and risque, and to come to the throne in a calm. It was the interest of a faction that they should come to it in a storm." Bolingbroke, Letter on the State of Parties at the Accession of George I.

P. 106, L. 10. *a peculiar venom and malignity,* &c. It might be said that Burke here pushes his point too far. The student should read the criticism of H. Walpole, Mem. Geo. III, vol. iv. pp. 129–147.

L. 15. *system unfavourable to freedom.* The allusion is to France.

L. 29. *energy of a Monarchy that is absolute.* "Le gouvernement monarchique a un grand avantage sur le républicain; les affaires étant menées par un seul, il y a plus de promptitude dans l'exécution." Montesquieu, Esp. des Lois, v. 10.

L. 33. *war is a situation,* &c. "Peace at any price" has generally been the maxim of a weak ministry.

P. 107, L. 5. *pious fear . . . such a fear, being the tender sensation of virtue:* cp. p. 195, "Timidity, with regard to the well-being of our country, is heroic virtue." Burke speaks elsewhere of "the fortitude of rational fear."

L. 9. *keeps danger at a distance,* &c.

The careful man
His reformation instantly began,
Began his state with vigour to reform,
And made a calm by laughing at the storm.
Crabbe "The Widow."

L. 15. *the conquest of Corsica.* Corsica had groaned in vain from century to century under the Republican tyranny of Genoa, patronised by France. Her last struggle was begun in 1755 under Pascal Paoli, and was advancing towards victory, when the proclamation of George III, in 1762, prohibited British subjects from rendering any assistance to the *Rebels of Corsica.* (The Mediterranean fleet had in former times given effectual help to the insurgents, having recovered from the Genoese, in 1745, the forts of St. Fiorenzo and Bastia.) This proclamation was a terrible blow to the Corsicans, and probably emboldened France to conclude the subsequent treaty with Genoa, by which the progress of the Corsican general was arrested in the midst of his victories. England was in a position to have [259] established by a single word the independence of Corsica. Had she uttered it, the name of Napoleon Buonaparte would probably never have been heard on the Continent of Europe. Thus the action of the cabinet in 1762, followed by the disgraceful treachery hinted at by Burke, on the union of the still unconquered island to France in 1768, is indirectly connected with the great European struggle of the early years of this century. See Belsham, Book xiv. Junius, Letter xii. Boswell's Corsica. On the acquisition of Lorraine and Corsica see Lord Chatham's speech, January 22, 1770.

L. 16. *professed enemies of the freedom of mankind.* The spirit of liberty which existed in France was unsuspected. "Il faut avouer que vos François sont un peuple bien servile, bien vendu à la tyrannie, bien cruel, et bien acharni sur les malheureux. S'ils savoient un homme libre à l'autre bout du monde, je crois qu'ils y iroient pour le seul plaisir de l'exterminer." Rousseau, Letter to M. de Leyre on the occasion of the Treaty of France and Genoa. Contemporary literature teems with allusions to the French people as the veriest slaves in the world.

L. 22. *Ransom of Manilla . . . East India prisoners.* Manilla was taken October 6, 1762, by General Draper and Admiral Cornish, and the enemy escaped with life, property, and liberty, on promising to pay a ransom of a million sterling. The East India prisoners were the garrison of Pondicherry, to the number of 1400 Europeans. See Ann. Reg. 1761, p. 56.

L. 30. *vinedresser.* Meaning "statesman."

P. 108, L. 2. *Foreign Courts and Ministers,* &c. "A letter from the Russian Minister to his Court was intercepted, urging his mistress not to conclude too hastily with Ministers, who could not maintain their ground. This the King denied, and assured Lord Rockingham that they had his confidence—having at that very moment determined on their speedy overthrow." Phillimore's Hist. of Geo. III, vol. i. p. 558. The belief in the still prevailing influence of Lord Bute, widely spread in England, was universally entertained on the Continent. Chatham was possessed of it till his dying day. The rumour of bribery on the occasion of the peace of 1762 probably gave other courts the cue for future transactions.

L. 25. *Lord Shelburne . . . is obliged to give up the seals.* Burke's hint that Lord Shelburne's removal was a penalty for the warmth of his remonstrances to the French court on the subject of Corsica, is disproved by the Duke of Grafton's MSS., and by other contemporary documents. See Lord Stanhope's Hist. of England, vol. v. p. 307.

P. 109, L. 21. *Therefore they turn their eyes,* &c. The Colonists rather attributed the encroaching policy of the government to the spirit of the majority of the nation.

L. 27. *not even friendly in their new independence.* The use of such terms in 1770 was truly prophetic.

P. 110, L. 4. *The Court Party resolve the whole into faction.* See the letters of Sir W. Draper to Junius. The cry of "faction!" was common from the Revolution until the Reform of Parliament. "In all political disputes the [260] word *faction* is much in esteem, and generally applied to the weaker side." North Briton, No. 30.

L. 15. *not the name of the roast beef of Old England*—alluding to the famous song in Fielding's "Grub-street Opera," Act iii. sc. 3.

L. 26. *season of fullness which opened our troubles in the time of Charles I.*

So doth the War and her impiety
Purge the imposthum'd humours of a Peace,
Which oft else makes good government decrease.
                    Lord Brooke, Treat. of Monarchie, sect. xii.

Sir W. Temple, in his Memoirs, p. 31, describes the yeomanry and lower gentry as in possession of the great bulk of the land, with "their Hearts high by ease and plenty." The gloomy picture here painted by Burke is in his most striking style. In the words of Churchill,

So nice the Master's touch, so great his care,
The colours boldly glow, not idly glare.

Macaulay compares this juncture with the lethargy which preceded in England the struggles of the Reformation. Burke in 1796 describes the English nation as "full even to plethory." Letters on Regicide Peace, No. I.

L. 35. *look upon this distracted scene,* &c. Cp. Goldsmith, Traveller:

Ferments arise, imprisoned factions roar,
Represt ambition struggles round her shore,
Till, over-wrought, the general system feels
Its motions stop, or phrenzy fire the wheels.

P. 111, L. 7. *the voice of law is not to be heard . . . it is the sword that governs.* "Inter arma leges silent." Cic. Pro. Milone. Cp. Bacon, Apophth. 235, and vol. ii. p. 118, l. 11.

L. 11. *perishes by the assistance,* &c. The case of the Britons and the Saxons, among many others, will occur to the student.

L. 17. *a* procedure *which at once.* Burke, like Swift, uses the term in the same comprehensive sense as in French.

L. 22. *protecting from the severity,* &c. The allusion is to the pardon of the convicted rioters at the Middlesex election.

P. 112, L. 6. *made a prisoner in his closet.* The common phrase. See note to p. 89, l. 28. The words put into the mouth of the monarch by Peter Pindar, twenty years afterwards (Ode to Burke), are substantially the language of his own letters at this time:

Alas! if majesty did gracious say,
"Burke, Burke, I'm glad, I'm glad you ran away;
I'm glad you left your party, very glad —
They wished to treat me like a boy at school;
Rope, rope me, like a horse, an ass, a mule —
That's very bad, you know, that's very bad."

Works, vol. ii. p. 289.

[261] **L. 28.** *picture of royal indigence which our Court has presented.* This was rather the effect of the simple and parsimonious tastes of the King and Queen, heightened by the regularity of family life. Compare the passage in the Speech on Economical Reform, "Our palaces are vast inhospitable halls," &c. Burke here alludes also to the debts of the Civil List, to the amount of 513,511*l.,* discharged by the House of Commons in 1769. See infra, p. 132.

P. 113, L. 1. *with a mean and mechanical rule.* "A parcel of mean, mechanical book-keepers." Speech on Impeachment of Hastings. "Vulgar and mechanical politicians." Infra, p. 288.

L. 18. *The whole is certainly not much short of a million annually.* In Almon's Parliamentary Register, 1777, vol. vii. p. 57, it is set down at 1,400,000*l.* per annum, including, however, items not mentioned by Burke. This is probably an exaggerated estimate. The general accuracy of Burke is witnessed by the following addition of the items here mentioned, estimated from later authorities, which comes exactly to a million. See Sir J. Sinclair's History of the Public Revenue, Third Edition, vol. ii. p. 81:

Civil List	£800,000
Ireland	90,000
Duchy of Lancaster	20,000
Duchy of Cornwall	25,000
American Quit-rents	15,000
Four and a half per cent. duty in West Indies	50,000
	£1,000,000

L. 23. *the Bishoprick of Osnabrug.* The infant Prince Frederick had been already made Bishop of Osnabrück. "The King, after keeping the bishoprick of Osnaburgh open near three years . . . bestowed it on his son, a new-born child, before it was christened. . . Of the revenue, which is about 25,000*l.* a year, only 2,000*l* belong to the Bishop till he is eighteen, and the rest is divided among the Popish chapter." Walpole, Mem. Geo. III, vol. i. p. 320. It is hardly necessary to add that the bishoprick was merely titular. Oct. 27, 1784, "His royal highness prince Frederick, Bishop of Osnaburgh, was gazetted colonel of the Coldstream Guards, vice the Earl of Waldegrave, and to be a lieutenant-general in the army."

P. 114, L. 1. *drawn away for the support of that Court Faction.* Burke writes as if there had been no such thing as Secret Service money in the days of Walpole. In the time of George II the debts of the Civil List had been paid without much scruple on the part of Parliament on this account. The introduction of the question of the foreign revenue is not happy.

L. 24. *expose him to a thousand contradictions and mortifications.* On the alleged outrageous behaviour of the Duke of Bedford to the King in 1765 ("*repeatedly gave him the lie, and left him in convulsions,*" Junius, Letter xxiii, note) see the remarks of Lord Russell, Bedford Correspondence, [262] vol. iii. But there is no reason to doubt that the Whig leaders took means to show the King that he was helplessly in their hands, while exacting from him concessions galling to his feelings, if not derogatory to his honour. See Percy Anecdotes, The Grenville Administration. "His (Grenville's) public acts," says Macaulay, most unfairly, "may be classed under two heads, outrages on the liberty of the people, and outrages on the dignity of the Crown."

NOTES

L. 30. *language of the Court but a few years ago, concerning most of the persons now in the external Administration*—consisting as it did mainly of Whigs, with a small remnant of the original Bute party.

L. 33. *keener instrument of mortification.* Burke justly credits the King with acute feelings on this subject. It is difficult however to see that he would have been less mortified by being in the hands of one body of Whig noblemen than of another. Still, the present difference between the Whig veterans Bedford, Temple, &c., and the youthful Lord Rockingham, who had held a post in the Bedchamber, was considerable.

P. 115, L. 7. *certain condescensions towards individuals.* The allusion seems to be to the seat at the Privy Council, and the lucrative contract, bestowed on Lord Mayor Harley for his activity and spirit during the Metropolitan riots of May 1768. See Walpole's Memoirs, vol. iii. pp. 207, 210, and Letter to Mann, May 12, 1768.

L. 29. *this refined project—this fine-wrought scheme.* "Refined policy ever has been the parent of confusion." Speech on Conciliation with America, p. 226. The spirit of *la fine politique,* of the School of Mazarin, was not likely to work well in England. Swift says, "I have frequently observed more causes of discontent arise from the practice of some refined Ministers, to act in common business out of the common road, than from all the usual topicks of displeasure against men in power."

P. 116, L. 9. *Have they not beggared his Exchequer,* &c. Burke sums up the conclusions of the previous pages.

L. 13. *It will be very hard, I believe,* &c. Burke throughout these pages uses the arguments employed by Swift, fifty years before, against the Whigs. After recalling the cases of Gaveston and the Spencers, Swift proceeds: "However, in the case of minions it must at least be acknowledged that the prince is pleased and happy, though his subjects be aggrieved; and he has the plea of friendship to excuse him, which is a disposition of generous minds. Besides, a wise minion, though he be haughty to others, is humble and insinuating to his master, and cultivates his favour by obedience and respect. But our misfortune has been a great deal worse; we have suffered for some years under the oppression, the avarice, and insolence of those for whom the queen had neither esteem nor friendship: who rather seem to snatch their own dues than receive the favour of their sovereign; and were so far from returning respect, that they forgot common good manners" (cp. p. 114). The Examiner, No. 30.

Ibid. *in what respect the King has profited,* &c. Burke has now fulfilled [263] one of the main objects of his pamphlet, the endeavour to convince the King that the old Whig system revived and worked by the Rockingham party would be more to his personal advantage than any other. The original Whig system rested, as on two pillars, on the Court and the People, both equally necessary to its support. The so-called People's Party accused the Whigs of quitting the people and veering to the Court, when they had less need of popular support. "Finally," says Mrs. Macaulay, in her answer to this pamphlet, "the Whigs themselves erected against the liberties and virtue of their trusting countrymen, the undermining and irresistible hydra, Court influence, in the room of the more terrifying, yet less formidable monster, prerogative!" (cp. pp. 77–78). The confusion of images is amusing.

L. 18. *partakers of his amusements.* An allusion to the origin of Lord Bute's influence with Frederick Prince of Wales.

L. 22. *these King's friends . . . May no storm ever come,* &c. Burke's rhetoric seems wasted when we learn that the number of King's Friends who held paid offices, all subordinate, did not at any time exceed a dozen, and that not more than thirty could at this time be counted in the House of Commons. That all ministers could be thwarted upon system by the instrumentality of a body in every way so insignificant, is incredible. But the name of King's Friends was also applied to a large number of loyal and independent peers and commoners, who certainly had never "deceived" the King's "benignity, into offices, pensions and grants"; men like Lord Dudley, "without a thought or wish of office for themselves, but who loved and revered the Crown with all their heart," &c. (Lord Stanhope, History of England, vol. v. p. 179), devoted to courts and ministers, but wholly indifferent to the favours that they had to bestow (p. 181). Such men formed much of the strength of the administrations of George III. The great question of the American War swelled the body of King's Friends in the House under the leading of Jenkinson and Rigby, the successors of Bradshaw (the "cream-coloured parasite") and Jeremiah or *Mungo* Dyson, who were supposed to head them in earlier days. With the termination of the American War they seemed to become extinct; but after Pitt's victory over the Coalition, and the New Parliament of 1784, were again found all over the House. The *rendezvous* of the party at this time seems to have been the Pay-office, where Rigby was wont to entertain them after the House adjourned. The sentiments of the party were thus embodied by Lord Barrington: "The King has long known that I am entirely devoted to him: having no political connexion with any man, being determined never to form one, and conceiving that in this age the country and its constitution are best served by an un-biassed attachment to the Crown." Foster's Life of Goldsmith, vol. ii. p. 90. Pope thus describes the "King's friends" of his time:

> A feather, shooting from another's head,
> Extracts his brain; and principle is fled;
> Lost is his God, his country, everything;
> And nothing left but homage to a King.
>
> Dunciad, iv. 521.

[264] **L. 31.** *Quantum infido scurrae,* &c. Hor. Epist. Lib. I. xviii. 2.

L. 34. *So far I have considered,* &c. The remainder of the pamphlet consists of an examination of the effects of the Royal policy on Parliament, and a spirited defence of the old Party System which that policy discountenanced. It appears strange that a politician who held these popular views on the nature of Parliament, and who saw so clearly that it had become hopelessly corrupt, should have opposed Parliamentary Reform. But Burke had from the beginning of his political career a theory of Reform, which was likely to commend itself to few practical politicians, viz. "by lessening the number, to add to the weight and independency, of our voters." Observations on Present State of Nation, 1769. "Every honest man," wrote Coleridge in 1795, "must wish that the lesser number of the House of Commons were elected as the majority (or actual legislative power), that is, by the 162 Peers, Gentlemen, and Treasury." The system on its old footing Burke did not regard as incurable, although in this pamphlet he expressed fears that symptoms of an incorrigible decay had appeared (p. 119). He fortified himself in this position by appealing to the widely different proposals of statesmen holding the same general views with himself. The Duke of Richmond and Sir George Savile were both members of the Rockingham party. The Duke was in favour of annual Parliaments, of universal suffrage at the age of eighteen, and of sweeping away at one stroke the privileges of every citizen, burgess, and freeholder, throughout the kingdom. This wild project, when embodied in a Bill, brought in at a most inopportune juncture (June 3, 1780), was negatived without a division. Savile, following the favourite idea of Lord Chatham, was for doubling the power of the freeholders, to swamp the corruption of the towns. "If I am asked," writes Burke, "who the Duke of Richmond and Sir George Savile are, I must fairly say that I look upon them to be the first men of their age and their country; and that I do not know men of more parts, or of more honour." Correspondence, ii. 386. When such men were advocates for opposite and sweeping measures, Burke deemed it his duty to throw all his weight into the Conservative scale. Reasonably, indeed, may a statesman revolt from change, on the ground of the partial, the ineffectual, and the contradictory methods, which may have been proposed for effecting it.

P. 117, L. 11. *In speaking of this body . . . I hope I shall be indulged in a few observations.* The expression reminds us of a speech. Burke, like Bolingbroke, carried with him into the closet the manner of the senate; most of his political writings are oratorical dissertations.

L. 20. *in the higher part of Government what juries are in the lower.* By this bold analogy Burke gives the key to the original parliamentary system. As each man was judged by his peers, so was each man to be taxed and legislated for by his peers. So Erskine: "The jury I regard as the Commons' House of the judicial system, as affording a safeguard to the people, &c." Speech on the Bill entitled, An Act to remove Doubts respecting the Functions of Juries, &c. And cp. Burke's Review of Blackstone, [265] Ann. Reg. 1768, p. 268, in which he traces the disuse of trial by jury, in Sweden and elsewhere on the continent, concurrently with the decline of free government.

P. 118, L. 10. *The King is the representative of the people; so are the Lords; so are the Judges. They all are trustees for the people, as well as the Commons.* Cp. the beautiful expression of Bolingbroke, Patriot King, p. 94, "Majesty is not an inherent, but a reflected light." Burke almost repeats the passionate words of John Adams in New England, in September 1765. "Rulers are no more than attorneys, agents, and trustees for the people: and if the trust is insidiously betrayed," &c. Bancroft, History of the United States, v. 325. Cp. the same arguments applied to commercial privileges and "self-derived trusts" in the opening of the Speech on the East-India Bill. Cp. p. 254, "the general trust of government," and vol. ii. p. 188. l. 31. "The Whigs, who consider them (the prerogatives of the Crown) as a trust for the people, a doctrine which the Tories themselves, when pushed in argument, will sometimes admit," &c. Fox, Hist. of James II, c. 1.

L. 20. *express image,* Hebrews i. 3.

L. 23. *control for the people.* The doctrine is not confined to the old Whiggism. "The House of Commons is properly speaking no more than a Court of Delegates, appointed and commissioned by the whole diffused body of the people of Great Britain to speak in their sense, and act in their name, in order to secure their rights and privileges against all incroachments of ill-disposed princes, rapacious ministers, or aspiring nobles." The Craftsman, No. 56.

L. 28. *miserably* appointed, i. e. furnished.

L. 35. *But an addressing House,* &c. "We may say, and cannot say it too often, that if the only road to honour and power is the mere personal favour of the sovereign, then that those men alone will be found from time to time possessed of honour and power who are favourable to the maxims of prerogative—to the principles of harsh government; who are very indulgent critics of the measures of ministers; who are very careless auditors of the public expense; who are not made very uneasy by sinecures, jobs, and pensions; who are not very ready to try or punish public defaulters, unless they be indeed the writers of libels; who are in a word always unwilling to assist, or rather who are always willing to impede in its operations, the democratic part of our mixed constitution." Professor Smyth, Lectures on Modern History, Lect. xxx.

P. 119, L. 1. *a petitioning nation.* It is but fair to commend the reader to Johnson's amusing description of the origin and progress of these Petitions, in The False Alarm, Works, vol. x. 25. The system of petitioning has, since the Reform Bill, lost most of its significance. At this time it was of considerable constitutional importance. "This unrestricted right of overawing the oligarchy of Parliament by constitutional expression of the general will, forms our liberty: it is the sole boundary that divides us from despotism. . . . By the almost winged communication of the Press, the whole nation [266] becomes one grand Senate, fervent yet untumultuous. By the right of meeting together to petition (which, Milton says, is good old English for *requiring*) the determinations of this Senate are embodied into legal form, and conveyed to the *executive* branch of government, the Parliament. The present Bills (the Treason and Sedition Bills) annihilate this right." S. T. Coleridge, The Plot Discovered, 1795, p. 44. The theory, practice, and history of petitions are well traced by the Craftsman, No. 53.

L. 6. *to grant, when the general voice demands account*—referring to the payment of the debts of the Civil List. Erskine quoted the whole of this eloquent passage in his Speech for Reform ("Sir, this is, in plain English, the degraded, disgraceful state of this assembly at this moment") 1797.

THOUGHTS ON THE PRESENT DISCONTENTS

P. 120, L. 1. *Parliaments must therefore sit every year.* On the technical necessity for this, see Hallam, Constitutional History, chap. xv, and the note to p. 288, l. 23, infra.

L. 3. *a septennial instead of a triennial duration.* "The enormous duration of seventeen years during which Charles II protracted his second Parliament, turned the thoughts of all who desired improvement in the constitution towards some limitation on a prerogative which had not hitherto been thus abused." Hallam, Constitutional History, chap. xv. Three years were at first deemed a sufficient limitation, without recurring to the ancient but inconvenient system of annual Parliaments. The substitution of septennial for triennial Parliaments, so frequently censured in later times, was based on the prevalent disaffection, and the general danger of the government in the early years of George I. "Nothing," says Mr. Hallam, "can be more extravagant, than what is sometimes confidently bolted out by the ignorant, that the Legislature exceeded its rights by this enactment. . . . The law for triennial Parliaments was of little more than twenty years' continuance. It was an experiment, which, as was argued, had proved unsuccessful; it was subject, like every other law, to be repealed entirely, or to be modified at discretion." Ib. chap. xvi.

L. 33. *Impeachment, that great guardian of the purity of the Constitution,* &c. Cp. Grattan, Dedic. of Baratariana. The liberty of impeaching ministers is the necessary corollary of the theorem that the King can do no wrong. See Bolingbroke, Dedication to Dissertation on Parties. But the practice of impeachment, which had been common from the reign of Edward III to the Revolution, naturally declined with the growth of the system of government by Party. A certain spirit of generosity sprang up between party and party, based, however, on the obvious business-principle of sparing the conquered on the understanding that you were entitled to similar mercy in return. Burke knew this well enough, but he wished to represent the ministry as a constitutional monster, waging a wicked war against all lawful parties. Cp. "the terrours of the House of Commons," &c., infra, p. 134, and p. 172, "These might have been serious matters formerly." On a subsequent occasion he spoke yet more menacingly. "There must be *blood,* I say BLOOD, to atone for the misconduct of those who have transacted [267] this dark affair, — the lives of some concerned in this business must make atonement to this injured nation." Speech in Debate on Falkland's Island, January 25, 1771.

NOTES

P. 121, L. 26. *an hardy attempt all at once, to alter the right of election itself,* in seating Luttrell a member for Middlesex in the place of Wilkes. Wilkes was duly elected in 1768, expelled February 3, 1769, "for having printed and published a seditious libel, and three obscene and impious libels"; elected a *second time,* February 16; election resolved to be void, February 17; elected a *third time,* March 16, when the intended opponent retired before the nomination; and a *fourth time,* April 13, on the election of March being declared void, and a new writ ordered. Colonel Luttrell had in the meantime been induced to vacate his seat and stand; he obtained 296 votes: Wilkes, who received 1143, was returned by the Sheriff. The House, on April 15, declared Luttrell lawfully elected. These unconstitutional votes were afterwards rescinded, and ordered to be expunged from the Journals of the House.

L. 35. *The arguments upon which this claim was founded and combated.* "If a few precedents, and those not before the year 1680, were to determine all controversies of Constitutional law, it is plain enough from the Journals, that the House *have* assumed the power of incapacitation. But as such an authority is highly dangerous, and unnecessary for any good purpose, and as, according to legal rules, so extraordinary a power could not be supported except by a sort of prescription which cannot be shown, the final resolution of the House of Commons, which condemned the votes, passed in times of great excitement, appears far more consonant to just principles." Hallam, Constitutional History, chap. xvi. "When we see this power so seldom exercised in old times, so grossly abused when it was, and so entirely abandoned since, we cannot but conclude that usage disclaims the power as much as reason protests against it, and that it does not exist in our constitution." Annual Register, 1769.

P. 122, L. 1. *Never has a subject been more amply and more learnedly handled.* See the Speech of George Grenville, February 3, 1769, Parliamentary History, xvi. 546; Burke's own summary in the Annual Register, 1769, and the masterly pamphlet An Enquiry into the Doctrine of Libels.

L. 4. *would not receive conviction though one arose,* &c. Luke xvi. 31.

L. 11. *by setting himself strongly in opposition to the Court Cabal.* Burke might have said, by assailing it with every weapon of calumny and ribaldry. The forcible feebleness of the *North Briton* is hardly redeemed by its occasional smartness. It derived its effect from a spirit in artful

THOUGHTS ON THE PRESENT DISCONTENTS

consilience with popular prejudice, and a blunt language, checkered with Billingsgate. Its circulation was enormous, being rivalled only, among works of that class, by the writings of Junius and Paine.

P. 123, L. 30. *It signifies very little how this matter,* &c. This paragraph should be noticed as a conspicuous example of Burke's method. He begins by an axiom parenthetically introduced. He goes on to put the case in the [268] strongest light, by altering its conditions to their polar opposites. The conclusion is then stated clearly at length; and as a final blow, this conclusion is *repeated* with a double antithesis, in the most concise and striking form attainable: "*Resistance to power has shut the door of the House of Commons to one man; obsequiousness and servility to none.*" See the forcible passage in vol. ii. p. 172. "But power, of some kind or other, will survive — *Kings will be tyrants from policy, when subjects are rebels from principle.*" And compare Bolingbroke's fine illustration of the "spots on the sun." "When they continue (for here is the danger, because, if they continue, they will increase) they are spots no longer. They spread a general shade, and obscure the light in which they were drowned before. *The virtues of the King are lost in the vices of the man.*" Patriot King, p. 224.

L. 31. *Example, the only argument,* &c. Cp. the extract in the Introduction, p. 46. ("Example is the school of mankind," &c.)

P. 124, L. 17. *temperaments.* In the French sense = restraints. "Il n'y a point de tempérament, de modification, d'accommodements." Montesquieu. "On prend des tempéraments, on s'arrange," &c., Ibid. Cp. p. 264, l. 8.

L. 22. *So the Star Chamber has been called by Lord Bacon*—who, of course, highly approves of it. History of Henry VII: "And as the Chancery had the praetorian power for equity; so the Star Chamber had the censorian power for offences under the degree of capital." The incorrect expression "Lord Bacon," justified only by the usage of lawyers (so "Lord Coke," "Lord Hale") has now become quasi-classical from common use since its adoption by Swift and Bolingbroke. Properly it should be "[Sir] Francis Bacon," "Lord Verulam," or "St. Albans," or "Lord Chancellor Bacon." Our classical writers down to Addison never use the expression "Lord Bacon."

L. 22. *all the evils of the Star Chamber.* In the remarkable passage in which public opinion is recognised as the "vehicle and organ of legislative omnipotence," as the power to which it is the duty of the legislature to give "a direction, a form, a technical dress, a specific sanction"

NOTES

(Letter to the Sheriffs of Bristol), the revival of the Star Chamber is introduced as an example of things which a legislative power, still remaining the same, would be powerless to effect, and insane to attempt.

L. 27. *Committee of Council.* The Star Chamber.

P. 125, L. 10. *never did an envenomed scurrility,* &c. This reminds the reader of Dr. Brown's lamentations on licentiousness and faction. See note to p. 88, l. 19.

L. 13. *To ruin one libeller.* "The destruction of *one* man has been, for many years, the sole object of your Government." Junius, December 19, 1769. Chatham used to say that in *his* time, the object was the destruction of France; now, it was the destruction of Wilkes.

L. 18. *The identical persons, who by their society,* &c., *have drawn this man into the very faults,* &c. Wilkes had, in other days, been the intimate associate of Dashwood (Bute's Chancellor of the Exchequer), and a member of his infamous Medmenham Club. It was one of their associates, Lord [269] Sandwich, who made the complaint in the Lords against the "Essay on Woman," and the "Veni Creator paraphrased." Sandwich was a notorious profligate. See Churchill's "Candidate," and "Duellist." Lord March, another of Wilkes's associates, joined in the attack upon him. The allusion is particularly to Dashwood. The meaningless title of Baron le Despenser was revived in his favour, and he became, *per saltum,* premier baron of England!

L. 23. *foedum crimen servitutis.* Tacitus, Hist. i. 1.

L. 32. *his unconquerable firmness,* &c. The virtues of Wilkes are freely acknowledged by Burke. He possessed more than the show of patriotism. He was the first to treat the King's Speech publicly as the work of his ministers. He contributed not a little to make an Englishman's home really his castle, by making his papers inviolable in all cases except high treason. He was less than a great man, but was honourably distinguished by characteristics which have been wanting to many great men; he could face exile and penury, despise a jail, and resist corruption. See the Annual Register, 1797.

P. 126, L. 10. *how he* adventures: Fr. *s'aventurer.* More correct than the modern word "venture."

L. 11. *Breves et infaustos populi Romani amores.* Tacitus, Ann., lib. ii. c. 41.

THOUGHTS ON THE PRESENT DISCONTENTS

L. 29. *Mayors and Aldermen, and Capital Burgesses.* Burke had an undisguised contempt for the rotten system which in his Whiggish Conservatism, he supported. "Intrusion into this important debate, of such company as *quo warranto,* and *mandamus,* and *certiorari; as* if we were on a trial about mayors, and aldermen, and capital burgesses; or engaged in a suit concerning the borough of Penryn, or Saltash, or St. Ives, or St. Mawes . . . matter of the lowest and meanest litigation." Speech on East India Bill, ad init.

L. 32. *indemnity from quarters,* i. e. from having soldiers quartered on inhabitants of his borough.

P. 127, L. 11. *wise and* knowing *men.* In the old classical sense = intelligent. So in Speech on Econ. Reform; "The inexperienced instruct the knowing." Now only used ironically.

L. 13. *without the* eclat. Dr. Johnson considers this word "not English."

L. 29. *unless they are controuled themselves by their constituents.* Burke's words are applicable enough now that there is a fair approximation to a genuine representation of the nation: but misleading in connexion with a House of Commons of which *three-fourths* were returned by themselves, the Peers and the Government. (Bentham's Works, vol. iii. p. 530.) "The people at large exercise no sovereignty either personally or by representation," &c. Coleridge, Plot Discovered, p. 39.

P. 128, L. 21. *We do not make laws . . . We only declare law,* &c. Cp. Bacon, Ess. of Judicature, ad init. The distinction between a legislative and a juridical act was thus traced by Burke, in a subsequent speech on this subject: "A legislative act has no reference to any rule but these two; [270] original justice, and discretionary application. Therefore it can give rights; rights where no rights existed before; and it can take away rights where they were before established. . . . But a judge, a person exercising a judicial capacity, is neither to apply to original justice, nor to a discretionary application of it. He goes to justice and discretion only at second hand, and through the medium of some superiors. He is to work neither upon his opinions of the one nor of the other; but upon a fixed rule, of which he has not the making, but singly and solely the application to the case." Speech on the motion for leave to bring in a Bill to ascertain the rights of Electors, &c., February 7, 1771.

P. 129, L. 15. *Titius, Maevius, John Doe, Richard Roe.* The fictitious parties to actions in Roman and English law respectively.

L. 26. *made as strained constructions.* Alluding to the methods of barring entails by levying a fine and suffering a recovery, abolished by 3 & 4 Will. IV, c. 74.

L. 34. *Statute of Westminster*—the Second, 13 Edw. I, c. 1.

P. 132, L. 4. *payment of the debts of Civil List* . . . 513,000*l.* The actual sum was 513,511*l.* (See Parliamentary History, xvi. 598.) The Civil List "includes all the civil offices and expenses of Government, and those, whether public or private, which are supposed necessary for the support and dignity of the court: except on extraordinary occasions, as the marriage of a princess, or the establishment of households for the younger branches of the family: when, in either case, the Parliament usually allots a suitable portion for the one, and a sufficient revenue for the support of the other." Burke, Annual Register, 1769. On an allusion made by Col. Barré, to a similar occasion in the reign of George I on which the King promised "to make enquiry how the exceedings came, and to remedy them for the future," Lord North, sure of his majority, coolly told the House he should make no such promise, as he was not sure that he could keep it. As Mr. Grenville and Mr. Dowdeswell concurred in demanding accounts, it is obvious that the existing ministry alone were responsible for this increase of expenditure. Lord North fulfilled his anticipation. On April 16, 1777, a second sum of 620,000*l.* was voted to pay off Civil List debts, and an addition of 100,000*l.* per annum was made to the income of the crown. This occasioned violent debates in Parliament, and general dissatisfaction throughout the country, which led to Burke's Scheme of Economical Reform, introduced in one of his greatest speeches, February 11, 1780.

P. 134, L. 21. *No man ever pays first, and calls for his account afterwards.* "Why, you great blockhead, was ever man so foolish? What, pay the debts first, and see the bills afterwards? did ever man in his senses do so before? Why you are not fit to be sent to London at all, &c. &c." Sir G. Savile's Speech, March 2, 1769.

P. 135, L. 25. *god in the machine.* (Deus ex machinâ.) A well-known allusion borrowed from the Greek drama.

P. 136, L. 10. *navy or exchequer bills.* Securities issued for raising money for [271] the various needs of public service, and bearing interest, like the funded debt of the nation. See Smith's Wealth of Nations, Book V, chap. 3.

P. 137, L. 4. *all manner of* dissipation = waste.

THOUGHTS ON THE PRESENT DISCONTENTS

L. 24. *the Sinking Fund the great buttress of all the rest.* A favourite image. Compare p. 174, "clumsy buttresses of arbitrary power."

L. 31. *prolific principle.* Burke generally insisted on the tendency of bad examples to propagate themselves. "Your people were despoiled; and your navy, by a new, dangerous, and prolific example, corrupted with the plunder of their countrymen." Address to the King.

L. 32. *the fruitful mother of an hundred more.* The inscription on a bag, containing a hundred pounds, represented under the arm of the figure, in the picture of Hobson the carrier (see Milton) at an inn frequented by him in Bishopsgate-street. See the letter of Hezekiah Thrift in the No. 509 of the Spectator.

P. 138, L. 13. *land-marks from the wisdom of our ancestors.* Cp. p. 252. "All this cant about our ancestors is merely an abuse of words, by transferring phrases true of contemporary men to succeeding ages. Whereas of living men the oldest has, *caeteris paribus,* the most experience; of generations, the oldest has, *caeteris paribus,* the least experience. Our ancestors, up to the Conquest, were children in arms; chubby boys, in the time of Edward the First; striplings, under Elizabeth; men, in the reign of Queen Anne; and *we* only are the white-bearded, silver-headed ancients, — who have treasured up and are prepared to profit by, all the experience which human life can supply." Sydney Smith, Review of Bentham's Book of Fallacies, Edinburgh Review, vol. xlii. p. 368. This amplification of Bacon's witty remark ("These times are the ancient times, when the world is ancient," Advancement of Learning, Book I), is directed rather against the abuse of this question-begging phrase (whether from policy, as by Lord Eldon, or from timidity and ignorance as by "agricolous persons in the Commons") than against the legitimate use so often made of it by Burke. Burke speaks thoroughly in the spirit of Bacon. "Antiquity deserveth that reverence," says the latter, "that men should make a stand thereupon, and discover what is the best way; but when the discovery is well taken, then to make progression." Burke "makes what the ancients call *mos majorum,* not indeed the sole, but certainly his principal rule of policy, to guide his judgment in whatever regards our laws. Uniformity and analogy can be preserved in them by this process only. That point being fixed, and laying fast hold of a strong bottom, our speculations may swing in all directions, without public detriment, because they will ride with sure anchorage." (Appeal from New to Old Whigs.) Modern philosophy identifies a recurrence to the wisdom of our forefathers with the custom of some savages, who solemnly go to weep at the tombs of their ancestors and invoke their direction in the affairs of daily life.

L. 26. *to shorten the duration of Parliaments.* The demands of the democratic party, embodied in the annual motions of Alderman Sawbridge (commenced in 1771) for shortening the duration of Parliaments, were based on [272] a complete misunderstanding of that supposed exemplification of the "wisdom of our ancestors," the Annual Parliament. This incorrect view seems to have been first promulgated by that versatile politician Lord Shaftesbury, in 1675, and after the Revolution taken up by Lord Warrington, Dr. Samuel Johnson the Whig, and others. "In the protest of Lord Nottingham and other Lords against the Septennial Act, it is alleged 'that frequent and *new* Parliaments are required by the fundamental constitution of the kingdom': and in the debate on that bill, the speakers in opposition appear to have taken the same view of the laws for Annual Parliaments that had been suggested by Lord Shaftesbury. The same topics were employed in the debate for the Repeal of the Septennial Act in 1734, and on the motion for Annual Parliaments in 1745." (Edinburgh Review, vol. xxviii. p. 132.) Chatham was inclined to yield to the popular demands. It is now admitted that the laws of Edward III were intended to secure not annual *elections,* but annual *sessions* of the House of Commons. Burke's view is that of Milton. "The Ship of the Commonwealth is always under sail; they sit at the stern, and if they steer well, what need is there to change them, it being rather dangerous? Add to this, that the Grand Council is both Foundation and main Pillar of the whole State; and to move Pillars and Foundations not faulty, cannot be safe for the Building. I see not, therefore, how we can be advantag'd by successive and transitory Parliaments: but that they are much likelier continually to unsettle rather than to settle a free Government, to breed Commotions, Changes, Novelties, and Uncertainties, to bring neglect upon present Affairs and Opportunities, while all Minds are suspense with expectation of a new Assembly, and the Assembly for a good space taken up with the new settling of it self," &c. The Ready and Easy Way to establish a Free Commonwealth. Milton's ideal political system was a combination of elements derived from the aristocratic Republics of mediaeval Italy.

L. 27. *to disqualify . . . placemen, from a seat in the House of Commons.* The expedient of multiplying offices, invented for the control of Parliament by William III, was from the first viewed with suspicion by the country party. In 1693 the first place-bill was introduced, and the principle at one time became law that no placeman or pensioner should sit in the House of Commons. This too stringent provision was repealed before it came into operation. An important Place Act provides that every holder of a *new* office, created after October 25, 1705, and every holder of a crown pension during pleasure, shall be excluded from Parliament, and that every member of the House, accepting any *old* office, shall vacate his seat, but be capable of re-election. The Act of 1742 limited still further the extent of Place influence. To carry out strictly the theory of a Place Bill would of course bring Parliament into hopeless conflict with the executive; but the following list will show that it has been the steady policy of Parliament to diminish the number of Placemen and Pensioners belonging to it:

[273] In the first Parliament of George I there were . 271

" " George II " . 257

" " George IV " . 89

In 1833 60

(Sir T. E. May's Const. History, i. 374.)

P. 140, L. 9. *habit of affairs,* &c. Cp. the character of Mr. Grenville, p. 186: "Their habits of office," &c.

L. 21. *infallibility of laws,* &c. Cp. note to p. 70, l. 32.

L. 32. *disqualification . . . of all the lower sorts of them from votes in elections.* A bill for this purpose, which had hitherto been an opposition measure, was finally carried by the Rockingham ministry in 1782. "Its imperative necessity was proved by Lord Rockingham himself, who stated that seventy elections chiefly depended on the votes of these officers: and that 11,500 officers of customs and excise were electors. In one borough, he said that 120 out of the 500 voters had obtained revenue appointments, through the influence of a single person." Sir T. E. May, i. 349.

P. 141, L. 9. open *them.* Lat. aperio.

L. 20. *It is no inconsiderable part of wisdom,* &c. Cp. the Aristotelian caution on Reform, ἐατέον ἐνίας ἁμαρτίας καὶ τῶν νομοθετῶν καὶ τῶν ἀρχόντων· οὐ γὰρ τοσοῦτον ὠφελήσεται κινήσας, &c. Pol. ii. 5. "Il ne faut pas tout corriger," Montesquieu. Dryden, Astraea Redux:

Wise leaches will not vain receipts intrude
While growing pains pronounce the humours crude;
Deaf to complaints, they wait upon the ill,
Till some safe crisis authorize their skill.

NOTES

L. 22. *degree of purity impracticable,* &c. Cp. p. 151, l. 2, and p. 153, l. 35.

L. 32. *influence of contracts, of subscriptions, of direct bribery,* &c. See May's Const. History, chap. v.

P. 142, L. 2. *Our Constitution stands on a nice equipoise.* An antiquated commonplace, in which sense it is alluded to ante, p. 86, l. 35; p. 88, l. 21, &c. "The true poise of our Constitution, on maintaining which our all depends." Diss. on Parties, Letter xvi. Cp. the last letters of this famous series. "That nicely-poised Constitution," Erskine, Speech on Reform.

L. 22. *interposition of the body of the people itself . . . to be used then only, when it is evident that nothing else can hold the constitution to its true principles.* Cp. the quotations from the speech of Sir Joseph Jekyl, in the Appeal from the New to the Old Whigs. And Bolingbroke, Dissertation on Parties, Letter xvii: "If you therefore put so extravagant a case, as to suppose the two houses of Parliament concurring to make at once a formal cession of their own rights and privileges, and of those of the whole nation, to the Crown, and ask who hath the right and the means to resist the supreme legislative power; I answer, the whole nation hath the right; and a people who deserve to enjoy liberty, will find the means." He goes on to put the case, in prophetic terms, of the exact conjuncture now in question; "Let us suppose our Parliaments, in some future generation, grown so corrupt, [274] and the Crown so rich, that a pecuniary influence constantly prevailing over the majority, they should assemble for little else than to establish grievances, instead of redressing them: to approve the measures of the Court, without information; to engage their country in alliances, in treaties, in wars, without examination; and to give money without account, and almost without stint. The case would be deplorable. Our constitution itself would become our grievance whilst this corruption prevailed; and if it prevailed long, our constitution could not last long; because this slow progress would lead to the destruction of it as surely as the more concise method of giving it up at once. But in this case the constitution would help itself, and effectually too, unless the whole mass of the people was tainted, and the electors were become no honester than the elected." Cp. the significant language of Lord Chatham, January 22, 1770. "Rather than the nation should surrender their birthright to a despotic Minister, I hope, my Lords, old as I am, I shall *see the question brought to issue,* and fairly tried between the People and the Government." Cp. the same expression as

Burke's in Paley's Principles of Moral and Political Philosophy, quoted in Erskine's Speech for Paine: "No usage, law, or authority whatever, is so binding, that it need or ought to be continued, when it may be changed with advantage to the community. The family of the prince, the order of succession, the prerogative of the crown, the form and parts of the legislature, together with the respective powers, office, duration and mutual dependency of the several parts; are all only so many laws, mutable like other laws, whenever expediency requires, either by the ordinary act of the legislature, or, if the occasion deserve it, *by the interposition of the people.*"

L. 27. *legal remedy.* So Locke, who expresses the popular Whig views, is of opinion that "there remains still inherent in the people a supreme power to remove or alter the legislative, when they find the legislative act contrary to the trust reposed in them; for, when such trust is abused, it is thereby forfeited, and devolves to those who gave it." On Government, Part II, ss. 149, 227. The doctrine is not denied by Blackstone, who expounds the views of the opposite party, but he maintains that it is impossible to carry it legally into execution.

P. 143, L. 9. *by an indiscriminate support of all Administrations.* It is the interest of the public that the amount of support received by a minister should depend wholly on the efficiency and honesty with which he executes his trust. Burke's criticism is justified not only by the maxims of the Whig system to which it primarily belongs, but by the general laws of the relation between people and government. *Caeteris paribus,* the supporters of government have the advantage over its adversaries; and it is for the public interest that a vigorous opposition should never be wanting. "A man of no party is, nine times out of ten, a man of no party but his own. Few, very few, can comprehend the whole truth; and it much concerns the general interest that every portion of that truth should have interested and passionate advocates." Hartley Coleridge, Essays, vol. i. p. 352. "There is no true [275] Whig," wrote Cowper, "who wishes all power in the hands of his own party." It was a characteristic sarcasm of Franklin's, that as Parliament at this time always followed the minister of the day, the country would be as well and cheaper governed without it.

L. 13. *compacting.* A lost verb. G. Herbert:

A box where sweets compacted lie.

L. 19. frighted *into the arms of the faction.* So Shakspeare, Milton, Waller, &c. The only authority quoted by Johnson for *frighten,* is Prior.

NOTES

P. 144, L. 2. *rock of adamant.* Paradise Regained, iv. 533. The old English proverb was "He that builds on the people builds on the dirt." (B. Jonson, Discoveries.) Shelley, perhaps directly contradicting this passage, speaks of Athens as "On the will of man as on a mount of diamond, set." (Ode to Liberty.) The trite images of sand and stubble are borrowed from St. Matt. vii. 25–27, and St. Paul 1 Cor. iii. 12. The latter occurs in Milton's lines,

> The pillar'd Firmament is rottenness,
> And Earth's base built on stubble.

L. 3. *its structure is of stubble.* "Her (the Church of England) walls . . . are constructed of other materials than of stubble and straw; are built up with the strong and stable matter of the gospel of liberty," &c. Speech on a Bill for the Relief of Protestant Dissenters, 1773.

P. 146, L. 2. *The doctrine . . . That all political connexions are in their nature factious*—strongly insisted on in the tract of Bolingbroke. "Faction is to party what the superlative is to the positive: party is a political evil, and faction is the worst of all parties." Patriot King, p. 162. The plausible cry against Party was fortified by the professions of respectable statesmen. Lord Lechmere, says the Craftsman (No. 54, July 15, 1727), "was of no party, nor attached to any interest, but that of his country, which he constantly made the rule and measure of his actions."

L. 34. *When bad men combine,* &c. "In fatti si danno la mano i malvagi per fare il male, non avrebbero a darsi la mano i buoni per fare il bene?" Silvio Pellico, "Dei doveri degli nomini."

> The more the bold, the bustling, and the bad
> Press to usurp the reins of power, the more
> Behoves it virtue with indignant zeal
> To check the combination. Shall low views
> Of sneaking interest, or luxurious vice,
> The villain's passions, quicken more to toil
> And dart a livelier vigour through the soul,
> Than those that, mingled with our truest good,
> With present honour and immortal fame,
> Involve the good of all? An empty form
> Is the weak virtue that amid the shade
> Lamenting lies, with future schemes amused,
> While wickedness and folly, kindred powers,
> Confound the world.
>
> Thomson, Lines on Lord Talbot.

[276] **L. 36.** *an unpitied sacrifice,* "the unpitied calamity," p. 161.

P. 147, L. 1. *It is not enough,* &c. This paragraph in particular alludes to Lord Chatham.

L. 9. *That duty demands,* &c. "Let a man have a hearty strong opinion, and strive by all fair means to bring it into action. . . . Divisions in a state are a necessary consequence of freedom, and the practical question is, not to dispense with party, but to make the most good of it. The contest may exist, but it may have something of generosity enough; and how is this to be? Not by the better kind of men abstaining altogether from any attention to politics, or shunning party connections altogether. Staying away from a danger which in many instances it is their duty to face would be but a poor way of keeping themselves safe. It would be a doubtful policy to encourage political indifference as a cure for the evils of party-spirit, even if it were a certain cure." Sir Arthur Helps, Essays at Intervals. Bishop Taylor, when speaking of ecclesiastical party, says: "From all this it comes to pass that it is hard for a man to chuse his side, and he that chuseth wisest takes that which hath in it least hurt, but some he must endure or live without communion." Sermon on Christian Prudence.

L. 10. *not only be made known,* &c. Cp. the Aristotelian οὐ γνῶσις ἀλλὰ πρᾶξις.

L. 22. *I admit that people frequently acquire,* &c. Cp. p. 206, l. 17.

L. 30. *Every profession . . . sacred one of a priest.* See the review of the clerical character, vol. ii. pp. 246, 247. Cp. also infra, p. 185, l. 26.

L. 33. *nor are those vices,* &c. Cp. p. 185, l. 30, "persons very happily born."

P. 148, L. 1. Burke's favourite moralist had endeavoured to show

That true self-love and social are the same.

Pope, Ess. on Man, iv. 396.

IB. *Commonwealths are made of families,* &c. Cp. Refl. on Fr. Rev. p. 136: "To be attached to the subdivision, to love the little platoon we belong to in society, is the first principle (the germ as it were) of public affections," &c. Cp. Churchill, Farewell:

Those ties of private nature, small extent,
In which the mind of narrow cast is pent,
Are only steps on which the generous soul
Mounts by degrees till she includes the whole.

Notes

L. 6. *some legislators,* &c. The allusion is to Solon. (See Plutarch's Life of Solon, and Aul. Gell. ii. 12.) Aulus Gellius quotes this law of Solon from Aristotle. The illustration is used in the same sense by Bolingbroke, Occasional Writer, No. 3 (4to. ed. vol. i. p. 180), and by Addison in the Spectator, No. 16.

L. 10. *Idem sentire de republica.* From Cic. de Amicitia, ch. x. At the end, in ch. xxvii, "consensus de republica" is again mentioned as an important element in the friendship of Laelius and Scipio. "*Idem sentire de republica,* to think alike about political affairs, hath been esteemed necessary to constitute and maintain private friendships. It is obviously more [277] essential in public friendships. Bodies of men in the same society can never unite, unless they unite on this principle," &c. Diss. on Parties, Letter i.

L. 14. *The Romans carried this principle a great way.* Burke often alludes to the similarity between Roman and English politics. Cp. the allusion to the Claudian and Valerian families in the Letter to the Duke of Richmond, Corr. i. 382. In the panegyric on the great families, in the *Letter to the Sheriffs of Bristol,* he seems to have had the Roman families in mind.

L. 17. *necessitudo sortis.* See note to p. 69.

L. 20. *The whole people . . . political societies.* The allusion is to the tribes and centuries, which were the *constituencies* of Roman politics. A separate canvass was carried on in each of them upon public questions.

L. 23. *to endeavour by every honest means.* See the tract attributed to Q. Cicero, "De Petitione Consulatus," and the remarks of Bacon, Advancement of Learning, Book II, ch. 23.

L. 34. *plus sages que les sages.* "Il sied mal de vouloir être plus sages que celles qui sont sages," Molière, La Critique de l'École des Femmes, Act i. sc. 3. Cp. Appeal from New to Old Whigs: "They (the Rockingham party) did not affect to be better Whigs than those were who lived in the days in which principle was put to the test."

P. 149, L. 9. *a poet who was in high esteem with them.* See Macaulay's Essay on the Life and Writings of Addison.

L. 15. *Thy favourites . . . friendship's holy ties.* From "The Campaign," near the beginning.

L. 18. *friendships holy ties.* "Let friendship's holy band some names assure." Dryden, Absalom and Achitophel.

THOUGHTS ON THE PRESENT DISCONTENTS

L. 19. *The Whigs of those days,* &c. The subjects of this energetic panegyric were far from being equally worthy of it. See note to next page, l. 1.

L. 21. experimented *fidelity,* Fr. "expérimenté" = tried. Fénélon: "Les hommes les moins recueillis et les moins expérimentez."

L. 23. *sacrifice of . . . connexions in private life.* "Some, perhaps, may expect that the fewer and weaker men's particular attachments are, the more extensive and the stronger will be their general benevolence; but experience shows the contrary. Break off the nearest ties of affection and you weaken proportionably all that remain," &c. Powell, Sermon I.

L. 25. *of* that *ingenious,* &c. Cp. the Lat. *is* for *talis.* See note to p. 193, l. 6.

L. 27. *patiently bearing the sufferings of your friends.* Third Letter on Reg. Peace: "In the disasters of their friends, people are seldom wanting in a laudable patience."

P. 150, L. 1. *These wise men,* &c. See the extracts from the History of the last four years of Queen Anne, published as the work of Swift, in the Ann. Reg., 1758, and the remarks on them, evidently by Burke.

L. 6. *called an ambitious Junto,* which was a term often applied to them [278] by the Tories, as in Swift. The immediate allusion is to its use in the pamphlet "Seasonable Hints." See note to p. 85, l. 27.

L. 9. *Party is a body of men united,* &c. Fox explains the principle of party union to be "that men of honour, who entertain similar principles, conceive that those principles may be more beneficially and successfully pursued by the force of mutual support, harmony, and confidential connexion." Speech on Reform, 1797. "Sir, I will tell gentlemen what description of party is beneficial; party united on public principle by the bond of certain specific public measures, which measures cannot be carried by individuals, and can only succeed by party." Grattan, Speech on Corruption by Government, February 11, 1790. "When the two parties that divide the whole Commonwealth come once to a rupture, without any hopes of forming a third on better principles to balance the others, it seems every man's duty to choose one of the two sides, though he cannot entirely approve of either: and all pretences to neutrality are justly exploded by both, being too stale and obvious, only intending the safety and ease of a few individuals, while the public is embroiled." Swift, Sentiments of a Church of England Man. Compare with the theory of Party at the end of this pamphlet, the powerful vindication of it, based on experience, at the end of the Letter to the Sheriffs of Bristol, 1777. "In the way which they call party, I worship the constitution of your fathers," &c. &c.

L. 26. *by no means, for private considerations, to accept any offers,* &c. For an equally able statement of the other side of the case, the reader is recommended to Swift's Letter to a Whig Lord, 1712: "Will you declare you cannot serve your queen unless you choose her ministry? Is this forsaking your principles? But that phrase has dropped of late, and they call it forsaking your friends. To serve your queen and country, while any but they are at the helm, is to forsake your friends. This is a new party figure of speech, which I cannot comprehend."

P. 151, L. 2. *professions incompatible with human practice . . . practices below the level of vulgar rectitude.* "Entre nous, ce sont choses que j'ay tousjours veues de singulier accord, les opinions supercelestes, et les moeurs soubterraines." Montaigne, Ess., Liv. iii. chap. 13. "Narrow theories, so coincident with the poorest and most miserable practice." Reynolds, Discourse xiii. "He (Fox) at once set about the purchase of the House of Commons. The lowest bribe given was £200. The treasury was the scene where the traffic was carried on by his emissaries. The demands of the representatives of England were so enormous, that money was actually wanting to defray the necessary expenses of the King's household. Such was the commentary on the specious professions of purity with which the new reign was ushered in." Phillimore, Hist. Geo. III, vol. i. p. 335. Cp. Sp. on the Econ. Reform: "I do not hesitate to say, that that state, which lays its foundation in rare and heroic virtues, will be sure to have its superstructure in the basest profligacy and corruption."

L. 6. *a plausible air . . . light and portable.* "Disposition towards a [279] perpetual recurrence to it, on account of its simplicity and superficial plausibility." Reynolds, Discourse xiii.

L. 8. *as current as copper coin: and about as valuable.* "It puts me in mind of a Birmingham button, which has passed through an hundred hands, and after all is not worth three halfpence a dozen." Speech, January 25, 1771. The illustration of "current coin" is applied to personal popularity, Correspondence, i. 108. Molière, Bourgeois Gent. Act i. sc. 2: "Ses louanges sont monnoyées—His praises are Current Coin." Works, French and English, viii. 15. Lord Brooke wished laws to be written in English, in order to prove "coyns for traffick general." Treat. of Monarchie, sect. vii. "The greatest part of these opinions, like current coin in its circulation, we are used to take without weighing or examining; but by this inevitable inattention, many adulterated pieces are received, which, when we seriously estimate our wealth, we must throw away. So the collector of popular opinions," &c. Reynolds, Discourse vii. Cp. Goldsmith, Traveller:

> Honour, that praise which real merit gains,
> Or e'en imaginary worth obtains,
> Here passes current; paid from hand to hand,
> It shifts in splendid traffic round the land.

Bacon wished the existing systems of philosophy, which he was undermining, to be still used as "current coin." Nov. Org. I. Aph. 128.

L. 11. *cant of "Not men but measures."* "I was always for Liberty and Property, Sir," says Bristle in the Craftsman's Dialogue (No. 58, Aug. 12, 1727), "and am so still; and that I thought was a Whiggish principle; but if the parties change sides, 'tis none of my fault d'ye see. I shall always follow the *Principles,* whatever the *Persons* may be that espouse them." Brown, Thoughts on Civil Liberty, &c., p. 124. "As to my future conduct, your Lordship will pardon me if I say, 'Measures, and not men,' will be the rule of it." Lord Shelburne to Lord Rockingham, refusing to join the administration, July 11, 1765; Rockingham Memoirs, i. 235. "How vain, then, how idle, how presumptuous is the opinion, that laws can do every thing! and how weak and pernicious the maxim founded upon it, that measures, not men, are to be attended to!" Fox, Hist. of James II, ch. i; cp. Canning's Speech on the Army Estimate, December 8, 1802. "Away with the cant of measures, not men—the idle supposition that it is the harness and not the horses that draw the chariot along. No, Sir; if the comparison must be made, if the distinction must be taken; measures are comparatively nothing, men everything. I speak, Sir, of times of difficulty and danger, of times when precedents and general rules of conduct fail. Then it is that not to this or that measure, however prudently desired, however blameless in execution, but to the energy and character of individuals a state must be indebted for its salvation." On the Whig maxim of "not measures but men," see the amusing discussion in Bentham's Book of Fallacies, part iv. ch. 14. Goldsmith (1768) puts [280] the Court phrase into the mouth of Lofty in the "Good-natured Man": "Measures, not men, have always been my mark," &c., Act ii.

L. 20. *a gentleman with great visible emoluments.* Most obviously applicable to General Conway, the brother of Lord Hertford. He came in as one of the Secretaries with the Rockingham party in 1765, and continued in office after their resignation under Lord Chatham, and afterwards under the Duke of Grafton, from whom in 1768 he accepted the military appointment of Lieutenant-General of the Ordnance. See the bitter allusions to him in the Speech on Taxation, p. 197, l. 32, and cp. note.

L. 30. *Would not such a coincidence of interest and opinion,* &c. Similarly argues a contemporary Whig divine: "He whose situation obliges him frequently to take a part in the public divisions, must be very fortunate if his sentiments constantly coincide with his interest; or very generous if he never pursues his interest in contradiction to his sentiments." Powell, Sermon on Public Virtue (1765).

P. 153, L. 2. *that partiality which becomes a well-chosen friendship.* The student will find the bold views of Burke on the important place of inclinations and prejudices in the philosophy of man and states more fully developed as he goes on. In this passage the peculiar happiness of the expression should be noticed. Cp. the expression of Reynolds, "Among the first moral qualities which the student ought to cultivate, is a just and manly confidence in himself," Discourse xii.

L. 22. *either an angel or a devil.* "*Homo solus aut Deus aut Daemon;* a man alone is either a Saint or a Devil; *mens ejus aut languescit aut tumescit,*" &c. Burton, Anat. Mel., Part 1, Sect. 2, Mem. 2, Subs. 7. "Whoever is delighted in solitude, is either a wild beast or a god." Quoted by Bacon, Essay of Friendship.

L. 29. *dispositions that are lovely.* St. Paul, Phil. iv. 8.

L. 32. *friendships . . . enmities . . . in the one, to be placable; in the other, immoveable.* "What Mr. Fox said finely of himself, could be affirmed with equal truth of his former rival (Lord Shelburne), 'Amicitiae sempiternae, inimicitiae placabiles.'" May, Const. History, ch. viii.

P. 154, L. 7. *There is, however, a time for all things.* In this paragraph Burke states in clear terms the menace he has foreshadowed at p. 74, l. 35, "Les Révolutions," &c.; p. 104, "While some politicians," &c.; p. 110, "A sullen gloom," &c., with the significant hint at the times of Charles I; and p. 142, in asserting the right of the body of the people to interposition.

IBID. *a time for all things.* Ecclesiastes, chap. iii.

L. 9. *critical* exigences. Burke sometimes, with Bolingbroke, uses the less classical *exigencies.* Similarly he uses both *inconveniences* and *inconveniencies.*

SPEECH ON AMERICAN TAXATION

P. 155, L. 2. *hearty concurrence of the people at large.* To be expressed by addresses and petitions. Cp. note to p. 119, l. 1.

L. 9. *every other,* i. e. "every one else."

L. 10. *This servitude is . . . "perfect freedom."* "Whose service is perfect [281] freedom," Liturgy. This passage seems to have been misunderstood by Mr. Bancroft, History of United States, v. 41. The coincidence of this passage with the close of Sir J. Reynolds's 12th Discourse is remarkable. "Those artists who have quitted the service of nature (whose service, when well understood, is *perfect freedom*), and have put themselves under the direction of I know not what capricious fantastical mistress, who fascinates and overpowers their whole mind, and from whose dominion there are no hopes of their being ever reclaimed (since they appear perfectly satisfied, and not at all conscious of their forlorn situation), like the transformed followers of Comus,

'Not once perceive their foul disfigurement,
But boast themselves more comely than before.' "

Compare Speech on Economical Reform: "We ought to *walk before them* with purity, plainness, and integrity of heart: with *filial love,* and not with slavish *fear,*" &c. And the animated appeal, in the peroration, to the House of Commons under the image of a faithless wife.

L. 18. *casting from it, with scorn, . . . all the false ornaments,* &c. "Let us cast away from us, with a generous scorn, ... all the other adulterous trinkets that are the pledges of our alienation, and the monuments of our shame." Ibid.

SPEECH ON AMERICAN TAXATION

P. 158, L. 3. *publication at this time.* The speech was sent to press about the Christmas vacation of 1774.

P. 159, L. 13. *the Honourable Gentleman who spoke last.* "Charles Wolfran Cornwall, Esq., lately appointed one of the Lords of the Treasury." (*Burke*). For a sketch of him, see Mr. Macknight's Life of Burke, ii. 52. He was "Member for Grampound, descended from an ancient Herefordshire family, and a sensible lawyer. He (according to Walpole) married a sister of the first Earl of Liverpool: became a Lord of the Treasury in 1774, and Lord Chatham upon the occasion of the offer being made him, writes, 'If he accepts, Government makes a very valuable and accredited instrument of public business. His character is respectable, and his manners and life amiable. Such men are not to be found every day.'" He continued a Junior Lord of the Treasury till 1780, when he was chosen Speaker. He thus figures in the Rolliad;

> There Cornewall sits, and oh! unhappy fate!
> Must sit for ever through the long debate.
> Painful preeminence! he hears, 'tis true,
> Fox, North, and Burke, but hears Sir Joseph too;
> Like sad Prometheus fastened to his rock,
> In vain he looks for pity to the clock;
> In vain the effects of strengthening porter tries,
> And nods to Bellamy for fresh supplies.
>
> —Rock. Mem., vol. ii.

[282] **L. 14.** *this subject is not new in this House.* "The long debates which have formerly happened upon this business. If this were a new question," &c. Cornwall's Speech. The present debate had begun in the dullest possible style, and had reached its meridian. Rose Fuller, Rice, Captain Phipps, Stephen Fox, and Cornwall had already well tried the patience of the House. The members had begun to disperse to the adjoining apartments, or places of refreshment. Hence the short, lashing, petulant exordium, contrasting strongly with those of the great speeches on the Economical Reform, and the Nabob of Arcot's Debts. It was necessary to arrest the attention of the House in the dullest part of a debate. The report of it spread rapidly, and members crowded back till the hall was filled to the utmost. It resounded throughout the speech with the loudest applause. The student should observe the contrast between this preamble and that of the speech which follows. The latter is full of touches of that ostentatious trifling which was so common in the speaking of the last century; what Hazlitt terms, "calling out the Speaker to dance a minuet with him before he begins."

L. 19. *occasional arguments.* Fr. "arguments d'occasion."

L. 26. *this* disgusting *argument.* The epithet means no more than "wearisome," "tedious." Cp. Goldsmith, Citizen of the World, Letter lvii: "A nobleman has but to take a pen, ink, and paper, write away through three large volumes, and then sign his name to the title page; though the whole might have been before more *disgusting* than his own rent-roll, yet signing his name and title gives value to the deed," &c.

L. 30. *I had long the happiness to sit at the same side of the House. . . . privilege of an old friendship.* Cornwall was a renegade from Lord Shelburne's party, and had spoken with effect on the side of opposition in the debates on the Nullum Tempus Bill, and on Lotteries, as well as on the American question. He accepted office March 12, 1774, together with Lord Beauchamp, afterwards Marquis of Hertford. His speech is reported in the Parliamentary History, vol. xvii.

P. 160, L. 22. *the most ample historical detail.* It is to this demand of Cornwall's that we are indebted for the second part of this speech — one of the most interesting passages in English literature. The student should supplement it by reading the Letter to the Sheriffs of Bristol, 1777.

L. 32. *to stick to that rule.* Classical, but not so good as *stick by.* Vide Johnson.

P. 161, L. 2. *He asserts, that retrospect is not wise.* "I think it (the re-opening of the whole question) wrong; and wish only to pursue the present expediency of the measure." Cornwall's Speech.

L. 14. *unpitied calamity of being repeatedly caught,* &c. See note to p. 77, ante.

L. 17. *without the least* management. In the French sense now disused. Dryden:

[283] Mark well what management their tribes divide:
     Some stick to you, and some to t'other side.

Burnet: "The managements of the present administration." Infra, p. 197, "He (Rockingham) practised no managements." "Plus il y a de gens dans une nation qui ont besoin d'avoir des *ménagements* entre eux et de ne pas déplaire, plus il y a de politesse." De l'Esprit des Lois, Liv. xix. c. 27. "Peut-être que ce fut un *ménagement* pour le clergé." Ibid. xxviii. 20.

L. 27. take post *on this concession,* i. e. take their stand on it as an argument for future concessions.

L. 29. *call for a repeal of the duty on wine.* "Let me ask, what answer will they give, when, after this, the Americans shall voluntarily apply to repeal the duty on wine, &c.? The same principle that operates for the repeal of this, will go to that," &c. Cornwall's Speech.

P. 162, L. 8. *or even any one of the articles which compose it.* At that time the Colonies would have not opposed duties imposed for the regulation of trade.

P. 163, L. 4. *had thus addressed* the Minister. Lord North, then Chancellor of the Exchequer.

L. 33. *left unfinished.* To give this paragraph its proper effect we must suppose it to be concluded among "cheers and laughter."

P. 164, L. 7. *and* he *is the worst of all the repealers, because he is the last,* i.e. Lord North. Lord Rockingham had repealed only one duty, while Lord North had repealed five. These four paragraphs must be understood in their true spirit of open irony in the form of an "argumentum ad hominem."

L. 13. *the lie direct.* Cp. Shakspeare, As You Like It, Act v. Sc. 4.

L. 18. *ancient household troops.* See note p. 96.

L. 19. *new recruits from this.* Alluding to the deserters from the various sections of the Whig party, who by this time had gone over to the Court in large numbers.

P. 165, L. 2. *Here Mr. Speaker,* is a precious *mockery.* Used thus ironically by Locke. "*Precious limbs* was at first an expression of great feeling: till vagabonds, draymen, &c., brought upon it the character of coarseness and ridicule." Lord Thurlow, Letter to Cowper.

L. 12. *the paper in my hand.* Lord Hillsborough's Circular Letter to the Governours of the Colonies, concerning the Repeal of some of the Duties laid in the Act of 1767. (*Burke.*)

P. 165, L. 33. *an advantage in Lead, that amounts to a monopoly.* The total exports of lead from England in 1852 were about 23,000 tons, of which the United States took nearly a third, being three times as much as any other customer; and this notwithstanding the working of the productive mines of Illinois and Wisconsin. "The lead mines of Granada," says Mr. Macculloch, "would, were they properly wrought, be among the most productive in the world." Spain is now a large producer, and the advantage of England no longer exists.

P. 166, L. 20. *Sir, it is not a pleasant consideration.* Burke here makes a [284] landing-place, as usual, out of a broad generalisation arising from a particularly striking point in his argument. The student should note the effective use of familiar terms in the body of the paragraph, and its contrast with the rhetorical sentence which concludes it. In the next paragraph he returns to the argument on the preamble, after a digression on the interests of the East India Company, who purchased tea in China with the silver of the Bengal revenue.

L. 22. *mischief of not having large and liberal ideas in the management of great affairs.* Cp. the peroration of the Speech on Conciliation (*Sursum Corda,* p. 289), and especially the following passage from the Second

Letter on a Regicide Peace: "In truth, the tribe of vulgar politicians are the lowest of our species. There is no trade so vile and mechanical as government in their hands. Virtue is not their habit. They are out of themselves in any course of conduct recommended only by conscience and glory. A large, liberal, and prospective view of the interests of states passes with them for romance; and the principles that recommend it, for the wanderings of a disordered imagination. The calculators compute them out of their senses. The jesters and buffoons shame them out of everything grand and elevated. Littleness in object and in means, to them appears soundness and sobriety. They think there is nothing worth pursuit, but that which they can handle; which they can measure with a two-foot rule; which they can tell upon ten fingers."

L. 31. *meanly to sneak out of difficulties, into which they had proudly strutted.* "He (Bute) as abjectly sneaked out of an ostensible office in the State, as he had arrogantly strutted into it." Public Advertiser, Aug. 30, 1776.

P. 167, L. 2. *irresistible operation of feeble counsels . . . circled the whole globe.* The device called by the rhetoricians *contentio* is here used by Burke with striking effect. Observe the same in the subsequent sentence: "The monopoly of the most lucrative trades . . . beggary and ruin." Cp. the passage in the Speech on Economical Reform, ending: "The judges were unpaid; the justice of the kingdom bent and gave way; the foreign ministers remained inactive and unprovided; the system of Europe was dissolved; the chain of our alliances was broken; all the wheels of government at home and abroad were stopped— *because the King's turnspit was a Member of Parliament.*"

L. 3. *so insignificant an article as Tea* in the eyes of a philosopher. In contrast with the paramount importance asserted for it from a commercial point of view in the previous paragraph.

L. 13. *with all the parade of indiscreet declamation.* The mover and seconder of the Address "expatiated largely on the enormous transgressions of the East India Company, and described their affairs, as being in the most ruinous and almost irretrievable situation." Ann. Reg. 1773.

L. 14. *monopoly of the most lucrative trades.* The whole commerce of the East with Great Britain was in the hands of the Company.

L. 15. *verge of beggary and ruin.* The Company had agreed to the payment of 400,000*l.* per annum to government. But in 1772, while

NOTES

many of their servants had returned to England with large fortunes, the Company became so involved in difficulties as not only to be unable to pay this sum, but to make it necessary that 1,400,000*l*. should be advanced to them by the public. The exhaustion of the country, and the expenses incurred in the war with Hyder Ali and France, involved the Company in fresh difficulties; and they were obliged, in 1783, to present a petition to Parliament, setting forth their inability to pay their annual sum of 400,000*l*., praying to be excused therefrom, and to be supported by a loan of 900,000*l*. (Macculloch.) At this crisis Fox brought in his India Bill, on which Burke made one of the most memorable of his speeches, the last but one of the five parliamentary orations which he gave to the world through the press.

L. 17. *Ten Millions of pounds . . . rotting in the warehouses.* It was said by Burke's critics on the opposite side, that the whole stock of tea in the Company's warehouses was estimated at this quantity, and that by comparing his own estimate (p. 178) of the American consumption, and taking tea at an average price of five shillings the pound, it would be seen that Burke here exaggerated. It was only a fraction of the whole stock, according to this view, that was "locked up by the operation of an injudicious tax." This [285] objection seems, on a careful examination, to be unfounded. In 1772 official reports showed that the warehouses of the Company contained 16,000,000 pounds of tea.

L. 19. *rotting in the warehouses.* The absurd regulation which made it necessary for the Company to keep a year's supply of tea in their warehouses, helped to raise its price and spoil its quality. Coarse teas deteriorate 5 per cent. in value by being kept a year.

L. 24. *next to a necessary of life.* The Secretary of the Treasury of the United States, in his Report for 1827, observed: "The use of tea has become so general throughout the United States, as to rank almost as a necessary of life." The same may be said of Russia and Australia. The duty on tea once formed one of the largest items in the American revenue, but it has for many years been wholly repealed.

L. 25. *our dear-bought East India Committees.* Alluding to the Select Committee of thirty-one members appointed in pursuance of a motion, April 13, 1772, and the Secret Committee appointed in November of the same year, shortly after the opening of the session. By "dear-bought" Burke means that the practical result of those Committees, represented by the East India Act of 1773, was but small, or at least incommensurate to the difficulties experienced in getting the

Committees appointed, and in procuring adequate information on the abuses they were intended to be instrumental in remedying. See Ninth Report from the Select Committee, &c., 25th June, 1783 (in Burke's Works).

L. 29. *through the American trade of Tea that your East India conquests are to be prevented from crushing you with their burthen,* &c. The [286] state of the recent conquest of Bengal was then exciting some not unreasonable apprehensions. Economists were alarmed by the gradual exhaustion of the circulating coin, military men by the attitude of the Mahrattas. Foreign critics described English rule in India as a brilliant illusion. From the origin of the tea trade in the reign of Charles II down to 1834, it was a monopoly in the hands of the East India Company. The history of this monopoly is a striking example of the mischiefs of the whole commercial system. "The teas sold by the Company," says Mr. Macculloch, in his Commercial Dictionary, "cost the people of Britain, during the last years of the monopoly, upwards of 1,500,000*l.* a year more than they would have cost had they been sold at the price at which teas of equal quality were sold, under a system of free competition, in New York, Hamburg, and Amsterdam." And yet several gentlemen of great experience, who carefully inquired into the state of the Company's affairs in 1830, expressed their decided conviction that they made nothing by the tea trade—the increased price at which they sold not being more that sufficient to balance the immense expenses incident to the monopoly! "But for the increased consumption of tea in Great Britain," writes Mr. Macculloch in another place, "the company would have entirely ceased to carry on any branch of trade with the East: and the monopoly would have excluded us as effectually from the markets of India and China as if the trade had reverted to its ancient channels, and the route by the Cape of Good Hope been relinquished." (Art. *East India Company.*)

L. 32. *must have that great country to lean upon.* The colonies consumed about one-third of the Company's total importations of tea, and the war forced on a corresponding diminution in the tea trade. The void, however, was speedily filled up by an increased importation of silk.

P. 168, L. 18. *Draw-back.* Exportation was encouraged sometimes by drawbacks, sometimes by bounties, sometimes by advantageous treaties of commerce with foreign states, and sometimes by the establishment of colonies in distant countries. Drawbacks were given upon two different occasions. When the home manufactures were subject to any duty or excise, either the whole or a part of it was frequently drawn back upon their exportation; and when foreign goods liable to a duty were imported in order to be exported again, either the whole or a part of this duty was sometimes given back upon such exportation. Wealth of Nations, book iv. chap i.

L. 24. *certain* litigation. In the general sense of quarrelling, not the special and more common one, of proceeding at law.

L. 27. *heavy excises on those articles.* "The duty varied (previously to 1836) on the different descriptions of first-class paper from about 25 or 30 per cent. on the finest, to about 200 per cent. on the coarsest!" (Macculloch.) That on glass was even more exorbitant. "After successive augmentations," says the same authority, "the duties were raised in 1813 to the amount of 98s. a cwt. on flint and plate glass! and the consequence was, that despite the increase of wealth and population in the interim, the consumption of both these sorts of glass was less than it had been in 1794, when the duty [287] was only 32s. 2¼d. a cwt.!" The income-tax enabled Peel to abolish this monstrous imposition.

P. 169, L. 2. *devour it to the bone.* Cp. Europ. Settlements in America, vol. ii. p. 215. "Therefore any failure in the sale of their goods brings them (the tobacco planters) heavily in debt to the merchants in London, who get mortgages on their estates, which are consumed to the bone, with the canker of an eight per cent. usury."

L. 3. *One spirit pervades,* &c. Cp. Speech on Conciliation, p. 288.

One common *soul—animates the whole.*
Dryden's Virgil, vi. 982.

Thy courage, like the universal *soul*
Darts thro' the troops, and *animates the whole.*
Rowe's Boileau's Lutrin, Canto 3.

This jingle is common in the poets of the century, and is parodied in Sydney Smith's Receipt for a Salad.

P. 170, L. 6. *neither abstract right, nor profitable enjoyment.* Cp. infra, p. 213, "Some honourable right, or some profitable wrong."

P. 171, L. 2. *a famous address for a revival.* Agreed to in the Commons, February 8, 1769, requesting the King to revive the powers given for this purpose under an obsolete Act of 35 Henry VIII. The excellent speech of Governor Pownall on this occasion should be referred to in illustration of Burke. See the first part of the Letter

SPEECH ON AMERICAN TAXATION

to the Sheriffs of Bristol. The expressions "well-considered address," "graciously pleased," &c., are of course ironical.

P. 172, L. 14. *canonical book . . . General Epistle to the Americans.* This is not mere raillery. Burke was justified in holding the ministry to so important a declaration.

LL. 17, 19, 21. *I pass by . . . I conceal,* &c. The classical reader will recognise the *occultatio* of the rhetoricians. "Et illud praetereo"; "Horum nihil dico"; "Furta, rapinas tuas omnes omitto." Rhet. ad Herenn., lib. iv. c. xxvii. s. 37.

L. 26. *These might have been serious matters formerly.* Cp. note, p. 120, ante.

P. 173, L. 33. *rather part with his crown, than preserve it by deceit.* A material point is omitted by Mr. Burke in this speech, viz. *the manner in which the Continent received this royal assurance.* The assembly of Virginia, in their Address in answer to Lord Botetourt's speech, express themselves thus: "We will not suffer our present hopes, arising from the pleasing prospect your Lordship hath so kindly opened and displayed to us, to be dashed by the bitter reflection that any *future* administration will entertain a wish to depart from that *plan* which affords the surest and most permanent foundation of public tranquillity and happiness. No, my Lord, we are sure *our most gracious Sovereign,* under whatever changes may happen in his confidential servants, will remain immutable in the ways of truth and justice, and that he is *incapable of deceiving his faithful subjects;* and we esteem your Lordship's [288] information not only as warranted, but even sanctified *by the royal word.*" (*Burke.*)

L. 35. *A glorious and true character!* &c. There is a lurking irony here, as in many of Burke's allusions to the King. Cp. p. 82.

P. 174, L. 6. *Noble Lord upon the floor.* Lord North, sitting in the front or lowest rank of the Treasury benches.

L. 29. *Session of 1768, that Session of idle terror and empty menaces.* The Session which commenced November 8, 1768, and ended May 9, 1769, is alluded to.

P. 175, L. 6. *mumping with a sore leg.* To *mump,* in cant language, "to go a begging." Johnson. The word may, however, be regarded as a classical vulgarism. "You it seems may mump it at your sister's." Echard's Terence. Cp. Third Letter on a Regicide Peace, "Our embassy of *shreds and patches,* with all its mumping cant."

L. 21. *send the Ministers . . . to America.* Burke perhaps had in mind the well-known occasion in the Samnite wars after the disgrace of the Caudine Forks. See Livy, ix. c. 8–11.

L. 22. *tarred and feathered.* A species of punishment peculiar to America. Mr. Flaw, in Foote's comedy of the "Cozeners," promises O'Flanagan that if he discharges properly his duty of a tidewaiter in the inland part of America, he will be "found in tar and feathers for nothing." "When properly mixed, they make a genteel kind of dress, which is sometimes wore in that climate—very light, keeps out the rain, and sticks extremely close to the skin."

L. 25. *preservation of this faith . . . red lead, white lead,* &c. By way of forcing his audience into some largeness of ideas, Burke often contrasts a great moral principle with a group of technical names. Cp. p. 288: "Your registers and your bonds, your affidavits and your sufferances, your cockets and your clearances," &c. Observations on State of Nation: "Visions of stamp duties on Perwannas, Dusticks, Kistbundees, and Hushbulhookums." Vol. ii. p. 193. "The State ought not to be considered nothing better than a partnership agreement in a trade of pepper and coffee, calico or tobacco, or some other such low concern," &c. Atlas-ordinary, &c., are papers of different qualities and sizes.

P. 176, L. 16. *disclaimer* = act of disclaiming.

L. 27. *I dare say the noble Lord,* &c. Ironical.

L. 32. *I suppose he made,* &c., i. e. I will suppose, for the sake of argument, that he made, &c.

P. 177, L. 14. *the very citadel of smuggling, the Isle of Man*—annexed to the Crown in 1765. "Just loaded yonder from Douglas in the Isle of Man—neat cognac," &c. Guy Mannering, ch. iv.

P. 178, L. 27. *the end of every visto.* Cp. vol. ii. p. 171, l. 27. Johnson only gives the more correct *vista.* Cp. the Sir Visto of Pope, Moral Essays, Ep. iv. Dyer, Grongar Hill:

And groves, and grottoes where I lay,
And vistoes shooting beams of day.

[289] "A long, dull, dreary, unvaried visto of despair and exclusion." Speech on Econ. Reform.

IBID. *Your commerce,* &c., *all jointly oblige you to this repeal.* "If any man," says Professor Goodrich, "has been accustomed to regard Mr. Burke as more of a rhetorician than a reasoner, let him turn back and study over the series of arguments contained in this first head. There is nothing in any of the speeches of Mr. Fox or Mr. Pitt which surpasses it for close reasoning on the facts of the case, or the binding force with which at every step the conclusion is linked to the premises. It is unnecessary to speak of the pungency of its application, or the power with which he brings to bear upon Lord North the whole course of his measures respecting the Colonies, as an argument for repealing this 'solitary duty on tea.' "

L. 29. *all* jointly *oblige you to this repeal.* Burke does not mean that it is only when taken together that these considerations led to the repeal, which would be the strict meaning of the adverb. The context shows that he meant *severally* as well as *jointly.*

P. 179, L. 14. *to say something on the historical part . . . open myself fully on that important and delicate subject.* The history of American taxation, which follows, is probably the best known section of all Burke's speeches and writings, and its parts are among the most popular "elegant extracts" of the English Classics. This portion of the speech bears marks of careful elaboration previous to delivery.

L. 22. *the Act of Navigation.* Passed by Cromwell in 1651, with the design of taking the carrying trade out of the hands of the Dutch. It prohibited amongst other things the importation into England and her Colonies, by foreign vessels, of any commodities which were not the growth and manufacture of the countries to which these vessels belonged. The policy of this Act, now totally repealed, was preserved in subsequent ones. See Smith's Wealth of Nations, book iv. chap. 2, and Macculloch's note.

IBID. *the corner-stone of the policy.* A common Scriptural image. "The income-tax—the corner-stone of our whole financial plan." Gladstone, financial statement, April 18, 1853.

L. 24. *the commercial system was wholly restrictive.* See Smith's Wealth of Nations, book iv. It is justly observed by Smith that though the policy of Great Britain, with regard to the trade of her Colonies, was dictated by the same mercantile spirit as that of other nations, it had, upon the whole, been less illiberal and oppressive than that of any of them.

L. 25. *the system of a monopoly.* "Prior to this era (the peace of Paris) you were content with drawing from us the wealth produced by our commerce. You restrained our trade in every way that could conduce to your emolument. You exercised unbounded sovereignty over the sea. You named the ports and nations to which alone our merchandise should be carried, and with whom alone we should trade; and, though some of these restrictions were grievous, we nevertheless did not complain; we looked up [290] to you as to our parent state, to which we were bound by the strongest ties, and were happy in being instrumental to your prosperity and your grandeur." Address of Congress to the people of Great Britain, September 5, 1774.

P. 180, L. 6. *your superintending legislative power.* Cp. infra, pp. 217, 218, 251.

L. 17. *your right . . . your settled policy.* This is the key to Burke's whole argument on the American question. Cp. p. 254.

P. 181, L. 27. *attended the Colonies from their infancy.* This is not strictly correct. "On the contrary, the charters granted to the founders of the settlement in Virginia *distinctly empower the colonists to carry on a direct intercourse with foreign states.* Nor were they slow to avail themselves of this permission; for they had, as early as 1620, established tobacco warehouses in Middelburg and Flushing." (See further on this subject, Macculloch, Art. *Colonies and Colony Trade.*) The Navigation Acts of Cromwell and of Charles II founded the monopoly system.

L. 28. *grew with their growth, and strengthened with their strength.* Pope, Essay on Man, ii. 136.

P. 182, L. 4. *this capital was a hot-bed to them.* It was in the sugar Colonies that English capital was most extensively employed. It is observed by Smith that the capital of the French sugar Colonies was, on the other hand, almost entirely the product of the industry of the Colonists themselves.

L. 12. *not so much sent as thrown out.* "The original relation between the government of the Mother-Country and the New England Colonists was that of tyrant and refugee. The ancient 'Art of Colonization,' which it is supposed we have lost and may recover, consisted in persecuting the Puritans till they fled to the New World. . . . That which James I gave the founders of New England, under the name of a charter, was the inestimable boon of his neglect. It made them the fathers of a great nation. Later governments were more beneficent. They forcibly endowed the Southern States with the slave trade—the root of the present war (1862). Let us bless Lord North and Mr. Grenville that the war is not on *our* hands." Goldwin Smith, The Empire, p. 84. The Puritans established the four Colonies of New England; the Catholics, treated with much greater injustice, that of Maryland; and the Quakers, that of Pennsylvania. The persecution of the Portuguese Jews by the Inquisition was the foundation of the prosperity of the

Brazils. "Upon all these different occasions," says Adam Smith, "it was not the wisdom and policy, but the disorder and injustice of the European Governments, which peopled and cultivated America."

L. 27. *sole disposal of her own internal government.* "The Colony Assemblies had not only the legislative, but a part of the executive power. In Connecticut and Rhode Island, they elected the governor. In the other Colonies, they appointed the revenue officers who collected the taxes imposed by those respective Assemblies, to whom those officers were immediately responsible. There is more equality, therefore, among the English [291] Colonists, than among the inhabitants of the mother-country." Adam Smith, book iv. ch. 7.

L. 29. *perfect freedom*—cp. p. 155, l. 12.

P. 183, L. 35. *close of the last war . . . a scheme of government new in many things.* Cp. the Present Discontents. American independence began to dawn upon the world with the rise of the Royal party. At the most unhappy juncture, just as the Colonists had been permanently freed from foreign danger by the acquisition of Canada, a plan was formed, and its execution commenced, to abolish the charters of the Colonies and "make them all royal governments." (Bancroft, v. 83, note.) This arbitrary policy required a standing army, which was to be maintained by those whom it was destined to oppress. Ibid. The fifth and sixth volumes of Bancroft should be studied by those who wish to understand this speech in all its bearings.

P. 184, L. 5. *the necessity was established,* i. e. was confidently asserted—thought to be established. The great accession of French territory, inhabited by French subjects, in Lower Canada, certainly justified some increase of the military establishment.

L. 6. *capable of seats in this House.* Cp. Present Discontents.

L. 13. *Country gentlemen, the great patrons of economy,* &c. The cry against standing armies and corrupt expenditure was a watchword of the country party in the early part of the century. Cp. Bolingbroke, Pref. to Diss. on Parties, p. xxxiv.

L. 19. *Townshend, in a brilliant harangue.* "No man in the House of Commons was thought to know America so well; no one was so resolved on making a thorough change in its constitutions and government. 'What schemes he will form,' said the proprietary of Pennsylvania (February 11, 1763), 'we shall soon see.' But there was no disguise about his schemes. He was always for making thorough work of it with the Colonies." Bancroft, v. 81.

L. 29. *considered his objects in lights that were rather too detached.* Burke's intimacy with Reynolds should be remembered. The art of painting often furnished Burke with admirable illustrations. "Reformation is one of those pieces which must be put at some distance in order to please." (Speech on Economical Reform.) "The works of malice and injustice are quite in another style. They are finished with a bold, masterly hand; touched as they are with the spirit of those vehement passions that call forth all our energies, whenever we oppress and persecute." (Speech at Bristol previous to the Election.) "A group of regicide and sacrilegious slaughter was indeed boldly sketched, but it was only sketched. It unhappily was left unfinished, in this great history-piece of the massacre of innocents. What hardy pencil of a great master will finish it," &c. Vol. ii. p. 166.

L. 30. *Whether the business of an American revenue was imposed upon him altogether.* The words of Walpole, "Grenville adopted, from Lord Bute, a plan of taxation formed by Jenkinson," seem to express the truth. George the Third forced it upon Grenville, who is said to have at first [292] positively declined the task. See Wraxall's Historical Memoirs, vol. 1. p. 418 sqq.

P. 185, L. 4. *to* lean on *the memory*—to be severe upon. So our colloquialism "to be hard upon." Erskine, Speech for Paine; "God forbid that I should be thought to *lean upon* her unfortunate monarch (Louis XVI)."

L. 7. *acted with more pleasure with him.* Grenville, when out of office, fell into the ranks of the general Whig opposition. In the Speech at Bristol at the Conclusion of the Poll, Burke speaks of his own share in Mr. Grenville's most beneficial plan of scrutiny for elections.

L. 8. *A first-rate figure in this country.* Mr. Grenville, though not a man of first-rate abilities, was a distinguished financier. His whole policy was directed to making the most of the revenue, and especially to do this by repressing smuggling both in England and the colonies. He was also a rigid economist, and made good bargains for the public with capitalists. He was, says Dr. Bisset, "a most frugal, faithful, and skilful steward to his country." In 1764, after the termination of a costly war of seven years, he was able to bring forward a budget which proposed no additional taxes.

L. 10. *undissipated* = unwasted.

L. 12. *as a pleasure he was to enjoy,* &c. Burke says the same of his own son. "He was made a public creature; and had no enjoyment what-

SPEECH ON AMERICAN TAXATION

ever, but in the performance of some duty." (Letter to a Noble Lord.) "No man," says South, "ever was, or can be, considerable in any art or profession whatsoever, which he does not take a particular delight in." "Use also such persons as affect (i. e. love) the business wherein they are employed." Bacon, Essay on Negotiating. "Pleasures are all alike, simply considered in themselves: he that hunts, or he that governs the commonwealth." Selden, Table-talk.

L. 16. *noble and generous* strain = breed. Spenser, Faery Queen, Book iv. Cant. 8: "Sprung of the ancient stocke of Princes' *straine*." "Intemperance and lust breed diseases, which propagated, spoil the *strain* of a nation." Tillotson, quoted by Johnson.

L. 17. *not by the low, pimping politicks of a Court.* Cp. the quotation from Addison, p. 149, ante.

L. 22. *if such a man fell into errors, it must be;* i. e. "it must *have been.*" Burke, following the Irish idiom, frequently neglects the proper sequence of tenses.

L. 23. *intrinsical.* Burke commonly follows the practice of the early part of the last century, in using such forms as intrinsic, intrinsical — ecclesiastic, ecclesiastical, almost indifferently.

L. 26. *He was bred to the law,* &c. With this portrait of Grenville, in which generosity to a deceased foe leads Burke, as in that of Townshend, to be onesided, should be compared those by Mr. Bancroft and Lord Macaulay. The North Briton, No. 46, contains a coarse sketch of him from Wilkes's point of view. Of Burke's sketch Professor Goodrich says, "It does not so much describe the objective qualities of the man, as the formative [293] principles of his character. The traits mentioned were *causes* of his being what he was, and doing what he did. They account (and for this reason they were brought forward) for the course he took in respect to America. The same also is true respecting the sketch of Lord Chatham. This is one of the thousand exhibitions of the philosophical tendencies of Mr. Burke's mind, his absorption in the idea of cause and effect, of the action and reaction of principles and feelings." Cp. the contrast of the functions of the lawyer and the legislator in the Letter to the Sheriffs of Bristol.

L. 30. *except in persons very happily born.* Bacon and Selden are rare examples.

P. 186, L. 2. *There is no knowledge which is not valuable.* "Burke was a strong advocate for storing the mind with multiform knowledge, rather than confining it to one narrow line of study." Life of Crabbe, by his Son.

L. 3. *men too much conversant,* &c. Of such men Professor Smyth says, "They mistake their craft for sagacity, their acquaintance with detail for more profound wisdom, . . . if any crisis of human affairs occurs, they are the most fatal counsellors, with or without their intention, that their king or their country can listen to." Lect. xxxii, on Modern History.

L. 9. *as long as things go on in their common order.* See Gordon's Discourses on Tacitus, No. iv. sect. 9, in which the ability derived from practice is contrasted with the powerlessness of extraordinary talents without it. Cp. vol. ii. p. 134: "It cannot escape observation, that when men are too much confined to professional and faculty habits, and as it were inveterate in the recurrent employment of that narrow circle, they are rather disabled than qualified for whatever depends on the knowledge of mankind, on experience in mixed affairs, on a comprehensive, connected view of the various complicated external and internal interests, which go to the formation of that multifarious thing called a State."

L. 10. *when the high roads are broken up, and the waters out.* The description of the Flood (Gen. vii. 11, &c.) seems to have afforded verbal hints for this celebrated sentence.

L. 20. *regulation to be commerce, and taxes to be revenue.* Such bold and easy touches are peculiarly characteristic of Burke. This sentence gives the key to the whole of his argument on Grenville's share in the American business.

L. 29. *After the war and in the last years of it,* &c. The enforcement of the Navigation Act had preceded the Stamp Act. The important trade in British manufactures which the English colonists carried on with those of France and Spain, was certainly against the letter of the Navigation Act, though not, perhaps, against its spirit. This trade was afterwards allowed, though under duties that were virtually prohibitory.

P. 187, L. 1. *It is the nature of all greatness not to be exact.* Cp. the fine amplification of this by Erskine; "It is the nature of everything that is great and useful, both in the animate and inanimate world, to be wild and irregular," &c., in the Speech for Stockdale (1789).

[294] **L. 27.** *appointment of Courts of Admiralty,* which were employed in enforcing the Navigation Act, so as to deprive the offenders

of trial by jury. This injudicious proceeding touched the sensibilities of the Colonists perhaps more keenly than anything else.

L. 29. *sudden extinction of the paper currencies.* The colonial assemblies during the war had issued notes, which were made a legal tender. To remedy the inconvenience produced by their natural depreciation, Mr. Grenville passed an act which took away from them the nature of a legal tender. Most of the bullion of the Colonies being employed in the trade to England (see Adam Smith), the extinction of the paper currencies must have caused a general stoppage in trade.

L. 33. *as their recent services in the war did not at all merit.* The Colonies had entered warmly into the war against France, and such was their zeal, that of their own accord they advanced for carrying it on much larger sums than were allotted to their quota by the British Government. (*Goodrich.*) See the citations in the next speech, p. 271.

P. 188, L. 27. *beginning of sorrows.* St. Matt. xxiv. 8.

P. 189, L. 5. *Great was the applause of this measure here,* i.e. throughout the country. Public opinion was from first to last in favour of taxing America. Cp. Burke to Lord Rockingham, Aug. 23, 1775. Rockingham to Burke, Sept. 24, 1775: "I see and lament that the generality of the nation are aiding and assisting in their own destruction; and I conceive that nothing but a degree of experience of the evils can bring about a right judgment in the public at large." See also Burke to the Duke of Richmond, Sept. 26, 1775.

L. 11. *did not object to the principle.* It is far from being true that the Americans "did not object to the principle" of the Act of 1764: nor is Mr. Burke correct in saying that they "touched it very tenderly." The first Act of the British Parliament for the avowed purpose of raising a revenue in America was passed April 5th, 1764. Within a month after the news reached Boston, the General Court of Massachusetts met, and on the 13th of June, 1764, addressed a letter to Mr. Mauduit, their agent in England, giving him spirited and decisive instructions on the subject. It seems he had misconstrued their silence respecting another law, and had not, therefore, come forward in their behalf against the Act. They say, "No agent of the province has power to make concessions in any case without express orders"; and that "the silence of the province should have been imputed to any cause, even to despair, rather than to have been construed into a tacit cession of their rights, or of an acknowledgment of a right in Parliament to impose duties and taxes upon a people who are not represented in the House of Commons." A Committee was also chosen with power to sit in the recess of the General Court, and directed to correspond with the other provinces on the subject, acquainting them with the instructions sent to Mr. Mauduit, and requesting the concurrence of the other provincial assemblies in resisting "any impositions and taxes upon this and the other American provinces." Accordingly, in November of the same year, the House of Burgesses in Virginia [295] sent an address to the House of Lords, and a remonstrance to the House of Commons on the same subject. Remonstrances were likewise sent from Massachusetts and New York to the Privy Council. James Otis also published during this year his pamphlet against the right of Parliament to tax the Colonies, while unrepresented in the House of Commons. This was printed in London in 1765, about the time when the Stamp Act was passed. See Holme's American Annals, 2nd ed., vol. ii. p. 225–6. (*Goodrich.*)

L. 12. *It was not a direct attack;* i.e. Their opposition was not that direct calling in question of the power of Parliament to impose taxes which was forced from them by the Stamp Act.

L. 15. *like those which they had been accustomed to bear.* The duties on rum, sugar, and molasses, imported from the West Indies; and on tobacco and indigo exported from the American continent to any of the other plantations.

P. 190, L. 7. *his own favourite governour.* Sir Francis Bernard, Governor of Massachuset's Bay. It was commonly supposed in America that it was he and his coadjutors who laid the original plans for establishing the American revenue, out of which they promised themselves large stipends and extensive patronage.

L. 18. *for four years longer.* See p. 272.

L. 25. *could not legally grant any revenue.* See pp. 269 sqq., where Burke contends that they could do so.

P. 191, L. 11. *Massachuset's Bay.* Massachuset was the collective name of a small Indian tribe.

P. 192, L. 9. *a common friend.* This expression should always be used instead of our vulgarism, "a mutual friend."

L. 11. *a situation of little rank.* That of private secretary.

L. 32. *was a direct violation,* &c., i.e. was represented as a direct violation, &c.

P. 193, L. 2. *the late Mr. Yorke, then Attorney-General.* Son of Lord Hardwicke. In an evil hour, casting aside all promises and obligations, he yielded to the offers of the Court and accepted the Chancellorship on the resignation of Lord Camden, 1770. His brother refused to admit him to his presence, and in his agitation and remorse he put an end to his life. See Junius, Letters xxxviii and xlix; Walpole's Mem., vol. iv. p. 52, and the note p. 53, on his subsequent interview with Burke, and Rockingham's conduct on the occasion.

L. 6. *of* that *constitution of mind.* Cp. Present Discontents, p. 149, "of *that* ingenious paradoxical morality." A latinism, using *is* for *talis*, not noticed in Johnson.

P. 194, L. 13. *political equity.* (See post, p. 198, l. 28). The principle which should correct and supplement the letter of the law. Cp. ante, p. 124, l. 23, where the idea of equity, of a "large and liberal construction," and a "discretionary power," which Burke approved in dealing with the *interests,* is reprobated as applied to the *offences,* of the subject.

L. 20. *crayoned out* = sketched. Fr. crayonné.

[296] **L. 31.** *A modification is the constant resource of weak, undeciding minds.* "Media sequitur, quod inter ancipitia teterrimum est," says Tacitus. De la Houssaie remarks the spirit of compromise in general policy as one of the causes of the decline of Venice. Compare the very different and truly philosophical view of compromise infra p. 278, l. 29.

P. 195, L. 5. *this labour did knight's service.* The expression "yeoman's service," as used in Hamlet, Act v. Sc. 2, is applied to the result of labours actually performed by a superior intelligence which might have been done though not so well, by an inferior. Burke gives this expression new dignity by substituting for the "yeoman" the "knight," whose service was under the feudal law the highest form of land tenure (abolished 12 Charles II). It was indeed in a great measure such "knight's service" as that here alluded to, which raised Burke so far above his contemporaries in political wisdom, because it brought him into actual contact with so large a mass of political and social facts, which the inferior statesman is content to accept at second-hand.

L. 6. *It opened the eyes of several.* Burke himself probably knew more about America than any one in England. He had read every accessible authority on the subject at the commencement of the Seven Years' War, when the attention of the public was strongly drawn to it, for his Account of the European Settlements in America (1757), which has been recognised from the first as a standard authority. Robertson commends it highly. It has not been reprinted in any of the English editions, but is to be found in the American edition.

NOTES

L. 14. *least garbled.* Used as now commonly, *in malam partem.* To "garble" meant originally to sift the good from the bad, and it is still used in this sense in the drug trade. "They garbled our army," Lyttelton, Persian Letters. Bolingbroke speaks of "garbling" corporations by prerogative, i.e. excluding the disaffected.

L. 19. *old mercenary Swiss of state . . . practised instruments of a Court.* See note, p. 96, *ante.* From the days of the battles of Granson and Morat in 1476, and Nanci in 1477, the Swiss mercenaries were highly valued throughout western Europe. Cp. Goldsmith, Traveller:

> No product here the barren hills afford,
> But man and steel, the soldier and his sword.

P. 196, L. 2. *glaring and dazzling influence at which the eyes of eagles have blenched*—alluding to the famous "eagle eye" of Chatham, which was often compared to that of Condé, and his submission to influence in 1766. "Blench, to shrink, to start back, to give way; *not used*" (Johnson). It occurs several times in Shakspeare, but is not used by Milton. Cp. vol. ii. p. 357: "It was wherewithal to dazzle the eye of an eagle. It was not made to entice the smell of a mole," &c.

L. 9. *whose aid was then particularly wanting.* The accession of either Chatham, Temple, or Shelburne, was the sole hope of the Rockingham party in their administration of 1765–6. See the speech of Chatham (then Mr. [297] Pitt) in the debate on the Address, January 14, 1766, containing the well-known passage, "I cannot give them my confidence: pardon me, Gentlemen (bowing to the Ministry), confidence is a plant of slow growth in an aged bosom," &c. Cp. Lord Chesterfield to his son, Letters, vol. iv. p. 401. "Here is a new political arch almost built, but of materials of so different a nature, and without a key-stone, that it does not, in my opinion, indicate either strength or duration. It will certainly require repairs, and a key-stone, next winter; and that key-stone will, and must necessarily, be Mr. Pitt. It is true, he might have been that key-stone now; and would have accepted it, but not without Lord Temple's consent: and Lord Temple positively refused." Chesterfield believes that this "heterogeneous jumble of youth and caducity" must "centre before long in Mr. Pitt and Co." Pitt was the only person who could have given strength to the Rockingham administration. June 13, 1766, Chesterfield writes: "It is a total dislocation and derangement, consequently, a total inefficiency." The Duke of Grafton said as much in the Lords, on resigning the Seals. While Pitt was extending to them a useless patronage, the Earl of Bute was cajoling Temple with the prospect of a carte blanche for himself.

Animated by the spirit of genuine Whiggism, this nobleman refused in 1770 and 1775 to "wear the livery" of the Court to which nearly all his adherents went over.

L. 23. *of a* complexion *to be bullied by Lord Chatham.* Constantly used by Burke in this sense = bodily temperament. "Their complexion, which might defy the rack, cannot go through such a trial." Letter to Member of the Assembly. "Our complexion is such, that we are palled with enjoyment, and stimulated with hope." Appeal from New to Old Whigs, &c., &c. He contrasts moral with *complexional* timidity, vol. ii. p. 364.

L. 29. *Lord Egmont, who acted,* &c. See Introduction.

L. 35. *household troops . . . allies.* See note, p. 96, l. 1.

P. 197, L. 10. *Earth below shook;* Ps. civ. 32, &c.

L. 32. *with a melancholy pleasure.* See note, p. 151, ante, l. 20.

P. 198, L. 1. *almost to a winter's return of light.* The Stamp Act was repealed March 18, 1766. "An event that caused more universal joy throughout the British dominions, than perhaps any other that can be remembered." Ann. Reg. 1766.

L. 12. *Hope elevated and joy brightened his crest.* Par. Lost, ix. 633.

L. 13. *expression of the Scripture.* Acts vi. 15. Lord Stanhope (vol. v. p. 213) criticises this comparison too severely. It is not a "metaphor" at all: and careful analysis on the ordinary principles of rhetoric discovers in it nothing "overstrained," "bordering on the ludicrous," or in the least resembling Pitt's allusion to the mother of mankind.

L. 16. *all that kings in their profusion could bestow.* General Conway must have felt this passage keenly, and he deserved it. He was now connected with Lord North, and had gratified the King by going the whole length of the most violent measures against Wilkes. About three weeks before, he had said respecting the Boston Port Bill, that he "was particularly [298] happy in the mode of punishment adopted in it." He was then enjoying his reward in the emoluments pertaining to the office of Governor of Jersey, to which he had been promoted, after holding for some years that of Lieutenant-General of the Ordnance. In justice to Conway, it ought, however, to be said, that notwithstanding his hasty remark in favour of the Boston Port Bill, he was always opposed to American taxation. He differed from Lord North at every step as to carrying on the war, and made the motion for ending it, February 22, 1782, which drove Lord North from power. (*Goodrich.*)

NOTES

P. 199, L. 10. *to revert to the ancient policy of this Kingdom.* Cp. pp. 213, 215, and the Speech on Conciliation, passim.

P. 201, L. 25. *vermin of Court reporters . . . bolt out of all their holes.* Cp. the expression of Oldham, Sat. i. on Jesuits:

Unkennel those state foxes where they lie
Working your speedy fate and destiny.

P. 202, L. 2. *an advocate of that faction, a Dr. Tucker.* Mr. Forster regards this as an "ill-considered attack" on Dean Tucker, "the only man of that day who thoroughly anticipated the judgment and experience of our own on the question of the American Colonies." Life of Goldsmith, i. 412. Tucker was for first coercing the Colonists into submission, obliging them to pay their debts, and then enfranchising them, and making alliances with them as so many independent states, on the principle that the gain of England from them would be just as great, and the expense connected with them less. Johnson's reply to this, is that by doing so before the war, many millions would have been saved. "One wild proposal is best answered by another. Let us restore to the French what we have taken from them. We shall see our Colonists at our feet, when they have an enemy so near them." Taxation no Tyranny, Works, x. 139. A sufficient account of Tucker's pamphlets will be found in Smyth's Lectures on Modern History, No. 32.

L. 3. *labours in this vineyard.* Alluding to a well-known parable.

P. 203, L. 7. *the Earl of Halifax.* Through this minister Burke had obtained the Irish Pension of 300*l.* a year, in the days of his attachment to Hamilton. It has been remarked, that on this account he spares his memory.

P. 204, L. 2. *their importunate buzzing.* "Importun" is a common French epithet for troublesome noises. Cp. vol. ii. p. 180, l. 15, "importunate chink." "Importunate guinea-fowls," First Letter on a Regicide Peace.

P. 205, L. 15. *in various ways demonstrated,* &c. "South Carolina voted Pitt a statue; and Virginia a statue to the King, with an obelisk." Bancroft, v. 457.

L. 29. *Another scene was opened.* Cp. ante, p. 186, "when a new and troubled scene is opened." The expression is common in Bolingbroke.

P. 206, L. 3. *Clarum et venerabile nomen,* &c. Lucan, l. ix. v. 202.

L. 6. *his* superior *eloquence.* Note the modern use of the term in a positive sense.

SPEECH ON AMERICAN TAXATION

L. 8. *fall from power . . . canonizes and sanctifies a great character.* "Il y a des tems où la disgrace est une manière de feu, qui purifie toutes les mauvaises qualitez, et qui illumine toutes les bonnes." Mémoires du Card. de Retz, Liv. ii.

[299] **L. 12.** *betrayed him by their adulation, insult him,* &c. Cp. p. 207, "As if it were to insult as well as to betray him."

L. 15. *governed too much by general maxims.* Burke himself appeals to the same maxims at page 131, l. 2.

L. 17. *maxims, flowing from an opinion not the most indulgent to our unhappy species.* "He made far too little distinction between gangs of knaves associated for the mere purpose of robbing the public, and confederacies of honourable men for the promotion of great public objects." Macaulay, Essay on Chatham. See the paragraph commencing at p. 147, l. 19.

L. 22. *an administration, so checkered and speckled.* "Miserable examples of the several administrations constructed upon the idea of systematic discord, monstrous and ruinous conjunctions." Obs. on a Late State of the Nation. "The last botching of Lord Chatham." Letter to Rockingham, Oct. 29, 1769. This passage has been called a specimen of "dictionary eloquence."

L. 25. *a* cabinet *so variously inlaid.* This frigid pun is probably not original. The image, however, as is usual with Burke, is quickly exchanged for a better.

L. 32. *Were obliged to ask,* &c. This dramatic manner must have been frequent in Burke's speeches, though there are naturally few traces of it in those which he prepared for the press. See, however, his Speech on being elected at Bristol, Nov. 3, 1774.

P. 207, L. 3. pigging *together,* i.e. lying huddled together, like pigs. One of the vulgarisms which, in the opinion of critics, too often disfigure Burke's pages.

IBID. *heads and points, in the same truckle-bed.* Supposed to allude to the Right Honourable Lord North and George Cooke, Esq., who were made joint paymasters in the summer of 1766, on the removal of the Rockingham administration. As a handful of pins shaken together will be found to have heads and points confused, so two persons get more space in a narrow bed by lying opposite ways. Cp. Erskine, Speech for Baillie; "Insulated passages, culled out and set *heads and points* in their wretched affidavits." The truckle-bed was "a bed that runs on wheels under a higher bed" (Johnson). Hence to "truckle" to another, in which sense Burke here employs the image. It suggested an amusing passage in the debate on the Reform Bill, 1866: "But I must protest against one portion of the Speech of my Right Hon. Friend (Mr. Lowe), and that is, the portion in which he treated largely of the honour of the Government, and gave his views of the Government as being persons who needed not to be particular, and who were not in a condition to be fastidious on that subject, and he spoke, I think, with marked emphasis of a *truckle-bed* in which they were to lie," &c. Mr. Gladstone, June 4, 1866. On Lord North's and Mr. Cooke's joint office, see note to Rockingham Memoirs, vol. i, p. 258.

L. 15. *When his face was* hid but for a moment. Isaiah liv. 8. Pitt's face was hid for three consecutive years.

L. 22. *Deprived of his guiding influence,* &c. Lord Macaulay thinks that on the whole, "the worst administration which has governed [300] England since the Revolution was that of George Grenville." Mr. Massey has happily transferred this compliment to the Grafton administration. To this Burke would certainly have assented. "The worst government which this country had experienced since the Revolution was the Rump administration of Lord Chatham. While that great man continued at the head of affairs and kept possession of his faculties, it mattered little that the other members of his cabinet were of slender capacity and experience. . . . Chatham had sketched the plan of a great administration, which his colleagues, deprived of his direction, were utterly unable to fulfil. For the perverse and calamitous measures which superseded the policy of Chatham, it would be a hard measure of justice to load the memory of his successor. The Duke of Grafton has been termed a minister by accident. . . . Grafton, unconnected with faction, and professing allegiance to Chatham alone, became as chief minister, a passive instrument in the hands of a determined will, in the furtherance of a definite policy. It was *the King* who insisted on the prosecution of Wilkes: and it was *the King* who urged measures of coercion towards the refractory Colonies." History of England, i. 402. (Compare, however, the note to p. 189.)

L. 35. *For even then, Sir, even before,* &c. Cp. p. 97, l. 1. This passage is acknowledged to contain the most gorgeous image in modern oratory. Burke perhaps borrowed the germ of it from Smollett's "Humphrey Clinker" (Letter of June 2): "Ha! there is the other great phenomenon, the grand pensionary, that weathercock of patriotism, that veers about in every point of the political compass, and still feels the wind of popularity in his tail. *He, too, like a portentous comet, has risen again above the*

*court horizon; but how long he will continue to ascend, it is not easy to foretell,
considering his great eccentricity.*" The name "grand pensionary" alludes
to the similarity between the position of Pitt and the minister of that
title in the Dutch Republic. It was sometimes significantly curtailed
to "grand pensioner." Cp. Bacon, Advice to Sir G. Villiers (afterwards
Duke of Buckingham): "You are as a new-risen star, and the eyes of
all men are upon you; let not your own negligence make you fall like
a meteor." The least rhetorical of writers makes free use of the image:
"In the session of 1714, when he had *become lord of the ascendant,*" &c.
Hallam, Const. Hist. ch. xvi, note. "The Whigs, *now lords of the ascendant,*" Ibid.

P. 208, L. 5. *you understand,* to be sure. Used as we now use *of
course.* "Oh, to be sure, it is some very great man that writes it." Ann.
Reg. 1760.

L. 6. *I speak of Charles Townshend.* With this affectionate panegyric
should be compared the juster portraiture of Horace Walpole, in his
Memoirs, vol. iii. p. 100, who would rank him with Churchill's "Men
void of Principle, and damn'd with Parts." He is, however, forced to
admit that "he seemed to create knowledge instead of searching for
it, with a wit so abundant that in him it seemed loss of time to think.
He had but to speak, and all he said seemed new, natural, and uncommon." On the other hand, Grattan, in his character of Pitt, describes
him as "for ever on the rack of exertion," and [301] contrasts his style
with Chatham's, "lightening upon the subject, and reaching the point
by the flashings of his mind, which like those of his eye, were felt, but
could not be followed." Smollett's character of Townshend is excellent: "At length, a person of a very prepossessing appearance coming
in, his grace (Newcastle) rose up, and, hugging him in his arms, with
the appellation of 'My dear Charles!' led him forth into the inner
apartment, or *sanctum sanctorum* of this political temple. That, said
Captain C——, is my friend Charles Townshend, almost the only man
of parts who has any concern in the present administration. Indeed, he
would have no concern at all in the matter if the ministry did not find
it absolutely necessary to make use of his talents upon some particular
occasions. As for the common business of the nation, it is carried on
in a constant routine, by the clerks of the different offices, otherwise
the wheels of Government would be wholly stopped amidst the abrupt
succession of ministers, every one more ignorant than his predecessor. I am thinking what a fine hobble we should be in, if all the clerks
of the Treasury, if the secretaries, the War Office, and the Admiralty,

should take it into their heads to throw up their places, in imitation of the great pensioner. But to return to Charles Townshend; he certainly knows more than all the Ministry and all the Opposition, if their heads were laid together, and talks like an angel on a vast variety of subjects. He would be really a great man, if he had any consistency or stability of character. Then, it must be owned, he wants courage, otherwise he would never allow himself to be cowed by the great political bully (Pitt), for whose understanding he has justly a very great contempt. I have seen him as much afraid of that overbearing Hector as ever schoolboy was of his pedagogue; and yet this Hector, I shrewdly suspect, is no more than a craven at bottom. Besides this defect, Charles has another, which he is at too little pains to hide. There's no faith to be given to his assertions, and no trust to be put in his promises. However, to give the devil his due, he is very good-natured, and even friendly when close urged in the way of solicitation. As for principle, that's out of the question. In a word, he's a wit and an orator, extremely entertaining; and he shines very often at the expense of those ministers to whom he is a retainer. This is a mark of great imprudence by which he has made them all his enemies, whatever face they may put upon the matter; and sooner or later he'll have cause to wish he had been able to keep his own counsel. I have several times cautioned him on this subject: but 'tis all preaching to the desert. His vanity runs away with his discretion." (Humphrey Clinker.) The following clever stanzas "by a Friend," are quoted from Belsham, v. 249:

> Behold that ship in all her pride,
> Her bosom swelling to the tide,
>   Each curious eye delighting:
> With colours flying, sails unfurl'd,
> From head to stern she'll match the world
>   For sailing or for fighting.
> [302] Alas, dear Charles! she cheats the sight,
> Though all appears so fair and tight,
>   For sea so trim and ready;
> Each breeze will toss her to and fro,
> Nor must she dare to face the foe
>   Till BALLAST makes her steady.

On Townshend's celebrated "Champagne Speech," see Walpole, vol. iii, p. 25, and Lord Stanhope's History, v. 272: "full of wit, comedy, quotation, &c., but not a syllable to the purpose. Upon this speech he had meditated a great while, and it only found utterance by accident on that particular day!"

SPEECH ON AMERICAN TAXATION

L. 9. *the delight and ornament of this House.* "It was Garrick writing and acting extempore scenes of Congreve." Walpole.

L. 14. *not so great a stock, as some have had who flourished formerly, of knowledge.* The allusion seems to be to Pulteney and Carteret, to whose school Townshend may be ascribed.

L. 23. *hit the House just* between wind and water. Fr. *entre deux eaux.* When a ship heels over to leeward a part of her *bottom* (that portion of the keel which is usually below the water-line), is uncovered. An attacking enemy bearing down on the wind naturally aims at this strip along her side, which is "between wind and water."

L. 24. *not being troubled with too anxious a zeal.* Villemain, in his Souvenirs, quotes Talleyrand on this point: "Talleyrand dit, 'Il faut en politique, comme ailleurs, ne pas engager tout son coeur, ne pas trop aimer; cela embrouille, cela nuit à la clarté des vues, et n'est pas toujours compté à bien. Cette excessive préoccupation d'autrui, ce dévouement qui s'oublie trop soi-même, nuit souvent à l'objet aimé, et toujours à l'objet aimant qu'il rend moins mésuré, moins adroit, et même moins persuasif.'"

L. 28. *He conformed exactly to the temper of the House.* Cp. infra, p. 211, "He was truly the child of the House," &c. Cp. Chesterfield, Character of Walpole: "He saw as by intuition the disposition of the House, and pressed or receded accordingly." Lord Dalling, Character of Canning: "At last, when he himself spoke, he seemed to a large part of his audience to be merely giving a striking form to their own thoughts."

L. 36. *the sole cause of all the public measures.* Further than this, Burke thought with Guicciardini that "any general temper in a nation" might always be traced to a few individuals. Letter to Rockingham, Aug. 23, 1775. "As well may we fancy," he writes in the First Letter on a Regicide Peace, "that of itself the sea will swell, and that without winds the billows will insult the adverse shore, as that the gross mass of the people will be moved, and elevated, and continue by a steady and permanent direction to bear upon one point, without the influence of superior authority, or superior mind." "It is the Few, which commonly give the turn to Affairs," Guicc. Maxim 83. Cp. Gordon's Discourses on Tacitus, ix, II.

P. 209, L. 15. *passion for fame; a passion,* &c. Cp. in the description of [303] the trial of Hastings, in Erskine's Speech for Stockdale, "the love of fame, which is the inherent passion of genius."

L. 26. *Obstinacy, Sir, is certainly a great vice,* &c. Pope, Essay on Man:

What crops of wit and honesty appear
From spleen, from obstinacy, hate or fear!

L. 29. *whole line of the great and masculine virtues.* Cp. Speech on the Econ. Reform, near beginning; "Indeed, the whole class of the severe and restrictive virtues are at a market almost too high for humanity. What is worse, there are very few of these virtues which are not capable of being imitated, and even outdone, by the worst of vices. Malignity and envy will carve much more deeply, and finish much more sharply, than frugality and prudence."

P. 210, L. 3. *Things and the disposition of men's minds were changed.* The opinion of most politicians was expressed in the application of a witty remark of Townshend on a former administration to the Rockingham ministry at the outset of its career, July 1765, as a "*lutestring* ministry; fit only for the summer," but he seems to have lent them an unconfiding support. Cp. Churchill, The Ghost, Book iv:

A slight shot silk, for summer wear,
Just as our modern Statesmen are,
If rigid honesty permit
That I for once purloin the wit
Of him, who, were we all to steal,
Is much too rich the theft to feel.

Macaulay errs in assigning the origin of the *bon-mot* to this particular occasion.

Ibid. *men's minds.* "*Men's* for the genitive plural of *men,* is not allowable. We say, a *man's mind,* but we can only say, the *minds of men.*" Hurd, note on Spect., No. 262. The solecism is now well established.

L. 7. *resolutions leading to the Repeal.* These Resolutions embraced also the principle of the Declaratory Act, without which it is not probable that Townshend would have supported them. The inconsiderate strictures of Lord Campbell (*Lives of the Chancellors, Camden*) on the exceeding "folly of accompanying the Repeal of the Stamp Act with the statutable declaration of the abstract right to tax," are amply refuted by this Speech (see pp. 217–18). Macaulay is more just. "The Stamp Act was indefensible, not because it was beyond the constitutional competence of Parliament, but because it was unjust and impolitic, sterile of revenue, and fertile of discontents."

L. 9. *if an illness, (not, as was then given out, a political, but . . . a very real illness).* Cp. the newspaper quotation in Chesterfield's Letters, vol.

SPEECH ON AMERICAN TAXATION

iv. p. 404: "We hear that the Right Hon. Mr. Charles Townshend is indisposed, at his house in Oxfordshire, of a pain in his side: but it is not said *in which side*."

L. 12. *as the fashion of this world passeth away.* St. Paul, 1 Cor. vii. 31; 1 John ii. 17.

L. 24. *then Chancellor of the Exchequer, found himself in great straits.* [304] Townshend had laughed at the weakness of the Rockingham ministry, but his own "tessellated" ministry was the first since the Revolution to endure the disgrace of being defeated on a Money Bill. Dowdeswell, his predecessor in the Exchequer, moved an amendment to the four-shilling Land Tax, and defeated him by 206 to 118. Rock. Mem., vol. ii. p. 34. It was the loss on the Land Tax of a shilling in the pound that his American taxes were intended partly to supply. Walpole, iii. 28.

P. 211, L. 1. *to counterwork.* Properly a military term, meaning to raise works in opposition to those of the enemy. Pope, Ess. on Man, ii. 239:

That counterworks each folly and caprice.

L. 6. *usual fate of all exquisite policy.* "Refined policy has ever been the parent of confusion," p. 226.

L. 16. *a race of men,* &c. The class known in Parliamentary slang as "outsiders," "loose fish," &c. Or, by the transfer of an epithet formerly appropriated to electors, "independent" members. An "independent" member has been described as one who can never be depended on. Such men have naturally ever been unpopular with the organizers of parties.

L. 27. *the Hear-hims.* The "Hear him, hear him" of applauding auditors has now become, by ecthlipsis, "Hear, hear."

L. 28. *to whom* they *fell*—i.e. the speakers.

L. 31. *A single whiff of incense withheld.* Pope, Character of Wharton:

Tho' wondering senates hung on all he spoke,
The club must hail him master of the joke.

P. 212, L. 20. *on a former occasion.* In moving his eight resolutions relating to the disorders in North America, May 8, 1770.

L. 22. *After all these changes and agitations.* The remarks of Professor Goodrich (see note to p. 178) might be repeated here. The speech is here summed up with great force and perspicuity. The peroration,

"If you do not fall in, &c." which immediately follows, continues this style, in arguments of a more general character. Of these arguments Mr. Hazlitt says, they are "so sensible, so moderate, so wise and beautiful, that I cannot resist the temptation of copying them out, though I did not at first intend it." Eloq. of the British Senate, vol. ii. p. 293. This peroration is a brilliant specimen of direct appeal. It unites, like the Theseus, the grace of the Apollo with the strength of the Hercules. Vehemently as the power is exerted, it is done so easily and temperately, as to suggest an infinite fund in store. The words are eloquent, but the eloquence appears to reside not in them, but in the subject.

P. 213, L. 24. *reason not at all.* Burke may have had in mind the impressive phrase of the Gospel, "Swear not at all."

L. 28. *On this solid basis.* Alluding to the δὸς ποῦ στῶ of Archimedes, to which Burke often appears to have had recourse as an illustration in his parliamentary speeches. It must have been after some such passage as this that Lord John Townshend exclaimed aloud, *Heavens! what a man this is! Where could he acquire such transcendent powers?*

[305] **P. 214, L. 9.** *summum jus.* Gr. ἀκριβοδίκαιον. The origin of the maxim *Summum jus summa injuria* is lost in antiquity. "That over-perfect kind of justice which has obtained, by its merits, the title of the opposite vice." Speech on Econ. Reform. Cp. Aristotle, Ethics, lib. v. Macaulay compares the Stamp Act with Acts of Attainder and Confiscation. "Parliament was legally competent to tax America, as Parliament was legally competent to confiscate the property of all the merchants in Lombard Street, or to attaint any man of high treason, without examining witnesses against him, or hearing him in his own defence." "There is no worse torture than the torture of laws." Bacon, Essay of Judicature.

L. 23. *destroying angel.* I Chron. xxi. 12. Cp. vol. ii. p. 138. "The hand that like a destroying angel," &c.

L. 33. *Let us, Sir, embrace some system.* This final appeal is said to have fallen with immense weight on the audience. Burke not only knew that on a prepared audience the blow must be redoubled to produce a corresponding effect, but, as this paragraph proves, he was able to do it at will.

P. 215, L. 7. *Seek peace and ensue it.* A favourite quotation of Burke's. Ps. xxxiv. 14.

L. 11. *metaphysical distinctions; I hate the very sound of them.* Burke, says Bentham, had good cause to hate metaphysics; "The power he

SPEECH ON AMERICAN TAXATION

trusted to was *oratory, rhetoric,* the art of misrepresentation, the art of misdirecting the judgment by agitating and inflaming the passions," Works, x. 510. Others have accused him of metaphysical subtleties. "Thus was this great man," says Hazlitt, "merely for disclaiming metaphysical distinctions, and shewing their inapplicability to practical questions, considered as an unintelligible reasoner; as if you were chargeable with the very folly of which you convict others. Burke understood metaphysics, and saw their true boundaries. When he saw others venturing blindly on this treacherous ground, and called out to them to stop, shewing them where they were, they said, 'This man is a metaphysician!' General, unqualified assertions, universal axioms, and abstract rules, serve to embody our prejudices. They are the watchwords of party, the strong-holds of the passions. It is therefore dangerous to meddle with them! Solid reason means nothing more than being carried away by our passions, and solid sense is that which requires no reflection to understand it!" Eloq. of Brit. Senate, vol. ii. p. 297.

L. 20. *not used to do so from the beginning.* St. Matt. xix. 8.

L. 32. *Nobody will be argued into slavery.* "Which government the English have best preserv'd, being a Nation too tenacious of their Libertys to be complemented out of 'em," &c. Tindal, Essay Concerning Obedience, ch. 2. Burke's happy expression reminds us of the equally happy phrase of Sherlock, "Never a man was reasoned out of his religion."

L. 34. *what one* character *of liberty.* In the primary signification of "a mark, a stamp" (Johnson).

P. 216, L. 10. *a noble Lord, who spoke.* Lord Carmarthen.

L. 14. *the Americans are our children,* &c. An old commonplace of [306] despotic theorists. Notice the gentle irony with which Burke receives its utterance by a young speaker.

L. 20. *children ask for bread . . . not to give a stone.* St. Matt. vii. 9.

L. 27. *beauteous countenance of British liberty,* &c. Apparently an allusion to Exodus xxxiii. 18–23.

P. 217, L. 19. her *extensive Empire.* Burke begins by personifying Great Britain in the feminine gender, which is common enough; but he goes on to do the same with Parliament, which seems a little ludicrous.

L. 23. *What I call her* imperial character. Cp. Speech on Conciliation, p. 279.

P. 218, L. 10. *stress of the draft.* The image is from draught-horses.

NOTES

L. 13. *backwardness . . . of Pennsylvania . . . internal dissensions in the Colony.* "Domestic faction impeded measures of defence," Bancroft, iv. 224–253.

P. 219, L. 2. *Sir William Temple says, that Holland,* &c. "Thus this stomachful People, who could not endure the least exercise of Arbitrary Power or Impositions, or the sight of any Foreign Troops under the *Spanish* Government; have been since inured to all of them in the highest degree, under their own popular magistrates: Bridled with hard Laws; Terrified with severe executions; Environed with Foreign Forces; and opprest with the most cruel Hardship and Variety of Taxes, that ever was known under any Government." Obs. upon the United Provinces, ch. ii. "Cette nation aimerait prodigieusement sa liberté, parce que cette liberté serait vraie; et il pouvrait arriver que, pour la défendre, elle sacrifierait son bien, son aisance, ses intérêts: et qu'elle se chargerait des impôts les plus durs, et tels que le prince le plus absolu n'oserait les faire supporter à ses sujets." De l'Esp. des Lois, xix. 27. "Règle générale: on peut lever des tributs plus forts, à proportion de la liberté des sujets; et l'on est forcé de les modérer à mesure que la servitude augmente." Id. xii. 12.

L. 4. *Tyranny . . . knows neither how to accumulate nor how to extract.* "Quand les sauvages de la Louisiane veulent avoir du fruit, ils coupent l'arbre au pied, et cueillent le fruit. Voilà le gouvernement despotique." Id. v. 13. Cp. infra, p. 262.

L. 10. *morally* certain. Johnson, "popularly, according to the common occurrences of life, according to the common judgment made of things." The term is a relic of the Schoolmen, who allowed three degrees of certainty—mathematical, metaphysical, and moral.

L. 26. *not* partial good, *but* universal evil. Pope, Essay on Man, i. 292.

P. 220, L. 8. *The* noble Lord *will as usual.* Lord North.

L. 19. *friend under me on the floor.* Mr. Dowdeswell.

SPEECH ON CONCILIATION WITH THE COLONIES

P. 221, L. 1. *I hope, Sir,* &c. See p. 283, l. 8. The personality of the address to the Speaker is more marked than is now usual. Cp. p. 229, l. 1.

[307] **P. 222, L. 6.** *grand penal Bill, by which we had passed sentence.*

SPEECH ON CONCILIATION WITH THE COLONIES

The Act to restrain the Commerce of the Provinces of Massachuset's Bay and New Hampshire, and Colonies of Connecticut and Rhode Island, and Providence Plantation, in North America, to Great Britain, Ireland, and the British Islands in the West Indies; and to prohibit such Provinces and Colonies from carrying on any Fishery on the Banks of Newfoundland, and other places therein mentioned, under certain conditions and limitations. (*Original ed.*)

L. 18. *incongruous mixture of coercion and restraint.* The coercion consisted in breaking the resistance to the Tea-duty; the restraint in prohibiting the New Englanders from the Newfoundland fisheries. The incongruity lay in the form, not in the spirit or method of these attempts.

L. 31. *I was obliged to take more than common pains.* Burke however had long before this taken more than common pains to instruct himself in the affairs of the Colonies. See note to p. 195, l. 5, ante.

P. 223, L. 3. *blown about by every wind of fashionable doctrine.* St. Paul to Eph. iv. 14. Cp. Reynolds, Discourse xii, "at the mercy of every gust of fashion." Burke elsewhere speaks of "hebdomadal politicians." Cp. p. 243, "Some rule which may give a little stability to our politicks."

L. 6. *in perfect concurrence with a large majority.* The numbers on the division were 275 and 161.

L. 30. *worthy Member of great Parliamentary experience.* Mr. Rose Fuller.

P. 224, L. 15. *a platform* = a ground-plan.

L. 21. *gave so far* into *his opinion*—i.e. assented to. So European Settlements in America, vol. i. p. 32: "This (the natural slavery of barbarians) was so general a notion, that Aristotle himself, with all his penetration, gave into it very seriously."

L. 26. *hazard Plans of Government,* &c. Cp. note to p. 70, l. 14. "We live in a nation where, at present, there is scarce a single head that does not teem with politics. The whole island is peopled with statesmen, and not unlike Trinculo's Kingdom of Viceroys. Every man has contrived a scheme of government for the benefit of his fellow subjects." The Whig-Examiner, No. 5.

L. 28. *disreputably.* In the limited sense of "with prejudice to the reputation of those who make them."

L. 30. *ambitious of ridicule—candidate for disgrace.* Young, Night Thoughts: "O thou, ambitious of disgrace alone!"

L. 33. *Paper government.* Burke possibly had in mind the original settlement of Carolina, with its "model of a constitution framed, and body of fundamental laws compiled by the famous philosopher, Mr. Locke." (European Settlements in America, vol. ii. p. 237.) This absurd specimen of modern feudalism settled the lands in large and inalienable fiefs, on three classes of nobility: barons, cassiques (earls), and landgraves (dukes), and was tolerated for two generations. Shaftesbury had a hand in it. Burke's resolutions would in effect have established a new charter for all the Colonies.

[308] **P. 225, L. 1.** *prevailed every day more and more.* Note the Scriptural cast of the sentence. Cp. Ps. lxxiv. 24.

L. 4. *Public calamity,* &c. Cp. ante, p. 70, l. 12.

L. 10. *ennoble the flights,* &c. Anywhere but in Burke, such an antithesis would appear trifling.

L. 23. *dazzle or delude.* These two ideas were generally connected by Burke. Cp. p. 184, l. 20. So elsewhere he speaks of the "dazzling and delusive wealth" of the Spanish and Portuguese Colonies (their gold, silver, and precious stones).

L. 25. *The proposition is Peace.* "What a pompous description is here! Mulier formosa superne Desinit in piscem. For after all, what is this Heaven-born pacific Scheme, of which we have heard so laboured an Encomium? Why truly; if we will grant the Colonies all that they shall require, and stipulate for nothing in Return; then they will be at Peace with us. I believe it; and on these simple Principles of simple Peace-making, I will engage to terminate every difference throughout the world." Tucker, Letter, p. 44.

L. 30. *precise marking the shadowy boundaries,* &c. Another allusion from the passage in the Essay on Man (see p. 255):

Tho' each by turns the other's bound invade,
As in some well-wrought picture, light and shade.

—ii. 207.

L. 35. *former unsuspecting confidence of the Colonies,* &c. These are the words of the Congress at Philadelphia in 1774. Letter to Sheriffs of Bristol, 1777: "Man is a creature of habit; and the first breach being of very short duration, the Colonies fell back exactly into their ancient state. The Congress has used an expression with regard to this pacification, which appears to me truly significant. After the repeal of the Stamp Act, 'the Colonies fell,' says this Assembly, 'into their ancient state of *unsuspecting confidence in the mother country.*' This *unsuspecting*

Speech on Conciliation with the Colonies

confidence is the true center of gravity amongst mankind, about which all the parts are at rest. It is this *unsuspecting confidence* that removes all difficulties, and reconciles all the contradictions, which occur in the complexity of all ancient, puzzled, political establishments. Happy are the rulers which have the secret of preserving it!" &c. Cp. with this passage, vol. ii. p. 333, on the tampering of the Assembly with the army: "They have touched the central point, about which the particles that compose armies are at repose."

P. 226, L. 10. *Genuine simplicity of heart is an healing*, &c. "Truth in its nature is healing, and productive of reflection." Glover's Speech at the Bar, March 16, 1775.

L. 16. *Project lately laid upon your table*, &c. "That when the Governor, Council, or Assembly, or General Court, of any of his Majesty's Provinces or Colonies in America, shall *propose* to make provision, *according to the condition, circumstances*, and *situation*, of such Province or Colony, for contributing their *proportion* to the *Common Defence* (such *proportion* to be raised under the Authority of the General Court, or General Assembly, of such [309] Province or Colony, and disposable by Parliament), and shall engage to make provision also for the support of the Civil Government, and the Administration of Justice, in such Province or Colony, it will be proper, *if such Proposal shall be approved by his Majesty, and the two Houses of Parliament,* and for so long as such Provision shall be made accordingly, to forbear, *in respect of such Province or Colony,* to levy any Duty, Tax, or Assessment, or to impose any further Duty, Tax, or Assessment, except such duties as it may be expedient to continue to levy or impose, for the Regulation of Commerce; the Nett Produce of the Duties last mentioned to be carried to the account of such Province or Colony respectively." — Resolution moved by Lord North in the Committee; and agreed to by the House, Feb. 27, 1775. (*Original ed.*) See post, p. 280 sq.

L. 17. *Blue Ribband.* Lord North was conspicuous among the members of the Lower House by this badge of a Knight of the Garter. The only other commoner who had then obtained the Garter was Sir R. Walpole. Castlereagh and Palmerston are the only other instances of this distinction being offered to and accepted by commoners.

P. 227, L. 28. *that time and those chances*, &c. An allusion to the well-known passage of Shakspeare:

There is a tide in the affairs of men
Which, taken at the flood, leads on to fortune.

NOTES

So Dryden, Absalom and Achitophel:

"Heaven has to all allotted, soon or late,
Some lucky revolution of their fate," &c.

P. 228, L. 10. arrant *trifling* = mere, downright.

L. 15. *The number of people in the Colonies.* The computation of Mr. Bancroft (vol. iv. p. 128), which fully justifies Burke's remarks, is as follows:

	Whites	Blacks	Total
1750	1,040,000	220,000	1,260,000.
1754	1,165,000	260,000	1,425,000.
1760	1,385,000	310,000	1,695,000.
1770	1,850,000	462,000	2,312,000.
1780	2,383,000	562,000	2,945,000.
1790	3,177,257	752,069	3,929,326.

Cp. Johnson's savage comment on this and other arguments; "We are told that the continent of North America contains three millions, not of men, merely, but of *Whigs;* of Whigs fierce for liberty, and disdainful of dominion (alluding to Chatham's Speech of January 20, 1775); that they multiply with the fecundity of their own rattlesnakes, so that every quarter of a century doubles their numbers. . . . When it is urged that they will shoot up like the hydra, he (the English politician) naturally considers how the hydra was destroyed." Taxation no Tyranny, Works, x. 96, 97.

L. 28. *whilst the dispute continues, the exaggeration ends.* Cp. note, p. 225, ante, on Burke's repetition of his proposition, now put in a few words at once terse in expression, but weighty with antithesis, and now [310] expanded in its fullest details. It is impossible to surpass the felicity of this antithesis.

P. 229, L. 4. *Occasional*—used *in malam partem.* Cp. ante p. 159, "occasional arguments." Dr. Johnson speaks of Browne's Hydriotaphia as "a treatise *occasionally* written." So the Occasional Writer, a paper to which Bolingbroke contributed.

L. 6. Minima *which are out of the eye of the law.* For the explanation and illustration of the maxim "De minimis non curat lex," see Broom's Legal Maxims, 2nd ed. p. 105.

L. 20. *trod some days ago . . . by a distinguished person.* Mr. Glover, who appeared at the bar (March 16), to support the petition of the West Indian Planters respecting the Non-Importation Agreement, praying that peace might be concluded with the Colonies, presented Febru-

SPEECH ON CONCILIATION WITH THE COLONIES

ary 2. His Speech, Parl. Hist. xviii. 461–478, is well worthy of study, as an illustration of Burke's relation to contemporary oratory. His *Leonidas* still survives; but few readers will be disposed to encounter his *Athenaid,* an epic in thirty books.

L. 22. *after Thirty-five years.* Probably therefore, on the occasion of the transactions which occasioned the war with Spain in 1739.

P. 230, L. 13. *Davenant*—Inspector-General's *office,* i.e. of Customs. Author of the *Discourses on Revenue and Trade,* &c.

L. 17. *The African, terminating almost wholly in the Colonies.* Because little more than a trade in slaves, who were paid for with English wares. See Burke's remarks on the African trade in his Account of America, vol. i. It was owing to the judgment with which the Portuguese carried on the trade in slaves that Brazil, in Burke's time, was looked on as the richest and most promising of the American Colonies.

L. 19. *the West Indian.* More important than the legitimate trade was that carried on, against the Act of Navigation, between the Spanish Colonies and the English West Indies. See Lord Stanhope's History, vol. ii.

L. 25. *the trade to the Colonies,* &c. Burke had employed the statistics of 1704 in his pamphlet of 1769 on the State of the Nation, to demonstrate the increase of the Colony trade. He there compares the total exports to the Colonies in 1704 (£483,265) with those to Jamaica in 1767 (£467,681).

P. 231, L. 23. *is not this American trade an unnatural protuberance.* "The people of the United States still constitute our largest and most valuable commercial connection. The business we carry on with them is nearly twice as extensive as that with any other people, and our transactions are almost wholly conducted on ready money terms." Cobden's Political Writings, vol. i. p. 98. The American official returns for the year ending June 30, 1873, shows that in that year *more than one-third of the whole imports* into the United States came from England, and that *more than one-half of their whole exports,* consisting chiefly of cotton, provisions, breadstuffs, and petroleum, were sent to England.

P. 232, L. 6. *Mr. Speaker,* &c. The transition, bold as it is, is happily managed. [311] It is difficult to pass from arithmetical to rhetorical figures, but Burke seems to fuse the two elements into one by the mere force of his reasoning.

L. 7. *It is good for us to be here.* St. Mark ix. 5 sq. The quotation is introduced with striking effect.

NOTES

L. 8. *Clouds, indeed, and darkness rest upon the future.*

The wide, th' unbounded Prospect lies before me,
And Shadows, Clouds, and Darkness, rest upon it.

> Addison, Cato, Act v. Sc. I.

IBID. *clouds,* indeed. "Indeed" is emphatic, not used conjunctively.

L. 14. *my Lord Bathurst.* The connexion of Lord Bathurst with English literature extends from Pope and Swift to Sterne (vide Sterne, Letters, p. 192). In 1704 he was more than "of an age at least to be made to comprehend," &c., having been born in 1684: he took his seat in Parliament in 1705.

L. 17. *acta parentum jam legere.* The tense in the quotation is adapted to this use of it. Virg. Ecl. iv. 26.

L. 21. *in the fourth generation,* i.e. of the House of Brunswick.

L. 24. *was to be made Great Britain*—in 1707.

L. 25. *his son.* The eldest, Henry, Lord Chancellor, created Baron Apsley 1771.

P. 233, L. 2. *stories of savage men,* &c. See Part II of Burke's Account of America.

L. 3. *before you* taste of death. St. Matt. xvi. 28, St. John viii. 52, Heb. ii. 9. Shakspeare, Julius Caesar, Act ii. Sc. 2:

The valiant never taste of death but once.

L. 15. *cloud the* setting *of his day,* i.e. sunset. Borrowed from Johnson, Vanity of Human Wishes:

But few there are whom hours like these await,
Who set unclouded in the gulphs of fate.

With this graceful figure Burke concludes one of the best-known of his passages, in a higher strain of rhetoric than is now permissible in Parliamentary speaking. This eloquent effort of imagination would have been better in place in the Address of Daniel Webster on the Landing of the Pilgrim Fathers. Dr. Johnson's extemporaneous travesty of it, which illustrates the general temper of the country, shall be given in the words of Mrs. Piozzi.

"It was in the year 1775 that Mr. Edmund Burke made the famous speech in Parliament, that struck even foes with admiration, and friends with delight. Among the nameless thousands who are contented to echo those praises they have not skill to invent, I ventured, before Dr. Johnson himself, to applaud with rapture the beautiful passage in it concerning Lord Bathurst and the Angel; which, said our Doctor, had I been in the House, I would have answered thus;

"'Suppose, Mr. Speaker, that to Wharton, or to Marlborough or to any of the eminent Whigs of the last age, the devil had, not with any great impropriety, consented to appear; he would perhaps in somewhat like these words have commenced the conversation;

[312] "'You seem, my Lord, to be concerned at the judicious apprehension, that while you are sapping the foundations of royalty at home, and propagating here the dangerous doctrine of resistance, the distance of America may secure its inhabitants from your arts, though active; but I will unfold to you the gay prospects of futurity. This people, now so innocent and harmless, shall draw the sword against their mother country, and bathe its point in the blood of their benefactors; this people, now contented with a little, shall then refuse to spare what they themselves confess they could not miss; and these men, now so honest and so grateful, shall, in return for peace and protection, see their vile agents in the house of Parliament, there to sow the seeds of sedition, and propagate confusion, perplexity, and pain. Be not dispirited, then, at the contemplation of their present happy state; I promise you that anarchy, poverty, and death shall, by my care, be carried even across the spacious Atlantic, and settle in America itself, the sure consequences of our beloved Whiggism.'" Anecdotes of Dr. Johnson, p. 42.

L. 26. *I choose, Sir, to enter,* &c. "I think I know America," wrote Burke to the Sheriffs of Bristol, in 1777. "If I do not, my ignorance is incurable, because I have spared no pains to understand it. . . . Everything that has been done there has arisen from a total misconception of the object."

L. 27. *generalities, which in all other cases,* &c. The thought is as original as the expression is striking.

L. 35. *deceive the burthen of life.* To match this elegant Latinism we may quote the final lines of Bowles's Inscription at Knoyle:

Laetare, et verno jamjam sub lumine, carpe,
Dum licet, ipse rosas, et fallas tristia vitae.
[So "gather its brief rosebuds," and deceive
The cares and crosses of humanity.]

P. 234, L. 9. comprehending *rice* = including. Cp. Fr. *y compris.*

L. 16. *with a Roman charity.* The story of Xanthippe and Cimon, as told by Hyginus, was universally known by the name of the *Roman*

NOTES

Charity. It afforded an effective subject to several artists. Some authors (Plin. Nat. Hist. vii. 36, Valerius Maximus v. 47) represent a mother instead of a father as the object. Valerius Maximus in another version, and Festus and Solinus, agree with Hyginus.

L. 22. *they seemed even to excite your envy.* George Grenville had by his budget of 1764, practically resigned the whale fishery to America. "This," says Mr. Bancroft, "is the most liberal act of Grenville's administration, of which the merit is not diminished by the fact that American whale fishery was superseding the English under every discouragement." England and Holland had formerly contested the whaling trade. The position of America was of course such that when the American fishery was freed from its burdens it overwhelmed both.

L. 25. *what in the world is equal to it.* At this time Massachusetts alone employed 183 vessels, carrying 13,820 tons, in the North, and 120 vessels, carrying 14,026 tons, in the South Atlantic fishery. The fishery was at first [313] carried on from the shores, and then, as whales became scarce, they were pursued to their haunts. Hence the advantage of the Americans. See an interesting article in the Quarterly Review, vol. lxiii. p. 318.

L. 30. *Hudson's Bay*—Henry Hudson, 1607; but discovered by Seb. Cabot, 1517. *Davis's Streights*—John Davis, 1585.

L. 31. *we hear that they have pierced into the opposite region of polar cold.* It is interesting to be able to trace to the eloquent appeal of Burke some of the most important events in Colonial history. In 1775 ships were apparently for the first time fitted out by English owners for the purpose of following the track of the Americans in the South Seas. The bounties abolished by Grenville were revived in 1776 to favour this new branch of adventure; but it was not until 1785 that our navigators discovered the haunts of the sperm whale, and attained a success equalling that of the Americans. The enterprise of Mr. Enderby in 1788 extended the fisheries to the Pacific, and in 1820 to Japan. The consequences were a constant intercourse with the Spanish Colonies, which had no small share in leading them to their independence — the introduction of civilization into Polynesia, and the foundation of the Australian and Tasmanian Colonies. The whalers preceded the missionaries.

P. 235, L. 1. *frozen Serpent of the south.* The Hydrus, or Water-serpent, a small constellation far to the south, within the Antarctic Circle.

SPEECH ON CONCILIATION WITH THE COLONIES

IBID. *Falkland Island.* A letter from Port Egmont, dated 1770, in the Grenville Papers, vol. iv. p. 505, gives a dismal account of the Falkland Islands. "Barren of everything except sea-lions and seals. There is not an inch of Braddock Down that is not better than the very best of any of these islands; there is not a stick so big as the pen I am writing with on any of them. The soil is turf chiefly, and in short is one wild heath wherever you turn your eye. . . . We have been ordered off the island by the Spaniards, the French having given up their pretensions to their settlements." This will explain the humour of an allusion in the first scene of Foote's comedy of the "Cozeners," where Mrs. Fleece'em promises an applicant for a place the surveyorship of the woods in Falkland's Island, with the loppings and toppings for perquisites.

L. 2. *too remote and romantic an object for the grasp of national ambition.* The Falkland Islands are about 200 in number, of which East and West Falkland were the chief. Discovered at the end of the sixteenth century, they were not considered worth occupation. In 1763 the French built Port Louis on East Falkland; England soon after built Port Egmont on West Falkland, but abandoned it in 1773. Through the whale-fishery they afterwards attained an unexpected importance. See Lord Stanhope's History, vol. v.

L. 8. *run the longitude;* i.e. sail south to the South American coast.

L. 9. vexed *by their fisheries.* Cp. Par. Lost, i. 305:

When with fierce winds Orion arm'd
Hath vex'd the Red-Sea coast,

[314] and the "still-vexed Bermoothes" of Shakspeare. The Latin cast of the phrase is noticeable. Cp. Ovid. Met. xi. 434:

Nil illis vetitum est, incommendataque tellus
Omnis, et omne fretum: coeli quoque nubila vexant.

IBID. *no climate,* &c. Virgil, Aen. i. 460:

Quae regio in terris nostri non plena laboris?

L. 13. hardy *industry* = bold, adventurous. So Goldsmith; "Bacon, that great and *hardy* genius." Cp. p. 121, l. 26, ante, "an hardy attempt." Burke however often used the word in the modern sense = patient of hardship.

P. 236, L. 5. *not as an odious, but as a feeble instrument.* The inability of European governments even to put down the buccaneers was doubtless present to Burke: "What armaments from England, Holland, and France have been sent in different times to America, whose remains returned without honour or advantage, is too clear, and perhaps too invidious a topic to be greatly insisted upon." Account of America, vol. ii. p. 12.

L. 9. *does not remove the necessity of subduing again.* So Milton:

who overcomes
By force, hath overcome but half his foe.
—Par. Lost, i. 648.

L. 13. *an armament is not a victory.* Burke perhaps alludes to the Spanish Armada.

L. 16. *Power and authority—can never be begged.* Cp. First Letter on Regicide Peace: "Power, and eminence, and consideration, are things not to be begged. They must be commanded; and they, who supplicate for mercy from others, can never hope for justice through themselves. What justice they are to obtain, as the alms of an enemy, depends upon his character; and that they ought well to know, before they implicitly confide."

L. 22. *I do not choose . . . the spirit that has made the country.* Cp. First Letter on Regicide Peace; "Nation is a moral essence, not a geographical arrangement, or a denomination of the nomenclator."

P. 237, L. 25. *emigrated from you when this part of your character was most predominant.* "The American freeholders at present are nearly, in point of condition, what the English Yeomen were of old, when they rendered us formidable to all Europe, and our name celebrated throughout the world. The former, from many obvious circumstances, are more enthusiastical lovers of liberty, than even our Yeomen were." Burke, Ann. Reg. 1775, p. 14. The New England colonies had their origin in the time of the great struggle against the Stuarts.

L. 31. *Liberty inheres in some sensible object.* The Whigs and the popular party indulged in so much vain talk about liberty that such observations were to the point. "It inheres in good and steady government, as in its substance and vital principle." Speech on arrival at Bristol, 1774.

L. 32. *Every nation, &c.* Burke adopts the well-known doctrine of Goldsmith's "Traveller," which belongs, however, rather to poetry than to political philosophy, though it is borrowed from Montesquieu. "The Traveller" was published in 1764.

[315] From art more various are the blessings sent,
Wealth, commerce, honour, liberty, content;
Yet these each others' power so strong contest,
That either seems destructive of the rest.

SPEECH ON CONCILIATION WITH THE COLONIES

Where wealth and freedom reign, contentment fails,
And honour sinks where commerce long prevails.
Hence every state, to one lov'd blessing prone,
Conforms and models life to that alone;
Each to the fav'rite happiness attends,
And spurns the plan that aims at other ends;
Till, carried to excess in each domain,
This fav'rite good begets peculiar pain.

P. 238, L. 3. *in the ancient commonwealths.* Notably in Rome, an example always present to Burke's mind. Read Swift's Discourse on the Contests and Dissensions in Athens and Rome, which, though opposing Burke's Whiggish doctrine of Party, furnished him with many hints.

L. 7. *the ablest pens, and most eloquent tongues.* Pym, Hampden, Selden, St. John, &c. See Raleigh's "Prerogative of Parliaments in England."

L. 17. *that in theory it ought to be so.* It is rare with Burke to cite deductive arguments approvingly. Cp. second note to p. 247, l. 26.

P. 239, L. 4. *pleasing error.* Virgil:

Indiscreta suis, gratusque parentibus error.

The "amabilis insania" of Horace, however, comes nearer in meaning. Cp. vol. ii. p. 125, "the delusion of this amiable error."

L. 6. *some are* merely *popular* = purely, entirely. "The one sort we may for distinction safe call *mixedly,* and the other *merely* humane." Hooker, Eccl. Pol. Book i. c. 10. New England was an aggregate of pure *democracies,* the foremost in spirit and popular organisation being Massachusett's Bay and Connecticut. New Hampshire, Rhode Island, and Maine, which was a part of Massachusetts, were the others. New York differed from New England chiefly from having been settled under large patents of land to individuals, instead of charters to towns. North of the Potomac were the two large *proprietary governments,* Pennsylvania with Delaware, under Thomas and Richard Penn, and Maryland, which belonged nominally to Lord Baltimore. There were five *royal governments,* the Carolinas, Georgia, Virginia, and New Jersey. See Bancroft, vol. iv. chap. 6. It was not, however, in the democratic governments that the most violent resolutions were passed. See Ann. Reg. 1775, p. 6.

L. 14. *Religion, always a principle of energy.* The incidents of the Anti-Slavery war show that this principle in the Americans is still in no way impaired.

L. 20. averseness from *all*, &c. The Addisonian "aversion" is more usual. *From* is the proper construction. Johnson considers *to* improper, and *towards* very improper. (Cp. note to p. 83, l. 3.) Swift uses "aversion against."

P. 240, L. 1. *dissidence of dissent,* &c. Cp. Hooker, Book iv. c. viii. "There [316] hath arisen a sect in England, which following still the self same rule of policy, seeketh to reform even the French reformation." Cp. Fourth Letter on a Regicide Peace, "They have apostatized from their apostasy."

L. 28. *as broad and general as the air.* "As broad and general as the casing air," Macbeth, Act iii. Sc. 4.

P. 241, L. 3. *Our Gothick ancestors.* Incorrect, but commonly used, even by Hallam. Our ancestors were Low-Dutch.

IBID. *such in our days were the Poles.* "Poland seems to be a country formed to give the most disadvantageous idea of liberty, by the extreme to which it is carried, and the injustice with which it is distributed," &c. See the rest of this interesting description of the state of affairs in Poland, Ann. Reg. 1763.

L. 4. *were the Poles*—until 1772.

L. 10. *In no country . . . is the law so general a study.* American authors have not insisted on this as a cause, though the history of the Revolution is full of proofs of it. "The Lawyers of this place (New York)," writes the Lieutenant-Governor, to Conway, in 1765, "are the authors and conductors of the present sedition." On the study of the law in the Italian Republics, see Hallam, Middle Ages, vol. iii. ch. 9, part 2. On the lawyers in the French Assembly, cp. vol. ii. p. 131.

L. 12. *numerous and powerful.* "In many of our settlements the lawyers have gathered to themselves the greatest part of the wealth of the country." Europ. Settlements in America, vol. ii. p. 304. Burke censured as the cause of this, the burdening of the colonies with the mass of our common law, and the old statute law, and their adoption, with very little choice or discretion, of a great part of the new statute law. He thought "all that load of matter, perhaps so useless at home, without doubt extremely prejudicial in the colonies. . . . These infant settlements surely demanded a more simple, clear, and determinate legislation, though it were somewhat of a homelier kind." Ibid.

L. 20. *printing them for their own use.* Burke says nothing of the general influence of the printing-press, which was by this time actively at work in the Colonies. "The press," he writes, in the First Letter on a

SPEECH ON CONCILIATION WITH THE COLONIES

Regicide Peace, "in reality has made every government, in its spirit, almost democratic."

L. 21. *Blackstone's Commentaries.* Then a new and popular work.

L. 25. *in Boston they have been enabled, by successful chicane.* General Gage, in pursuance of the powers given him by the coercive statutes, had prohibited the *calling* of town meetings after August 1, 1774. A town meeting was, however, held, and asserted to be legal, not having been called, but adjourned over. "By such means," said Gage, "you may keep your meeting alive these ten years." He brought the subject before the new Council. "It is a point of law," said they, "and should be referred to the Crown lawyers," &c. Bancroft, vol. vii. ch. 8. Cp. Ann. Reg. 1775, p. 11.

IBID. *successful* chicane. Cp. the protest against this and other French words in the Ann. Reg. 1758, p. 374.

[317] **L. 30.** *my Hon. and Learned Friend on the floor.* The Attorney-General (Thurlow).

P. 242, L. 2. *Abeunt studia in mores.* Ovid, Heroid. Ep. xv. 83. The quotation is evidently adopted from Bacon's Essay of Studies.

L. 9. *snuff the approach of tyranny,* &c. The metaphor is from hunting. The phrases are a reminiscence of Addison, the Campaign. (Cp. p. 149, l. 15.)

> So the stanch hound the trembling deer pursues,
> And smells his footsteps in the *tainted* dews,
> The tedious track unravelling by degrees:
> But when the scent comes warm in *every breeze,*
> Fired at the near *approach,* he shoots away
> On his full stretch, and bears upon his prey.

L. 16. *Seas roll, and months pass.* The student will note the striking effect of the zeugma.

L. 19. *winged ministers of vengeance, who carry your bolts in their pounces,* &c. "Winged ministers of vengeance" is a compound of Milton's "ministers of vengeance" (Par. Lost, i. 170), and "winged messengers" (ib. iii. 229). Cp. ante, p. 236. "Those who wield the thunder of the State." The image is borrowed from Lord Chatham's Speech of January 22, 1770; "They have disarmed the imperial bird, the *ministrum fulminis alitem.*[1] The army is the thunder of the Crown—the ministry have tied up the hand which should direct the bolt." Burke

---

1. Horace, Odes iv. 1.

NOTES

happily transfers it to the navy. The student should compare the beautiful expansion and application of this image by Canning, introduced with exquisite propriety in the speech made within sight of Plymouth docks, 1823.

L. 21. *a power steps in . . .* "So far shalt thou go and no farther." The allusion is to the story of Canute and his courtiers, then recently popularized by Hume.

L. 27. *In large bodies,* &c. But cp. Letter to W. Elliott, Esq. "These analogies between bodies natural and politic, though they may sometimes illustrate arguments, furnish no argument of themselves." The same observation occurs in the First Letter on a Regicide Peace. Mill has apparently made use of the latter passage in his account of "Fallacies of Generalization."

L. 28. *The Turk,* &c. Notice the foresight which these observations imply.

P. 243, L. 1. *in all his borders—watches times.* These are well known Scriptural expressions. See note to p. 98, l. 32. "Temporibus servire" is a common maxim of Cicero.

IBID. *Spain, in her provinces—*i.e. in South America. The necessity of reform in the Spanish Colonial system was by this time obvious. In 1778 the monopoly of Cadiz was abolished, and a great stimulus was thus given to the Spanish Colony trade.

L. 3. *this is the immutable condition,* &c. Burke generalises from two bad instances, but the weakness of Spain and Turkey was then far less [318] apparent than now. The Czar is as well obeyed on the Pacific shore as on the Baltic, and English government is as strong on the Ganges as on the Thames.

L. 10. *grown with the growth,* &c. Cp. p. 181, l. 28.

L. 17. *causes which produce it—*i.e. produce the excess, not the spirit.

L. 22. *held in trust.* Cp. note to p. 118, l. 10.

L. 28. *with all its imperfections on its head.* Hamlet, Act i. Sc. 5.

P. 244, L. 28. *Obedience is what makes Government.* Cp. note to p. 105, l. 11.

P. 246, L. 4. *Sir, if I were capable,* &c. This perhaps indicates that the Speaker exhibited an appearance of weariness or inattention, on Burke's proposal to "go patiently round and round the subject."

SPEECH ON CONCILIATION WITH THE COLONIES

L. 20. *It is* radical *in its principle.* "The objects which I proposed were *radical,* systematic economy," &c. Letter to Mr. Harford, April 4, 1780. It was Burke who brought the term into parliamentary if not into general use—not Pitt, as commonly asserted: cp. Fischel, English Const., p. 551.

P. 247, L. 5. *The people would occupy without grants.* See Bancroft, ch. xviii. and xxvii. "But the prohibition only set apart the Great Valley as the sanctuary of the unhappy, the adventurous and the free; of those whom enterprise, or curiosity, or disgust at the forms of life in the old plantations, raised above royal edicts. . . . The boundless West became the poor man's City of Refuge," &c. Vol. vi. p. 33, where see note.

L. 11. *Already they have topped the Apalachian mountains*—better known as the Alleghanies, the western frontier of the British settlements. The germ of the description which follows is in the Annual Register, vol. i. p. 2. Burke doubtless remembered with some vividness a passage on which he had bestowed much pains.

L. 13. *an immense plain—a square of five hundred miles:* the other boundaries being the Mississippi and the lakes.

L. 17. *Hordes of English Tartars.* This idea seems to have been suggested by the history of the Buccaneers of St. Domingo, "a considerable number of men transformed by necessity into downright savages," an account of whom, from the pen of Burke, is to be found in the Annual Register for 1761.

L. 24. *Encrease and Multiply.* Burke quotes from Milton, Par. Lost. x. 730. Authorised Version, "Be fruitful and multiply"; Vulgate (used by Milton), "Crescite et multiplicamini."

L. 26. *which God by an express Charter,* &c. Cp. More's Utopia (Bp. Burnet's translation), Book ii: "They account it a very just cause of war for a nation to hinder others from possessing a part of the soil of which they make no use, but which is suffered to lie idle and uncultivated; since every man has, by the law of nature, a right to such a waste portion of the earth as is necessary for his subsistence."

[319] **IBID.** *given to the children of men.* Ps. cxv. 16. This is one of the rare instances in which Burke employs the arguments of what he called the "metaphysical" school. He evidently had in mind Locke, of Civil Government, Book ii. ch. v. The phrase is used in the Letter to a Bristol firm, May 2, 1778. Blackstone similarly deduces the rights of property from the "dominion over all the earth," &c., conferred upon

mankind at the creation. "This is the only true and solid foundation of man's dominion over external things, whatever airy metaphysical notions may have been started by fanciful writers on this subject." Cp. the expression "charter of nature," p. 254.

P. 248, L. 6. *a more easy task.* Because the system of commercial restriction was well established.

L. 20. *beggar its subjects into submission.* Cp. p. 73, l. 27, and note.

L. 26. *Spoliatis arma supersunt.* Juvenal, Sat. viii. 124. The phrase seems also to have stuck in the memory of Hallam. "Arms, says the poet, remain to the plundered," he writes in chapter xviii. of the Constitutional History. "Les nations doivent jouir de cette indépendance qu'on peut leur arracher un moment, mais qu'elles finissent toujours par reconquérir: *spoliatis arma supersunt.*" Chateaubriand, De la Monarchie selon la Charte, ch. xlvi.

L. 33. *your speech would betray you.* St. Matt. xxvi. 73.

L. 34. *argue another Englishman into slavery.* Cp. p. 215, l. 32.

P. 249, L. 2. *to substitute the Roman Catholic, as a penalty.* Why should Burke introduce this, which seems mere redundance? He casts an oblique glance at Ireland, and "counterchanges" the unjust penal laws which were there in force.

L. 4. *inquisition and dragooning*—alluding to the measures adopted by Spain to reduce the Netherlands, in the sixteenth century, and by Louis XIV, in the next, to conquer the Huguenots.

L. 8. *burn their books of curious science.* Acts xix. 12. Cp., in the pathetic Defence of Strafford, "It will be wisdom for yourselves and your posterity to cast into the fire these bloody and mysterious volumes of constructive and arbitrary treason, as the primitive Christians did their books of curious arts, and betake yourselves to the plain letter of the law and statute," &c.

L. 15. *more* chargeable—i.e. more expensive.

L. 21. *any opinion of it*—an elliptical expression, still in use—equivalent to "any *favourable* opinion of it." Cp. the expression "to have no idea of a thing," i.e. to disapprove it (found in Pitt's speeches).

L. 26. *both these pleasing tasks.* A masterly stroke. Cp. p. 215, l. 32.

L. 30. *a measure to which other people have had recourse.* See Aristoph. Ran. 27, from which it appears that the slaves who had distinguished themselves at the battle of Arginusae, were presented with their freedom. Plutarch says that Cleomenes armed 2,000 Helots to oppose the Macedonian Leucaspedae, in his war with that people and the Achaeans. According to [320] Pausanias, the Helots were present at the battle of Marathon. Among the Romans, as Virgil (Aen. ix. 547) tells us, it was highly criminal for slaves to enter the army of their masters, but in the Hannibalian War, after the battle of Cannae, 8,000 of them were armed, and by their valour in subsequent actions, earned their liberty. See Livy, Book xxiv.

L. 33. *Slaves as these,* &c. Burke, in his Account of the Settlements in America, was the first to point out that on English soil there were slaves enduring "a slavery more complete, and attended with far worse circumstances, than what any people in their condition suffer in any part of the world, or have suffered in any period of time." The passage is quoted in Dr. Ogden's Sermon against Oppression.

IBID. *dull as all men are from slavery.* It was shown by Adam Smith that slave labour was so much dearer than free labour that none but the most lucrative trades could bear the loss it involved.

P. 250, L. 13. *Ye gods, annihilate but space and time,* &c. This piece of fustian is taken from Martinus Scriblerus, of the Art of Sinking in Poetry, where it is cited without name. It is said to come from one of Dryden's plays. Cp. the humorous paper in the Ann. Reg. 1761, p. 207, in which, alluding to the "stage-coaches, machines, flys, and post-chaises," which were plying about this time in great numbers on the improved turnpike-roads, the author says, "The lover now can almost literally *annihilate time and space,* and be with his mistress, before she dreams of his arrival."

P. 251, L. 2. *method of drawing up an indictment,* &c. Cp. vol. ii. p. 189. (Quidquid multis peccatur inultum.)

L. 4. *Sir Edward Coke—Sir W. Rawleigh.* See Howell's State Trials, vol. ii. p. 7. sq. (Pronounce *Cooke.* Similarly, "Bolingbroke" should be pronounced *Bullingbrook.* Both names indeed were at one time spelt in this way.)

L. 8. *same title that I am*—i.e. that of popular election as a representative.

L. 12. *my idea of an Empire.* Cp. sup. p. 217. With the extension of the Colonies, this "idea" of Burke's has acquired a new significance.

P. 252, L. 15. *as often decided against the superior,* &c. Cp. ante, pp. 74, 75.

NOTES

L. 19. *rights which, in their exercise,* &c. Cp. note to p. 214, l. 9.

P. 253, L. 10. *these* juridical *ideas.* Cp. note, p. 225, l. 30, ante.

L. 20. *for my life* = if my life depended on the effort. A vulgarism, now nearly obsolete. So Shakspeare often uses the phrase "for my heart."

P. 254, L. 8. *Sir, I think you must perceive.* It is difficult to select any passage in this oration for special notice in point of style: but no one can fail to be struck with fresh admiration at the method of this paragraph, in which the "right of Taxation" is excluded from the discussion. The delicate irony with which the theorists are passed over gives place, by way of a surprising antithesis ("right to render your people miserable"—"interest to make them happy"), to the earnest remonstrance with which the passage [321] concludes. The continuous irony of the first part of the paragraph seems to contribute to rather than detract from the general elevation of treatment.

L. 10. *Some gentlemen* startle—intransitive. Classical. Cp. Addison's Cato, Act iii. Sc. 2:

> my frighted thoughts run back,
> And *startle* into Madness at the Sound.

Young, Satire on Women:

> How will a miser *startle,* to be told
> Of such a wonder as insolvent gold!

L. 11. *it is less than nothing.* Isaiah xl. 17. "In matters of State, a constitutional competence to act, is, in many cases, the smallest part of the Question." First Letter on a Regicide Peace.

L. 22. *deep questions . . . great names, high and reverend authorities,* &c. "As to the right of taxation, the gentlemen who opposed it produced many learned authorities from Locke, Selden, Harrington, and Puffendorf, shewing that the very foundation and ultimate point in view of all government, is the good of society," &c. Annual Register, 1766. "These arguments were answered with great force of reason, and knowledge of the constitution, by the other side." Ibid. The whole of this able summary, which is from the pen of Burke, is also to be read in the Parliamentary History, vol. xvi.

L. 23. *militate against.* The proper construction; though Burke also uses the modern "militate with." (Not in Johnson.)

L. 27. *the great Serbonian bog,* &c. Par. Lost, ii. 592. "He climbed and descended precipices on which vulgar mortals tremble to look:

he passed marshes like the *Serbonian bog,* where *armies whole have sunk,* &c." The Idler, No. 49. Cp. "the Serbonian bog of this base oligarchy," vol. ii. p. 305. See Herodotus, iii. 5.

P. 255, L. 8. *assertion of my title . . . loss of my suit.* "It would have been a poor compensation that we had triumphed in a dispute, whilst we lost an Empire." Letter to Sheriffs of Bristol.

What were defeat, when victory must appal?

Shelley, Hellas.

L. 11. *Unity of spirit—diversity of operations.* 1 Cor. xii. 4 sq.

L. 13. *sealed a regular compact.* To *seal,* i.e. to affix one's seal, implies a higher degree of formality than merely to *sign.*

L. 15. *rights of citizens . . . posterity to all generations.* The allusion is to a question which is fully discussed in vol. ii. p. 106, where Burke takes the contrary view to that which is implied here.

L. 19. *two million of men.* The old plural. So "two thousand," "two hundred," "two score," "two dozen."

L. 21. *the general character,* &c. The doctrine was then novel. Its currency is due to the French philosophers.

P. 256, L. 19. *a gentleman of real moderation.* Mr. Rice.

P. 257, L. 17. *The pamphlet from which he seems to have borrowed*—by Dean Tucker, see note to p. 202, ante.

[322] **L. 19.** *without idolizing them.* "His (Grenville's) idol, the Act of Navigation," p. 186.

L. 33. *real, radical cause.* See note to p. 246, l. 20.

P. 258, L. 15. *will go further . . . fact and reason.* For the *fact* alluded to, see pp. 203–4, and for the *reason,* p. 178, ante.

P. 259, L. 10. *consult the genius,* &c. Chatham was fond of "consulting the genius of the English constitution." Notice the method of the paragraph.

L. 28. *roots of our primitive constitution.* From which the representation of the Commons naturally sprang. Burke is correct, and in his time such a view implied some originality.

L. 31. *gave us at least,* &c., i. e. the liberties secured by Magna Charta gave the people at once some weight and consequence in the state, and this weight and consequence were felt in Parliament when the people attained distinct representation.

Notes

P. 260, L. 3. *your standard could never be advanced an inch beyond your* privileges; i. e. the privileges of the Pale. See Hallam's Const. Hist., ch. xviii.

L. 4. *Sir John Davies.* "Discoverie of the true Causes why Ireland was never entirely subdued until the beginning of his Majestie's happy reign." 4to., 1612. Davies was in this year made Speaker of the first Irish House of Commons. He was afterwards Lord Chief Justice of England. He is still remembered as the author of a curious metaphysical poem on the Immortality of the Soul, and as a legal reporter.

L. 24. *strength and ornament.* The most indulgent critic will complain that this is carrying the argument too far.

L. 25. *formally taxed her.* Queen Elizabeth attempted to tax the Irish landowners by an Order in Council, which was resisted. On the question of the competency of the Parliament of England to tax Ireland, see the last pages of Hallam's Constitutional History.

P. 261, L. 5. *my next example is Wales.* "Perhaps it is not generally known that Wales was once the Ireland of the English Government." O'Connell, Speech at Waterford, August 30, 1826. He applies to Ireland, with much ingenuity, all that Burke here says of Wales. O'Connell also quoted this part of the Speech at length in his Speech at the Association, February 2, 1827. The "strange heterogeneous monster, something between hostility and government," he marked as "an epitome of Irish history—I love to repeat it."

L. 11. *put into the hands of Lords Marchers.* See Scott's "The Betrothed," and the Appendix to Pennant's Tour in Wales. The conquest of Wales by ordinary military operations having been found impossible, the kings of England granted to these lords "such lands as they could win from the Welshmen." The first conquests were made in the neighbourhood of the great frontier towns; and the lords were "suffered to take upon them such prerogative and authority as were fit for the quiet government of the country." No actual [323] records of these grants remain, as the writs from the King's Courts did not run into Wales, nor were there any sheriffs to execute such writs. The towns of Wales grew up around the castles of the Lords Marchers. They executed the English laws, for the most part, within their lordships; but where the ancient laws of the land were sufficiently ascertained, they seem to a certain extent to have respected them: there being in many lordships separate Courts for the Welsh and English. The text must not be understood to imply that the governments by Lords Marchers were

SPEECH ON CONCILIATION WITH THE COLONIES

established by Edward I. On the contrary, after Edward II was made Prince of Wales, no more Lordships Marchers were created, and no Lord Marcher could claim any liberty or prerogative more than they had before, without a grant. These lordships were held of the King in chief, and not of the principality of Wales.

L. 16. *secondary.* Lat. *secundarius,* a deputy, alluding to the delegation of the supreme power to him during a state of war.

P. 262, L. 4. *fifteen acts of penal regulation.* In addition to those specified by Burke, no Welshman might be a burgess, or purchase any land in a town, 2 Henry IV, c. 12 and 20. No Welshman was to have any castle or fortress, save such as was in the time of Edward I, except bishops and temporal lords.

L. 35. *day-star—arisen in their hearts.* 2 Peter i. 19. The image is forced; but we forget the discordance in the admirable quotation which follows.

P. 263, L. 3. *simul alba nautis,* &c. Hor. Odes, Lib. I. xii. 27.

L. 18. *shewen*—the third person plural of "shew."

P. 264, L. 3. *What did Parliament,* &c. Notice the method of the paragraph.

L. 26. *Now if the doctrines,* &c. Burke's argument would be weightier if he were not obliged to abandon it when confronted with the question "How can America be represented in a British Parliament?"

P. 265, L. 24. *Opposuit natura.* Juv. x. 152. Canning borrowed this quotation in his eloquent speech on the Roman Catholic Disability Removal Bill, March 16, 1821.

L. 29. *arm . . . not shortened.* Isaiah lix. i.

P. 266, L. 4. *Republick of Plato . . . Utopia of More* (pronounce *Moore*) *. . . Oceana of Harrington.* Adam Smith and many others class the Utopia and the Oceana together as idle schemes. Nothing, however, can be more contrary than the spirit of the works of Plato and More on the one hand, and of Harrington on the other. More's work is pervaded by Greek ideas, and, like Plato's Republic, was intended to form a bright artificial picture, with the view of exhibiting more clearly by contrast the dark mass of contemporary realities. Beyond this, both works contain much sound sense and many practical suggestions. The "Utopia," even in its English dress, is a fine model of the method of composition. The "Oceana" is quite a different thing. It is a complete, pragmatical scheme of what Burke calls "paper government," constructed as if human beings were so many counters, and [324] the human soul some common machine: the work of an ingenious but unimaginative man, who knew too much of history, and too little of the nature of men.

L. 6. *and the rude swain,* &c. Comus, l. 633, slightly misquoted.

L. 27. *temple of British concord.* A grand and appropriate image. There is an allusion to the Temple of Concord at Rome, so celebrated in the story of the Conspiracy of Catiline. Cp. p. 287, "The sacred temple consecrated to our common faith."

P. 267, L. 13. *like unto the first.* St. Matt. xxii. 39.

L. 19. *by lack whereof . . . within the same.* These words were, by an amendment which was carried, omitted in the motion.

L. 23. *Is this description,* &c. A paragraph in Burke's best style. The copiousness of thought and the economy of words are equally remarkable, and both contribute to the general effect of weight and perspicuity.

L. 28. *Non meus hic sermo,* &c. Hor. Serm. ii. 2. 3.

L. 30. *homebred sense.* "The 'squire . . . had some homebred sense." Third Letter on Regicide Peace.

L. 33. *touch with a tool the stones,* &c. Exodus xx. 25.

P. 268, L. 2. *violate . . . ingenuous and noble roughness.* A curious reminiscence of a passage in Juvenal. See Sat. iii. 20.

L. 4. *guilty* of tampering. Absolutely used, in the old and classical sense, not noticed in Johnson = "variis remediorum generibus curam morbi tentare." (Bailey.) So in the pamphlet on the State of the Nation the "injudicious tampering" of the ministers at one time, is contrasted with their supine negligence at another.

L. 8. *not to be wise beyond what was written.* τὸ μὴ ὑπὲρ ὃ γέγραπται φρονεῖν. St. Paul, 1 Ep. to Cor. iv. 6. Whether Burke is the author of this elegant mistranslation, which has now become a classical phrase, or whether he adopted it from some English divine, I cannot say. The authorized translation seems to be correct, though Professor Scholefield supports that given by Burke. "That he is resolved not 'to be wise beyond what is written' in the legislative record and practice." App. from New to Old Whigs.

L. 9. *form of sound words.* "Religiously adheres to 'the form of sound words.'" App. from New to Old Whigs. (St. Paul, 2 Tim. i. 13.)

SPEECH ON CONCILIATION WITH THE COLONIES

P. 270, L. 1. *Those who have been pleased.* Alluding to Grenville. See p. 190.

L. 31. *on that solid basis.* Cp. p. 113, "on this solid basis fix your machines."

P. 272, L. 14. *passions of the misguided people.* Public opinion in England was certainly in favour of American taxation. The extent in which the English people were overwhelmed with taxes, and the difficulty of devising new ones, should not be forgotten.

L. 24. *this* state = statement, the sense which the word properly bears in the phrase "state of the case."

[325] **P. 276, L. 26.** *and to provide for . . . Judges in the same.* These words were also, by an amendment which was carried, omitted in the motion.

P. 277, L. 33. *Ought I not from hence to presume,* &c. Ingeniously brought in to vindicate the middle line taken by the Rockingham administration.

P. 278, L. 19. *mistake to imagine,* &c. Arnold says of Popery, that men "judge it naturally from the tendency of its most offensive principles; supposing that all men will carry their principles into practice, and ignorant of the checks and palliatives which in actual life neutralise their virulence." On Christian duty of conceding the Roman Catholic Claims. Macaulay more than once refers to this variation between theory and action; once at great length in the Essay on Hallam's Constitutional History. There is a remarkable passage much to the same effect at the close of Jeremy Taylor's second sermon on the "Miracles of the Divine Mercy."

L. 29. *We give and take—we remit some rights,* &c. "Of one thing I am perfectly clear, that it is not by deciding the suit, but by compromising the difference, that peace can be restored or kept." Letter to Sheriffs of Bristol.

L. 32. *As we must give away,* &c. To enter fully into this bold and just analogy refer to vol. ii. p. 151.

P. 279, L. 1. *The* purchase *paid* = purchase-money. So the Spectator, No. 152: "Short labours or dangers are but a cheap purchase of jollity, triumph, victory," &c. Cp. Europ. Sett. in America, vol. ii. p. 197: "Not aiming at a sudden profit, he (Penn) disposed of his land at a very light purchase." Young's Night Thoughts: "Insolvent worlds the purchase cannot pay."

NOTES

L. 2. *immediate jewel of his soul.* From Burke's favourite play, Othello, Act iii. Sc. 5. Cp. p. 70, "Reputation, the most precious possession of every individual." So in Fourth Letter on Regicide Peace, "Our ruin will be disguised in profit, and the sale of a few wretched baubles will bribe a degenerate people to barter away the most precious jewel of their souls."

L. 3. *"a great house is apt to make slaves haughty."* Juvenal, Sat. v. 66:

Maxima quaeque domus servis est plena superbis.

L. 8. *But although there are some,* &c. Cp. note to p. 116, l. 34.

L. 13. *what we are to lose*—i.e. what we stand the risk of losing.

L. 16. *cords of man.* Hosea xi. 4. "To draw them without persecuting the others, by the cords of love into the pale of the Church," &c. Bolingbroke, Diss. on Parties, Letter ii.

L. 18. *Aristotle.* Ethics, Book I. See note, p. 215, ante.

L. 26. *which is itself the security,* &c. Similarly, on the subject of Jacobinism, Burke points out that the large masses of property are natural ramparts which protect the smaller ones.

P. 280, L. 9. *promoted the union of the whole.* Burke lived to see this pleasant state of things reversed, and to approve the abolition of a separate Irish legislature.

P. 281, L. 3. *Experimentum in corpore vili.* This well-known saying seems to have had its origin from an anecdote of Muretus. He was attacked by [326] sickness when on a journey, and two physicians, who attended him, supposing him some obscure person, agreed to use a novel remedy, with the remark, "Faciamus periculum in anima vili." Muretus tranquilly asked, "Vilem animam appelas, pro qua Christus non dedignatus est mori?" (Menagiana, 3rd ed. p. 129.)

L. 7. *fatal in the end to our Constitution.* Burke apprehends that the taxation of the mother country, following such an example, might escape the direct control of Parliament.

L. 19. *back door of the Constitution*—i.e. through a Select Committee.

P. 283, L. 29. A *Treasury* Extent—a writ of Commission for valuing lands to satisfy a Crown debt.

P. 284, L. 24. *full of hazard*—"periculosae plenum opus aleae," Hor. Lib. ii. Carm. 1.

P. 285, L. 11. *richest mine,* &c. Mr. Hallam, comparing the grants of revenue before and after the Revolution, says: "The supplies meted out with niggardly caution by former parliaments to sovereigns whom they could not trust, have flowed with redundant profuseness, when they could judge of their necessity, and direct their application." Const. Hist. ch. xv.

L. 16. *Posita luditur arca.* Juvenal i. 90.

L. 17. *time of day* = of history. Used from the time of Shakspeare in more than one metaphorical sense.

L. 31. *stock* = capital.

L. 34. *voluntary flow of heaped-up* luxuriance. "He that will milk his Cattle, must feed them well; and it encourages men to gather and lay up when they have law to hold by what they have." N. Bacon (Henry VIII). So Lord Brooke, Treatise of Monarchie, sect. x.:

Rich both in people's treasures and their loves;
What Midas wish, what dreams of Alchimy
Can with these true crown-mines compared be?

Burke's metaphor is borrowed from the wine-press. The "mustum sponte defluens antequam calcentur uvae" was highly valued by the ancients, and is still prized in some varieties of modern wine. "Among the many excellent parts of this speech, I find you have got many proselytes by so cleverly showing that the way to get most revenue, is to let it come freely from them." Duke of Richmond to Burke, June 16, 1775.

P. 286, L. 15. *Ease would retract,* &c. It should be "recant." Par. Lost, iv. 96. Quoted by Mr. Gladstone from Burke, April 12, 1866.

L. 18. *immense, ever-growing, eternal Debt.* "The debt immense of endless gratitude." Par. Lost, iv. 53.

L. 30. *return in loan . . . taken in imposition.* See note to p. 167, l. 15.

P. 287, L. 8. *enemies that we are most likely to have.* France and Spain, then usually allied against England. The interests of France in the West Indies were at this time great and increasing.

L. 11. *For that service, for all service,* &c. No passage affords a more [327] curious illustration of the manner in which Burke in his more impassioned appeals, refunds his "rich thievery" of the Bible and the English poets. The remarkable independence of Burke's usual style makes the contrast striking. The concluding sentence is a reminiscence of Virg. Aen. vi. 726, &c.:

The active mind, *infus'd* thro' all the space,
Unites and mingles with the *mighty mass.*

Dryden's transl. ll. 984, 985.

Burke evidently borrowed this use of it from Bacon, Adv. of Learning, xxiii. 47, where it is applied to government in general: "We see, all governments are obscure and invisible;

Totamque infusa per artus
Mens agitat molem, et magno se corpore miscet.

Such is the description of governments." South uses it in the same way: "The spirit which animates and acts the universe, is the spirit of government." (Sermon on the Episcopal Function.) Shakespeare and the Bible supply most of the other phrases in the passage. "My trust is in her," &c., Psalms. "Light as air, strong," &c., Othello. "Grapple to you," Hamlet, &c. "No force under heaven will be of power to tear you," &c., St. Paul. "Chosen race," Tate and Brady. "Turn their faces toward you," 1 Kings ix. 44, 5; Dan. vi. 10. "Perfect obedience"; "mysterious whole," Pope. Cp. note to p. 236, l. 22.

L. 20. *your government one thing, and their privileges another . . . the cement is gone,* &c. Cp. the passage in Erskine's speech for Stockdale; "Your government—having no root in consent or affection, no foundation in similarity of interests, nor support from any one principle which cements men together in society, could only be upheld by alternate strategem and force."

L. 29. *multiply . . . ardently love liberty.* Notice this masterly reference to previous arguments.

P. 288, L. 5. *must still preserve:* "still" = ever.

L. 6. *Do not entertain so weak an imagination:* "imagination" = thought. "Nobody was so unacquainted with the world as to entertain so puerile an imagination." Ann. Reg. 1763, p. 40.

L. 7. *registers . . . bonds,* &c. Alluding to the official routine of the Custom-houses.

L. 8. *Cockets.* The term "cocket" designates primarily the custom-house seal, and secondarily the sealed parchment delivered by the officer to the merchant as warrant that the goods have been customed.

L. 12. *these things,* &c. The genial animation of this skilful appeal is admirable.

L. 20. *Land Tax Act.* The Land Tax was formerly a much more important item in the Revenue than now: it used to contribute more than a third of the whole, but it now yields about a sixty-fourth. Until 1798 it fluctuated, in peace being assessed at two or three shillings, in war, at four; but in 1798 it was made permanent at four shillings in the pound.

L. 23. *Mutiny Bill.* "The people of England, jealous on all subjects which relate to liberty, have exceeded, on the subject of the army, their usual caution. [328] They have in the preamble of their annual Mutiny Bill claimed their birthright; they recite part of the Declaration of Right, 'that standing armies and martial law in peace, without the consent of Parliament, are illegal'; and having stated the simplicity and purity of their ancient constitution, and having set forth a great principle of Magna Charta, they admit a partial and temporary repeal of it; they admit an army and a law for its regulation, but they limit the number of the former, and the duration of both; confining all the troops themselves, the law that regulates, and the power that commands them, to *one year.* Thus is the army of England rendered a Parliamentary army; the constitutional ascendancy of the subject over the soldier preserved; the military rendered effectually subordinate to the civil magistrate; the government of the sword controlled in its exercise, because limited in its duration; and the King entrusted with the command of the army during good behaviour only." Grattan, "Observations on the [Irish] Mutiny Bill," 1781.

L. 25. *deep stake they have in such a glorious institution.* The Conservative commonplace, *a stake in the country,* usually attributed to Canning, was borrowed by him in his Speech at Liverpool, March 18, 1820, from Burke: "Those who have the greatest stake in the country," Speech on Fox's Bill for the Repeal of the Marriage Act, 1781 (among the fragments).

L. 31. *profane herd.* The "profanum vulgus" of Horace.

L. 32. *no place*—i. e. no right.

P. 289, L. 4. *all in all.* St. Paul, 1 Cor. xv. 28.

IBID. *Magnanimity in politics,* &c. "It is a true saying, and has often been repeated, that a very moderate share of human wisdom is sufficient for the guidance of human affairs. But there is another truth, equally indisputable, which is, that a man who aspires to govern mankind ought to bring to the task generous sentiments, compassionate sympathies, and noble and elevated thoughts." Lord Palmerston, Debate on the Claims against Greece, 1850.

Notes

L. 9. *Sursum corda!* The canticle of the Church, "Lift up your hearts." Cp. Gordon, Discourses on Tacitus, Disc. iv; "Great souls are always sincere. . . . Good sense and greatness of mind are always found together, and justice is inseparable from either." Burke's works are full of lofty appeals in this strain. "But if we make ourselves too little for the sphere of our duty; if, on the contrary, we do not stretch and expand our minds to the compass of their object: be well assured, that everything about us will dwindle by degrees, until at length our concerns are shrunk to the dimensions of our minds." Speech on Nabob of Arcot's Debts. Cp. Mr. Gladstone, Speech on Irish Church, March 1, 1869: "Every man who proceeds to the discussion is under the most solemn obligation to raise the level of his vision, and to expand its scope in proportion to the greatness of the object."

L. 12. *this high calling.* St. Paul, Phil. iii. 14.

The typeface used for this book is ITC New Baskerville, which was created for the International Typeface Corporation and is based on the types of the English type founder and printer John Baskerville (1706–75). Baskerville is the quintessential transitional face: it retains the bracketed and oblique serifs of old style faces such as Caslon and Garamond, but in its increased lowercase height, lighter color, and enhanced contrast between thick and thin strokes, it presages modern faces.

Printed on paper that is acid-free and meets the requirements of the American National Standard for Permanence of Paper for Printed Library Materials, z39.48-1992. ∞

Book design by Martin Lubin, New York
Composition by Tseng Information Systems, Inc.,
Durham, North Carolina
Printed and bound by Worzalla Publishing Co.,
Stevens Point, Wisconsin